Conformity & Conflict

Conformity & Conflict
READINGS IN CULTURAL ANTHROPOLOGY

Eighth Edition

JAMES P. SPRADLEY
LATE

DAVID W. McCURDY
MACALESTER COLLEGE

HarperCollinsCollegePublishers

To Barbara Spradley and Carolyn McCurdy

Part-Opening Photo Credits
Page 2, © Delevingne, Stock, Boston; p. 12, DeVore, Anthro-Photo; p. 56, Keery, Stock, Boston; p. 106, Holland, Stock, Boston; p. 156, Redenius, Monkmeyer Press Photo; p. 196, Francois, Gamma-Liaison; p. 236, Smucker, Anthro-Photo; p. 274, Smolan, Stock, Boston; p. 318, Grant, Monkmeyer Press Photo; p. 370, Devore, Anthro-Photo.

Senior Editor: Alan McClare
Project Editor: Ellen MacElree
Design Supervisor: John Callahan
Text and Cover Design: John Callahan
Cover Photos: *Top left:* © Paul Conklin, Monkmeyer Press; *top right:* © Guy Marche, FPG International; *bottom left:* © Al Michaud, FPG International; *bottom right:* © Haroldo Castro, FPG International.
Photo Researcher: Mira Schachne
Production Manager: Willie Lane
Compositor: Circle Graphics Typographers
Printer and Binder: Malloy Lithographing Inc.
Cover Printer: The Lehigh Press, Inc.

Conformity & Conflict: Readings in Cultural Anthropology, Eighth Edition
Copyright © 1994 by Barbara A. Spradley and David W. McCurdy

Library of Congress Cataloging-in-Publication Data
Conformity & conflict : readings in cultural anthropology / [edited by] James P. Spradley, David W. McCurdy.—8th ed.
     p.   cm.
   ISBN 0-673-52312-8
   1. Ethnology.   I. Spradley, James P.   II. McCurdy, David W.
GN325.C69   1994
305.8—dc20   93-46206
                                                                      CIP

94 95 96 97 9 8 7 6 5 4 3 2 1

CONTENTS

v

World Map and Geographical Placement of Readings

The numbers on this map correspond to the reading numbers and indicate the places on which the articles focus. Screened maps also accompany readings themselves, and white areas on these maps highlight the subject locations. Readings labeled as *world* on this global map do not include white areas.

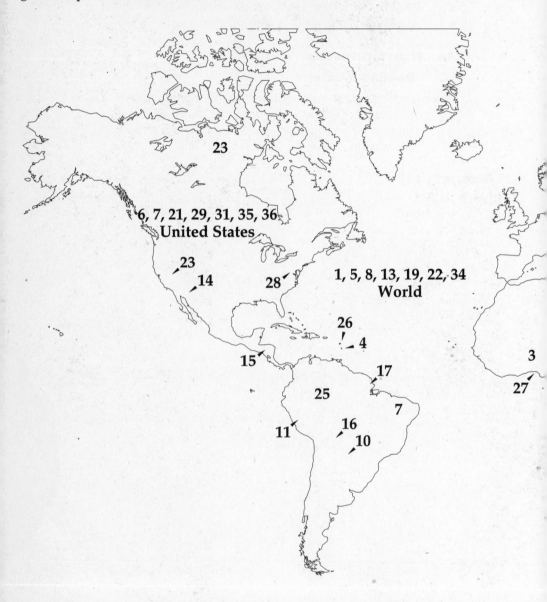

23

6, 7, 21, 29, 31, 35, 36
United States

23
14
28

1, 5, 8, 13, 19, 22, 34
World

26
4

15

3

27

17

25

7

11
16
10

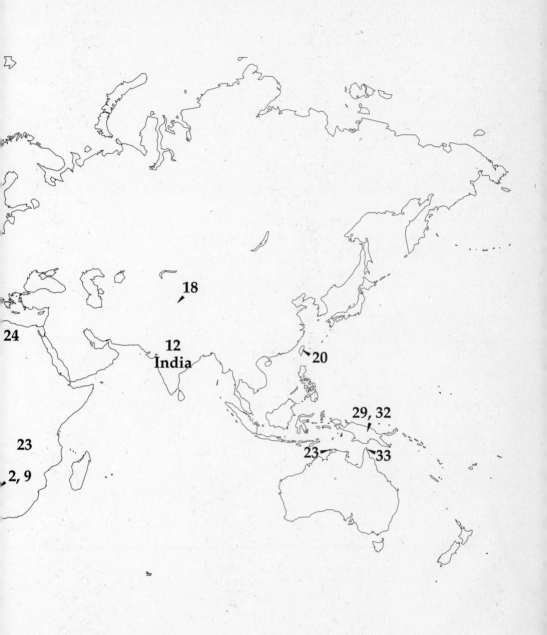

PREFACE

Cultural anthropology has a twofold mission: to understand other cultures and to communicate that understanding. Twenty-four years ago, in preparing the first edition of this book, we sought to make communication easier and more enjoyable for teachers and students alike. We focused on the twin themes stated in the title—conformity, or order, and conflict, or change—while organizing selections into sections based on traditional topics. We balanced the coverage of cultures between non-Western and Western (including American) so students could make their own cultural comparisons and see the relation between anthropology and their lives. We chose articles that reflected interesting topics in anthropology, but we also looked for selections that illustrated important concepts and theories because we believed that anthropology provides a unique and powerful way to look at experience. We searched extensively for scholarly articles written with insight and clarity. Students and instructors in hundreds of colleges and universities responded enthusiastically to our efforts, and a pattern was set that carried through six subsequent editions.

This eighth edition retains the features of earlier editions: the focus on stability and change, the coverage of a broad range of societies, the combination of professionalism and readability in selections, the view that anthropology provides a perspective on experience, and carefully integrated organization. As in previous editions, we have revamped topics and added or subtracted selections in response to the suggestions of instructors and students across the country.

Anthropology and the world it seeks to understand have changed since the first edition of *Conformity & Conflict*. New articles were chosen to reflect these changes. Most new selections were written within the last four years; several were created especially for this volume and two are updated versions of previous selections. Many new articles are written by women, reflecting a change from the time when anthropology was largely a male enterprise. There are major revisions to the sections on language and communication, kinship and family, roles and inequality, and law and politics. The section on economic systems now follows the one on cultural ecology, reflecting the organization of most popular textbooks. In all, there are 14 new articles and two others brought back from earlier editions. Every section has at least one new selection.

We have also retained some older classic articles in this edition. Many of these teach fundamental concepts and theories that we believe are timeless in anthropology and that are essential ideas for students who are new to the discipline.

We have also continued the expanded special features that have appeared in past editions. Part introductions include discussion of many basic anthropological definitions for instructors who do not wish to use a standard textbook but find it helpful to provide students with a terminological foundation.

Several student aids are retained in the eighth edition. Lists of key terms accompany each part introduction. Each article is followed by several review questions. Maps locating societies discussed in articles accompany each selection. There is also a glossary and subject index at the end of the book.

A complimentary instructor's manual and test bank is available from the publisher. The manual contains a summary of each article along with a large selection of true or false and multiple-choice questions for articles and part introductions.

It has always been our aim to provide a book that meets the needs of students and instructors. To help us with this goal we encourage you to send us your comments and ideas for improving *Conformity & Conflict*.

Many people have made suggestions that guided this revision of *Conformity & Conflict*. We are especially grateful to Brian L. Foster, Arizona State University; Kathleen Godel Gengenbach, Red Rocks Community College; Barry H. Michie, Kansas State University; Richard H. Moore, The Ohio State University; and John Alan Ross, Eastern Washington University for their advice. We would also like to thank Alan McClare, Michael Kimball, Ellen MacElree, and Julie Conway for their editorial support, and Kathryn Hyduke, Meridith Cooley, and Samantha Grosby for their advice and help in production. Finally, we are grateful to our students at Macalester College for their advice and inspiration.

David W. McCurdy

Conformity & Conflict

CULTURE AND THE CONTEMPORARY WORLD

Many students associate cultural anthropology with the study of primitive peoples. They picture the anthropologist as that slightly peculiar person who, dressed in khaki shorts and pith helmet, lives among some exotic tribe in order to record the group's bizarre and not altogether pleasant customs. Like most stereotypes, this one is not completely true but it does reflect anthropology's traditional interest in describing the culture of less complex societies. In the last century, when anthropology became a recognized discipline, its members collected and analyzed the growing numbers of reports on non-Western peoples by missionaries, travelers, and colonial administrators. This tradition continued into the twentieth century, although the collection of data was refined by actual fieldwork. Impressed by the variety of human behavior, anthropologists sought to record these cultures that were vanishing before the onslaught of Western civilization. Such studies continue among remote groups, and reports of this research are regularly found in professional journals.

During recent decades, however, anthropologists have developed wider interests. As primitive groups have been obliterated or assimilated, anthropologists have increasingly studied subcultures within more complex societies. Certainly World War II and the Cold War stimulated this trend. The United States government employed anthropologists to describe societies in whose territories we fought. The Cold War years, marked by competition with the Russians for influence in developing nations, led to studies of peasant lifestyles and culture change.

Today, however, our position in the world has changed. Americans are less welcome in developing nations. Concurrently, problems in our own country have multiplied and taken the center stage of national concern. It is not surprising that anthropologists have extended their attention to subcultures within our own society.

3

But what can anthropology contribute to an understanding of American life? After all, other social scientists have been doing research in this country for years. Is there anything special about anthropology? In many ways the answer to this question is no. The various social sciences often share the same interests. Yet, as a result of their intensive cross-cultural experience, anthropologists have developed a unique perspective on the nature and the significance of *culture*. This view has emerged from over a century of fieldwork among populations whose behavior was dramatically different from the anthropologists' own. Why, for example, did Iroquois women participate with apparent relish in the gruesome torture of prisoners? How could Bhil tribesmen put chili powder in the eyes of witches, blindfold them, and swing them over a smoky fire by their feet? What possessed Kwakiutl chiefs to destroy their wealth publicly at potlatch ceremonies? Why did Rajput widows cast themselves upon their husbands' funeral pyres? Why did Nagas engage in raids to acquire human heads? In every case, anthropologists were impressed by the fact that this "bizarre" behavior was intentional and meaningful to the participants. Bhils wanted to swing witches; to them it was appropriate. Kwakiutl chiefs made careful investments to increase the wealth they destroyed. These acts were planned; people had a notion of what they were going to do before they did it, and others shared their expectations.

CULTURE

The acquired knowledge that people use to interpret their world and generate social behavior is called *culture*. Culture is not behavior itself, but the knowledge used to construct and understand behavior. It is learned as children grow up in society and discover how their parents, and others around them, interpret the world. In our society we learn to distinguish objects such as cars, windows, houses, children, and food; to recognize attributes like sharp, hot, beautiful, and humid; to classify and perform different kinds of acts; to evaluate what is good and bad and to judge when an unusual action is appropriate or inappropriate. How often have you heard parents explain something about life to a child? Why do you think children are forever asking why? During socialization children learn a culture, and because they learn it from others, they share it with others, a fact that makes human social existence possible.

Culture is thus the system of knowledge by which people design their own actions and interpret the behavior of others. It tells an American that eating with one's mouth closed is proper, while an Indian knows that to be polite one must chew with one's mouth open. There is nothing preordained about culture categories; they are arbitrary. The same act can have different meanings in various cultures. For example, when adolescent Hindu boys walk holding hands, it signifies friendship, while to Americans the same act may suggest homosexuality. This arbitrariness is particularly important to remember if we are to understand our own complex society. We tend to think that the norms we follow represent the "natural" way human beings do things. Those who behave otherwise are judged morally wrong. This viewpoint is *ethnocentric,* which means that people think their own culture represents the best, or at least the most appropriate, way for human beings to live.

Although in our complex society we share many cultural norms with everyone, each of us belongs to a number of groups possessing exclusive cultural knowledge. We share some categories and plans with family members alone. And our occupational group, ethnic group, voluntary society, and age group each have their distinctive culture. Instead of assuming that another's behavior is reasonable to him, that it is motivated by a different set of cultural norms, we frequently assume that he has intentionally violated accepted conventions. In their attempt to build bridges of understanding across cultural barriers, anthropologists identified the universality of ethnocentrism many years ago. The study of subcultures in our own society is another attempt to further mutual understanding, as some of the selections in this volume indicate.

How do anthropologists discover and map another culture? Are their methods applicable in the United States? Typically, anthropologists live among the people of the society that interests them. They learn the culture by observing, asking questions, and participating in daily activities—a process resembling childhood socialization or enculturation. Obviously, the anthropologist cannot become a child and must try to learn the norms in a strange group despite his or her foreign appearance and advanced age. Those who study in the United States have followed a similar procedure.

More than anything else, the study of culture separates anthropologists from other social scientists. Other scholars do not ignore culture; they assume their subjects have it, but their main interest is to account for human behavior by plotting correlations among variables. Some social scientists have explained the rise in the American divorce rate as a function of industrialization; this hypothesis can be tested by seeing if higher divorce rates are associated with industrialization and mobility. Anthropologists share a concern with this kind of explanation; for example, many have employed the Human Relations Area Files, a collection of ethnographies describing several hundred societies, as data for testing more general hypotheses. Almost every anthropologist starts with an *ethnography,* the description of a particular culture, and such studies are required to understand the complexity within American society.

As anthropologists have encountered, studied, and compared the world's societies, they have learned more about the concept of culture itself. As we have seen, culture is the knowledge people use to generate behavior, not behavior itself; it is arbitrary, learned, and shared. In addition, culture is adaptive. Human beings cope with their natural and social environment by means of their traditional knowledge. Culture allows for rapid adaptation because it is flexible and permits the invention of new strategies—although change often appears to be painfully slow to those who are in a hurry for it. By the same token, the adaptive nature of culture accounts for the enormous variety of the world's distinct societies.

Culture is a system of interrelated parts. If Americans were to give up automobiles, then other modes of travel, places for courtship, marks of status, and sources of income would have to be found. Culture meets personal needs; through it, people seek security and a sense of control over experience. Indeed, every tradition includes ways to cure the sick, to prepare for the unexpected, and to support the individual. In a complex society with many ways of life in contact with each other, change is persistent. It may be illusion to think that people can control the course of change or can modify the resulting culture conflict. But if we can understand human cultures—including our own—the illusion may become reality.

It is easy for people to feel that their own way of life is natural and God-given. One's culture is not like a suit of clothing that can be discarded easily or exchanged for each new lifestyle that comes along. It is rather like a security blanket, and though to some it may appear worn and tattered, outmoded and ridiculous, it has great meaning to its owner. Although there are many reasons for this fact, one of the most important is the value-laden nature of what we learn as members of society. Whether it is acquired in a tribal band, a peasant village, or an urban neighborhood, each culture is like a giant iceberg. Beneath the surface of rules, norms, and behavior patterns there is a system of values. Some of these premises are easily stated by members of a society, while others are outside their awareness. Because many difficulties in the modern world involve values, we must examine this concept in some detail.

A value is an arbitrary conception of what is *desirable* in human experience. During socialization all children are exposed to a constant barrage of evaluations—the arbitrary "rating system" of their culture. Nearly everything they learn is labeled in terms of its desirability. The value attached to each bit of information may result from the pain of a hot stove, the look of disapproval from a parent, the smile of appreciation from a teacher, or some specific verbal instruction. When parents tell a child, "You should go to college and get a good education," they are expressing a value. Those who do not conform to society's rating system are identified with derogatory labels or are punished in a more severe way. When a Tlingit Indian says to his nephew, "You should marry your father's sister," he is expressing one of the core values of his culture. When a young couple save income for future emergencies, they are conforming to the American value that the future is more important than the present. When a tramp urinates in an alley, he is violating the value attached to privacy. All these concepts of what is desirable combine cognitive and affective meanings. Individuals internalize their ideas about right and wrong, good and bad, and invest them with strong feelings.

Why do values constitute an inevitable part of all human experience? That human potential is at odds with the requirements of social life is well known. Behavior within the realm of possibility is often outside the realm of necessity. There are numerous ways to resolve the conflict between what people *can do* by themselves and what they *must do* as members of society. It is a popular notion that prisons and other correctional institutions are the primary means by which our society enforces conformity, but this is not the case. Socialization may be ineffective for a few who require such drastic action, but for the vast majority in any society, conformity results from the internalization of values. As we learn through imitation, identification, and instruction, values are internalized. They provide security and contribute to a sense of personal and social identity. For this reason, individuals in every society cling tenaciously to the values they have acquired and feel threatened when confronted with others who live according to different conceptions of what is desirable.

CULTURAL RELATIVISM

A misconception about values has been spawned by science and, in particular, by the anthropological doctrine of cultural relativism. Some have maintained that it is possible to separate values from facts and, since science is limited to facts, that it is possible to do "value-free" research. By an exercise in mental gymnastics, the very scholars who admit the influence of values in the behavior of others sometimes deny it in themselves. Preferences operate whenever an individual must *select* one action from a multitude of possible courses. Anyone who decides to observe one thing and not another is making that decision on the basis of an implicit or explicit conception of desirability. Science is an activity that makes many value judgments—including which approaches to information gathering are the best. When biologists decide to examine the structure of the DNA molecule using an empirical approach, rather than a mystical, intuitive, or religious one, they are doing so with reference to their sense of what is desirable. Even the decision to study DNA rather than some other substance involves an exercise of values. When doing research on human behavior, the influence of one's values is undeniable. The "objective observer" who is detached from the subject matter, who refrains from allowing values to influence observations, is a myth. This fact does not suggest a retreat from the *quest for objectivity*. It does not mean that social scientists are free to disparage the customs encountered in other societies, or to impose their morals on those being studied. Skilled anthropologists are aware of their own values and then approach other cultures with tolerance and respect. They *identify* rather than *deny* the influence of their own viewpoints. They strive to achieve the ideal of value-free research but realize that it would be naive to assume such a goal possible.

Cultural relativism rests on the premise that it is possible to remain aloof and free from making value judgments. Put simply, this doctrine is based on four interrelated propositions.

1. Each person's value system is a result of his or her experience; that is, it is learned.
2. The values that individuals learn differ from one society to another because of different learning experiences.
3. Values, therefore, are relative to the society in which they occur.
4. There are no universal values, but we should respect the values of each of the world's cultures.

Cultural relativism has enabled the uninformed to understand what appears to be strange and immoral behavior. Although we may not believe it is good to kill infants, for example, we have found it intelligible in the context of a native Australian band. Although Americans generally believe in the desirability of monogamous marriage (or at least serial monogamy), we have found the practice of polygamy in other societies to be comprehensible when related to their cultures. This view presents numerous difficulties. Does one respect a society that believes it best to murder 6 million of its members who happen to be Jewish? How do anthropologists respect the values of a head-hunting tribe when their own heads are at stake?

Moreover, all the statements in this doctrine of relativism are either based on implicit values (that is, empiricism), or they are outright statements of desirability. The belief that it is good to *respect* the ideals of each of the world's cultures is itself a "relative" value. An extreme relativism is based on the philosophy that it is best to "let everyone do his or her own thing." Given unlimited resources and space this might have been possible, but in the modern world this philosophy represents a retreat from the realities facing us. It absolves the believer from the responsibility of finding some way to resolve conflicts among the world's different value systems. What is needed today is not a "live and let live" policy but a commitment to a higher, more inclusive value system, and this requires changes that are extremely difficult to achieve.

CONFORMITY AND CONFLICT

Every social system is a moral order; shared values act as the mortar binding together the structure of each human community. Rewards and punishments are based on commonly held values; those persons achieving high status do so in terms of cultural rating systems. These values are expressed in symbolic ways—through food, clothing, wealth, language, behavior—all of which carry implicit messages about good and bad. The pervasiveness of values gives each person a sense of belonging, a sense of being a member of a community, the feeling of joining other human beings who share a commitment to the good life. But the moral nature of every culture has two sides: it facilitates adaptation and survival on the one hand, but it often generates conflict and destruction on the other. Let us examine each of these possibilities.

For almost a million years, people have successfully adapted to a variety of terrestrial environments. From the frozen tundra to the steaming jungle, people have built their homes, reared their children, performed their rituals, and buried their dead. In recent years we have escaped the thin layer of atmosphere surrounding the earth to live, if only for a few days, in outer space and beneath the ocean. All these achievements have been possible because of a unique endowment, our capacity for culture. Wherever people wandered, they developed patterns for organizing behavior, using natural resources, relating to others, and creating a meaningful life. A genetic inheritance did not channel behavior into specialized responses but instead provided a reservoir of plasticity that was shaped by values into one of the many ways to be human. Children in every society do not learn the entire range of potential human behavior—they are taught to *conform* to a very limited number of behavior patterns that are appropriate to a particular society. Human survival depends on cultural conformity, which requires that every individual become a specialist, be committed to a few values, and acquire knowledge and skills of a single society.

This very specialization has led to diversity, resulting in a myriad of contrasting cultures. This volume contains only a small sample of the different symbolic worlds created by people in their attempt to cope with the common problems of human existence. We will see how the generosity of the American Christmas spirit stands in contrast to the daily sharing among the !Kung. Chicago suburbanites and natives of the Brazilian jungle both adorn their bodies with paint, clothing, and rings, but neither can comprehend how the other defines these symbols. All elements of human experience—kinship, marriage, age, race, sexuality, food, warfare—are socially defined and valued. The difficulty of moving from one cultural world to another is immense.

Cultural diversity has fascinated people for centuries. The study of strange and exotic peoples has attracted the curious for many generations. In the isolation of a remote jungle village or South Sea island, anthropologists found a natural laboratory for carrying out research. Their research reports often seemed more like novels than scientific studies and were read by both professionals and laypeople; seldom did any reader feel threatened by the strange behavior of far-off "savages."

But isolation rapidly disappeared, sometimes by virtue of the anthropologists' intrusion! Exploration gave way to colonization, trade, and the massive troop movements of modern warfare. Today it is impossible to find groups of people who are isolated from the remainder of the world.

Instead we have a conglomeration of cultures within a single nation, and often within a single city. Anthropologists need only walk down the street from the university to encounter those who have learned a culture unlike their own. Individuals with different language styles, sexual practices, religious rituals, and a host of other strange behavior patterns sit in their classrooms or play with their children on the urban playgrounds. Anthropology today is a science concerned with understanding how people can survive in a world where village, hamlet, city, and nation are all *multicultural*. In isolation, each value system is interesting. Crowded into close and intimate contact, these distinct culture patterns often lead to conflict, oppression, and warfare. Barbara Ward has eloquently summed up our situation:

> In the last few decades, mankind has been overcome by the most change in its entire history. Modern science and technology have created so close a network of communication, transport, economic interdependence—and potential nuclear destruction—that planet Earth, on its journey through infinity, has acquired the intimacy, the fellowship and the vulnerability of a spaceship.[1]

In a sense, our greatest resource for adapting to different environments—the capacity to create different cultures—has become the source of greatest danger. Diversity is required for survival in the ecological niches of earth, but it can be destructive when all people suddenly find themselves in the same niche. Numerous species have become extinct because of their inability to adapt to a changing *natural* environment. Culture was the survival kit that enabled us to meet fluctuating natural conditions with flexibility, but now we are faced with a radically altered *human* environment. Successful adaptation will require changes that fly in the face of thousands of years of cultural specialization. Our ingenuity has been used to develop unique cultures, but thus far we have failed to develop satisfactory patterns and rules for articulating these differences. Can we survive in a world where our neighbors and even our children have different cultures? Can we adapt to the close, intimate fellowship of a spaceship when each group of passengers lives by different values?

TOWARD A MULTICULTURAL SOCIETY

What is required? In the first place, instead of suppressing cultural diversity by stressing assimilation into the mainstream of American life, we must recognize the extent to which our culture is pluralistic. We must accept the fact that groups within our society are committed to disparate and sometimes conflicting values. The second requirement for a truly multi-

---

[1]Barbara Ward, *Spaceship Earth* (New York: Columbia University Press, 1966), vii.

cultural society is that we continuously examine the *consequences* of each value system. What is the long-range effect of our commitment to a "gospel of growth"? What are the results of a belief in male superiority? How do our values of privacy affect those without homes? What is the consequence for minority groups when all students are taught to use "standard English"? As we study American culture we must discover the effect of our dominant values on every sector of life. The ideals that have made this country what it is have also been destructive to some citizens. In our efforts to assimilate ethnic groups, we have destroyed their pride and self-identity. In our attempt to offer the advantages of education to American Indians, we have induced them to become failures because our schools are not able to educate for diversity. In order to demonstrate the tolerance built into American values, we have created the "culturally deprived," but the sophistication of labels does not conceal our prejudice. The absence of men in the families of the urban poor is a logical consequence of welfare institutions created from a single value system. The consumer suffers from dangerous products because in our culture productive enterprise is more important than consumer protection. We have only begun to understand some of the consequences of our values, and during the next few decades our survival will demand that the study of values be given top priority.

Finally, the most difficult task for the contemporary world is to induce people to relinquish those values with destructive consequences. This will not be simple, and it probably will not occur without a better understanding of the nature and the function of the world's many value systems. People's capacity to learn has not yet reached its full potential. In every society, children learn to shift from *egocentric* behavior to *ethnocentric* behavior. In deference to desirable community standards, individuals give up those things they desire, and life in a particular society becomes secure and meaningful, with conventional values acting as warp and woof of social interaction.

Can we now learn to shift from *ethnocentric* to *homocentric* behavior? Can we relinquish values desirable from the standpoint of a single community but destructive to the wider world? This change will require a system of ideals greater than the conventions of any localized culture. The change will necessitate a morality that can articulate conflicting value systems and create a climate of tolerance, respect, and cooperation. Only then can we begin to create a culture that will be truly adaptive in today's world.

CULTURE AND ETHNOGRAPHY

Culture, as its name suggests, lies at the heart of cultural anthropology. And the concept of *culture*, along with ethnography, sets anthropology apart from other social and behavioral sciences. Let us look more closely at these concepts.

To understand what anthropologists mean by culture, imagine yourself in a foreign setting, such as a market town in India, forgetting what you might already know about that country. You step off a bus onto a dusty street where you are immediately confronted by strange sights, sounds, and smells. Men dress in Western clothes, but of a different style. Women drape themselves in long shawls that entirely cover their bodies. They peer at you through a small gap in this garment as they walk by. Buildings are one- or two-story affairs, open at the front so you can see inside. Near you some people sit on wicker chairs eating strange foods. Most unusual is how people talk. They utter vocalizations unlike any you have ever heard, and you wonder how they can possibly understand each other. But obviously they do, since their behavior seems organized and purposeful.

Scenes such as this confronted early explorers, missionaries, and anthropologists, and from their observations an obvious point emerged. People living in various parts of the world looked and behaved in dramatically different ways. And these differences correlated with groups. The people of India had customs different from those of the Papuans; the British did not act and dress like the Iroquois.

Two possible explanations for group differences came to mind. Some argued that group behavior was inherited. Dahomeans of the African Gold Coast, for example, were characterized as particularly "clever and adaptive" by one British colonial official, while, according to the same authority, another African group was "happy-go-lucky and improvident." Usually implied in such statements was the idea that group members were born that way. Such thinking persists to the present and in its least discriminating guise takes the form of racism.

But a second explanation also emerged. Perhaps, rather than a product of inheritance, the behavior characteristic of a group was learned. The way people dressed, what they ate, how they talked—all these could more easily be explained as acquisitions. Thus, a baby born on the African Gold Coast would, if immediately transported to China and raised like other children there, grow up to dress, eat, and talk like a Chinese. Cultural anthropologists focus on the explanation of learned behavior.

The idea of learning, and a need to label the lifestyles associated with particular groups, led to the definition of culture. In 1871, British anthropologist Sir Edward Burnet Tylor argued that "Culture . . . is that complex whole which includes knowledge, belief, art, law, morals, custom, and any other capabilities and habits acquired by man as a member of society."[1]

The definition we present here places more emphasis on the importance of knowledge than does Tylor's. We will say that *culture is the acquired knowledge that people use to generate behavior and interpret experience.*

Important to this definition is the idea that culture is a kind of knowledge, not behavior. It is in people's heads. It reflects the mental categories they learn from others as they grow up. It helps them *generate* behavior and *interpret* what they experience. At the moment of birth, we lack a culture. We don't yet have a system of beliefs, knowledge, and patterns of customary behavior. But from that moment until we die, each of us participates in a kind of universal schooling that teaches us our native culture. Laughing and smiling are genetic responses, but as infants we soon learn when to smile, when to laugh, and even how to laugh. We also inherit the potential to cry, but we must learn our cultural rules for when crying is appropriate.

As we learn our culture, we acquire a way to interpret experience. For example, we Americans learn that dogs are like little people in furry suits. Dogs live in our houses, eat our food, share our beds. They hold a place in our hearts; their loss causes us to grieve. Villagers in India, on the other hand, view dogs as pests that admittedly are useful for hunting in those few parts of the country where one still can hunt, and as watchdogs. Quiet days in Indian villages are often punctuated by the yelp of a dog that has been threatened or actually hurt by its master or a bystander.

Clearly, it is not the dogs that are different in these two societies. Rather, it is the meaning that dogs have for people that varies. And such meaning is cultural; it is learned as part of growing up in each group.

Ethnography is the process of discovering and describing a particular culture. It involves anthropologists in an intimate and personal activity as they attempt to learn how the members of a particular group see their worlds.

---

[1] Edward Burnet Tylor, *Primitive Culture* (New York: Harper Torchbooks, Harper & Row, 1958; originally published by John Murray, London, 1871), 1.

But which groups qualify as culture-bearing units? How does the anthropologist identify the existence of a culture to study? This was not a difficult question when anthropology was a new science. As Tylor's definition notes, culture was the whole way of life of a people. To find it, one sought out distinctive ethnic units, such as Bhil tribals in India or Apaches in the American Southwest. Anything one learned from such people would be part of their culture.

But discrete cultures of this sort are becoming more difficult to find. The world is increasingly divided into large national societies, each subdivided into a myriad of subgroups. Anthropologists are finding it increasingly attractive to study such subgroups, because they form the arena for most of life in complex society. And this is where the concept of the microculture enters the scene.

Microcultures are systems of cultural knowledge characteristic of subgroups within larger societies. Members of a microculture will usually share much of what they know with everyone in the greater society but will possess a special cultural knowledge that is unique to the subgroup. For example, a college fraternity has a microculture within the context of a university and a nation. Its members have special daily routines, jokes, and meanings for events. It is this shared knowledge that makes up their microculture and that can serve as the basis for ethnographic study. More and more, anthropologists are turning to the study of microcultures, using the same ethnographic techniques they employ when they investigate the broader culture of an ethnic or national group.

More than anything else, it is ethnography that is anthropology's unique contribution to social science. Most scientists, including many who view people in social context, approach their research as *detached observers*. As social scientists, they observe the human subjects of their study, categorize what they see, and generate theory to account for their findings. They work from the outside, creating a system of knowledge to account for other people's behavior. Although this is a legitimate and often useful way to conduct research, it is not the main task of ethnography.

Ethnographers seek out the insider's viewpoint. Because culture is the knowledge people use to generate behavior and interpret experience, the ethnographer seeks to understand group members' behavior from the inside, or cultural, perspective. Instead of looking for a *subject* to observe, ethnographers look for an *informant* to teach them the culture. Just as a child learns its native culture from parents and other people in its social environment, the ethnographer learns another culture by inferring folk categories from the observation of behavior and by asking informants what things mean.

Anthropologists employ many strategies during field research to understand another culture better. But all strategies and all research ultimately rest on the cooperation of *informants*. An informant is neither a subject in a scientific experiment nor a *respondent* who answers the investigator's questions. An informant is a teacher who has a special kind of pupil: a professional anthropologist. In this unique relationship a transformation occurs in the anthropologist's understanding of an alien culture. It is the informant who transforms the anthropologist from a tourist into an ethnographer. The informant may be a child who explains how to play hopscotch, a cocktail waitress who teaches the anthropologist to serve drinks and to encourage customers to leave tips, an elderly man who teaches the anthropologist to build an igloo, or a grandmother who explains the intricacies of Zapotec kinship. Almost any individual who has acquired a repertoire of cultural behavior can become an informant.

Ethnography is not as easy to do as we might think. For one thing, Americans are not taught to be good listeners. We prefer to observe and draw our own conclusions. We like a sense of control in social contexts; passive listening is a sign of weakness in our culture. But listening and learning from others is at the heart of ethnography, and we must put aside our discomfort with the student role.

It is also not easy for informants to teach us about their cultures. Culture is often *tacit*; it is so regular and routine that it lies below a conscious level. A major ethnographic task is to help informants remember their culture, to make their knowledge part of their *explicit culture*.

But, in some cases, it is necessary to infer cultural knowledge by observing an informant's behavior because the cultural rules governing it cannot be expressed in language. Speaking distances, which vary from one culture to the next, and language sound categories, called *phonemes*, are good examples of this kind of tacit culture.

Naive realism may also impede ethnography. *Naive realism* is the belief that people everywhere see the world in the same way. It may, for example, lead the unwary ethnographer to assume that beauty is the same for all people everywhere or, to use our previous example, that dogs should mean the same thing in India as they do in the United States. If an ethnographer fails to control his or her own naive realism, inside cultural meanings will surely be overlooked.

Culture shock and ethnocentrism may also stand in the way of ethnographers. *Culture shock* is a state of anxiety that results from cross-cultural misunderstanding. Immersed alone in another society, the ethnographer understands few of the culturally defined rules for behavior and interpretation used by his or her hosts. The result is anxiety about proper action and an inability to interact appropriately in the new context.

Ethnocentrism can be just as much of a liability. *Ethnocentrism* is the belief and feeling that one's own culture is best. It reflects our tendency to judge other people's beliefs and behavior using values of our own native culture. Thus, if we come from a society that abhors painful treatment of animals, we are likely to react with anger when an Indian villager hits a dog with a rock. Our feeling is ethnocentric.

It is impossible to rid ourselves entirely of the cultural values that make us ethnocentric when we do ethnography. But it is important to control our ethnocentric feeling in the field if we are to learn from informants. Informants resent negative judgment.

Finally, the role assigned to ethnographers by informants affects the quality of what can be learned. Ethnography is a personal enterprise, as all the articles in this section illustrate. Unlike survey research using questionnaires or short interviews, ethnography requires prolonged social contact. Informants will assign the ethnographer some kind of role and what that turns out to be will affect research.

The selections in Part II illustrate several points about culture and ethnography discussed in the preceding section. The first piece, by the late James Spradley, takes a close look at the concept of culture and its role in ethnographic research. The second, by Richard Lee, illustrates how a simple act of giving can have a dramatically different cultural meaning in two societies, leading to cross-cultural misunderstanding. Laura Bohannan's article deals with the concept of naive realism and its role in cross-cultural misunderstanding. When she tells the classic story of *Hamlet* to African Tiv elders, the plot takes on an entirely different meaning as they use their own cultural knowledge to interpret it. Finally, the fourth article, by George Gmelch, explores how fieldwork in another culture can increase understanding of one's own.

KEY TERMS

culture	informant
enthnocentrism	respondent
ethnography	tacit culture
microculture	explicit culture
detached observer	naive realism
subject	culture shock

READINGS IN THIS SECTION

1

Ethnography and Culture

James P. Spradley

Most Americans associate science with detached observation; we learn to observe whatever we wish to understand, introduce our own classification of what is going on, and explain what we see in our own terms. In this selection, James Spradley argues that cultural anthropologists work differently. Ethnography is the work of discovering and describing a particular culture; culture is the learned, shared knowledge that people use to generate behavior and interpret experience. To get at culture, ethnographers must learn the meanings of action and experience from the insider's or informant's point of view. Many of the examples used by Spradley also show the relevance of anthropology to the study of culture in this country.

E thnographic fieldwork is the hallmark of cultural anthropology. Whether in a jungle village in Peru or on the streets of New York, the anthropologist goes to where people live and "does fieldwork." This means participating in activities, asking questions, eating strange foods, learning a new language, watching ceremonies, taking fieldnotes, washing clothes, writing letters home, tracing out genealogies, observing play, interviewing informants, and hundreds of other things. This vast range of activities often obscures the nature of the most fundamental task of all fieldwork: doing ethnography.

Ethnography is the work of describing a culture. The central aim of ethnography is to understand another way of life from the native point of view. The goal of ethnography, as Malinowski put it, is "to grasp the native's point of view, his relation to life, to realize *his* vision of *his* world."[1] Fieldwork, then, involves the disciplined study of what the world is like to people who have learned to see, hear, speak, think, and act in ways that are different. Rather than *studying people*, ethnography means *learning from people*. Consider the following illustration.

George Hicks set out, in 1965, to learn about another way of life, that of the mountain people in an Appalachian valley.[2] His goal was to discover their culture, to learn to see the world from their perspective. With his family he moved into Little Laurel Valley, his daughter attended the local school, and his wife became one of the local Girl Scout leaders. Hicks soon discovered that stores and storekeepers were at the center of the valley's communication system, providing the most important social arena for the entire valley. He learned this by watching what other people did, by following their example, and slowly becoming part of the groups that congregated daily in the stores. He writes:

> At least once each day I would visit several stores in the valley, and sit in on the groups of gossiping men or, if the storekeeper happened to be alone, perhaps attempt to clear up puzzling points about kinship obligations. I found these hours, particularly those spent in the presence of the two or three excellent storytellers in the Little Laurel, thoroughly enjoyable. . . . At other times, I helped a number of local men gather corn or hay, build sheds, cut trees, pull and pack galax, and search for rich stands of huckleberries. When I needed aid in, for example, repairing frozen water pipes, it was readily and cheerfully provided.[3]

In order to discover the hidden principles of another way of life, the researcher must become a *student*. Storekeepers and storytellers and local farmers become *teachers*. Instead of studying the "climate," the "flora," and the "fauna" that made up the environment of this Appalachian valley, Hicks tried to discover how these mountain people defined and evaluated trees and galax and huckleberries. He did not attempt to describe social life in terms of what most Americans know about "marriage," "family," and "friendship"; instead he sought to discover how these mountain people identified relatives and friends. He tried to learn the obligations they felt toward kinsmen and discover how they felt about friends. Discovering the *insider's view* is a different species of knowledge from one that rests

---

[1] Bronislaw Malinowski, *Argonauts of the Western Pacific* (London: Routledge, 1922), 22.
[2] George Hicks, *Appalachian Valley* (New York: Holt, Rinehart, and Winston, 1976).
[3] Hicks, 3.

mainly on the outsider's view, even when the outsider is a trained social scientist.

Consider another example, this time from the perspective of a non-Western ethnographer. Imagine an Eskimo woman setting out to learn the culture of Macalester College. What would she, so well schooled in the rich heritage of Eskimo culture, have to do in order to understand the culture of Macalester College students, faculty, and staff? How would she discover the patterns that made up their lives? How would she avoid imposing Eskimo ideas, categories, and values on everything she saw?

First, and perhaps most difficult, she would have to set aside her belief in *naive realism*, the almost universal belief that all people define the *real* world of objects, events, and living creatures in pretty much the same way. Human languages may differ from one society to the next, but behind the strange words and sentences, all people are talking about the same things. The naive realist assumes that love, snow, marriage, worship, animals, death, food, and hundreds of other things have essentially the same meaning to all human beings. Although few of us would admit to such ethnocentrism, the assumption may unconsciously influence our research. Ethnography starts with a conscious attitude of almost complete ignorance: "I don't know how the people at Macalester College understand their world. That remains to be discovered."

This Eskimo woman would have to begin by learning the language spoken by students, faculty, and staff. She could stroll the campus paths, sit in classes, and attend special events, but only if she consciously tried to see things from the native point of view would she grasp their perspective. She would need to observe and listen to first-year students during their week-long orientation program. She would have to stand in line during registration, listen to students discuss the classes they hoped to get, and visit departments to watch faculty advising students on course selection. She would want to observe secretaries typing, janitors sweeping, and maintenance personnel plowing snow from walks. She would watch the more than 1600 students crowd into the post office area to open their tiny mailboxes, and she would listen to their comments about junk mail and letters from home and no mail at all. She would attend faculty meetings to watch what went on, recording what professors and administrators said and how they behaved. She would sample various courses, attend "keggers" on weekends, read the *Mac Weekly*, and listen by the hour to students discussing things like their "relationships," the "football team," and "work study." She would want to learn the *meanings* of all these things. She would have to listen to the members of this college community, watch what they did, and participate in their activities to learn such meanings.

The essential core of ethnography is this concern with the meaning of actions and events to the people we seek to understand. Some of these meanings are directly expressed in language; many are taken for granted and communicated only indirectly through word and action. But in every society people make constant use of these complex meaning systems to organize their behavior, to understand themselves and others, and to make sense out of the world in which they live. These systems of meaning constitute their culture; ethnography always implies a theory of culture.

CULTURE

When ethnographers study other cultures, they must deal with three fundamental aspects of human experience: what people do, what people know, and the things people make and use. When each of these is learned and shared by members of some group, we speak of them as *cultural behavior, cultural knowledge,* and *cultural artifacts.* Whenever you do ethnographic fieldwork, you will want to distinguish among these three, although in most situations they are usually mixed together. Let's try to unravel them.

Recently I took a commuter train from a western suburb to downtown Chicago. It was late in the day, and when I boarded the train, only a handful of people were scattered about the car. Each was engaged in a common form of *cultural behavior: reading.* Across the aisle a man held the *Chicago Tribune* out in front of him, looking intently at the small print and every now and then turning the pages noisily. In front of him a young woman held a paperback book about twelve inches from her face. I could see her head shift slightly as her eyes moved from the bottom of one page to the top of the next. Near the front of the car a student was reading a large textbook and using a pen to underline words and sentences. Directly in front of me I noticed a man looking at the ticket he had purchased and reading it. It took me an instant to survey this scene, and then I settled back, looked out the window, and read a billboard advertisement for a plumbing service proclaiming it would open any plugged drains. All of us were engaged in the same kind of cultural behavior: reading.

This common activity depended on a great many *cultural artifacts,* the things people shape or make from natural resources. I could see artifacts like books and tickets and newspapers and billboards, all of which contained tiny black marks arranged into intricate patterns called "letters." And these tiny artifacts were arranged into larger patterns of words, sentences, and paragraphs. Those of us on that commuter train could read, in part, because of still other artifacts: the bark of trees made into paper; steel made into printing presses; dyes of various colors made into ink; glue used to hold book pages together; large wooden frames to hold billboards. If an ethnographer wanted to understand the full cultural meaning in our society, it would involve a careful study of these and many other cultural artifacts.

Although we can easily see behavior and artifacts, they represent only the thin surface of a deep lake. Beneath the surface, hidden from view, lies a vast reservoir of *cultural knowledge.* Think for a moment what the people on that train needed to know in order to read. First, they had to know the grammatical rules for at least one language. Then they had to learn what the little marks on paper represented. They also had to know the meaning of space and lines and pages. They had learned cultural rules like "move your eyes from left to right, from the top of the page to the bottom." They had to know that a sentence at the bottom of a page continues on the top of the next page. The man reading a newspaper had to know a great deal about columns and the spaces between columns and what headlines mean. All of us needed to know what kinds of messages were intended by whoever wrote what we read. If a person cannot distinguish the importance of a message on a billboard from one that comes in a letter from a spouse or child, problems would develop. I knew how to recognize when other people were reading. We all knew it was impolite to read aloud on a train. We all knew how to feel when reading things like jokes or calamitous news in the paper. Our culture has a large body of shared knowledge that people learn and use to engage in this behavior called *reading* and make proper use of the artifacts connected with it.

Although cultural knowledge is hidden from view, it is of fundamental importance because we all use it constantly to generate behavior and interpret our experience. Cultural knowledge is so important that I will frequently use the broader term *culture* when speaking about it. Indeed, I will define culture as *the acquired knowledge people use to interpret experience and generate behavior.* Let's consider another example to see how people use their culture to interpret experience and do things.

One afternoon in 1973 I came across the following news item in the *Minneapolis Tribune:*

Crowd Mistakes Rescue Attempt, Attacks Police

Nov. 23, 1973. Hartford, Connecticut. Three policemen giving a heart massage and oxygen to a heart attack victim Friday were attacked by a crowd of 75 to 100 persons who apparently did not realize what the policemen were doing.

Other policemen fended off the crowd of mostly Spanish-speaking residents until an ambulance arrived. Police said they tried to explain to the crowd what they were doing, but the crowd apparently thought they were beating the woman.

Despite the policemen's efforts the victim, Evangelica Echevacria, 59, died.

Here we see people using their culture. Members of two different groups observed the same event, but their *interpretations* were drastically different. The crowd used their cultural knowledge (a) to interpret the behavior of the policemen as cruel and (b) to act on the woman's behalf to put a stop to what they perceived as brutality. They had acquired the cultural principles for acting and interpreting things in this way through a particular shared experience.

The policemen, on the other hand, used their cultural knowledge (a) to interpret the woman's condition as heart failure and their own behavior as a life-saving effort and (b) to give her cardiac massage and oxygen. They used artifacts like an oxygen mask and an ambulance. Furthermore, they interpreted the actions of the crowd in an entirely different manner from how the crowd saw their own behavior. The two groups of people each had elaborate cultural rules for interpreting their experience and for acting in emergency situations, and the conflict arose, at least in part, because these cultural rules were so different.

We can now diagram this definition of culture and see more clearly the relationships among knowledge, behavior, and artifacts (Figure I). By identifying cultural knowledge as fundamental, we have merely shifted the emphasis from behavior and artifacts to their *meaning.* The ethnographer observes behavior but goes beyond it to inquire about the meaning of

Figure I
The two levels of cultural knowledge.

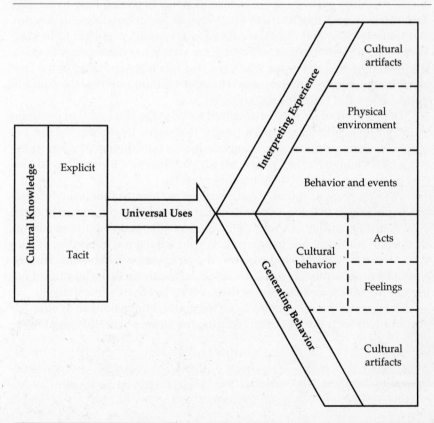

that behavior. The ethnographer sees artifacts and natural objects but goes beyond them to discover what meanings people assign to these objects. The ethnographer observes and records emotional states but goes beyond them to discover the meaning of fear, anxiety, anger, and other feelings.

As represented in Figure I, cultural knowledge exists at two levels of consciousness. *Explicit culture* makes up part of what we know, a level of knowledge people can communicate about with relative ease. When George Hicks asked storekeepers and others in Little Laurel Valley about their relatives, he discovered that any adult over fifty could tell him the genealogical connections among large numbers of people. They knew how to trace kin relationships and the cultural rules for appropriate behavior among kins. All of us have acquired large areas of cultural knowledge such as this which we can talk about and make explicit.

At the same time, a large portion of our cultural knowledge remains *tacit*, outside our awareness. Edward Hall has done much to elucidate the nature of tacit cultural knowledge in his books *The Silent Language* and *The Hidden Dimension*.[4] The way each culture defines space often occurs at the level of tacit knowledge. Hall points out that all of us have acquired thousands of spatial cues about how close to stand to others, how to arrange furniture, when to touch others, and when to feel cramped inside a room. Without realizing that our tacit culture is operating, we begin to feel uneasy when someone from another culture stands too close, breathes on us when talking, touches us, or when we find furniture arranged in the center of the room rather than around the edges. Ethnography is the study of both explicit and tacit cultural knowledge. . . .

The concept of culture as acquired knowledge has much in common with symbolic interactionism, a theory that seeks to explain human behavior in terms of meanings. Symbolic interactionism has its roots in the work of sociologists like Cooley, Mead, and Thomas. Blumer has identified three premises on which this theory rests.

The first premise is that "human beings act toward things on the basis of the meanings that the things have for them."[5] The policemen and the crowd in our earlier example interacted on the basis of the meanings things had for them. The geographic location, the types of people, the police car, the policemen's movements, the sick woman's behavior, and the activities of the onlookers—all were *symbols* with special meanings. People did not act toward the things themselves, but to their meanings.

The second premise underlying symbolic interactionism is that the "meaning of such things is derived from, or arises out of, the social inter-

---

[4] Edward T. Hall, *The Silent Language* (Garden City, NY: Doubleday, 1959); *The Hidden Dimension* (Garden City, NY: Doubleday, 1966).

[5] Herbert Blumer, *Symbolic Interactionism* (Englewood Cliffs, NJ: Prentice-Hall, 1969), 2.

action that one has with one's fellows."[6] Culture, as a shared system of meanings, is learned, revised, maintained, and defined in the context of people interacting. The crowd came to share their definitions of police behavior through interacting with one another and through past associations with the police. The police officers acquired the cultural meanings they used through interacting with other officers and members of the community. The culture of each group was inextricably bound up with the social life of their particular communities.

The third premise of symbolic interactionism is that "meanings are handled in, and modified through, an interpretive process used by the person dealing with the things he encounters."[7] Neither the crowd nor the policemen were automatons, driven by their culture to act in the way they did. Rather, they used their cultural knowledge to interpret and evaluate the situation. At any moment, a member of the crowd might have interpreted the behavior of the policemen in a slightly different way, leading to a different reaction.

We may see this interpretive aspect more clearly if we think of culture as a cognitive map. In the recurrent activities that make up everyday life, we refer to this map. It serves as a guide for acting and for interpreting our experience; it does not compel us to follow a particular course. Like this brief drama between the policemen, a dying woman, and the crowd, much of life is a series of unanticipated social occasions. Although our culture may not include a detailed map for such occasions, it does provide principles for interpreting and responding to them. Rather than a rigid map that people must follow, culture is best thought of as

> a set of principles for creating dramas, for writing script, and of course, for recruiting players and audiences. . . . Culture is not simply a cognitive map that people acquire, in whole or in part, more or less accurately, and then learn to read. People are not just map-readers; they are map-makers. People are cast out into imperfectly charted, continually revised sketch maps. Culture does not provide a cognitive map, but rather a set of principles for map making and navigation. Different cultures are like different schools of navigation to cope with different terrains and seas.[8]

If we take *meaning* seriously, as symbolic interactionists argue we must, it becomes necessary to study meaning carefully. We need a theory of meaning and a specific methodology designed for the investigation of it. . . .

---

[6] Blumer, 2.

[7] Blumer, 2.

[8] Charles O. Frake, "Plying Frames Can Be Dangerous: Some Reflections on Methodology in Cognitive Anthropology," *Quarterly Newsletter of the Institute for Comparative Human Development* 3 (1977): 6–7.

REVIEW QUESTIONS

1. What is the definition of *culture?* How is this definition related to the way anthropologists do ethnographic fieldwork?
2. What is the relationship among cultural behavior, cultural artifacts, and cultural knowledge?
3. What is the difference between tacit and explicit culture? How can anthropologists discover these two kinds of culture?
4. What are some examples of naive realism in the way Americans think about people in other societies?

2

Eating Christmas in the Kalahari

Richard Borshay Lee

What happens when an anthropologist living among the !Kung of Africa decides to be generous and to share a large animal with everyone at Christmastime? This compelling account of the misunderstanding and confusion that resulted takes the reader deeper into the nature of culture. Richard Lee carefully traces how the natives perceived his generosity and taught the anthropologist something about his own culture.

The !Kung Bushmen's knowledge of Christmas is thirdhand. The London Missionary Society brought the holiday to the southern Tswana tribes in the early nineteenth century. Later, native catechists spread the idea far and wide among the Bantu-speaking pastoralists, even in the remotest corners of the Kalahari Desert. The Bushmen's idea of the Christmas story, stripped to its essentials, is "praise the birth of white man's god-chief"; what keeps their interest in the holiday high is the Tswana-Herero custom of slaughtering an ox for his Bushmen neighbors as an annual goodwill gesture. Since the 1930s, part of the Bushmen's an-

Originally published as "A Naturalist at Large: Eating Christmas in the Kalahari." With permission from *Natural History*, December 1969; Copyright © the American Museum of Natural History, 1969.

nual round of activities has included a December congregation at the cattle posts for trading, marriage brokering, and several days of trance dance
feasting at which the local Tswana headman is host.

As a social anthropologist working with !Kung Bushmen, I found that
the Christmas ox custom suited my purposes. I had come to the Kalahari
to study the hunting and gathering subsistence economy of the !Kung, and
to accomplish this it was essential not to provide them with food, share my
own food, or interfere in any way with their food-gathering activities.
While liberal handouts of tobacco and medical supplies were appreciated,
they were scarcely adequate to erase the glaring disparity in wealth between the anthropologist, who maintained a two-month inventory of
canned goods, and the Bushmen, who rarely had a day's supply of food
on hand. My approach, while paying off in terms of data, left me open to
frequent accusations of stinginess and hardheartedness. By their lights, I
was a miser.

The Christmas ox was to be my way of saying thank you for the cooperation of the past year; and since it was to be our last Christmas in the
field, I determined to slaughter the largest, meatiest ox that money could
buy, insuring that the feast and trance dance would be a success.

Through December I kept my eyes open at the wells as the cattle were
brought down for watering. Several animals were offered, but none had
quite the grossness that I had in mind. Then, ten days before the holiday,
a Herero friend led an ox of astonishing size and mass up to our camp. It
was solid black, stood five feet high at the shoulder, had a five-foot span
of horns, and must have weighed 1,200 pounds on the hoof. Food consumption calculations are my specialty, and I quickly figured that bones
and viscera aside, there was enough meat—at least four pounds—for
every man, woman, and child of the 150 Bushmen in the vicinity of /ai/ai
who were expected at the feast.

Having found the right animal at last, I paid the Herero £20 ($56) and
asked him to keep the beast with his herd until Christmas day. The next
morning word spread among the people that the big solid black one was
the ox chosen by /ontah (my Bushman name; it means, roughly, "whitey")
for the Christmas feast. That afternoon I received the first delegation. Ben!a,
an outspoken sixty-year-old mother of five, came to the point slowly.

"Where were you planning to eat Christmas?"

"Right here at /ai/ai," I replied.

"Alone or with others?"

"I expect to invite all the people to eat Christmas with me."

"Eat what?"

"I have purchased Yehave's black ox, and I am going to slaughter and
cook it."

"That's what we were told at the well but refused to believe it until we
heard it from yourself."

"Well, it's the black one," I replied expansively, although wondering what she was driving at.

"Oh, no!" Ben!a groaned, turning to her group. "They were right." Turning back to me she asked, "Do you expect us to eat that bag of bones?"

"Bag of bones! It's the biggest ox at /ai/ai."

"Big, yes, but old. And thin. Everybody knows there's no meat on that old ox. What did you expect us to eat off it, the horns?"

Everybody chuckled at Ben!a's one-liner as they walked away, but all I could manage was a weak grin.

That evening it was the turn of the young men. They came to sit at our evening fire. /gaugo, about my age, spoke to me man-to-man.

"/ontah, you have always been square with us," he lied. "What has happened to change your heart? That sack of guts and bones of Yehave's will hardly feed one camp, let alone all the Bushmen around /ai/ai." And he proceeded to enumerate the seven camps in the /ai/ai vicinity, family by family. "Perhaps you have forgotten that we are not few, but many. Or are you too blind to tell the difference between a proper cow and an old wreck? That ox is thin to the point of death."

"Look, you guys," I retorted, "that is a beautiful animal, and I'm sure you will eat it with pleasure at Christmas."

"Of course we will eat it; it's food. But it won't fill us up to the point where we will have enough strength to dance. We will eat and go home to bed with stomachs rumbling."

That night as we turned in, I asked my wife, Nancy, "What did you think of the black ox?"

"It looked enormous to me. Why?"

"Well, about eight different people have told me I got gypped; that the ox is nothing but bones."

"What's the angle?" Nancy asked. "Did they have a better one to sell?"

"No, they just said that it was going to be a grim Christmas because there won't be enough meat to go around. Maybe I'll get an independent judge to look at the beast in the morning."

Bright and early, Halingisi, a Tswana cattle owner, appeared at our camp. But before I could ask him to give me his opinion on Yehave's black ox, he gave me the eye signal that indicated a confidential chat. We left the camp and sat down.

"/ontah, I'm surprised at you; you've lived here for three years and still haven't learned anything about cattle."

"But what else can a person do but choose the biggest, strongest animal one can find?" I retorted.

"Look, just because an animal is big doesn't mean that it has plenty of meat on it. The black one was a beauty when it was younger, but now it is thin to the point of death."

"Well, I've already bought it. What can I do at this stage?"

"Bought it already? I thought you were just considering it. Well, you'll have to kill it and serve it, I suppose. But don't expect much of a dance to follow."

My spirits dropped rapidly. I could believe that Ben!a and /gaugo just might be putting me on about the black ox, but Halingisi seemed to be an impartial critic. I went around that day feeling as though I had bought a lemon of a used car.

In the afternoon it was Tomazo's turn. Tomazo is a fine hunter, a top trance performer . . . and one of my most reliable informants. He approached the subject of the Christmas cow as part of my continuing Bushman education.

"My friend, the way it is with us Bushmen," he began, "is that we love meat. And even more than that, we love fat. When we hunt we always search for the fat ones, the ones dripping with layers of white fat: fat that turns into a clear, thick oil in the cooking pot, fat that slides down your gullet, fills your stomach and gives you a roaring diarrhea," he rhapsodized.

"So, feeling as we do," he continued, "it gives us pain to be served such a scrawny thing as Yehave's black ox. It is big, yes, and no doubt its giant bones are good for soup, but fat is what we really crave, and so we will eat Christmas this year with a heavy heart."

The prospect of a gloomy Christmas now had me worried, so I asked Tomazo what I could do about it.

"Look for a fat one, a young one . . . smaller, but fat. Fat enough to make us //gom (evacuate the bowels), then we will be happy."

My suspicions were aroused when Tomazo said that he happened to know a young, fat, barren cow that the owner was willing to part with. Was Tomazo working on commission, I wondered? But I dispelled this unworthy thought when we approached the Herero owner of the cow in question and found that he had decided not to sell.

The scrawny wreck of a Christmas ox now became the talk of the /ai/ai water hole and was the first news told to the outlying groups as they began to come in from the bush for the feast. What finally convinced me that real trouble might be brewing was the visit from u!au, an old conservative with a reputation for fierceness. His nickname meant spear and referred to an incident thirty years ago in which he had speared a man to death. He had an intense manner; fixing me with his eyes, he said in clipped tones:

"I have only just heard about the black ox today, or else I would have come here earlier. /ontah, do you honestly think you can serve meat like that to people and avoid a fight?" He paused, letting the implications sink in. "I don't mean fight you, /ontah; you are a white man. I mean a fight between Bushmen. There are many fierce ones here, and with such a small quantity of meat to distribute, how can you give everybody a fair share? Someone is sure to accuse another of taking too much or hogging all the choice pieces. Then you will see what happens when some go hungry while others eat."

The possibility of at least a serious argument struck me as all too real. I had witnessed the tension that surrounds the distribution of meat from a kudu or gemsbok kill, and had documented many arguments that sprang up from a real or imagined slight in meat distribution. The owners of a kill may spend up to two hours arranging and rearranging the piles of meat under the gaze of a circle of recipients before handing them out. And I knew that the Christmas feast at /ai/ai would be bringing together groups that had feuded in the past.

Convinced now of the gravity of the situation, I went in earnest to search for a second cow; but all my inquiries failed to turn one up.

The Christmas feast was evidently going to be a disaster, and the incessant complaints about the meagerness of the ox had already taken the fun out of it for me. Moreover, I was getting bored with the wisecracks, and after losing my temper a few times, I resolved to serve the beast anyway. If the meat fell short, the hell with it. In the Bushmen idiom, I announced to all who would listen:

"I am a poor man and blind. If I have chosen one that is too old and too thin, we will eat it anyway and see if there is enough meat there to quiet the rumbling of our stomachs."

On hearing this speech, Ben!a offered me a rare word of comfort. "It's thin," she said philosophically, "but the bones will make a good soup."

At dawn Christmas morning, instinct told me to turn over the butchering and cooking to a friend and take off with Nancy to spend Christmas alone in the bush. But curiosity kept me from retreating. I wanted to see what such a scrawny ox looked like on butchering, and if there *was* going to be a fight, I wanted to catch every word of it. Anthropologists are incurable that way.

The great beast was driven up to our dancing ground, and a shot in the forehead dropped it in its tracks. Then, freshly cut branches were heaped around the fallen carcass to receive the meat. Ten men volunteered to help with the cutting, I asked /gaugo to make the breast bone cut. This cut, which begins the butchering process for most large game, offers easy access for removal of the viscera. But it also allows the hunter to spot-check the amount of fat on an animal. A fat game animal carries a white layer up to an inch thick on the chest, while in a thin one, the knife will quickly cut to bone. All eyes fixed on his hand as /gaugo, dwarfed by the great carcass, knelt to the breast. The first cut opened a pool of solid white in the black skin. The second and third cut widened and deepened the creamy white. Still no bone. It was pure fat; it must have been two inches thick.

"Hey /gau," I burst out, "that ox is loaded with fat. What's this about the ox being too thin to bother eating? Are you out of your mind?"

"Fat?" /gau shot back. "You call that fat? This wreck is thin, sick, dead!" And he broke out laughing. So did everyone else. They rolled on

the ground, paralyzed with laughter. Everybody laughed except me; I
was thinking.

I ran back to the tent and burst in just as Nancy was getting up. "Hey,
the black ox. It's fat as hell! They were kidding about it being too thin to
eat. It was a joke or something. A put-on. Everyone is really delighted
with it."

"Some joke," my wife replied. "It was so funny that you were ready to
pack up and leave /ai/ai."

If it had indeed been a joke, it had been an extraordinarily convincing
one, and tinged, I thought, with more than a touch of malice, as many jokes
are. Nevertheless, that it was a joke lifted my spirits considerably, and I returned to the butchering site where the shape of the ox was rapidly disappearing under the axes and knives of the butchers. The atmosphere had
become festive. Grinning broadly, their arms covered with blood well past
the elbow, men packed chunks of meat into the big cast-iron cooking pots,
fifty pounds to the load, and muttered and chuckled all the while about
the thinness and worthlessness of the animal and /ontah's poor judgment.

We danced and ate that ox two days and two nights; we cooked and
distributed fourteen potfuls of meat and no one went home hungry and no
fights broke out.

But the "joke" stayed in my mind. I had a growing feeling that something important had happened in my relationship with the Bushmen and
that the clue lay in the meaning of the joke. Several days later, when most
of the people had dispersed back to the bush camps, I raised the question
with Hakekgose, a Tswana man who had grown up among the !Kung,
married a !Kung girl, and who probably knew their culture better than any
other non-Bushman.

"With us whites," I began, "Christmas is supposed to be the day of
friendship and brotherly love. What I can't figure out is why the Bushmen
went to such lengths to criticize and belittle the ox I had bought for the
feast. The animal was perfectly good and their jokes and wisecracks practically ruined the holiday for me."

"So it really did bother you," said Hakekgose. "Well, that's the way
they always talk. When I take my rifle and go hunting with them, if I miss,
they laugh at me for the rest of the day. But even if I hit and bring one
down, it's no better. To them, the kill is always too small or too old or too
thin; and as we sit down on the kill site to cook and eat the liver, they keep
grumbling, even with their mouths full of meat. They say things like, 'Oh,
this is awful! What a worthless animal! Whatever made me think that this
Tswana rascal could hunt!'"

"Is this the way outsiders are treated?" I asked.

"No, it is their custom; they talk that way to each other, too. Go and
ask them."

/gaugo had been one of the most enthusiastic in making me feel bad
about the merit of the Christmas ox. I sought him out first.

"Why did you tell me the black ox was worthless, when you could see that it was loaded with fat and meat?"

"It is our way," he said, smiling. "We always like to fool people about that. Say there is a Bushman who has been hunting. He must not come home and announce like a braggart, 'I have killed a big one in the bush!' He must first sit down in silence until I or someone else comes up to his fire and asks, 'What did you see today?' He replies quietly, 'Ah, I'm no good for hunting. I saw nothing at all [pause] just a little tiny one.' Then I smile to myself," /gaugo continued, "because I know he has killed something big.

"In the morning we make up a party of four or five people to cut up and carry the meat back to the camp. When we arrive at the kill we examine it and cry out, 'You mean to say you have dragged us all the way out here in order to make us cart home your pile of bones? Oh, if I had known it was this thin I wouldn't have come.' Another one pipes up, 'People, to think I gave up a nice day in the shade for this. At home we may be hungry, but at least we have nice cool water to drink.' If the horns are big, someone says, 'Did you think that somehow you were going to boil down the horns for soup?'

"To all this you must respond in kind. 'I agree,' you say, 'this one is not worth the effort; let's just cook the liver for strength and leave the rest for the hyenas. It is not too late to hunt today and even a duiker or a steenbok would be better than this mess.'

"Then you set to work nevertheless; butcher the animal, carry the meat back to the camp and everyone eats," /gaugo concluded.

Things were beginning to make sense. Next, I went to Tomazo. He corroborated /gaugo's story of the obligatory insults over a kill and added a few details of his own.

"But," I asked, "why insult a man after he has gone to all that trouble to track and kill an animal and when he is going to share the meat with you so that your children will have something to eat?"

"Arrogance," was his cryptic answer.

"Arrogance?"

"Yes, when a young man kills much meat he comes to think of himself as a chief or a big man, and he thinks of the rest of us as his servants or inferiors. We can't accept this. We refuse one who boasts, for someday his pride will make him kill somebody. So we always speak of his meat as worthless. This way we cool his heart and make him gentle."

"But why didn't you tell me this before?" I asked Tomazo with some heat.

"Because you never asked me," said Tomazo, echoing the refrain that has come to haunt every field ethnographer.

The pieces now fell into place. I had known for a long time that in situations of social conflict with Bushmen I held all the cards. I was the only source of tobacco in a thousand square miles, and I was not incapable of cutting an individual off for noncooperation. Though my boycott never lasted longer than a few days, it was an indication of my strength. People resented my presence at the water hole, yet simultaneously dreaded my leaving. In short I was a perfect target for the charge of arrogance and for the Bushman tactic of enforcing humility.

I had been taught an object lesson by the Bushmen; it had come from an unexpected corner and had hurt me in a vulnerable area. For the big black ox was to be the one totally generous, unstinting act of my year at /ai/ai and I was quite unprepared for the reaction I received.

As I read it, their message was this: There are no totally generous acts. All "acts" have an element of calculation. One black ox slaughtered at Christmas does not wipe out a year of careful manipulation of gifts given to serve your own ends. After all, to kill an animal and share the meat with people is really no more than the Bushmen do for each other every day and with far less fanfare.

In the end, I had to admire how the Bushmen had played out the farce—collectively straight-faced to the end. Curiously, the episode reminded me of the *Good Soldier Schweik* and his marvelous encounters with authority. Like Schweik, the Bushmen had retained a thoroughgoing skepticism of good intentions. Was it this independence of spirit, I wondered, that had kept them culturally viable in the face of generations of contact with more powerful societies, both black and white? The thought that the Bushmen were alive and well in the Kalahari was strangely comforting. Perhaps, armed with that independence and with their superb knowledge of their environment, they might yet survive the future.

REVIEW QUESTIONS

1. What was the basis of the misunderstanding experienced by Lee when he gave an ox for the Christmas feast held by the !Kung?
2. Construct a model of cross-cultural misunderstanding, using the information presented by Lee in this article.
3. Why do you think the !Kung ridicule and denigrate people who have been successful hunters or who have provided them with a Christmas ox? Why do Americans expect people to be grateful to receive gifts?

3

Shakespeare in the Bush

Laura Bohannan

All of us use the cultural knowledge we acquire as members of our own society to organize our perception and behavior. Most of us are also naive realists: we tend to believe our culture mirrors a reality shared by everyone. But cultures are different, and other people rarely behave or interpret experience according to our cultural plan. In this article, Laura Bohannan describes her attempt to tell the classic story of Hamlet *to Tiv elders in West Africa. At each turn in the story, the Tiv interpret the events and motives in* Hamlet *using their own cultural knowledge. The result is a very different version of the classic play.*

J ust before I left Oxford for the Tiv in West Africa, conversation turned to the season at Stratford. "You Americans," said a friend, "often have difficulty with Shakespeare. He was, after all, a very English poet, and one can easily misinterpret the universal by misunderstanding the particular."

I protested that human nature is pretty much the same the whole world over; at least the general plot and motivation of the greater tragedies would always be clear—everywhere—although some details

Reprinted with permission by the author from *Natural History*, August/September 1966. Copyright © 1966 by Laura Bohannan.

of custom might have to be explained and difficulties of translation
might produce other slight changes. To end an argument we could not
conclude, my friend gave me a copy of *Hamlet* to study in the African bush:
it would, he hoped, lift my mind above its primitive surroundings, and
possibly I might, by prolonged meditation, achieve the grace of correct
interpretation.

It was my second field trip to that African tribe, and I thought myself
ready to live in one of its remote sections—an area difficult to cross even
on foot. I eventually settled on the hillock of a very knowledgeable old
man, the head of a homestead of some hundred and forty people, all of
whom were either his close relatives or their wives and children. Like the
other elders of the vicinity, the old man spent most of his time performing
ceremonies seldom seen these days in the more accessible parts of the
tribe. I was delighted. Soon there would be three months of enforced isolation and leisure, between the harvest that takes place just before the rising of the swamps and the clearing of new farms when the water goes
down. Then, I thought, they would have even more time to perform ceremonies and explain them to me.

I was quite mistaken. Most of the ceremonies demanded the presence
of elders from several homesteads. As the swamps rose, the old men found
it too difficult to walk from one homestead to the next, and the ceremonies
gradually ceased. As the swamps rose even higher, all activities but one
came to an end. The women brewed beer from maize and millet. Men,
women, and children sat on their hillocks and drank it.

People began to drink at dawn. By midmorning the whole homestead
was singing, dancing, and drumming. When it rained, people had to sit inside their huts: there they drank and sang or they drank and told stories.
In any case, by noon or before, I either had to join the party or retire to my
own hut and my books. "One does not discuss serious matters when there
is beer. Come, drink with us." Since I lacked their capacity for the thick native beer, I spent more and more time with *Hamlet*. Before the end of the
second month, grace descended on me. I was quite sure that *Hamlet* had
only one possible interpretation, and that one universally obvious.

Early every morning, in the hope of having some serious talk before
the beer party, I used to call on the old man at his reception hut—a circle
of posts supporting a thatched roof above a low mud wall to keep out
wind and rain. One day I crawled through the low doorway and found
most of the men of the homestead sitting huddled in their ragged cloths on
stools, low plank beds, and reclining chairs, warming themselves against
the chill of the rain around a smoky fire. In the center were three pots of
beer. The party had started.

The old man greeted me cordially. "Sit down and drink." I accepted a
large calabash full of beer, poured some into a small drinking gourd, and
tossed it down. Then I poured some more into the same gourd for the man
second in seniority to my host before I handed my calabash over to a

young man for further distribution. Important people shouldn't ladle beer themselves.

"It is better like this," the old man said, looking at me approvingly and plucking at the thatch that had caught in my hair. "You should sit and drink with us more often. Your servants tell me that when you are not with us, you sit inside your hut looking at a paper."

The old man was acquainted with four kinds of "papers": tax receipts, bride price receipts, court fee receipts, and letters. The messenger who brought him letters from the chief used them mainly as a badge of office, for he always knew what was in them and told the old man. Personal letters for the few who had relatives in the government or mission stations were kept until someone went to a large market where there was a letter writer and reader. Since my arrival, letters were brought to me to be read. A few men also brought me bride price receipts, privately, with requests to change the figures to a higher sum. I found moral arguments were of no avail, since in-laws are fair game, and the technical hazards of forgery difficult to explain to an illiterate people. I did not wish them to think me silly enough to look at any such papers for days on end, and I hastily explained that my "paper" was one of the "things of long ago" of my country.

"Ah," said the old men. "Tell us."

I protested that I was not a storyteller. Storytelling is a skilled art among them; their standards are high, and the audiences critical—and vocal in their criticism. I protested in vain. This morning they wanted to hear a story while they drank. They threatened to tell me no more stories until I told them one of mine. Finally, the old man promised that no one would criticize my style "for we know you are struggling with our language." "But," put in one of the elders, "you must explain what we do not understand, as we do when we tell you our stories." Realizing that here was my chance to prove *Hamlet* universally intelligible, I agreed.

The old man handed me some more beer to help me on with my storytelling. Men filled their long wooden pipes and knocked coals from the fire to place in the pipe bowls; then, puffing contentedly, they sat back to listen. I began in the proper style, "Not yesterday, not yesterday, but long ago, a thing occurred. One night three men were keeping watch outside the homestead of the great chief, when suddenly they saw the former chief approach them."

"Why was he no longer their chief?"

"He was dead," I explained. "That is why they were troubled and afraid when they saw him."

"Impossible," began one of the elders, handing his pipe on to his neighbor, who interrupted, "Of course it wasn't the dead chief. It was an omen sent by a witch. Go on."

Slightly shaken, I continued. "One of these three was a man who knew things"—the closest translation for scholar, but unfortunately it also meant witch. The second elder looked triumphantly at the first. "So he spoke to the dead chief, saying, 'Tell us what we must do so you may rest in your grave,' but the dead chief did not answer. He vanished, and they could see him no more. Then the man who knew things—his name was Horatio—said this event was the affair of the dead chief's son, Hamlet."

There was a general shaking of heads around the circle. "Had the dead chief no living brothers? Or was this son the chief?"

"No," I replied. "That is, he had one living brother who became the chief when the elder brother died."

The old men muttered: such omens were matters for chiefs and elders, not for youngsters; no good could come of being behind a chief's back; clearly Horatio was not a man who knew things.

"Yes, he was," I insisted, shooing a chicken away from my beer. "In our country the son is next to the father. The dead chief's younger brother had become the great chief. He had also married his elder brother's widow only about a month after the funeral."

"He did well," the old man beamed and announced to the others, "I told you that if we knew more about Europeans, we would find they really were very like us. In our country also," he added to me, "the younger brother marries the elder brother's widow and becomes the father of his children. Now, if your uncle, who married your widowed mother, is your father's full brother, then he will be a real father to you. Did Hamlet's father and uncle have one mother?"

His question barely penetrated my mind; I was too upset and thrown too far off balance by having one of the most important elements of *Hamlet* knocked straight out of the picture. Rather uncertainly I said that I thought they had the same mother, but I wasn't sure—the story didn't say. The old man told me severely that these genealogical details made all the difference and that when I got home I must ask the elders about it. He shouted out the door to one of his younger wives to bring his goatskin bag.

Determined to save what I could of the mother motif, I took a deep breath and began again. "The son Hamlet was very sad because his mother had married again so quickly. There was no need for her to do so, and it is our custom for a widow not to go to her next husband until she has mourned for two years."

"Two years is too long," objected the wife, who had appeared with the old man's battered goatskin bag. "Who will hoe your farms for you while you have no husband?"

"Hamlet," I retorted without thinking, "was old enough to hoe his mother's farms himself. There was no need for her to remarry." No one looked convinced. I gave up. "His mother and the great chief told Hamlet not to be sad, for the great chief himself would be a father to Hamlet. Furthermore, Hamlet would be the next chief: therefore he must stay to learn the things of a chief. Hamlet agreed to remain, and all the rest went off to drink beer."

While I paused, perplexed at how to render Hamlet's disgusted soliloquy to an audience convinced that Claudius and Gertrude had behaved
in the best possible manner, one of the younger men asked me who had
married the other wives of the dead chief.

"He had no other wives," I told him.

"But a chief must have many wives! How else can he brew beer and
prepare food for all his guests?"

I said firmly that in our country even chiefs had only one wife, that
they had servants to do their work, and that they paid them from tax
money.

It was better, they returned, for a chief to have many wives and sons
who would help him hoe his farms and feed his people; then everyone
loved the chief who gave much and took nothing—taxes were a bad thing.

I agreed with the last comment, but for the rest fell back on their favorite way of fobbing off my questions: "That is the way it is done, so that
is how we do it."

I decided to skip the soliloquy. Even if Claudius was here thought
quite right to marry his brother's widow, there remained the poison motif, and I knew they would disapprove of fratricide. More hopefully I resumed, "That night Hamlet kept watch with the three who had seen his
dead father. The dead chief again appeared, and although the others were
afraid, Hamlet followed his dead father off to one side. When they were
alone, Hamlet's dead father spoke."

"Omens can't talk!" The old man was emphatic.

"Hamlet's dead father wasn't an omen. Seeing him might have been
an omen, but he was not." My audience looked as confused as I sounded.
"It *was* Hamlet's dead father. It was a thing we call a 'ghost.'" I had to use
the English word, for unlike many of the neighboring tribes, these people
didn't believe in the survival after death of any individuating part of the
personality.

"What is a 'ghost'? An omen?"

"No, a 'ghost' is someone who is dead but who walks around and can
talk, and people can hear him and see him but not touch him."

They objected. "One can touch zombis."

"No, no! It was not a dead body the witches had animated to sacrifice
and eat. No one else made Hamlet's dead father walk. He did it himself."

"Dead men can't walk," protested my audience as one man.

I was quite willing to compromise. "A 'ghost' is a dead man's
shadow."

But again they objected. "Dead men cast no shadows."

"They do in my country," I snapped.

The old man quelled the babble of disbelief that rose immediately and
told me with that insincere, but courteous, agreement one extends to the
fancies of the young, ignorant, and superstitious, "No doubt in your coun-

try the dead can also walk without being zombis." From the depths of his bag he produced a withered fragment of kola nut, bit off one end to show it wasn't poisoned, and handed me the rest as a peace offering.

"Anyhow," I resumed, "Hamlet's dead father said that his own brother, the one who became chief, had poisoned him. He wanted Hamlet to avenge him. Hamlet believed this in his heart, for he did not like his father's brother." I took another swallow of beer. "In the country of the great chief, living in the same homestead, for it was a very large one, was an important elder who was often with the chief to advise and help him. His name was Polonius. Hamlet was courting his daughter, but her father and her brother . . . [I cast hastily about for some tribal analogy] warned her not to let Hamlet visit her when she was alone on her farm, for he would be a great chief and so could not marry her."

"Why not?" asked the wife, who had settled down on the edge of the old man's chair. He frowned at her for asking stupid questions and growled, "They lived in the same homestead."

"That was not the reason," I informed them. "Polonius was a stranger who lived in the homestead because he helped the chief, not because he was a relative."

"Then why couldn't Hamlet marry her?"

"He could have," I explained, "but Polonius didn't think he would. After all, Hamlet was a man of great importance who ought to marry a chief's daughter, for in his country a man could have only one wife. Polonius was afraid that if Hamlet made love to his daughter, then no one else would give a high price for her."

"That might be true," remarked one of the shrewder elders, "but a chief's son would give his mistress's father enough presents and patronage to more than make up the difference. Polonius sounds like a fool to me."

"Many people think he was," I agreed. "Meanwhile Polonius sent his son Laertes off to Paris to learn the things of that country, for it was the homestead of a very great chief indeed. Because he was afraid that Laertes might waste a lot of money on beer and women and gambling, or get into trouble by fighting, he sent one of his servants to Paris secretly, to spy out what Laertes was doing. One day Hamlet came upon Polonius's daughter Ophelia. He behaved so oddly he frightened her. Indeed"—I was fumbling for words to express the dubious quality of Hamlet's madness—"the chief and many others had also noticed that when Hamlet talked one could understand the words but not what they meant. Many people thought that he had become mad." My audience suddenly became much more attentive. "The great chief wanted to know what was wrong with Hamlet, so he sent for two of Hamlet's age mates [school friends would have taken long explanation] to talk to Hamlet and find out what troubled his heart. Hamlet, seeing that they had been bribed by the chief to betray him, told them nothing. Polonius, however, insisted that Hamlet was mad because he had been forbidden to see Ophelia, whom he loved."

"Why," inquired a bewildered voice, "should anyone bewitch Hamlet on that account?"

"Bewitch him?"

"Yes, only witchcraft can make anyone mad, unless, of course, one sees the beings that lurk in the forest."

I stopped being a storyteller, took out my notebook and demanded to be told more about these two causes of madness. Even while they spoke and I jotted notes, I tried to calculate the effect of this new factor on the plot. Hamlet had not been exposed to the beings that lurk in the forest. Only his relatives in the male line could bewitch him. Barring relatives not mentioned by Shakespeare, it had to be Claudius who was attempting to harm him. And, of course, it was.

For the moment I staved off questions by saying that the great chief also refused to believe that Hamlet was mad for the love of Ophelia and nothing else. "He was sure that something much more important was troubling Hamlet's heart."

"Now Hamlet's age mates," I continued, "had brought with them a famous storyteller. Hamlet decided to have this man tell the chief and all his homestead a story about the man who had poisoned his brother because he desired his brother's wife and wished to be chief himself. Hamlet was sure the great chief could not hear the story without making a sign if he was indeed guilty, and then he would discover whether his dead father had told him the truth."

The old man interrupted, with deep cunning. "Why should a father lie to his son?" he asked.

I hedged: "Hamlet wasn't sure that it really was his dead father." It was impossible to say anything, in that language, about devil-inspired visions.

"You mean," he said, "it actually was an omen, and he knew witches sometimes send false ones. Hamlet was a fool not to go to one skilled in reading omens and divining the truth in the first place. A man-who-sees-the-truth could have told him how his father died, if he really had been poisoned, and if there was witchcraft in it; then Hamlet could have called the elders to settle the matter."

The shrewd elder ventured to disagree. "Because his father's brother was a great chief, one-who-sees-the-truth might therefore have been afraid to tell it. I think it was for that reason that a friend of Hamlet's father—a witch and an elder—sent an omen so his friend's son would know. Was the omen true?"

"Yes," I said, abandoning ghosts and the devil; a witch-sent omen it would have to be. "It was true, for when the storyteller was telling his tale before all the homestead, the great chief rose in fear. Afraid that Hamlet knew his secret, he planned to have him killed."

The stage set of the next bit presented some difficulties of translation. I began cautiously. "The great chief told Hamlet's mother to find out from her son what he knew. But because a woman's children are always first in her heart, he had the important elder Polonius hide behind a cloth that hung against the wall of Hamlet's mother's sleeping hut. Hamlet started to scold his mother for what she had done."

There was a shocked murmur from everyone. A man should never scold his mother.

"She called out in fear, and Polonius moved behind the cloth. Shouting 'A rat!' Hamlet took his machete and slashed through the cloth." I paused for a dramatic effect. "He had killed Polonius!"

The old men looked at each other in supreme disgust. "That Polonius truly was a fool and a man who knew nothing! What child would not know enough to shout, 'It's me!'" With a pang, I remembered that these people are ardent hunters, always armed with bow, arrow, and machete; at the first rustle in the grass an arrow is aimed and ready, and the hunter shouts "Game!" If no human voice answers immediately, the arrow speeds on its way. Like a good hunter Hamlet had shouted, "A rat!"

I rushed in to save Polonius's reputation. "Polonius did speak. Hamlet heard him. But he thought it was the chief and wished to kill him to avenge his father. He had meant to kill him earlier that evening. . . ." I broke down, unable to describe to these pagans, who had no belief in individual afterlife, the difference between dying at one's prayers and dying "unhousell'd, disappointed, unaneled."

This time I had shocked my audience seriously. "For a man to raise his hands against his father's brother and the one who has become his father—that is a terrible thing. The elders ought to let such a man be bewitched."

I nibbled at my kola nut in some perplexity, then pointed out that after all the man had killed Hamlet's father.

"No," pronounced the old man, speaking less to me than to the young men sitting behind the elders. "If your father's brother has killed your father, you must appeal to your father's age mates; *they* may avenge him. No man may use violence against his senior relatives." Another thought struck him. "But if his father's brother had indeed been wicked enough to bewitch Hamlet and make him mad, that would be a good story indeed, for it would be his fault that Hamlet, being mad, no longer had any sense and thus was ready to kill his father's brother."

There was a murmur of applause. *Hamlet* was again a good story to them, but it no longer seemed quite the same story to me. As I thought over the coming complications of plot and motive, I lost courage and decided to skim over dangerous ground quickly.

"The great chief," I went on, "was not sorry that Hamlet had killed Polonius. It gave him a reason to send Hamlet away, with his two treacherous age mates, with letters to a chief of a far country, saying that Hamlet should be killed. But Hamlet changed the writing on their papers, so that the chief killed his age mates instead." I encountered a reproachful glare from one of the men whom I had told undetectable forgery was not merely immoral but beyond human skill. I looked the other way.

"Before Hamlet could return, Laertes came back for his father's funeral. The great chief told him Hamlet had killed Polonius. Laertes swore to kill Hamlet because of this, and because his sister Ophelia, hearing her father had been killed by the man she loved, went mad and drowned in the river."

"Have you already forgotten what we told you?" The old man was reproachful. "One cannot take vengeance on a madman; Hamlet killed Polonius in his madness. As for the girl, she not only went mad, she was drowned. Only witches can make people drown. Water itself can't hurt anything. It is merely something one drinks and bathes in."

I began to get cross. "If you don't like the story, I'll stop."

The old man made soothing noises and himself poured me some more beer. "You tell the story well, and we are listening. But it is clear that the elders of your country have never told you what the story really means. No, don't interrupt! We believe you when you say your marriage customs are different, or your clothes and weapons. But people are the same everywhere; therefore, there are always witches and it is we, the elders, who know how witches work. We told you it was the great chief who wished to kill Hamlet, and now your own words have proved us right. Who were Ophelia's male relatives?"

"There were only her father and her brother." Hamlet was clearly out of my hands.

"There must have been many more; this also you must ask of your elders when you get back to your country. From what you tell us, since Polonius was dead, it must have been Laertes who killed Ophelia, although I do not see the reason for it."

We had emptied one pot of beer, and the old men argued the point with slightly tipsy interest. Finally one of them demanded of me, "What did the servant of Polonius say on his return?"

With difficulty I recollected Reynaldo and his mission. "I don't think he did return before Polonius was killed."

"Listen," said the elder, "and I will tell you how it was and how your story will go, then you may tell me if I am right. Polonius knew his son would get into trouble, and so he did. He had many fines to pay for fighting, and debts from gambling. But he had only two ways of getting money quickly. One was to marry off his sister at once, but it is difficult to find a man who will marry a woman desired by the son of a chief. For if the chief's heir commits adultery with your wife, what can you do? Only a fool calls a case against a man who will someday be his judge. Therefore Laertes had to take the second way: he killed his sister by witchcraft, drowning her so he could secretly sell her body to the witches."

I raised an objection. "They found her body and buried it. Indeed Laertes jumped into the grave to see his sister once more—so, you see, the body was truly there. Hamlet, who had just come back, jumped in after him."

"What did I tell you?" The elder appealed to the others. "Laertes was up to no good with his sister's body. Hamlet prevented him, because the chief's heir, like a chief, does not wish any other man to grow rich and powerful. Laertes would be angry, because he would have killed his sister without benefit to himself. In our country he would try to kill Hamlet for that reason. Is this not what happened?"

"More or less," I admitted. "When the great chief found Hamlet was still alive, he encouraged Laertes to try to kill Hamlet and arranged a fight with machetes between them. In the fight both the young men were wounded to death. Hamlet's mother drank the poisoned beer that the chief meant for Hamlet in case he won the fight. When he saw his mother die of poison, Hamlet, dying, managed to kill his father's brother with his machete."

"You see, I was right!" exclaimed the elder.

"That was a very good story," added the old man, "and you told it with very few mistakes. There was just one more error, at the very end. The poison Hamlet's mother drank was obviously meant for the survivor of the fight, whichever it was. If Laertes had won, the great chief would have poisoned him, for no one would know that he arranged Hamlet's death. Then, too, he need not fear Laertes's witchcraft; it takes a strong heart to kill one's only sister by witchcraft.

"Sometime," concluded the old man, gathering his ragged toga about him, "you must tell us some more stories of your country. We, who are elders, will instruct you in their true meaning, so that when you return to your own land your elders will see that you have not been sitting in the bush, but among those who know things and who have taught you wisdom."

REVIEW QUESTIONS

1. In what ways does Bohannan's attempt to tell the story of *Hamlet* to the Tiv illustrate the concept of naive realism?
2. Using Bohannan's experience of telling the story of *Hamlet* to the Tiv and the response of the Tiv elders to her words, illustrate cross-cultural misunderstanding.
3. What are the most important parts of *Hamlet* that the Tiv found it necessary to reinterpret?

4

Lessons from the Field

George Gmelch

Ethnographic fieldwork is a valued tradition in anthropology. Most anthropologists believe that the experience of living and working in another culture is essential to successful research. They also realize, however, that there is more to the experience than discovering and describing the culture of others. Like a rite of passage, fieldwork is an intense personal experience, one that yields deeper insight into one's own culture and personal life. It is this reflexive power of fieldwork that George Gmelch discusses below. He bases his analysis on the experiences of undergraduate students he has sent to do fieldwork in Barbados since 1978. He argues that, after a stressful beginning, students gain valuable new insight into their own racial and national identity, social position, urban existence, and materialism.

S ara, Eric, and Kristen throw their backpacks and suitcases—all the gear they'll need for the next 10 weeks—into the back of the institute's battered Toyota pickup. Sara, a tense grin on her face, gets up front with me; the others climb in the back and make themselves comfortable on the soft luggage.

This article was written especially for this volume. Copyright © by George Gmelch, 1993. Reprinted by permission of the author.

Leaving Bellairs Research Institute on the west coast of the island of Barbados, we drive north past the posh resort hotels. The scene changes abruptly as we move from tourism to agriculture, from the hustle and noise of the coast to the green and quiet of sugar cane fields. There are no more white faces.

Graceful cabbage palms flank a large plantation house, one of the islands "great" houses. On the edge of its cane fields is a tenantry, a cluster of small board houses whose inhabitants are the descendants of the slaves who once worked on the plantation.

Entering the village of Mile and a Quarter, so named because that is the distance from the village to the nearby town of Speightstown, I point out the small orange and blue chattel house that one of my first students lived in. Sara and the others know of Ellen, as she became a documentary filmmaker and has made several films about the island that they have seen.

Two monkeys emerge from a cane field and scamper across the road. I mention that monkeys came to Barbados on early slave ships, 300 years ago. But Sara, absorbed in her own thoughts, doesn't seem to hear me. I've taken enough students to the "field" to have an idea of what's on her mind. She is wondering what her village will be like—the one we just passed through looked unusually poor. And will she like the family she is going to live with? Will they like her? Many people are walking along the road; clusters of men sit and stand outside the rum shop shouting loudly while slamming dominoes down. She is wondering how she will ever make friends with these people and gain their acceptance, which as a student anthropologist she must do.

Earlier in the day, Eric told me that many of the 10 students on the field program thought they had made a mistake coming to Barbados. If they had not chosen to go on the term abroad to Greece, or England, or even Japan, they mused, they would be together on campus, among friends, and safe. They wouldn't have to live in a village; they wouldn't have to go out and make friends with all these strange people; and to do it all alone now seems more of a challenge than many want.

We drive toward the northeastern corner of the island to the village of Pie Corner, where I have arranged for Sara to live with a family. This is the unsheltered side of the island. From several miles off, we can see huge swells rolling in off the Atlantic and beat against the cliffs. The village has only a few hundred people but six small wooden churches, one of which, Bennett's Temple, has windows painted on the wall instead of real glass. Marcus Hinds and his family all come out to the truck to welcome Sara. Mrs. Hinds gives her a big hug, as though she were a returning relative, and daughter Yvette takes Sara into the backyard to show her the pigs and chickens. I explain to the Hindses, for a second time, the nature of the program: Sara, like the other students, will be spending most of her time in the village talking to people and as much as possible participating in the life of the community, which means everything from attending church to cutting sugar cane. He is puzzled as my description doesn't fit his conception of what a university education is all about. The lives of Caribbean villagers is not something he thinks worthy of a university students' attention.

As we drive away from the village, Eric and Kristen comment on the curiosity of the children and the stares from the houses we pass. But they also appear relieved by seeing the warm welcome and friendliness of the family.

Things are different at Eric's village. Chalky Mount sits high on a narrow ridge, on land unsuitable for cultivation. The land drops away so abruptly that most residents have little flat ground and many activities take place on the road. Most houses are simple wooden affairs with corrugated metal roofs. Eric's homestay "mother" shows him around. I see the disappointment in Eric's face when we are shown his bedroom. It is more cramped than he had ever imagined, barely larger than the bed. His new "mother," mostly out of her nervousness and uncertain over what to do with a foreigner, much less a white man, seems aloof and uncaring. Later, Eric writes about his arrival in his fieldnotes:

> It was just awful. I expected my homestay mother to welcome me with open arms and be so excited. But she had nothing to say. The only solution was to go to my room and unpack.

Back in the truck, Kristen, who seemed more relaxed after meeting Sara's family at the first drop-off, begins to bite her nails.

For 15 years I have been taking students to the field, and like most anthropologists, I know a good deal about what they will learn about the foreign culture in which they will live. But it wasn't until this last year, while serving on a committee that evaluated my college's foreign study programs, that I ever thought much about what it is that they learn about their own culture by living in another. The notion that you have to live in another culture before you can understand your own has gained wide acceptance. But what is it that we learn?

I questioned other anthropologists who also take students to the field, and they, too, were unclear about its lessons. A search through the literature didn't help. All the research on the educational outcomes of foreign study has been among students who study at universities in foreign countries.

As a result, I decided to examine the experiences of my own students in Barbados. Using a variety of techniques, including questionnaires, tape-recorded interviews, and analysis of their daily fieldnotes and journals, I looked at their adjustment to the new culture and to being student anthropologists, and at what they learned about their America while living in Barbados and how they learned it. It is primarily the latter—the lessons one learns by living in another culture—that I wish to address here.

Typically, my students go to Barbados expecting to learn a great deal about the culture, about how people there live and think. What they don't expect is that they will also learn much about themselves and their own society. Nor do they imagine that they will discover in this still-developing society attitudes and perspectives that they will take back home and incorporate into their own lives.

RACE

In Barbados the students become members of a racial minority for the first time in their lives. About 95% of the population of the island is of African descent, and 100% of the population of the small villages in which the students live is black. Before going to Barbados, most of my students have had little contact with black people, and as a result they hold negative stereotypes (e.g., blacks are more inclined than whites to use drugs, commit crimes, and collect welfare). The students have little understanding of racial prejudice. During their first few weeks in the field, they become acutely aware of race: of their being white and of everyone around them being dark. Characteristically, during the second week one student wrote:

> I have never been in a situation before where I was a minority purely due to the color of my skin and treated differently because of it. When I approach people, I am very conscious of having white skin. Before, I never thought of myself as having color. (Senior Female)

Some students become hypersensitive to race, especially during the early weeks. When students leave their villages, they travel by bus. The buses are often crowded, and the student is usually the only white person on board. Often, the students are stared at. They notice that, as the bus fills up, the seats next to them are usually the last to be taken, and one common reaction is for them to feel shame or guilt. For example, here is the comment of a female student who went by bus to a remote area to visit a village of potters during her first week in Barbados. There she encountered a woman who stared at her:

> The woman glared at me as if she was seeing the evil white woman who has been responsible for the oppression of her people. I felt like I had chained, maimed, and enslaved every black person who had ever lived. The feelings were so strange . . . somehow I felt responsible for the entire history of the relationship between blacks and whites. I carried this woman's face with me for the rest of the day. When I got on the bus to go back to my village, I felt very alone and very unwanted, as if the mere presence of my color was making a lot of people very uneasy.

But concerns about race, even the very awareness of race, diminish rapidly as the students become integrated into their villages. In fact, by the end of the term, most students have said they were "rarely" aware of being white. Several students have described incidents in which they had become so unaware of skin color that they were shocked when someone made a remark or did something that reminded them of their being different. Sara was startled when, after shaking the hand of someone in her village, the person remarked that she had never touched the hand of a white person before. Several students reported being surprised when they walked by a mirror and got a glimpse of their white skin. One student wrote that, although she knew she wasn't black, she no longer felt white.

What is the outcome of all this? Do these students now have an understanding of what it means to be a minority, and does this translate into their having more empathy for blacks at home in America? Yes, I think so. All the students from the previous five Barbados programs whom I have questioned about the impact of their experiences mentioned a heightened awareness of race. Many said they now felt an affinity with black people. Several innocently revealed that, when they first returned home, they wanted to go up to any black person they saw and have a conversation. "But I kept having to remind myself," said one student, "that most blacks in America are not West Indians and they wouldn't understand where I was coming from." Another said that her first, admittedly naive, reaction on coming home and seeing black people was to want to hug every one of them.

SOCIAL CLASS

In *The Closing of the American Mind,* Leonard Bloom said that American students, particularly compared to their European counterparts, have little understanding of social class. My students are no exception. Even after several weeks in Barbados, most students see class primarily as a division between the tiny white minority who control the island's commerce and the black majority. They typically view the black population, especially the people of their villages, as being homogeneous. They do not yet see that within the black population there are distinct middle and working classes. For example, early in the term, one student wrote:

> Most Barbadians come from the same social-economic strata and they have similar values, religious beliefs, and heritage, which they can all look back on as a unifying force.

The students also do not have a clear idea of what distinguishes working-class from middle-class occupations. One student described everyone in his village, a village in which the most of the people work as carpenters and hotel waiters and maids, as "middle-class."

It is largely from the comments that their home-stay families make about other people, from travel to other villages, and from visits to several schools that draw their pupils from the different social classes that the students gradually become aware of class distinctions. But equally, students learn about class and status by making mistakes and by violating norms concerning relationships between different categories of people. As in most field situations, the first villagers to offer the students friendship are often marginal members of the community, and this kind of friendship creates special problems in that the students are guests in the homes of "respectable" and often high-status village families.

The home-stay parents become upset when they discover their student has been seeing a disreputable man or woman. The most serious difficulties arise when female students date lower-class local men. The women enter into these relationships oblivious of what the local reaction may be, and equally oblivious of how little privacy there is in a village where everyone knows everyone else's business. One student said she wrongly assumed that people would look favorably on her going with a local man because it would show she wasn't prejudiced, that she thought blacks were just as desirable as whites. Another female student befriended some Rastas—orthodox Rastas, who wore no clothes, lived off the land, and slept in caves in the hills above her village. When villagers discovered she had been seeing the Rastas, her home-stay mother nearly evicted her, and others gave her the cold shoulder. The student wrote:

> I have discovered the power of a societal norm: nice girls don't talk to Rastas. When girls who were formerly nice talk to Rastas, they cease to be known as nice. Exceptions none.

RURALISM

There were also some lessons in the difference between rural and urban. Over 80% of my students come from suburbs or cities and have never lived in the countryside before. For them, a significant part of the experience is rural life, living among people who are close to the land. The home-stay families, like most villagers, grow crops and raise animals. Each morning, well before dawn, the students are awakened by the sounds of animals in the yard. Students learn something of the behavior of chickens, pigs, sheep, and cows. They witness animals giving birth and being slaughtered. They see the satisfaction their families get from consuming food they have produced themselves. One senior female wrote about the effect of an everyday occurrence:

> I was in Mrs S's kitchen and she was making sugar cakes. The recipe calls for a lime, and when she didn't have any in the kitchen, she just walked into the yard and pulled a few off the nearest tree. It was nothing to her, but I was amazed, and I thought how, in that situation, I would've had to drive to the supermarket.

In the villages, most students live close to nature for a prolonged period of time. They become aware of how different are the sounds of the countryside and are struck by the darkness of the sky and the brightness of the stars as there are no city lights to diminish their intensity. A student from Long Island described it as being "like living in a planetarium."

Most of the students come from families in which their fathers or mothers work at a single job, while in Barbados most village men and women depend on multiple sources of income to make ends meet: a pattern known as "occupational pluralism." The home-stay father of one student, for example, was a rural postman, a Pentecostal minister, and a small farmer, while his wife ran a small shop and was mother to six children. How hard many people must work to make a living leaves an impression on most students and makes them realize how much easier they have it in the United States.

The social world of the village is even more alien from the student's background than is its economy. In doing a household census, for example, students discover that not only does everybody seem to know everybody else, and that many families are related to one another, but that they know one another in more than one context. The man who runs the local shop is not just shopkeeper to the home-stay family, he is also a member of the family's church, plays on the same cricket team with the home-stay father, and is a distant cousin. People are tied to one another in multiple ways; relationships are not single-stranded as they often are in the urban United States the students come from.

Students have never known a place of such intimacy, where relationships are so embedded with different meanings and a shared history. Some students reflect on and compare the warmth, friendliness, and frequent sharing of food and other resources with the impersonality, individualism, and detachment of urban life at home.

But they also learn there are drawbacks to living in small communities: there is no anonymity. People are nosy and unduly interested in the affairs of their neighbors. As the students become integrated into the community, they soon discover that they, too, may be the object of local gossip. Three of the four female students this year learned from village friends that there were stories afoot that they were either mistresses to their home-stay fathers or sleeping with their home-stay brothers. The gossip hurt, as the students had worked hard to gain acceptance, greatly valued the friendships they had made, and were concerned about the damage such rumors might do to their reputations.

One of the biggest adjustments that the students must make to village life is to the slow pace, and to the absence of the diversions and entertainment that they are accustomed to at home. Early in their stay, there seems to be little to do apart from their research. At times they are desperate to escape the village, but they are not allowed to leave except on designated days (all students initially hate this restriction, but by the end of the term, they recommend that it be continued). The outcome of their forced isolation is that the students must satisfy their needs for companionship and recreation within their communities. They must learn to be resourceful in finding ways to entertain themselves. They spend a good deal of time just hanging out, socializing with people in the village, which strengthens friendships and results in a good deal of informal education about culture.

By the midpoint in the term, the students have adapted well enough to village life so that they no longer report being bored or desperate to get away. And many no longer leave the village on their day off.

NEW PERSPECTIVES ON THE UNITED STATES

In learning about another culture, the students inevitably make comparisons with their own culture. Especially in the early stages of fieldwork, the students think about Barbadian customs in terms of how similar they are to or how different from those at home. The students are often assisted in such comparisons by the villagers, who know a lot about the United States themselves: much of their television programming comes from the United States, many North Americans vacation in Barbados, and because of high rates of outmigration, nearly every village household has a relative in North America. Many Barbadians have also been abroad themselves.

Students quickly discover that the villagers' perspectives on the United States are often at odds with their own. Early in the term, students often report having defended their country against criticism. For example, one student who became involved in a debate over the invasion of Panama wrote, "I didn't really believe we were right going into Panama, but I felt as if I had to stand up to him." Another student described getting very annoyed by a guest at the dinner table who talked about American chicken being adulterated with chemicals, even though she knew him to be right.

Over time, the students become less eager to defend their own society. Indeed, many become quite critical of the United States, or at least aspects of it. Why? What causes them to think differently about their country after a few months in a Barbadian village? Part of the answer is found in the students' growing appreciation of many aspects of Barbadian life and their identification with the local people. The students come to see many things from the perspective of their village friends.

Another factor is the students' exposure to North American tourists, and to the effect of their presence on Barbados. Nearly 500,000 tourists, mostly North American and British, visit Barbados annually. That figure is about twice the population of the island. Several cruise ships arrive weekly, and tourist hotels crowd much of the island's south and west coasts. Students hear tales from their village informants who work in the hotels about the misbehavior of tourists. When the students go to the beach or to town, they encounter tourists themselves and are sometimes appalled by what they see and hear. Aware of how staunchly conservative Barbadians are about dress and the exposure of flesh, the students witness middle-class Americans enter shops and grocery stores and walk the streets in the skimpiest of beach attire. They hear the loudness of American voices, decibels above and more intrusive than the voices of Barbadians. They observe white women coming to Barbados for sex as much as for sun, availing themselves of the local beach bums.

The students are surprised by how little many tourists know about the country they have come to visit. How could someone come all this way, they ask, and not know what language is spoken, or that most of the people are black, or that Barbados is no longer a colony of Great Britain. They discover that most American visitors, unlike themselves, aren't really very interested in learning about the people or their culture:

> The tourists don't really care about Barbadians. They're here for a quick fix. They get off the tour buses, have a quick look around, snap a few pictures, and off they go, and they think they've seen Barbados. They haven't even scratched the surface. We're (the United States) a society with blinkers; we don't take the time to look at things, or try to understand things. (Junior Male)

From a variety of sources, students learn about the social impact of tourism: increased crime, drug abuse, prostitution, and the Americanization of culture, as readily seen in the arrival of McDonalds, Kentucky Fried Chicken, CNN, and so on. Viewing tourism as part of a broader Americanization of the region, many students become critical not only of tourists themselves but of the U.S. presence abroad generally.

MATERIALISM

Living in a village, combined with exposure to tourists, leads many students to a new awareness of wealth and materialism. One of the strongest initial perceptions that the students have of their villages is that people are poor—that their houses are tiny, their diets are restricted, and they have few of the amenities and comforts the students are accustomed to. (In reality, Barbadians are among the most affluent people in the Eastern Caribbean, but the students don't realize that until much later, when they visit several other islands.) A frequent response of the students to the poverty they perceive around them is to feel embarrassed and even guilty that they, like many Americans, have so much wealth and the villagers have so little.

However, such feelings are short-lived, for as the students get to know the families better, they no longer see poverty, and the houses no longer seem so small. They discover that most people not only manage quite well on what they have but are also reasonably content. In fact, most students eventually come to believe that the villagers are, on the whole, actually more satisfied with their lives than are most Americans. Whether or not this is true, it's an important perception for students whose ideas about happiness have been shaped by an ethos that measures success and satisfaction by material gain. About his home-stay family, Eric said:

> I ate off the same plate and drank from the same cup every night. We only had an old fridge, an old stove, an old TV, and a few dishes and pots and pans. But that was plenty. Mrs. H. never felt like she needed any more. And after a while I never felt like I needed any more either.

I believe that one result of this awareness is that many students become less materialistic. Many students have said that when they came back to campus after Barbados, they didn't bring nearly as many things with them as they usually do. A junior female student said:

> When I came back, I saw how out-of-control the students here are. It's just crazy. They want so much; they talk about how much money they need to make, as if these things are necessities and you'll never be happy without them. Maybe I was like that, too, but now I know I don't need those things; sure, I'd like a great car, but I don't need it.

Many students have said that when they returned home from Barbados they were surprised by how many possessions they owned. Several said they went through their drawers and closets and gave away to the Good Will or the Salvation Army all the things they didn't really need. Most said they would no longer take for granted the luxuries, such as hot showers, that they have on campus and at home.

FIELDWORK AND EDUCATION

Students learn about more than just cultural difference from their experience of living and doing anthropology alone in a Caribbean village. Most return from Barbados with a more positive attitude toward education. This appears to stem both from their own experiences in doing research and from their seeing the high value the villagers place on formal education. Barbadians view education as the principal means of upward mobility. In a society in which whites control most sectors of the economy, the best jobs available to nonwhites are in government, and civil service positions require diplomas and the passing of competitive exams. My students not only become aware of the villagers' esteem for education but also see that they themselves are accorded respect and adult status largely because they are working toward a university degree.

Also, as the weeks pass, most students become deeply involved in their own research, to the point where it becomes the focus of their existence. They are surprised by how much satisfaction they get from doing something that they previously regarded as "work." A number of the students from past terms have said that they hadn't seen education as an end in itself until their Barbados experience. One student wrote about her new attitude after returning from the field:

> I feel isolated from many of my old friends on campus, and I no longer feel guilty missing social events. . . . I appreciate my education more, and I do much more work for my own understanding and enjoyment rather than just for the exam or grades. I find myself, on a daily basis, growing agitated with those who don't appreciate what is being offered to them here. Several of my classmates blow off class and use others people's notes. A lot of what I feel is from seeing how important education was to my Bajan friends in Barbados compared to the lax attitude of my Union [College] friends here.

Students spend much of their time in the field talking to people; a good part of each day is spent in conversations that they must direct onto the topics that they are investigating. To succeed at their studies, they must learn to be inquisitive, to probe sensitively, to concentrate and listen to what they are being told, and later to be able to recall it so that they may record it in fieldnotes. The students become proficient in maintaining lengthy conversations with adults and in asking pertinent questions. These are interpersonal skills that they bring back with them and make use of in many aspects of their own lives.

As the world's economies intertwine and its societies move closer to the "global village" Marshall McLuhan envisioned, it is more imperative than ever that we seek to understand other peoples and cultures. Without understanding, there can be neither respect, nor prosperity, nor lasting peace. My students, in the course of becoming part of village life, invariably arrive at the notion that, beneath differences in race and culture, Barbadians and Americans are all one. In the words of a male student:

> If I had to sum up my whole trip in one experience, it would be this: It was late at night, a full moon, and I sat in a pasture with a local Rastafarian. After hours of talking, about everything from love to politics, the two of us came to an interesting conclusion. Although we lived a thousand miles away from each other, and that our skin color, hair style, and many personal practices were quite different, at heart we were the same people.

While this may seem like common sense, I assure you that it is not a notion that many 20-year-old college students share today. "The tragedy about Americans," noted Mexican novelist Carlos Fuentes, "is that they understand others so little." Students who study abroad, like those described in these pages, not only enrich themselves but in countless small ways help bridge the gulf between us and those we regard as "foreign."

REVIEW QUESTIONS

1. What are the main ways that fieldwork in Barbados has changed students' perceptions of their own culture and personal lives?
2. How has the behavior of U.S. tourists in Barbados changed students' perception of their own nation?
3. How has life in a Barbadian rural community affected students' views of U.S. materialism and social class?
4. How do you think fieldwork achieves the personal transformations described by Gmelch in the students he has sent to Barbados?

LANGUAGE AND COMMUNICATION

Culture is a system of symbols that allows us to represent and communicate our experience. We are surrounded by symbols: the flag, a new automobile, a diamond ring, billboard pictures, and, of course, spoken words.

A *symbol* is anything that we can perceive with our senses that stands for something else. Almost anything we experience can come to have symbolic meaning. Every symbol has a referent that it calls to our attention. The term *mother-in-law* refers to a certain kind of relative, the mother of a person's spouse. When we communicate with symbols, we call attention not only to the referent but also to numerous connotations of the symbol. In our culture, *mother-in-law* connotes a stereotype of a person who is difficult to get along with, who meddles in the affairs of her married daughter or son, and who is to be avoided. Human beings have the capacity to assign meaning to anything they experience in an arbitrary fashion. This fact gives rise to limitless possibilities for communication.

Symbols greatly simplify the task of communication. Once we learn that a word like *barn,* for example, stands for a certain type of building, we can communicate about a whole range of specific buildings that fit into the category. And we can communicate about barns in their absence; we can even invent flying barns and dream about barns. Symbols make it possible to communicate the immense variety of human experience, whether past or present, tangible or intangible, good or bad.

Many channels are available to human beings for symbolic communication: sound, sight, touch, and smell. Language, our most highly developed communication system, uses the channel of sound (or, for some deaf people, sight). *Language* is a system of cultural knowledge used to generate and interpret speech. It is a feature of every culture and a distinctive characteristic of the human animal. *Speech* refers to the behavior that produces vocal sounds. Our distinction between language and speech is like the one made between culture and behavior. Language is part of culture, the system of knowledge that generates behavior. Speech is the behavior generated and interpreted by language.

Every language is composed of three subsystems for dealing with vocal symbols: phonology, grammar, and semantics. Let's look briefly at each of these.

Phonology consists of the categories and rules for forming vocal symbols. It is concerned not directly with meaning but with the formation and recognition of the vocal sounds to which we assign meaning. For example, if you utter the word *bat*, you have followed a special set of rules for producing and ordering sound categories characteristic of the English language.

A basic element defined by phonological rules for every language is the phoneme. *Phonemes* are the minimal categories of speech sounds that serve to keep utterances apart. For example, speakers of English know that the words *bat, cat, mat, hat, rat*, and *fat* are different utterances because they hear the sounds /b/, /c/, /m/, /h/, /r/, and /f/ as different categories of sounds. In English each of these is a phoneme. Our language contains a limited number of phonemes from which we construct all our vocal symbols.

Phonemes are arbitrarily constructed, however. Each phoneme actually classifies slightly different sounds as though they were the same. Different languages may divide up the same range of speech sounds into different sound categories. For example, speakers of English treat the sound /t/ as a single phoneme. Hindi speakers take the same general range and divide it into four phonemes: /t/, /t^h/, /T/, and /T^h/. (The lowercase *t*'s are made with the tongue against the front teeth, while the uppercase *T*'s are made by touching the tongue to the roof of the mouth further back than would be normal for an English speaker. The *h* indicates a puff of air, called *aspiration*, associated with the *t* sound.) Americans are likely to miss important distinctions among Hindi words because they hear these four different phonemes as a single one. Hindi speakers, on the other hand, tend to hear more than one sound category as they listen to English speakers pronounce *t*'s. The situation is reversed for /w/ and /v/. We treat these as two phonemes, whereas Hindi speakers hear them as one. For them, the English words *wine* and *vine* sound the same.

Phonology also includes rules for ordering different sounds. Even when we try to talk nonsense, we usually create words that follow English phonological rules. It would be unlikely, for example, for us ever to begin a word with the phoneme /ng/ usually written in English as "ing." It must come at the end or in the middle of words.

Grammar is the second subsystem of language. *Grammar* refers to the categories and rules for combining vocal symbols. No grammar contains rules for combining every word or element of meaning in the language. If this were the case, grammars would be so unwieldy that no one could learn all the rules in a lifetime. Every grammar deals with *categories* of symbols, such as the ones we call *nouns* and *verbs*. Once you know the rules covering a particular category, you can use it in appropriate combinations.

Morphemes are the categories in any language that carry meaning. They are minimal units of meaning that cannot be subdivided. Morphemes occur in more complex patterns than you may think. The term *bats,* for example, is actually two morphemes, /bat/ meaning a flying mammal and /s/ meaning plural. Even more confusing, two different morphemes may have the same sound shape. /Bat/ can refer to a wooden club used in baseball as well as a flying mammal.

The third subsystem of every language is semantics. *Semantics* refers to the categories and rules for relating vocal symbols to their referents. Like the rules of grammar, semantic rules are simple instructions for combining things; they instruct us to combine words with what they refer to. A symbol can be said to *refer* because it focuses our attention and makes us take account of something. For example, /bat/ refers to a family of flying mammals, as we have already noted.

Language regularly occurs in a social context, and to understand its use fully, it is important to recognize its relation to sociolinguistic rules. *Sociolinguistic rules* combine meaningful utterances with social situations into appropriate messages.

Although language is the most important human vehicle for communication, almost anything we can sense may represent a *nonlinguistic symbol* that conveys meaning. The way we sit, how we use our eyes, how we dress, the car we own, the number of bathrooms in our house—all these things carry symbolic meaning. We learn what they mean as we acquire culture. Indeed, a major reason we feel so uncomfortable when we enter a group with a strange culture is our inability to decode our hosts' symbolic world.

The articles in this section illustrate several important aspects of language and communication. The first selection, by Edward and Mildred Hall, shows the significance of nonverbal symbols. The authors describe how tacit behaviors, such as eye contact and speaking distance, form powerful channels for communication in human groups. The second article, by David Thomson, describes the hypothesis generated in the 1930s by a young linguist named Benjamin Lee Whorf. Whorf argued that, instead of merely labeling reality, the words and grammatical structure of a language can actually determine the way its speakers perceive the world. Thomson reviews and evaluates this hypothesis and asserts that, although language may not create reality, it affects our perceptions, as illustrated by the use of words in American advertising and political doublespeak. In the third selection, Conrad Kottak looks at the role played by "teleconditioning" in the creation of American cultural behavior. He argues that the ways people relate to their television sets inappropriately carry over into other social settings, such as university classrooms, and that television is a major enculturating force in American life. The final article, by Jared Diamond, discusses the accelerating rate of language extinctions around the world. Describing the process and causes of language loss, Diamond argues for bilingualism as a way to preserve the rich cultural and linguistic heritage contained in the world's 6,000 remaining tongues.

KEY TERMS

symbol	grammar
language	morpheme
speech	semantics
phonology	sociolinguistic rules
phoneme	nonlinguistic symbols

READINGS IN THIS SECTION

5

The Sounds of Silence

Edward T. Hall and Mildred Reed Hall

*People communicate with more than just words. An important part
of every encounter is the messages we send with our bodies and
faces: the smile, the frown, the slouch of the shoulders, or the tightly
crossed legs are only a few gestures that add another dimension to
our verbal statements. These gestures as well as their cultural meaning change from one culture to another. They also vary over time as
styles and meanings change. Often, nonverbal symbols, such as
speaking distances, operate outside the awareness of actors and represent good examples of* tacit culture *(see Part II). In this classic article, Edward and Mildred Hall, pioneers in the study of nonverbal
communication, describe and explain the function of nonverbal symbols and their meanings for social encounters observed by them and
other researchers during the 1960s.*

Bob leaves his apartment at 8:15 A.M. and stops at the corner drug-
store for breakfast. Before he can speak, the counterman says, "The
usual?" Bob nods yes. While he savors his Danish, a fat man pushes onto
the adjoining stool and overflows into his space. Bob scowls and the man

pulls himself in as much as he can. Bob has sent two messages without speaking a syllable.

Henry has an appointment to meet Arthur at 11 o'clock; he arrives at 11:30. Their conversation is friendly, but Arthur retains a lingering hostility. Henry has unconsciously communicated that he doesn't think the appointment is very important or that Arthur is a person who needs to be treated with respect.

George is talking to Charley's wife at a party. Their conversation is entirely trivial, yet Charley glares at them suspiciously. Their physical proximity and the movements of their eyes reveal that they are powerfully attracted to each other.

José Ybarra and Sir Edmund Jones are at the same party and it is important for them to establish a cordial relationship for business reasons. Each is trying to be warm and friendly, yet they will part with mutual distrust and their business transaction will probably fall through. José, in Latin fashion, moved closer and closer to Sir Edmund as they spoke, and this movement was miscommunicated as pushiness to Sir Edmund, who kept backing away from this intimacy, and this was miscommunicated to José as coldness. The silent languages of Latin and English cultures are more difficult to learn than their spoken languages.

In each of these cases, we see the subtle power of nonverbal communication. The only language used throughout most of the history of humanity (in evolutionary terms, vocal communication is relatively recent), it is the first form of communication you learn. You use this preverbal language, consciously and unconsciously, every day to tell other people how you feel about yourself and them. This language includes your posture, gestures, facial expressions, costume, the way you walk, even your treatment of time and space and material things. All people communicate on several different levels at the same time, but are usually aware of only the verbal dialog and don't realize that they respond to nonverbal messages. But when a person says one thing and really believes something else, the discrepancy between the two can usually be sensed. Nonverbal communication systems are much less subject to the conscious deception that often occurs in verbal systems. When we find ourselves thinking, "I don't know what it is about him, but he doesn't seem sincere," it's usually this lack of congruity between a person's words and his behavior that makes us anxious and uncomfortable.

Few of us realize how much we all depend on body movement in our conversation or are aware of the hidden rules that govern listening behavior. But we know instantly whether or not the person we're talking to is "tuned in" and we're very sensitive to any breach in listening etiquette. In white middle-class American culture, when someone wants to show he is listening to someone else, he looks either at the other person's face or, specifically, at his eyes, shifting his gaze from one eye to the other.

If you observe a person conversing, you'll notice that he indicates he's listening by nodding his head. He also makes little "Hmm" noises. If he

agrees with what's being said, he may give a vigorous nod. To show pleasure or affirmation, he smiles; if he has some reservations, he looks skep-
tical by raising an eyebrow or pulling down the corners of his mouth. If a
participant wants to terminate the conversation, he may start shifting his
body position, stretching his legs, crossing or uncrossing them, bobbing
his foot or diverting his gaze from the speaker. The more he fidgets, the
more the speaker becomes aware that he has lost his audience. As a last
measure, the listener may look at his watch to indicate the imminent end
of the conversation.

Talking and listening are so intricately intertwined that a person cannot do one without the other. Even when one is alone and talking to oneself, there is part of the brain that speaks while another part listens. In all
conversations, the listener is positively or negatively reinforcing the speaker all the time. He may even guide the conversation without knowing it, by
laughing or frowning or dismissing the argument with a wave of his hand.

The language of the eyes—another age-old way of exchanging feelings—is both subtle and complex. Not only do men and women use their
eyes differently but there are class, generation, regional, ethnic, and national cultural differences. Americans often complain about the way foreigners stare at people or hold a glance too long. Most Americans look
away from someone who is using his eyes in an unfamiliar way because it
makes them self-conscious. If a man looks at another man's wife in a certain way, he's asking for trouble, as indicated earlier. But he might not be
ill-mannered or seeking to challenge the husband. He might be a European in this country who hasn't learned our visual mores. Many American
women visiting France or Italy are acutely embarrassed because, for the
first time in their lives, men really look at them—their eyes, hair, nose, lips,
breasts, hips, legs, thighs, knees, ankles, feet, clothes, hairdo, even their
walk. These same women, once they have become used to being looked at,
often return to the United States and are overcome with the feeling that
"No one ever really looks at me anymore."

Analyzing the mass of data on the eyes, it is possible to sort out at least
three ways in which the eyes are used to communicate: dominance vs.
submission, involvement vs. detachment, and positive vs. negative attitude. In addition, there are three levels of consciousness and control,
which can be categorized as follows: (1) conscious use of the eyes to communicate, such as the flirting blink and the intimate nose-wrinkling
squint; (2) the very extensive category of unconscious but learned behavior governing where the eyes are directed and when (this unwritten set of
rules dictates how and under what circumstances the sexes, as well as people of all status categories, look at each other); and (3) the response of the
eye itself, which is completely outside both awareness and control—
changes in the cast (the sparkle) of the eye and the pupillary reflex.

The eye is unlike any other organ of the body, for it is an extension of
the brain. The unconscious pupillary reflex and the cast of the eye have
been known by people of Middle Eastern origin for years—although most

are unaware of their knowledge. Depending on the context, Arabs and others look either directly at the eyes or deeply *into* the eyes of their interlocutor. We became aware of this in the Middle East several years ago while looking at jewelry. The merchant suddenly started to push a particular bracelet at a customer and said, "You buy this one." What interested us was that the bracelet was not the one that had been consciously selected by the purchaser. But the merchant, watching the pupils of the eyes, knew what the purchaser really wanted to buy. Whether he specifically knew *how* he knew is debatable.

A psychologist at the University of Chicago, Eckhard Hess, was the first to conduct systematic studies of the pupillary reflex. His wife remarked one evening, while watching him reading in bed, that he must be very interested in the text because his pupils were dilated. Following up on this, Hess slipped some pictures of nudes into a stack of photographs that he gave to his male assistant. Not looking at the photographs but watching his assistant's pupils, Hess was able to tell precisely when the assistant came to the nudes. In further experiments, Hess retouched the eyes in a photograph of a woman. In one print, he made the pupils small, in another, large; nothing else was changed. Subjects who were given the photographs found the woman with the dilated pupils much more attractive. Any man who has had the experience of seeing a woman look at him as her pupils widen with reflex speed knows that she's flashing him a message.

The eye-sparkle phenomenon frequently turns up in our interviews of couples in love. It's apparently one of the first reliable clues in the other person that love is genuine. To date, there is no scientific data to explain eye sparkle; no investigation of the pupil, the cornea, or even the white sclera of the eye shows how the sparkle originates. Yet we all know it when we see it.

One common situation for most people involves the use of the eyes in the street and in public. Although eye behavior follows a definite set of rules, the rules vary according to the place, the needs and feelings of the people, and their ethnic background. For urban whites, once they're within definite recognition distance (16–32 feet for people with average eyesight), there is mutual avoidance of eye contact—unless they want something specific: a pickup, a handout, or information of some kind. In the West and in small towns generally, however, people are much more likely to look at and greet one another, even if they're strangers.

It's permissible to look at people if they're beyond recognition distance; but once inside this sacred zone, you can only steal a glance at strangers. You *must* greet friends, however; to fail to do so is insulting. Yet, to stare too fixedly even at them is considered rude and hostile. Of course, all of these rules are variable.

A great many blacks, for example, greet each other in public even if they don't know each other. To blacks, most eye behavior of whites has the effect of giving the impression that they aren't there, but this is due to white avoidance of eye contact with *anyone* in the street.

Another very basic difference between people of different ethnic backgrounds is their sense of territoriality and how they handle space. This is the silent communication, or miscommunication, that caused friction between Mr. Ybarra and Sir Edmund Jones in our earlier example. We know from research that everyone has around himself an invisible bubble of space that contracts and expands depending on several factors: his emotional state, the activity he's performing at the time and his cultural background. This bubble is a kind of mobile territory that he will defend against intrusion. If he is accustomed to close personal distance between himself and others, his bubble will be smaller than that of someone who's accustomed to greater personal distance. People of North European heritage—English, Scandinavian, Swiss, and German—tend to avoid contact. Those whose heritage is Italian, French, Spanish, Russian, Latin American, or Middle Eastern like close personal contact.

People are very sensitive to any intrusion into their spatial bubble. If someone stands too close to you, your first instinct is to back up. If that's not possible, you lean away and pull yourself in, tensing your muscles. If the intruder doesn't respond to these body signals, you may then try to protect yourself, using a briefcase, umbrella, or raincoat. Women—especially when traveling alone—often plant their pocketbook in such a way that no one can get very close to them. As a last resort, you may move to another spot and position yourself behind a desk or a chair that provides screening. Everyone tries to adjust the space around himself in a way that's comfortable for him; most often, he does this unconsciously.

Emotions also have a direct effect on the size of a person's territory. When you're angry or under stress, your bubble expands and you require more space. New York psychiatrist Augustus Kinzel found a difference in what he calls Body-Buffer Zones between violent and nonviolent prison inmates. Dr. Kinzel conducted experiments in which each prisoner was placed in the center of a small room and then Dr. Kinzel slowly walked toward him. Nonviolent prisoners allowed him to come quite close, while prisoners with a history of violent behavior couldn't tolerate his proximity and reacted with some vehemence.

Apparently, people under stress experience other people as looming larger and closer than they actually are. Studies of schizophrenic patients have indicated that they sometimes have a distorted perception of space, and several psychiatrists have reported patients who experience their body boundaries as filling up an entire room. For these patients, anyone who comes into the room is actually inside their body, and such an intrusion may trigger a violent outburst.

Unfortunately, there is little detailed information about normal people who live in highly congested urban areas. We do know, of course, that the noise, pollution, dirt, crowding, and confusion of our cities induce feelings of stress in most of us, and stress leads to a need for greater space. The man who's packed into a subway, jostled in the street, crowded into an elevator, and forced to work all day in a bull pen or in a small office without auditory or visual privacy is going to be very stressed at the end of his day. He needs places that provide relief from constant overstimulation of his nervous system. Stress from overcrowding is cumulative and people can tolerate more crowding early in the day than later; note the increased bad temper during the evening rush hour as compared with the morning melee. Certainly one factor in people's desire to commute by car is the need for privacy and relief from crowding (except, often, from other cars); it may be the only time of the day when nobody can intrude.

In crowded public places, we tense our muscles and hold ourselves stiff, and thereby communicate to others our desire not to intrude on their space and, above all, not to touch them. We also avoid eye contact, and the total effect is that of someone who has "tuned out." Walking along the street, our bubble expands slightly as we move in a stream of strangers, taking care not to bump into them. In the office, at meetings, in restaurants, our bubble keeps changing as it adjusts to the activity at hand.

Most white middle-class Americans use four main distances in their business and social relations: intimate, personal, social, and public. Each of these distances has a near and a far phase and is accompanied by changes in the volume of the voice. Intimate distance varies from direct physical contact with another person to a distance of six to eighteen inches and is used for our most private activities—caressing another person or making love. At this distance, you are overwhelmed by sensory inputs from the other person—heat from the body, tactile stimulation from the skin, the fragrance of perfume, even the sound of breathing—all of which literally envelop you. Even at the far phase, you're still within easy touching distance. In general, the use of intimate distance in public between adults is frowned on. It's also much too close for strangers, except under conditions of extreme crowding.

In the second zone—personal distance—the close phase is 1½ to 2½ feet; it's at this distance that wives usually stand from their husbands in public. If another woman moves into this zone, the wife will most likely be disturbed. The far phase—2½ to 4 feet—is the distance used to "keep someone at arm's length" and is the most common spacing used by people in conversation.

The third zone—social distance—is employed during business transactions or exchanges with a clerk or repairman. People who work together tend to use close social distance—4 to 7 feet. This is also the distance for conversation at social gatherings. To stand at this distance from someone who is seated has a dominating effect (for example, teacher to pupil, boss to secretary). The far phase of the third zone—7 to 12 feet—is where people stand when someone says, "Stand back so I can look at you." This distance lends a formal tone to business or social discourse. In an executive office, the desk serves to keep people at this distance.

The fourth zone—public distance—is used by teachers in classrooms or speakers at public gatherings. At it farthest phase—25 feet and beyond—it is used for important public figures. Violations of this distance can lead to serious complications. During his 1970 U.S. visit, the president of France, Georges Pompidou, was harassed by pickets in Chicago, who were permitted to get within touching distance. Since pickets in France are kept behind barricades a block or more away, the president was outraged by this insult to his person, and President Nixon was obliged to communicate his concern as well as offer his personal apologies.

It is interesting to note how American pitchmen and panhandlers exploit the unwritten, unspoken conventions of eye and distance. Both take advantage of the fact that once explicit eye contact is established, it is rude to look away, because to do so means to brusquely dismiss the other person and his needs. Once having caught the eye of his mark, the panhandler then locks on, not letting go until he moves through the public zone, the social zone, and, finally, into the intimate sphere, where people are most vulnerable.

Touch also is an important part of the constant stream of communication that takes place between people. A light touch, a firm touch, a blow, a caress are all communications. In an effort to break down barriers among people, there's been a recent upsurge in group-encounter activities, in which strangers are encouraged to touch one another. In special situations such as these, the rules for not touching are broken with group approval and people gradually lose some of their inhibitions.

Although most people don't realize it, space is perceived and distances are set not by vision alone but with all the senses. Auditory space is perceived with the ears, thermal space with the skin, kinesthetic space with the muscles of the body, and olfactory space with the nose. And, once again, it's our culture that determines how our senses are programmed— which sensory information ranks highest and lowest. The important thing to remember is that culture is very persistent. In this country, we've noted the existence of cultural patterns that determine distance between people in the third and fourth generations of some families, despite their prolonged contact with people of very different cultural heritages.

Whenever there is great cultural distance between two people, there are bound to be problems arising from differences in behavior and expectations. An example is the American couple who consulted a psychiatrist about their marital problems. The husband was from New England and had been brought up by reserved parents who taught him to control his emotions and to respect the need for privacy. His wife was from an Italian family and had been brought up in close contact with all the members of her large family, who were extremely warm, volatile, and demonstrative.

When the husband came home after a hard day at the office, dragging his feet, and longing for peace and quiet, his wife would rush to him and smother him. Clasping his hands, rubbing his brow, crooning over his weary head, she never left him alone. But when his wife was upset or anxious about her day, the husband's response was to withdraw completely and leave her alone. No comforting, no affectionate embrace, no attention—just solitude. The woman became convinced her husband didn't love her and, in desperation, she consulted a psychiatrist. Their problem wasn't basically psychological but cultural.

Why have we developed all these different ways of communicating messages without words? One reason is that people don't like to spell out certain kinds of messages. We prefer to find other ways of showing our feelings. This is especially true in relationships as sensitive as courtship. Men don't like to be rejected and most women don't want to turn a man down bluntly. Instead, we work out subtle ways of encouraging or discouraging each other that save face and avoid confrontations.

How a person handles space in dating others is an obvious and very sensitive indicator of how he or she feels about the other person. On a first date, if a woman sits or stands so close to a man that he is acutely conscious of her physical presence—inside the intimate-distance zone—the man usually construes it to mean that she is encouraging him. However, before the man starts moving in on the woman, he should be sure what message she's really sending; otherwise, he risks bruising his ego. What is close to someone of North European background may be neutral or distant to someone of Italian heritage. Also, women sometimes use space as a way of misleading a man, and there are few things that put men off more than women who communicate contradictory messages—cuddling up and then acting insulted when a man takes the next step.

How does a woman communicate interest in a man? In addition to such familiar gambits as smiling at him, she may glance shyly at him, blush, and then look away. Or she may give him a real come-on look and move in very close when he approaches. She may touch his arm and ask for a light. As she leans forward to light her cigarette, she may brush him lightly, enveloping him in her perfume. She'll probably continue to smile at him and she may use what ethnologists call preening gestures—touching the back of her hair, thrusting her breasts forward, tilting her hips as she stands or crossing her legs if she's seated, perhaps even exposing one thigh or putting a hand on her thigh and stroking it. She may also stroke her wrists as she converses or show the palm of her hand as a way of gaining his attention. Her skin may be unusually flushed or quite pale, her eyes brighter, the pupils larger.

If a man sees a woman whom he wants to attract, he tries to present himself by his posture and stance as someone who is self-assured. He moves briskly and confidently. When he catches the eye of the woman, he may hold her glance a little longer than normal. If he gets an encouraging smile, he'll move in close and engage her in small talk. As they converse, his glance shifts over her face and body. He, too, may make preening gestures—straightening his tie, smoothing his hair, or shooting his cuffs.

How do people learn body language? The same way they learn spoken language—by observing and imitating people around them as they're growing up. Little girls imitate their mothers or an older female. Little boys imitate their fathers or a respected uncle or a character on television. In this way, they learn the gender signals appropriate for their sex. Regional, class, and ethnic patterns of body behavior are also learned in childhood and persist throughout life.

Such patterns of masculine and feminine body behavior vary widely from one culture to another. In America, for example, women stand with their thighs together. Many walk with their pelvis tipped slightly forward and their upper arms close to their body. When they sit, they cross their legs at the knee or, if they are well past middle age, they may cross their ankles. American men hold their arms away from their body, often swinging them as they walk. They stand with their legs apart (an extreme example is the cowboy, with legs apart and thumbs tucked into his belt). When they sit, they put their feet on the floor with legs apart and, in some parts of the country, they cross their legs by putting one ankle on the other knee.

Leg behavior indicates sex, status, and personality. It also indicates whether or not one is at ease or is showing respect or disrespect for the other person. Young Latin American males avoid crossing their legs. In their world of *machismo*, the preferred position for young males when with one another (if there is no older dominant male present to whom they must show respect) is to sit on the base of their spine with their leg muscles relaxed and their feet wide apart. Their respect position is like our military equivalent; spine straight, heels and ankles together—almost identical to that displayed by properly brought up young women in New England in the early part of this century.

American women who sit with their legs spread apart in the presence of males are *not* normally signaling a come-on—they are simply (and often unconsciously) sitting like men. Middle-class women in the presence of other women to whom they are very close may on occasion throw themselves down on a soft chair or sofa and let themselves go. This is a signal that nothing serious will be taken up. Males, on the other hand, lean back and prop their legs up on the nearest object.

The way we walk, similarly, indicates status, respect, mood, and ethnic or cultural affiliation. The many variants of the female walk are too well known to go into here, except to say that a man would have to be blind not to be turned on by the way some women walk—a fact that made Mae West rich before scientists ever studied these matters. To white Americans, some French middle-class males walk in a way that is both humorous and suspect. There is a bounce and looseness to the French walk, as though the parts of the body were somehow unrelated. Jacques Tati, the French movie actor, walks this way; so does the great mime, Marcel Marceau.

Blacks and whites in America—with the exception of middle- and upper-middle-class professionals of both groups—move and walk very differently from each other. To the blacks, whites often seem incredibly stiff, almost mechanical in their movements. Black males, on the other hand, have a looseness and coordination that frequently makes whites a little uneasy; it's too different, too integrated, too alive, too male. Norman Mailer has said that squares walk from the shoulders, like bears, but blacks and hippies walk from the hips, like cats.

All over the world, people walk not only in their own characteristic way but have walks that communicate the nature of their involvement with whatever it is they're doing. The purposeful walk of North Europeans is an important component of proper behavior on the job. Any male who has been in the military knows how essential it is to walk properly (which makes for a continuing source of tension between blacks and whites in the Service). The quick shuffle of servants in the Far East in the old days was a show of respect. On the island of Truk, when we last visited, the inhabitants even had a name for the respectful walk that one used when in the presence of a chief or when walking past a chief's house. The term was *sufan*, which meant to be humble and respectful.

The notion that people communicate volumes by their gestures, facial expressions, posture, and walk is not new; actors, dancers, writers, and psychiatrists have long been aware of it. Only in recent years, however, have scientists begun to make systematic observations of body motions. Ray L. Birdwhistell of the University of Pennsylvania is one of the pioneers in body-motion research and coined the term *kinesics* to describe this field. He developed an elaborate notation system to record both facial and body movements, using an approach similar to that of the linguist, who studies the basic elements of speech. Birdwhistell and other kinesicists such as Albert Sheflen, Adam Kendon, and William Condon take movies of people interacting. They run the film over and over again, often at reduced speed for frame-by-frame analysis, so that they can observe even the slightest body movements not perceptible at normal interaction speeds. These movements are then recorded in notebooks for later analysis.

To appreciate the importance of nonverbal communication systems, consider the unskilled inner-city black looking for a job. His handling of time and space alone is sufficiently different from the white middle-class pattern to create great misunderstandings on both sides. The black is told to appear for a job interview at a certain time. He arrives late. The white interviewer concludes from his tardy arrival that the black is irresponsible and not really interested in the job. What the interviewer doesn't know is that the black time system (often referred to by blacks as C.P.T.—colored people's time) isn't the same as that of whites. In the words of a black student who had been told to make an appointment to see his professor: "Man, you *must* be putting me on. I never had an appointment in my life."

The black job applicant, having arrived late for his interview, may further antagonize the white interviewer by his posture and his eye behavior. Perhaps he slouches and avoids looking at the interviewer; to him, this is playing it cool. To the interviewer, however, he may well look shifty and sound uninterested. The interviewer has failed to notice the actual signs of interest and eagerness in the black's behavior, such as the subtle shift in the quality of the voice—a gentle and tentative excitement—an almost imperceptible change in the cast of the eyes and a relaxing of the jaw muscles.

Moreover, correct reading of black-white behavior is continually complicated by the fact that both groups are comprised of individuals—some of whom try to accommodate and some of whom make it a point of pride *not* to accommodate. At present, this means that many Americans, when thrown into contact with one another, are in the precarious position of not knowing which pattern applies. Once identified and analyzed, nonverbal communications systems can be taught, like a foreign language. Without this training, we respond to nonverbal communications in terms of our own culture; we read everyone's behavior as if it were our own, and thus we often misunderstand it.

Several years ago in New York City, there was a program for sending children from predominantly black and Puerto Rican low-income neighborhoods to summer school in a white upper-class neighborhood on the East Side. One morning, a group of young black and Puerto Rican boys raced down the street, shouting and screaming and overturning garbage cans on their way to school. A doorman from an apartment building nearby chased them and cornered one of them inside a building. The boy drew a knife and attacked the doorman. This tragedy would not have occurred if the doorman had been familiar with the behavior of boys from low-income neighborhoods, where such antics are routine and socially acceptable and where pursuit would be expected to invite a violent response.

The language of behavior is extremely complex. Most of us are lucky to have under control one subcultural system—the one that reflects our sex, class, generation, and geographic region within the United States. Because of its complexity, efforts to isolate bits of nonverbal communication and generalize from them are in vain; you don't become an instant expert on people's behavior by watching them at cocktail parties. Body language isn't something that's independent of the person, something that can be donned and doffed like a suit of clothes.

Our research and that of our colleagues have shown that, far from being a superficial form of communication that can be consciously manipulated, nonverbal communication systems are interwoven into the fabric of the personality and, as sociologist Erving Goffman has demonstrated, into society itself. They are the warp and woof of daily interactions with others and they influence how one expresses oneself, how one experiences oneself as a man or a woman.

Nonverbal communications signal to members of your own group what kind of person you are, how you feel about others, how you'll fit into and work in a group, whether you're assured or anxious, the degree to which you feel comfortable with the standards of your own culture, as well as deeply significant feelings about the self, including the state of your own psyche. For most of us, it's difficult to accept the reality of another's behavioral system. And, of course, none of us will ever become fully knowledgeable of the importance of every nonverbal signal. But as long as each of us realizes the power of these signals, this society's diversity can be a source of great strength rather than a further—and subtly powerful—source of division.

REVIEW QUESTIONS

1. What are the ways people communicate with each other nonverbally, according to Edward and Mildred Hall?
2. What are the four culturally learned speaking distances used by Americans?
3. How does the nonverbal communication described by the Halls relate to the concept of tacit culture discussed in the last section?
4. Why is nonverbal communication so likely to be a source of cross-cultural misunderstanding?

6

Worlds Shaped by Words

David S. Thomson

*For many people, language mirrors reality. Words are labels for
what we sense; they record what is already there. This view, which is
another manifestation of what we have called* naive realism, *is
clearly challenged by previous selections in this book. We have seen,
for example, that members of different societies may not share cultural categories; words from one language often cannot be translated
directly into another. In the 1930s, a young linguist named Benjamin Lee Whorf took the objection to the "words label reality"
assertion one step further by arguing that words and grammatical
structure actually shape reality. This piece by David Thomson describes Whorf's theory, shows how linguists have evaluated it, and
applies it in modified form to the use of words, euphemisms, and
doublespeak in the modern United States.*

The scene is the storage room at a chemical plant. The time is evening.
A night watchman enters the room and notes that it is partially
filled with gasoline drums. The drums are in a section of the room where
a sign says "Empty Barrels." The watchman lights a cigarette and throws
the still-hot match into one of the empty barrels.

From *Human Behavior: Language* by David S. Thomson and the Editors of Time-Life
Books (New York: Time-Life Books, 1975). Copyright © 1975 Time-Life Books, Inc.

The result: an explosion.

The immediate cause of the explosion, of course, was the gasoline fumes that remained in the barrels. But it could be argued that a second cause of the explosion was the English language. The barrels were empty of their original contents and so belonged under the empty sign. Yet they were not empty of everything—the fumes were still present. English has no word—no single term—that can convey such a situation. Containers in English are either empty or they are not; there is no word describing the ambiguous state of being empty and yet not empty. There is not term in the language for "empty but not quite" or "empty of original contents but with something left over." There being no word for such an in-between state, it did not occur to the watchman to think of the explosive fumes.

This incident is hypothetical, but the questions about language it raises are real. The example of the gasoline drums often was cited by Benjamin Lee Whorf to illustrate a revolutionary theory he had about language. Whorf was an unusual man who combined two careers, for he was both a successful insurance executive and a brilliant (and largely self-taught) linguistic scholar. Language, he claimed, may be shaped by the world, but it in turn shapes the world. He reasoned that people can think about only those things that their language can describe or express. Without the words or structures with which to articulate a concept, that concept will not occur. To turn the proposition around, if a language is rich in ways to express certain sorts of ideas, then the speakers of that language will habitually think along those linguistic paths. In short, the language that humans speak governs their view of reality; it determines their perception of the world. The picture of the universe shifts from tongue to tongue.

The originator of this startling notion came from an intellectually active New England family. Whorf's brother John became an artist of note and his brother Richard a consummately professional actor. Benjamin's early bent was not for drawing or acting but photography, especially the chemistry that was involved in developing pictures, and this interest may have influenced his choice of the Massachusetts Institute of Technology, where he majored in chemical engineering. After he was graduated from M.I.T. he became a specialist in fire prevention and in 1919 went to work for the Hartford Fire Insurance Company. His job was to inspect manufacturing plants, particularly chemical plants, that the Hartford insured to determine whether they were safe and thus good insurance risks. He quickly became highly skilled at his work. "In no time at all," wrote C. S. Kremer, then the Hartford's board chairman, "he became in my opinion as thorough and fast a fire prevention inspector as there ever has been."

Whorf was a particularly acute chemical engineer. On one occasion he was refused admittance to inspect a client's building because, a company official maintained, a secret process was in use here. "You are making such-and-such a product?" asked Whorf. "Yes," said the official. Whorf pulled out a pad and scribbled the formula of the supposedly secret process, adding coolly, "You couldn't do it any other way." Needless to say, he was allowed to inspect the building. Whorf rose in the Hartford hierarchy to the post of assistant secretary of the company in 1940. But then in 1941 his health, never strong, gave way, and he died at the early age of forty-four.

While Whorf was becoming a successful insurance executive, he was also doing his revolutionary work in linguistics. He started by studying Hebrew but then switched to Aztec and other related languages of Mexico. Later he deciphered Maya inscriptions, and tried to reconstruct the long-lost language of the ancient Maya people of Mexico and Central America. Finally he tackled the complexities of the still-living language of the Hopi Indians of Arizona. He published his findings in respected anthropological and linguistic journals, earning the praise and respect of scholars in the two fields—all without formal training in linguistic science. As his fame as a linguist spread, the Hartford obligingly afforded him vacations and leaves to travel to the Southwest in pursuit of the structure and lexicon of the Hopi. He also put in countless hours in the Watkinson Library in Connecticut, a rich repository of Mexican and Indian lore.

It was primarily his study of Hopi that impelled Whorf toward his revolutionary ideas. He was encouraged and aided by the great cultural anthropologist and linguist of Yale, Edward Sapir, and the idea that language influences a person's view of the world is generally known as the Sapir-Whorf hypothesis. Whorf formulated it a number of times, but perhaps his clearest statement comes from his 1940 essay "Science and Linguistics": "The background linguistic system (in other words, the grammar) of each language is not merely a reproducing instrument for voicing ideas but rather is itself the shaper of ideas. . . . We dissect nature along lines laid down by our native language. The categories and types that we isolate from the world of phenomena we do not find there because they stare every observer in the face; on the contrary, the world is presented in a kaleidoscopic flux of impressions which has to be organized by our minds—and this means largely by the linguistic systems in our minds."

These ideas developed from Whorf's study of the Hopi language. He discovered that it differs dramatically from languages of the Indo-European family such as English or French, particularly in its expression of the concept of time. English and its related languages have three major tenses—past, present, and future ("it was," "it is," "it will be")—plus the fancier compound tenses such as "it will have been." Having these tenses, Whorf argued, encourages Europeans and Americans to think of time as so many ducks in a row. Time past is made up of uniform units of time—days, weeks, months, years—and the future is similarly measured out.

This division of time is essentially artificial, Whorf said, since people can only experience the present. Past and future are only abstractions, but Westerners think of them as real because their language virtually forces them to do so. This view of time has given rise to the fondness in Western cultures for diaries, records, annals, histories, clocks, calendars, wages paid by the hour or day, and elaborate timetables for the use of future time. Time is continually quantified. If Westerners set out to build a house they establish a deadline; the work will be completed at a specified time in the future, such as May 5 or October 15.

Hopis do not behave this way; when they start to weave a mat they are not concerned about when it will be completed. They work on it desultorily, then quit, then begin again; the finished product may take weeks. This casual progress is not laziness but a result of the Hopi's view of time—one symptom of the fact that their language does not have the past, present, and future tenses. Instead it possesses two modes of thought: the objective, that is, things that exist now, and the subjective, things that can be thought about and therefore belong to a state of becoming. Things do not become in terms of a future measured off in days, weeks, months. Each thing that is becoming has its own individual life rhythms, growing or declining or changing in much the same manner as a plant grows, according to its inner nature. The essence of Hopi life, therefore, Whorf said, is preparing in the present so that those things that are capable of becoming can in fact come to pass. Thus weaving a mat is preparing a mat to become a mat; it will reach that state when its nature so ordains—whenever that will be.

This view of the future is understandable, Whorf noted, in an agricultural people whose welfare depends on the proper preparing of earth and seeds and plants for the hoped-for harvest. It also helps explain why the Hopi have such elaborate festivals, rituals, dances, and magic ceremonies: All are intended to aid in the mental preparation that is so necessary if the crops, which the Hopi believe to be influenced by human thought, are to grow properly. This preparing involves "much visible activity," Whorf said, "introductory formalities, preparing of special food . . . intensive sustained muscular activity like running, racing, dancing, which is thought to increase the intensity of development of events (such as growth of crops), mimetic and other magic preparations based on esoteric theory involving perhaps occult instruments like prayer sticks, prayer feathers, and prayer meal, and finally the great cyclic ceremonies and dances, which have the significance of preparing rain and crops." Whorf went on to note that the very noun for *crop* is derived from the verb that means "to prepare." *Crop* therefore is in the Hopi language literally "the prepared." Further, the Hopi prayer pipe, which is smoked as an aid in concentrating good thoughts on the growing fields of corn and wheat, is named *na'twanpi*, "instrument of preparing."

The past to the Hopi, Whorf believed, is also different from the chrono-logical time sense of the speakers of Indo-European languages. The past is not a uniform row of days or weeks to the Hopi. It is rather an undifferen-tiated stream in which many deeds were done that have accumulated and prepared the present and will continue to prepare the becoming that is ahead. Everything is connected, everything accumulates. The past is not a series of events, separated and completed, but is present in the present.

To Whorf these striking differences in the Hopi language and sense of time implied that the Hopi live almost literally in another world from the speakers of Indo-European languages. The Hopi language grew out of its speakers' peculiar circumstances: As a geographically isolated agricul-tural people in a land where rainfall was scanty, they did the same things and prayed the same prayers year after year and thus did not need to have past and future tenses. But the language, once it had developed, perpetu-ated their particular and seemingly very different world view.

Many linguists and anthropologists who have worked with American In-dians of the Southwest have been convinced that Whorf's theories are by and large correct. Other linguists are not convinced, however, and through the years since Whorf's death they have attacked his proposals. The controversy is unlikely to be settled soon, if ever. One of the prob-lems is the difficulty of setting up an experiment that would either prove or disprove the existence of correlations between linguistic struc-ture and nonlinguistic behavior. It would be fruitless to go about asking people of various cultures their opinions as to whether the language they spoke had determined the manner in which they thought, had dictated their view of the world. Nobody would be able to answer such a question, for a people's language is so completely embedded in their conscious-ness that they would be unable to conceive of any other way of interpret-ing the world.

Despite the near impossibility of proving or disproving Whorf's the-ory, it will not go away but keeps coming back, intriguing each succeeding generation of linguists. It is certainly one of the most fascinating theories created by the modern mind. It is comparable in some ways to Einstein's theory of relativity. Just as Einstein said that how people saw the phe-nomena of the universe was relative to their point of observation, so Whorf said that a people's world view was relative to the language they spoke.

And demonstrations of Whorf's ideas are not entirely lacking. They come mainly from studies of color—one of the very few aspects of reality that can be specified by objective scientific methods and also is rather pre-cisely specified by people's naming of colors. In this instance it is possible to compare one person's language, expressing that person's view of the world, with another's language for exactly the same characteristic of the world. The comparison can thus reveal different views that are linked to different descriptions of the same reality. English-speakers view purple as a single relatively uniform color; only if pressed and then only with difficulty will they make any attempt to divide it into such shades as lavender and mauve. But no English-speaker would lump orange with purple; to the users of English, those colors are completely separate, for no single word includes both of them. If other languages made different distinctions in the naming of color—if lavender and mauve were always separate, never encompassed by a word for purple, or if orange and purple were not distinguished but were called by a name that covered both—then it would seem that the users of those languages interpreted those colors differently.

Such differences in color-naming, it turns out, are fairly widespread. Linguist H. A. Gleason compared the color spectrum as described by English-speaking persons to the way it was labeled by speakers of Bassa, a language spoken in Liberia, and by speakers of Shona, spoken in Rhodesia. English-speaking people, when seeing sunlight refracted through a prism, identify by name at least six colors—purple, blue, green, yellow, orange, and red. The speakers of Shona, however, have only three names for the colors of the spectrum. They group orange, red, and purple under one name. They also lump blue and green-blue under one of their other color terms and use their third word to identify yellow and the yellower hues of green. The speakers of Bassa are similarly restricted by a lack of handy terms for color, for they have only two words for the hues of the spectrum.

Gleason's observations prompted psychologists to perform an experiment that also showed the influence words can have on the way colors are handled intellectually and remembered. It was an ingenious and complex experiment with many checks and double checks of the results, but in essence it boiled down to something like this: English-speaking subjects were shown a series of color samples—rather like the little "chips" provided by a paint store to help customers decide what color to paint the living room. The subjects were then asked to pick out the colors they had seen from a far larger array of colors. It turned out that they could more accurately pick out the right colors from the larger selection when the color involved had a handy, ordinary name like "green." The subjects had difficulty with the ambiguous, in-between colors such as off-purples and misty blues. In other words, a person can remember a color better if that person's language offers a handy label for it, but has trouble when the language does not offer such a familiar term. Again the human ability to differentiate reality seemed to be affected by the resources offered by language.

Richness of linguistic resource undoubtedly helps people to cope with subtle gradations in the things they deal with every day. The Hanunóo people of the Philippine Islands have different names for ninety-two varieties of rice. They can easily distinguish differences in rice that would be all but invisible to English-speaking people, who lump all such grains under the single world *rice*. Of course, English-speakers can make distinctions by resorting to adjectives and perhaps differentiate long-grain, brown rice from small-grain, yellow rice, but surely no European or American would, lacking the terms, have a sufficiently practiced eye to distinguish ninety-two varieties of rice. Language is essentially a code that people use both to think and to communicate. As psychologist Roger Brown sums up the rice question: "Among the Hanunóo, who have names for ninety-two varieties of rice, any one of those varieties is highly codable in the array of ninety-one other varieties. The Hanunóo have a word for it and so can transmit it efficiently and presumably can recognize it easily. Among speakers of English one kind of rice among ninety-one other kinds would have very low codability."

Brown goes on to suppose that the Hanunóo set down in New York would be baffled by the reality around them partly because they would then be the ones lacking the needed words. "If the Hanunóo were to visit the annual Automobile Show in New York City, they would find it difficult to encode distinctively any particular automobile in that array. But an American having such lexical resources as *Chevrolet, Ford, Plymouth, Buick, Corvette, hard-top, convertible, four-door, station wagon,* and the like could easily encode ninety-two varieties."

The very existence of so many different languages, each linked to a distinctive culture, is itself support of a sort for Whorf's hypothesis. At least since the time of the Tower of Babel, no single tongue has been shared by all the people of the world. Many attempts have been made to invent an international language, one so simply structured and easy to learn it would be used by everyone around the globe as a handy adjunct to their native speech. Yet even the most successful of these world languages, Esperanto, has found but limited acceptance.

There are international languages, however, to serve international cultures. The intellectual disciplines of music, dance, and mathematics might be considered specialized cultures; each is shared by people around the world, and each has an international language, used as naturally in Peking as in Paris. English is a world language in certain activities that straddle national boundaries, such as international air travel; it serves for communications between international flights and the ground in every country— a Lufthansa pilot approaching Athens talks with the airport control tower neither in German nor in Greek but in English.

The trouble with most attempts to lend credence to the Sapir-Whorf hypothesis is that, while they indicate connections between culture and language, they do not really prove that a language shaped its users' view of the world. Just because the speakers of Shona have only three main distinctions of color does not mean that their "world view" is all that different from that of the English-speaker who has more convenient color terms. Shona speakers obviously see all the colors in the rainbow that English-speakers see. Their eyes are physiologically the same. Their comparative poverty of words for those colors merely means that it is harder for them to talk about color. Their "code" is not so handy; the colors' codability is lower.

Critics also point out that Whorf may have mistaken what are called dead metaphors for real differences in the Hopi language. All languages are loaded with dead metaphors—figures of speech that have lost all figurative value and are now just familiar words. The word "goodbye" is a dead metaphor. Once it meant "God be with you," but in its contracted form it conjures up no thought or picture of God. If a Whorfian linguist who was a native speaker of Hopi turned the tables and analyzed English he might conclude that English-speakers were perpetually thinking of religion since this everyday word incorporates a reference to God—a ridiculous misreading of a term that has lost all of its original religious significance. In like fashion, perhaps Whorf was reading too much into the Hopi lexicon and grammar, seeing significances where there were none.

The argument about how far Whorf's ideas can be stretched has gone on for several decades and promises to go on for several more. Most psychologists believe that all people see pretty much the same reality; their languages merely have different words and structures to approximate in various idiosyncratic ways a picture of that reality. And yet the experts accept what might be called modified Whorfism—a belief in the power of language to affect, if not to direct, the perception of reality. If a language is rich in terms for certain things or ideas—possesses extensive codability for them—then the people speaking that language can conceive of, and talk about, those things or ideas more conveniently. If different languages do not give their speakers entirely different world views, they certainly influence thinking to some degree.

Even within the Indo-European family of languages, some tongues have words for concepts that other tongues lack. German is especially rich in philosophical terms that have no exact counterparts in English, French, Italian—or any known language. One is *Weltschmerz,* which combines in itself meanings that it takes three English phrases to adequately convey— "weariness of life," "pessimistic outlook," and "romantic discontent." Another German word that has no direct translation is *Weltanschauung.* To approximate its meaning in English requires a number of different terms—"philosophy of life," "world outlook," "ideology"—for all of these elements are included in the German word. "Weltanschauung" is untranslatable into any single English term. It represents an idea for which only German has a word. Possessing the convenient term, German writers can develop this idea more easily than the users of other languages, and thus explore its ramifications further.

Even when a word from one language may seem to be easily translatable into another, it often is not really equivalent. The French term *distingué* would appear to translate easily enough into the English *distinguished*. But the French use their word in ways that no English-speaker would ever employ for *distinguished*. A Frenchman might reprimand his son by saying that his impolite behavior was not *distingué* or he might tell his wife that a scarf she has worn out to dinner is charmingly *distingué*. The word does not mean "distinguished" as English-speakers employ the term, but something more like "suitable," or "appropriate," or "in keeping with polite standards." It is simply not the same word in the two languages no matter how similar the spelling. It represents a different idea, connoting a subtle difference in mental style.

In some cases the existence of a word leads users of it down tortured logical paths toward dead ends. The common word nothing is one example. Since there is a word for the concept, points out philosopher George Pitcher, it tempts people to think that "nothing" is a real entity, that somehow it exists, a palpable realm of not-being. It has in fact led a number of philosophers, including the twentieth-century French thinker Jean-Paul Sartre, to spend a great deal of effort speculating about the nature of "nothing." The difficulty of this philosophic dilemma is indicated by a typical Sartre sentence on the subject: "The Being by which Nothingness arrives in the world must nihilate. Nothingness in its Being, and even so it still runs the risk of establishing Nothingness as a transcendent in the very heart of immanence unless it nihilates Nothingness in its being in connection with its own being." Sartre could hardly have gotten himself tangled up in such agonized prose had French lacked a noun for le neant, nothing, and the value to human welfare of his attempt to explain is open to question.

The power of language to influence the world can be seen not only in comparisons of one tongue to another, but also within a single language. The way in which people use their native tongue—choosing one term over another to express the same idea or action, varying structures or phrases for different situations—has a strong effect on their attitudes toward those situations. Distasteful ideas can be made to seem acceptable or even desirable by careful choices of words, and language can make actions or beliefs that might otherwise be considered correct appear to be obsolescent or naive. Value judgments of many kinds can be attached to seemingly simple statements. Shakespeare may have believed that "a rose by any other name would smell as sweet," but he was wrong, as other theatrical promoters have proved repeatedly. A young English vaudevillian known as Archibald Leach was a minor comedian until he was given the more romantic name of Cary Grant. The new name did not make him a star, but it did create an atmosphere in which he could demonstrate his talent, suggesting the type of character he came to exemplify.

If the power of a stage name to characterize personality seems of relatively minor consequence in human affairs, consider the effect of a different sort of appellation: "boy." It was—and sometimes still is—the form of address employed by whites in the American South in speaking to black males of any age. This word, many authorities believe, served as an instrument of subjugation. It implied that the black was not a man but a child, someone not mature enough to be entrusted with responsibility for himself, let alone authority over others. His inferior position was thus made to seem natural and justified, and it could be enforced without compunction.

Characterizing people by tagging them with a word label is a worldwide practice. Many peoples use a single word to designate both themselves and the human race. "The Carib Indians, for example, have stated with no equivocation, 'We alone are people,'" reported anthropologist Jack Conrad. "Similarly, the ancient Egyptians used the word *romet* (men) only among themselves and in no case for strangers. The Lapps of Scandinavia reserve the term 'human being' for those of their own kind, while the Cherokee Indians call themselves *Ani-Yunwiya*, which means 'principal people.' The Kiowa Indians of the Southwest are willing to accept other peoples as human, but the very name, *Kiowa*, meaning 'real people,' shows their true feeling." The effect of reserving a term indicating "human" to one group is far-reaching. It alters the perception of anyone from outside that group. He is not called "human," and need not be treated as human. Like an animal, he can be entrapped, beaten, or even killed with more or less impunity. This use of a word to demote whole groups from the human class is often a wartime tactic—the enemy is referred to by a pejorative name to justify killing him.

While language can be twisted to make ordinarily good things seem bad, it can also be twisted in the opposite direction to make bad things seem good or run-of-the-mill things better than they really are. The technique depends on the employment of euphemisms, a term derived from the Greek for "words of good omen." A euphemism is roundabout language that is intended to conceal something embarrassing or unpleasant. Some classes of euphemism—little evasions that people use every day—are inoffensive enough. It is when such cloudy doubletalk invades the vital areas of politics and foreign affairs that it becomes perilous.

A large and commonly used—and relatively harmless—class of euphemism has to do with bodily functions. Many people shy away from frank talk about excretion or sex; in fact, many of the old, vivid terms—the four-letter words—are socially taboo. So people for centuries have skirted the edge of such matters, inventing a rich vocabulary of substitute terms. Americans offered turkey on Thanksgiving commonly say "white meat" or "dark meat" to announce their preference. These terms date back to the nineteenth century when it was considered indelicate to say "breast" or "leg." *Toilet,* itself a euphemism coined from the French *toilette* ("making oneself presentable to the outside world"), long ago became tainted and too graphic for the prudish. The list of euphemistic substitutes is almost endless, ranging from the commonplace *washroom, bathroom,* and *restroom* (whoever rests in a restroom?) to *john, head,* and *Chic Sale* in the United States, and in England *the loo. Loo* may be derived from a mistaken English pronunciation of the French *l'eau,* water. Or it may be a euphemism derived from a euphemism. The French, with Gallic delicacy, once commonly put the number 100 on bathroom doors in hotels. It is easy to see how an English person might have mistaken the number for the word *loo.* Meanwhile, ladies in restaurants have adopted "I'm going to powder my nose" or, in England, where it once cost a penny to use public toilets, "I'm going to spend a penny."

Another generally harmless use of euphemistic language is the practice, especially notable in the United States, of giving prestigious names to more-or-less ordinary trades. As H. L. Mencken pointed out in *The American Language,* his masterly examination of English as spoken in the United States, ratcatchers are fond of calling themselves "exterminating engineers" and hairdressers have long since showed a preference for "beautician." The *-ician* ending, in fact, has proved very popular, doubtless because it echoes "physician" and thus sounds both professional and scientific. In the late nineteenth century undertakers had already begun to call themselves "funeral directors," but starting in 1916 ennobled themselves even further by battening on the newer euphemistic coinage, "mortician." Meanwhile a tree trimmer became a "tree surgeon" (that love of medicine again) and a press agent became a "publicist" or, even more grandly, a "public relations counsel."

Americans (and the English, too) not only chose high-sounding euphemisms for their professions but also gave new and gaudy names to their places of business. Thus pawn shops became "loan offices," saloons became "cocktail rooms," pool halls became "billiard parlors," and barber shops "hair-styling salons."

Purists might say that such shading or blunting of the stark truth leads to moral decay, but it is difficult to see why anybody should be the worse for allowing women to excuse themselves by pleading that they must powder their noses. There are euphemisms, however, that are clearly anything but harmless. These are evasive, beclouding phraseologies that hide truths people must clearly perceive if they are to govern themselves intelligently and keep a check on those in positions of power. Slick phrases, slippery evasions—words deliberately designed to hide unpleasant truth rather than reveal it—can so becloud political processes and so easily hide mistaken policies that the entire health of a nation is imperiled.

The classic treatise on the political misuse of language in modern times is the 1946 essay "Politics and the English Language" by the British writer George Orwell. "In our time, political speech and writing are largely the defence of the indefensible," Orwell said. "Thus political language has to consist largely of euphemism, question-begging and sheer cloudy vagueness." He concluded, "Such phraseology is needed if one wants to name things without calling up mental pictures of them. . . . When there is a gap between one's real and one's declared aims, one turns as it were instinctively to long words and exhausted idioms, like a cuttle-fish squirting out ink."

Orwell supplied numerous examples to buttress his charges. "Defenceless villages are bombarded from the air, the inhabitants driven out into the countryside, the cattle machine-gunned, the huts set on fire with incendiary bullets: this is called *pacification*." He went on to observe that in Stalin's Russia people were "imprisoned for years without trial or shot in the back of the neck or sent to die of scurvy in Arctic lumber camps: this is called *elimination of unreliable elements*."

Orwell, who died at the age of forty-six in 1950, did not live to collect even more deplorable distortions of language. The French clothed their brutal war in Algeria with a veil of euphemism; the North Koreans accused the South Koreans of "aggression" when the North invaded the South. The United States invented a whole lexicon of gobbledygook to disguise the horror of the war in Vietnam: "protective reaction strike" (the bombing of a Vietnamese village); "surgical bombing" (the same as protective reaction strike); "free-fire zone" (an area in which troops could shoot anything that moved, including helpless villagers); "new life hamlet" (a refugee camp for survivors of a surgical bombing).

Perhaps the most appalling use of this type of euphemism was the word employed by the Nazis for their program to exterminate all of Europe's Jews. The word is *Endlösung*, which means final solution. Behind that verbal façade the Nazis gassed, burned, shot, or worked to death some six million Jews from Germany, France, Poland, and other conquered parts of Europe. Hitler and Gestapo chief Himmler often employed the euphemism among themselves, and it was always used in official records—but not necessarily to preserve secrecy for purposes of state security. Apparently the euphemism shielded the Nazis from themselves. Openly brutal and murderous as they were, they could not face up to the horrible reality of what they were doing, and they had to hide it in innocuous language.

Such distortion of language can do more than disguise truth. It can turn truth around, so that the idea conveyed is the opposite of actuality. After the USSR savagely crushed the Hungarian rebellion in 1956 the Soviet aggression was made to seem, in the twisted language used by other Communist dictatorships, an expression of friendship. The Peking radio commented after the rebellion was put down: "The Hungarian people can see that Soviet policy toward the people's democracies is truly one of equality, friendship, and mutual assistance, not of conquest, aggression, and plunder."

The possibility that such topsy-turvy language might ultimately make the world topsy-turvy—an ironic demonstration of the fundamental truth of Benjamin Lee Whorf's insights—was raised in a dramatic way by George Orwell. His novel *1984,* a chilling and convincing description of life in a totalitarian society, shows how language might destroy reality. In the imaginary nation of Oceania the official language is Newspeak, which is intended to facilitate "doublethink," the ability to accept simultaneously ideas contradicting each other. The Oceania state apparatus includes a Ministry of Truth, its headquarters building emblazoned with three slogans: "WAR IS PEACE"; "FREEDOM IS SLAVERY"; "IGNORANCE IS STRENGTH." There are also other ministries, Orwell explained: "The Ministry of Peace, which concerned itself with war; the Ministry of Love, which maintained law and order." Anyone who would use language this way, Orwell made clear, denies the meaning of his or her words. He or she has lost touch with reality and substituted for it an emptiness concealed in sounds that once had meaning.

There is another threat to language besides the intentional twisting of words by demagogues and others who would control people's thoughts. It is less obvious, but a danger nevertheless: simple imprecision, slovenliness, mindlessness in the use of the language. It seems a small matter that English-speakers increasingly confuse *uninterested* with *disinterested,* for example. But these words do not mean the same thing. *Disinterested* means impartial, not taking sides. *Uninterested* means lacking in interest, bored. A judge should be *disinterested* but never *uninterested.* Many such changes result from the inevitable evolution of language as it changes over the years, but the change can be a loss. The slow erosion of distinctions, visible in much writing, audible in many conversations, makes language imprecise and thus clumsy and ineffective as communication.

Among the symptoms of such erosion are stock phrases that people mindlessly repeat, substituting noise for thought. Everyone has heard speechmakers use such clichés as "having regard to," "play into the hands of," "in the interest of," "no axe to grind.," Although this brief list is drawn from Orwell's essay of 1946 these exhausted clichés are still heard. Such verbal dead limbs do not distort thought but rather tend to obliterate it in a cloud of meaninglessness. "The slovenliness of our language makes it easier for us to have foolish thoughts," wrote Orwell. And ultimately, as has been pointed out by commentator Edwin Newman in his book *Strictly Speaking,* "Those for whom words have lost their value are likely to find that ideas have also lost their value."

REVIEW QUESTIONS

1. According to Thomson, what is the Sapir-Whorf hypothesis? Give some examples.
2. According to Whorf, how can grammar affect people's perceptions? Give examples.
3. The Sapir-Whorf hypothesis has been tested in several ways. What are some of the tests of the hypothesis described by Thomson, and how have these modified the theory?
4. What are some of the ways in which language affects or modifies perception in modern America? Can you add examples from your own experience to those presented by Thomson?

7

Television and Cultural Behavior

Conrad Phillip Kottak

The previous article dealt with the manipulation of meaning, especially the power of words to affect perception. This selection by Conrad Kottak looks at a medium for communication: television. Arguing that television is a much more important subject for anthropological study than most would think, Kottak notes that the repeated act of watching television has modified the cultural behavior of Americans in nontelevision settings such as university classrooms. In large classes, "teleconditioned" students are likely to treat instructors like TV sets, getting up for breaks, reading, talking, and occasionally turning off the "set" by leaving class early. Televiewing also has an important enculturative function. It teaches Americans a broad inventory of cultural knowledge. Because it is seen by almost everyone, television may be the most effective instrument of social solidarity in American life.

W hy should a cultural anthropologist, trained to study primitive societies, be interested in television, which is the creation of a complex, industrial society? My interest in television's impact on human social behavior arose mainly through contacts with young Americans. These include my children, their friends, and particularly the college students at the University of Michigan to whom I have been teaching introductory anthropology since 1968.

I teach my introductory course, which enrolls 600 students a semester, in a large auditorium. A microphone is necessary if the perennial instructor wants to avoid cancer of the larynx. One or two semesters a year, I stand on a stage in front of these massed undergraduates. In 13–14 weeks of lecturing I survey the field of anthropology, one of the broadest in the college curriculum. I cover not only cultural anthropology, which is my own specialty, but also the other three subdisciplines—prehistoric archeology, biological anthropology, and anthropological linguistics. Introductory anthropology is among the first courses taken at Michigan. Many students take it to satisfy their social science distribution requirement. Most do not plan to major in anthropology, and many will never take another anthropology course.

For these reasons, the lecturer must work hard to keep students' attention, and my evaluations usually give me good marks for making lectures interesting. However, students in this setting perceive a successful lecturer not simply as a teacher, but as something of an entertainer. My efforts to keep them interested sometimes have the side effect of creating a less formal and more relaxed atmosphere than is usual in a lecture. The combination of large lecture hall, electronic voice amplification, and relative informality sometimes prompts students to relax too much for my taste. Nevertheless, changes in students' behavior over the past decade, particularly their more relaxed classroom comportment, helped turn my attention to television's effects on human behavior.

TELECONDITIONING

Most of the freshmen I have taught during the past decade were born after 1955. They belong to the first generation raised after the almost total diffusion of television into the American home. Most of these young Americans have never known a world without TV. The tube has been as much a fixture in their homes as mom or dad. Considering how common divorce has become, the TV set even outlasts the father in many homes. American kids now devote 22–30 hours to television each week. By the end of high school, they will have spent 22,000 hours in front of the set, versus only 11,000 in the classroom. Such prolonged exposure must modify Americans' behavior in several ways.

I have discussed the behavior modification I see in my classroom with university colleagues, and many say they have observed similar changes in students' conduct. The thesis to be defended in this book is somewhat different from those of other studies about television's effects on behavior. Previous researchers have found links between exposure to media content (for example, violence) and individual behavior (hyperactivity, aggression, "acting out"). I also believe that content affects behavior. However, I make a more basic claim: The very habit of watching television has modified the behavior of Americans who have grown up with the tube.

Anyone who has been to a movie house recently has seen examples of TV-conditioned behavior—*teleconditioning.* People talk, babies cry, members of the audience file in and out getting snacks and going to the bathroom. Students act similarly in college courses. A decade ago, there was always an isolated student who did these kinds of things. What is new is a behavior pattern, characteristic of a group rather than an individual. This cultural pattern is becoming more and more pronounced, and I link it directly to televiewing. Stated simply, the pattern is this: *Televiewing causes people to duplicate inappropriately, in other areas of their lives, behavior styles developed while watching television.*

Some examples are in order. Almost nothing bothers professors more than having someone read a newspaper in class. If lecturers take their message and teaching responsibilities seriously, they are understandably perturbed when a student shows more interest in a sports column or "Doonesbury." I don't often get newspapers in class, but one day I noticed a student sitting in the front row reading a paperback novel. Irritated by her audacity, I stopped lecturing and asked, "Why are you reading a book in my class?" Her answer: "Oh, I'm not in your class. I just came in here to read my book."

How is this improbable response explained? Why would someone take the trouble to come into a classroom in order to read? The answer, I think, is this: Because of televiewing, many young Americans have trouble reading unless they have background noise. Research confirms that most Americans do something else while watching television. Often they read. Even I do it. When I get home from work I often turn on the television set, sit down in a comfortable chair, and go through the mail or read the newspaper.

Research on television's impact in other countries confirms that televiewing evolves through certain stages. The first stage, when sets are introduced, is rapt attention, gazes glued to the screen. Some of us can remember from the late 1940s and 1950s sitting in front of our first TV, dumbly watching even test patterns. Later, as the novelty diminishes, viewers become progressively less attentive. Televiewers in Brazil, whom I began studying systematically in 1983, had already moved past the first stage, but they were still much more attentive than Americans.

A study done in Brazil's largest city, São Paulo, illustrates the contrast. The study shocked Rede Globo, Brazil's dominant network (and the most watched commercial TV network in the world). It revealed that half the viewers were not paying full attention when commercials were shown. Afraid of losing advertising revenues, Rede Globo attacked the accuracy of the research. American sponsors are so accustomed to inattention and, nowadays, to remote control tune-outs, that it would probably delight them if even half the audience stayed put.

The student who came to my class to read her novel was simply an extreme example of a culture pattern derived from television. Because of her lifelong TV dependency, she had trouble reading without background noise. It didn't matter to her whether the background hum came from a stereo, a TV set, or a live professor. Accustomed to machines that don't talk back, she probably was amazed that I noticed her at all. Perhaps my questioning even prompted her to check her set that night to see if someone real was lurking inside.

Another example of a televiewing effect is students' increasing tendency to enter and leave classrooms at will. Of course, individual students do occasionally get sick or have a dentist's appointment. But here again I'm describing a group pattern rather than individual idiosyncrasies. Only during the past few years have I regularly observed students getting up in mid-lecture, leaving the room for a few minutes, then returning. Sometimes they bring back a canned soft drink.

These students intend no disrespect. They are simply transferring a home-grown pattern of snack-and-bathroom break from family room to classroom. They perceive nothing unusual in acting the same way in front of a live speaker and fellow students as they do when they watch television. (A few students manage to remain seated for only 10–15 minutes. Then they get up and leave the classroom. They are exhibiting a less flattering pattern. Either they have diarrhea, as one student told me he did, or they have decided to shut off the "set" or "change channels.")

Today, almost all Americans talk while watching television. Talking is becoming more common in the classroom, as in the movie house, and this also illustrates television's effects on our collective behavior. Not only do my students bring food and drink to class, some lie down on the floor if they arrive too late to get a seat. I have even seen couples kissing and caressing just a few rows away.

New examples of teleconditioning pop up all the time. In each of the past two semesters I've taught introductory anthropology, at least one student has requested that I say publicly "Happy Birthday" to a friend in the class. These students seem to perceive me as a professional analog of Willard Scott, NBC's *Today* show weatherman, who offers birthday greetings (to people 100 and over). Long ago I put into my syllabus injunctions against reading newspapers and eating crunchy foods in class. Last semester I felt compelled to announce that I "don't do birthdays."

All these are examples of effects of televiewing on social behavior of young Americans. They are not individual idiosyncrasies (the subject matter of psychology) but new *culture patterns* that have emerged since the 1950s. As such they are appropriate objects for anthropological analysis. *Culture,* as defined by anthropologists, consists of knowledge, beliefs, perceptions, attitudes, expectations, values, and patterns of behavior that people learn by growing up in a given society. Above all else, culture consists of *shared* learning. In contrast to education, it extends well beyond what we learn in school, to encompass everything we learn in life. Much of the information that contemporary Americans share comes from their common exposure to the mass media, particularly television.

TV CONTENT'S CULTURAL IMPACT

TV *content*'s impact on American culture enters the story when we consider that contemporary Americans share common information and experiences because of the programs they have seen. Again, I learn from my students. The subject matter of introductory anthropology includes the kinship systems of the United States and other societies. One habit I acquired about five years ago takes advantage of my students' familiarity with television. My practice is to illustrate changes in American family structure and household organization by contrasting television programs of the 1950s with more recent examples.

Three decades ago, the usual TV family was a nuclear family consisting of employed father (who often knew best), homemaker mother, and children. Examples include *Father Knows Best, Ozzie and Harriet,* and *Leave It to Beaver.* These programs, which were appropriate for the 1950s, are out of sync with the social and economic realities of the late 1980s. Only 16 million American women worked outside the home in 1950, compared with three times that number today. By the mid-1980s, fewer than 10 percent of American households had the composition that was once considered normal: breadwinner father, homemaker mother, and two children. Still, today's college students remain knowledgeable about these 1950s shows through syndicated reruns. Afternoon television is a pop culture museum that familiarizes kids with many of the same images, characters, and tales that their parents saw in recent days of yore.

Virtually all my students have seen reruns of the series *The Brady Bunch.* Its family organization provides an interesting contrast with earlier programs. It illustrates what anthropologists call "blended family organization." A new (blended) family forms when a widow with three daughters marries a widower with three sons. Blended families have been increasing in American society because of more frequent divorce and remarriage. However, a first spouse's death may also lead to a blended family, as in *The Brady Bunch.* During *The Brady Bunch*'s first run, divorce remained controversial and thus could not give rise to the Brady household.

The occupation of Mike, the Brady husband-father, a successful architect, illustrates a trend toward upper-middle-class jobs and life-styles that continues on American television today. TV families tend to be more professional, more successful, and richer than the average real-life family. More recent examples include the Huxtables (*The Cosby Show*) and the Keatons (*Family Ties*). There are also ultra-rich night-time soap families such as the Carringtons of *Dynasty* and the Ewings of *Dallas*. Mike and Carol Brady were wealthy enough to employ a housekeeper, Alice. Mirroring American culture when the program was made, the career of the wife-mother was part time and subsidiary, if it existed at all. Back then, women like Carol Brady who had been lucky enough to find a wealthy husband didn't compete with other women—even professional housekeepers—in the work force.

I use familiar examples like *The Brady Bunch* to teach students how to draw the genealogies and kinship diagrams that anthropologists use routinely in fieldwork and in making cross-cultural comparisons. TV family relationships may be represented with the same symbols and genealogical charts used for the Bushmen of the Kalahari Desert of southern Africa, or any other society. In particular, I chart changes in American family organization, showing how real-life changes have been reflected in television content, with which students tend to be familiar. *The Brady Bunch*, for example, illustrates a trend toward showing nontraditional families and households. We also see this trend in day-time soaps and in prime time, with the marital breakups, reconciliations, and extended family relationships of *Dallas, Dynasty, Falcon Crest,* and *Knot's Landing.* The trend toward newer household types is also obvious in *Kate & Allie* and *The Golden Girls.*

Students enjoy learning about anthropological techniques with culturally familiar examples. Each time I begin my kinship lecture, a few people in the class immediately recognize (from reruns) the nuclear families of the 1950s. They know the names of all the Cleavers—Ward, June, Wally, and Beaver. However, when I begin diagramming the Bradys, my students can't contain themselves. They start shouting out "Jan," "Bobby," "Greg," "Cindy," "Marsha," "Peter," "Mike," "Carol," "Alice." The response mounts. By the time we get to Carol and Alice, almost everyone is taking part in my blackboard kinship chart. Whenever I give my Brady Bunch lecture, Anthropology 101 resembles a revival meeting. Hundreds of young natives shout out in unison names made almost as familiar as their parents' through television reruns.

As the natives take up this chant—learned by growing up in post-1950s America—there is an enthusiasm, a warm glow, that my course will not recapture until next semester's rerun of my Brady Bunch lecture. It is as though my students find nirvana, religious ecstasy, through their collective remembrance of the Bradys, in the rituallike incantation of their names.

Given my own classroom experiences, I was hardly surprised to read that in a 1986 survey of 1550 American adults, more people said they got pleasure from TV than from sex, food, liquor, money, or religion. In that survey, people indicated which of the following "give you a great deal of pleasure and satisfaction." The percentages were as follows:

Watching TV	68
Friends	61
Helping others	59
Vacations	58
Hobbies	56
Reading	55
Marriage	45
Sexual relationships	42
Food	41
Money	40
Sports	32
Religion	32

"Furthermore, when people were asked what they liked to do for relaxation, watching TV again topped the list, followed by just relaxing and doing nothing, vacationing, music, reading and going out to eat. Sex and religion were each chosen by a mere one percent."[1]

THE CULTURAL DIMENSION

I often wonder how my more traditional colleagues in anthropology have managed to avoid becoming interested in television—so striking are the behavioral modifications it has wrought in the natives we see and talk to most frequently: our fellow citizens in modern society. Nationwide and ubiquitous, television cuts across demographic boundaries. It presents to diverse groups a set of common symbols, vocabularies, information, and shared experiences. Televiewing encompasses men and women of different ages, colors, classes, ethnic groups, and levels of educational achievement. Television is seen in cities, suburbs, towns, and country—by farmers, factory workers, and philosophers (although the last may be loath to admit it).

Television is stigmatized as trivial by many people (particularly orthodox intellectuals). However, it is hardly trivial that the average Amer-

---

[1] "More Enjoy TV Than Sex, Says Ad Agency Study," *TV Guide,* News Update Section (July 12–18, 1986), p. A1.

ican household has more television sets (2.2 per home) than bathrooms. Given the level of television's penetration of the modern home, we should hardly ignore its effects on socialization and enculturation. The common information that members of a mass society come to share as a result of watching the same thing is indisputably *culture* as anthropologists use the term. This anthropological definition of culture encompasses a much broader spectrum of human life than the definition that focuses on "high culture"—refinement, cultivation, taste, sophistication, education, and appreciation of the fine arts. From the anthropological perspective, not just university graduates, but all people are cultured.

Anthropology's subject matter must include features of modern culture that some regard as too trivial to be worthy of serious study, such as commercial television. As a cultural product and manifestation, a rock star may be as interesting as a symphony conductor, a comic book as significant as a book-award winner. It is axiomatic in anthropology that the most significant cultural forces are those that affect us every day of our lives. Particularly important are those features influencing children during *enculturation*—the process whereby one grows up in a particular society and absorbs its culture.

Culture is collective, shared, meaningful. It is transmitted by conscious and unconscious learning experiences. People acquire it not through their genes, but as a result of growing up in a particular society. Hundreds of culture-bearers have passed through the Anthropology 101 classroom over the past decade. Many have been unable to recall the full names of their parents' first cousins. Some have forgotten a grandmother's maiden name, and few contemporary students know many biblical or Shakespearean characters. Most, however, have no trouble identifying names and relationships in mythical families that exist only in televisionland.

As the Bible, Shakespeare, and classical mythology did in the past, television influences the names we bestow on our children and answer to all our lives. For example, "Jaime" rose from 70th to 10th most popular girl's name within two years of the debut of *The Bionic Woman,* whose title character was Jaime Sommers. The first name of the program's star, Lindsay Wagner, also became popular. *Charlie's Angels* boosted "Tiffany" and "Sabrina." Younger kids are named "Blake," "Alexis," "Fallon," and "Krystle" (spellings vary) after *Dynasty*'s Carringtons. In other cultures children still receive names of gods (Jesus, Mohammed) and heroes (Ulysses). The comparably honored Olympians of contemporary America lead their glamorous, superhuman lives not on a mountaintop, but in a small square box. We don't even have to go to church to worship them, because we can count on them to come to us in weekly visitations.

Psychologists are still debating the precise effects of television on *individual* behavior and psychopathology; TV murders and car chases may indeed influence kids toward aggressive or destructive behavior. However, television's *cultural* effects are indubitable. Examples of the medium's impact on U.S. culture—on the collective behavior and knowledge of contemporary Americans—are everywhere. . . .

My conclusions about television can be summarized as follows: New culture patterns related to television's penetration of the American home have emerged since the 1950s. As *technology*, television affects collective behavior, as people duplicate, in many areas of their lives, habits developed while watching TV. Television *content* also influences mass culture because it provides widely shared common knowledge, beliefs, and expectations.

I became interested in television because I saw that its effects are comparable to those of humanity's most powerful traditional institutions—family, church, state, and education. Television is creating new cultural experiences and meanings. It is capable of producing intense, often irrationally based, feelings of solidarity and *communitas* ("community feeling") shared widely by people who have grown up within the same cultural tradition. Nothing so important to natives could long escape the eye of the anthropologist. . . .

REVIEW QUESTIONS

1. What does Conrad Kottak mean by the term *teleconditioning?* What are some examples of teleconditioning.
2. According to Kottak, habitual televiewing results in a special form of cultural behavior. What is this behavior, and why does Kottak call it *cultural* rather than *personal?*
3. What is enculturation, and how does television contribute to the enculturation of American TV watchers?
4. Kottak feels that television is an instrument of solidarity in American society. How does televiewing achieve this outcome?

8

Losing Languages:
Speaking with a Single Tongue

Jared Diamond

Six thousand languages are spoken by the world's 5.5 billion people, but it is likely that only two hundred of these will survive 100 years from now. In this article, Jared Diamond looks at the process of language extinction and the effect language loss will have on ethnic groups, the conservation of cultural knowledge, linguistic studies, and government responsibilities. He concludes by saying that the advantages of preserving linguistic diversity outweigh any benefits of requiring all people to speak with a single tongue.

"**K**ópipi! Kópipi!" In jungle on the Pacific island of Bougainville, a man from the village of Rotokas was excitedly pointing out the most beautiful birdsong I had ever heard. It consisted of silver-clear whistled tones and trills, grouped in slowly rising phrases of two or three notes, each phrase different from the next. The effect was like one of Schubert's deceptively simple songs. I never succeeded in glimpsing the singer, nor have any of the other ornithologists who have subsequently visited Bougainville and listened spellbound to its song. All we know of the kópipi bird is that name for it in the Rotokas language and descriptions of it by Rotokas villagers.

As I talked with my guide, I gradually realized that the extraordinary music of Bougainville's mountains included not only the kópipi's song but also the sounds of the Rotokas language. My guide named one bird after another: *kópipi, kurupi, vokupi, kopikau, kororo, keravo, kurue, vikuroi.* . . . The only consonant sounds in those names are *k, p, r,* and *v.* Later I learned that the Rotokas language has only six consonant sounds, the fewest of any known language in the world. English, by comparison, has 24, while other languages have 80 or more. Somehow the people of Rotokas, living in a tropical rain forest on one of the highest mountains of the southwest Pacific, have managed to build a rich vocabulary and communicate clearly while relying on fewer basic sounds than any other people.

But the music of their language is now disappearing from Bougainville's mountains, and from the world. The Rotokas language is just one of 18 languages spoken on an island roughly three-quarters the size of Connecticut. At last count it was spoken by only 4,320 people, and the number is declining. With its vanishing, a 30,000-year history of human communication and cultural development is coming to an end.

That vanishing exemplifies a little-noticed tragedy looming over us: the possible loss of 90 percent of our creative heritage, linked with the loss of 90 percent of our languages. We hear much anguished discussion about the accelerating disappearance of indigenous cultures as our Coca-Cola civilization spreads over the world. Much less attention has been paid to the disappearance of languages themselves and to their essential role in the survival of those indigenous cultures. Each language is the vehicle for a unique way of thinking, a unique literature, and a unique view of the world. Only now are linguists starting seriously to estimate the world's rate of language loss and to debate what to do about it.

If the present rate of disappearance continues, our 6,000 modern languages could be reduced within a century or two to just a few hundred. Time is running out even to study the others. Hence linguists face a race against time similar to that faced by biologists, now aware that many of the world's plant and animal species are in danger of extinction.

To begin to understand the problem, we should take a look at how the world's languages are divvied up. If the global population of about 5.5 billion humans were equally distributed among its 6,000 tongues, then each language would have roughly 900,000 speakers—enough to give each language a fair chance of survival. Of course, the vast majority of people use only one of a few "big" languages, such as Mandarin Chinese, English, or Spanish, each with hundreds of millions of native speakers. The vast majority of languages are "little" ones, with a median number of perhaps only 5,000 speakers.

Our 6,000 languages are also unevenly distributed over the globe. Western Europe is especially poorly endowed, with about 45 native languages. In 1788, when European settlement of Australia began, aboriginal Australia was considerably richer: it had 250 languages, despite having far fewer people than Western Europe. The Americas at the time of Columbus's arrival were richer yet: more than 1,000 languages. But the richest region of the globe, then and now, is New Guinea and other Pacific islands, with only 8 million people, or less than .2 percent of the world's population, but about 1,400 languages, or almost 25 percent of the world's total! While New Guinea itself stands out with about 1,000 of those languages, other neighboring archipelagoes are also well endowed—Vanuatu, for example, with about 105, and the Philippines with 160.

Many New Guinea languages are so distinctive that they have no proven relationship with any other language in the world, not even with any other New Guinea language. As I travel across New Guinea, every 10 or 20 miles I pass between tribes with languages as different as English is from Chinese. And most of those languages are "tiny" ones, with fewer than 1,000 speakers.

How did these enormous geographic differences in linguistic diversity arise? Partly, of course, from differences in topography and human population density. But there's another reason as well: the original linguistic diversity of many areas has been homogenized by expansions of political states in the last several thousand years, and by expansions of farmers in the last 10,000 years. New Guinea, Vanuatu, the Philippines, and aboriginal Australia were exceptional in never having been unified by a native empire. To us, the British and Spanish empires may be the most familiar examples of centralized states that imposed their state language on conquered peoples. However, the Inca and Aztec empires similarly imposed Quechua and Nahuatl on their Indian subjects before A.D. 1500. Long before the rise of political states, expansions of farmers must have wiped out thousands of hunter-gatherer languages. For instance, the expansion of Indo-European farmers and herders that began around 4000 B.C. eradicated all preexisting Western European languages except Basque.

I'd guess that before expansions of farmers began in earnest around 6000 B.C. the world harbored tens of thousands of languages. If so, then we may *already* have lost much of the world's linguistic diversity. Of those vanished languages, a few—such as Etruscan, Hittite, and Sumerian—lingered long enough to be written down and preserved for us. Far more languages, though, have vanished without a trace. Who knows what the speech of the Huns and the Picts, and of uncounted nameless peoples, sounded like?

As linguists have begun surveying the status of our surviving languages, it has become clear that prognoses for future survival vary enormously.

Here are some calculations made by linguist Michael Krauss of the University of Alaska at Fairbanks. Presumably among the languages with the most secure futures are the official national languages of the world's sovereign states, which now number 170 or so. However, most states have officially adopted English, French, Spanish, Arabic, or Portuguese, leaving only about 70 states to opt for other languages. Even if one counts regional languages, such as the 15 specified in India's constitution, that yields at best a few hundred languages officially protected anywhere in the world. Alternatively, one might consider languages with over a million speakers as secure, regardless of their official status, but that definition also yields only 200 or so secure languages, many of which duplicate the list of official languages. What's happening to the other 5,800 of the world's 6,000?

As an illustration of their fates, consider Alaska's 20 native Eskimo and Indian languages. The Eyak language, formerly spoken by a few hundred Indians on Alaska's south coast, had declined by 1982 to two native speakers, Marie Smith (age 72) and her sister Sophie Borodkin. Their children speak only English. With Sophie Borodkin's death last year at the age of 80, the language world of the Eyak people reached its final silence—except when Marie Smith speaks Eyak with Michael Krauss. Seventeen other native Alaskan languages are moribund, in that not a single child is learning them. Although they are still being spoken by older people, they too will meet the fate of Eyak when the last of those speakers dies; in addition, almost all of them have fewer than 1,000 speakers each. That leaves only two native Alaskan languages still being learned by children and thus not yet doomed: Siberian Yupik, with 1,000 speakers, and Central Yupik, with a grand total of 10,000 speakers.

The situation is similar for the 187 Indian languages surviving in North America outside Alaska, such as Chickasaw, Navajo, and Nootka. Krauss estimates that 149 of these are already moribund. Even Navajo, the language with by far the largest number of speakers (around 100,000), has a doubtful future, as many or most Navajo children now speak only English. Language extinction is even further advanced in aboriginal Australia, where only 100 of the original 250 languages are still spoken or even remembered, and only 7 have more than 1,000 speakers. At best, only 2 or 3 of those aboriginal languages will retain their vitality throughout our lifetime.

In monographs summarizing the current status of languages, one encounters the same types of phrase monotonously repeated. "Ubykh [a language of the northwest Caucasus] . . . one speaker definitely still alive, perhaps two or three more." "Vilela [sole surviving language of a group of Indian languages in Argentina] . . . spoken by only two individuals." "The last speaker of Cupeño [an Indian language of southern California], Roscinda Nolasquez of Pala, California, died in 1987 at the age of 94." Putting these status reports together, it appears that up to half of the world's surviving languages are no longer being learned by children. By some time in the coming century, Krauss estimates, all but perhaps a few hundred languages could be dead or moribund.

Why is the rate of language disappearance accelerating so steeply now, when so many languages used to be able to persist with only a few hundred speakers in places like traditional New Guinea? Why do declining languages include not only small ones but also ones with many speakers, including Breton (around 100,000) and even Quechua (8.5 million)? Just as there are different ways of killing people—by a quick blow to the head, slow strangulation, or prolonged neglect—so too are there different ways of eradicating a language.

The most direct way, of course, is to kill almost all its speakers. This was how white Californians eliminated the Yahi Indian language between 1853 and 1870, and how British colonists eliminated all the native languages of Tasmania between 1803 and 1835. Another direct way is for governments to forbid and punish use of minority languages. If you wondered why 149 out of 187 North American Indian languages are now moribund, just consider the policy practiced until recently by the U.S. government regarding those languages. For several centuries we insisted that Indians could be "civilized" and taught English only by removing children from the "barbarous" atmosphere of their parents' homes to English-language-only boarding schools, where use of Indian languages was absolutely forbidden and punished with physical abuse and humiliation.

But in most cases language loss proceeds by the more insidious process now underway at Rotokas. With political unification of an area formerly occupied by sedentary warring tribes comes peace, mobility, intermarriage, and schools. Mixed couples may have no common language except the majority language (for example, English or Pidgin English in Papua New Guinea, the nation to which Bougainville belongs). Young people in search of economic opportunity abandon their native-speaking villages and move to mixed urban centers, where again they have no option except to speak the majority language. Their children's schools speak the majority language. Even their parents remaining in the village learn the majority language for its access to prestige, trade, and power. Newspapers, radio, and TV overwhelmingly use majority languages understood by most consumers, advertisers, and subscribers. (In the United States, the only native languages regularly broadcast are Navajo and Yupik.)

The usual result is that minority young adults tend to become bilingual, then their children become monolingual in the majority language. Eventually the minority language is spoken only by older people, until the last of them dies. Long before that end is reached, the minority language has degenerated through loss of its grammatical complexities, loss of forgotten native words, and incorporation of foreign vocabulary and grammatical features.

Those are the overwhelming facts of worldwide language extinction. But now let's play devil's advocate and ask, So what? Are we really so sure this loss is a terrible thing? Isn't the existence of thousands of languages positively harmful, first because they impede communication, and second because they promote strife? Perhaps we should actually *encourage* language loss.

The devil's first objection is that we need a common language to understand each other, to conduct commerce, and to get along in peace. Perhaps it's no accident that the countries most advanced technologically are ones with few languages. Multiple languages are just an impediment to communication and progress—at least that's how the devil would argue.

To which I answer: Of course different people need some common language to understand each other! But that doesn't require eliminating minority languages; it only requires bilingualism. We Americans forget how exceptional our monolingualism is by world standards. People elsewhere routinely learn two or more languages as children, with little effort. For example, Denmark is one of the wealthiest and most contented nations in the world. Danes have no problem doing business profitably with other countries, even though practically no one except the 5 million Danes speaks Danish. That's because almost all Danes also speak English, and many speak other foreign languages as well. Still, Danes have no thought of abandoning their tongue. The Danish language, combined with polylingualism, remains indispensable to Danes being happily Danish.

Perhaps you're thinking now, All right, so communication doesn't absolutely require us all to have a single language. Still, though, bilingualism is a pain in the neck that you yourself would rather be spared.

But remember that bilingualism is practiced especially by minority language speakers, who learn majority languages. If they choose to do that extra work, that's their business; monolingual speakers of majority languages have no right or need to prevent them. Minorities struggling to preserve their language ask only for the freedom to decide for themselves—without being excluded, humiliated, punished, or killed for exercising that freedom. Inuits (Eskimos) aren't asking U.S. whites to learn Inuit; they're just asking that Inuit schoolchildren be permitted to learn Inuit along with English.

The devil's second objection is that multiple languages promote strife by encouraging people to view other peoples as different. The civil wars tearing apart so many countries today are determined by linguistic lines. Whatever the value of multiple languages, getting rid of them may be the price we have to pay if we're to halt the killing around the globe. Wouldn't the world be a much more peaceful place if the Kurds would just agree to speak Arabic or Turkish, if Sri Lanka's Tamils would consent to speak Sinhalese, and if the Armenians would switch to Azerbaijani (or vice versa)?

That seems like a very strong argument. But pause and consider: language differences aren't the sole cause, or even the most important cause, of strife. Prejudiced people will seize on any difference to dislike others, including differences of religion, politics, ethnicity, and dress. One of the world's most vicious civil wars today, that in the land that once was Yugoslavia, pits peoples unified by language but divided by religion and ethnicity: Orthodox Serbs against Catholic Croats and Muslim Bosnians, all speaking Serbo-Croatian. The bloodiest genocide of history was that carried out under Stalin, when Russians killed mostly other Russians over supposed political differences. In the world's bloodiest genocide since World War II, Khmer-speaking Cambodians under Pol Pot killed millions of other Khmer-speaking Cambodians.

If you believe that minorities should give up their languages in order to promote peace, ask yourself whether you believe that minorities should also promote peace by giving up their religions, their ethnicities, their political views. If you believe that freedom of religion but not of language is an inalienable human right, how would you explain your inconsistency to a Kurd or an Inuit? Innumerable examples besides those of Stalin and Pol Pot warn us that monolingualism is no safeguard of peace. Even if the suppression of differences of language, religion, and ethnicity did promote peace (which I doubt), it would exact a huge price in human suffering.

Given that people do differ in language, religion, and ethnicity, the only alternative to tyranny or genocide is for people to learn to live together in mutual respect and tolerance. That's not at all an idle hope. Despite all the past wars over religion, people of different religions do coexist peacefully in the United States, Indonesia, and many other countries. Similarly, many countries that practice linguistic tolerance find that they can accommodate people of different languages in harmony, for example, three languages in Finland (Finnish, Swedish, and Lapp), four in Switzerland (German, French, Italian, and Romansh), and nearly a thousand in Papua New Guinea.

All right, so there's nothing inevitably harmful about minority languages, except the nuisance of bilingualism for the minority speakers. What are the positive advantages of linguistic diversity, to justify that minor nuisance?

One answer is that languages are the most complex products of the human mind, each differing enormously in its sounds, structure, and pattern of thought. But a language itself isn't the only thing lost when a language goes extinct. Each language is indissolubly tied up with a unique culture, literature (whether written or not), and worldview, all of which also represent the end point of thousands of years of human inventiveness. Lose the language and you lose much of that as well. Thus the eradication of most of the world's accumulation of languages would be an overwhelming tragedy, just as would be the destruction of most of the world's accumulated art or literature. We English-speakers would regard the loss of Shakespeare's language and culture as a loss to humanity; Rotokas villagers feel a similar bond to their own language and culture. We are putting millions of dollars into the effort to save one of the world's

8,600 bird species, the California condor. Why do we care so little about most of the world's 6,000 languages, or even desire their disappearance? What makes condors more wonderful than the Eyak language?

A second answer addresses two often-expressed attitudes: "One language is really as good as another," or conversely, "English is much better than any of those fiendishly complicated Indian languages." In reality, languages aren't equivalent or interchangeable, and there's no all-purpose "best language." Instead, as everyone fluent in more than one language knows, different languages have different advantages, such that it's easier to discuss or think about certain things, or to think and feel in certain ways, in one language than another. Language loss doesn't only curtail the freedom of minorities, it also curtails the options of majorities.

Now perhaps you're thinking, Enough of all this vague talk about linguistic freedom, unique cultural inheritance, and different options for thinking and expressing. Those are luxuries that rate low priority amid the crises of the modern world. Until we solve the world's desperate socioeconomic problems, we can't waste our time on bagatelles like obscure Indian languages.

But think again about the socioeconomic problems of the people speaking all those obscure Indian languages (and thousands of other obscure languages around the world). Their problems aren't just narrow ones of jobs and job skills, but broad ones of cultural disintegration. They've been told for so long that their language and everything else about their culture are worthless that they believe it. The costs to our government, in the form of welfare benefits and health care, are enormous. At the same time, other impoverished groups with strong intact cultures—like some recent groups of immigrants—are already managing to contribute to society rather than take from it.

Programs to reverse Indian cultural disintegration would be far better than welfare programs, for Indian minorities and for majority taxpayers alike. Similarly, those foreign countries now wracked by civil wars along linguistic lines would have found it cheaper to emulate countries based on partnerships between proud intact groups than to seek to crush minority languages and cultures.

Those seem to me compelling cultural and practical benefits of sustaining our inherited linguistic diversity. But if you're still unconvinced, let me instead try to persuade you of another proposition: that we should at least record as much information as possible about each endangered language, lest all knowledge of it be lost. For hundreds, perhaps thousands, of the world's 6,000 languages, we have either no written information at all, or just brief word lists. If many of those languages do indeed vanish, at least we'd have preserved as much knowledge as possible from irreversible loss.

What is the value of such knowledge? As one example, consider that relationships of the languages that survive today serve to trace the history of human development and migrations, just as relationships of existing animal and plant species trace the history of biological evolution. All linguists agree, for instance, that we can trace existing Indo-European languages back to an ancestral Proto-Indo-European language spoken somewhere in Europe or western Asia around 6,000 years ago. Now some linguists are trying to trace languages and peoples back much further in time, possibly even back to the origin of all human language. Many tiny modern languages, the ones now most at risk of vanishing unrecorded, have proved disproportionately important in answering that question that never fails to interest each of us: Where did I come from?

Lithuanian, for example, is an Indo-European language with only 3 million speakers, and until recently it struggled against Russian for survival. It's dwarfed by the combined total of 2 billion speakers of the approximately 140 other Indo-European languages. Yet Lithuanian has proved especially important in understanding Indo-European language origins because in some respects it has changed the least and preserved many archaic features over the past several thousand years.

Of course. Dictionaries and grammars of Lithuanian are readily available. If the Lithuanian language were to go extinct, at least we'd already know enough about it to use it in reconstructing Indo-European language origins. But other equally important languages are at risk of vanishing with much less information about them recorded. Why should anyone care whether four tiny languages, Kanakanabu, Saaroa, Rukai, and Tsou, spoken by 11,000 aborigines in the mountains of Taiwan, survive? Other Asians may eventually come to care a lot, because these languages may constitute one of the four main branches of the giant Austronesian language family. That family, consisting of some 1,000 languages with a total of 200 million speakers, includes Indonesian and Tagalog, two of Asia's most important languages today. Lose those four tiny aboriginal languages and these numerous Asian peoples may lose one-quarter of the linguistic data base for reconstructing their own history.

If you now at last agree that linguistic diversity isn't evil, and might even be interesting and good, what can you do about the present situation? Are we helpless in the face of the seemingly overwhelming forces tending to eradicate all but a few big languages from the modern world?

No, we're not helpless. First, professional linguists themselves could do a lot more than most of them are now doing. Most place little value on the study of vanishing languages. Only recently have a few linguists, such as Michael Krauss, called our attention to our impending loss. At minimum, society needs to train more linguists and offer incentives to those studying the languages most at risk of disappearing.

As for the rest of us, we can do something individually, but fostering sympathetic awareness of the problem and by helping our children become bilingual in any second language that we choose. Through government, we can also support the use of native languages. The 1990 Native

American Languages Act actually *encourages* the use of those languages. And at least as a start, Senate Bill 2044, signed by former President Bush last October, allocates a small amount of money—$2 million a year—for Native American language studies. There's also a lot that minority speakers themselves can do to promote their languages, as the Welsh, New Zealand Maori, and other groups have been doing with some success.

But these minority efforts will be in vain if strongly opposed by the majority, as has happened all too often. Should some of us English-speakers not choose actively to promote Native American languages, we can at least remain neutral and avoid crushing them. Our grounds for doing so are ultimately selfish: to pass on a rich, rather than a drastically impoverished, world to our children.

REVIEW QUESTIONS

1. What are the main reasons suggested by Diamond for the increased rate of language extinction?
2. According to Diamond, what are the advantages of conserving world linguistic diversity?
3. Some argue that the consolidation of linguistically distinctive groups around a single national language is desirable. What reasons do they use to support this view?
4. How can people facilitate world and national communication and at the same time preserve linguistic diversity, according to Diamond? What can individuals do about the problem?

ECOLOGY AND SUBSISTENCE

Ecology is the relationship of an organism to other elements within its environmental sphere. Every species, no matter how simple or complex, fits into a larger complex ecological system; each adapts to its ecological niche unless rapid environmental alterations outstrip the organism's ability and potential to adapt successfully. An important aim of ecological studies is to show how organisms fit within particular environments. Such studies also look at the effect environments have on the shape and behavior of life forms.

Every species has adapted biologically through genetically produced variation and natural selection. For example, the bipedal (two-footed) locomotion characteristic of humans is one possible adaptation to walking on the ground. It also permitted our ancestors to carry food, tools, weapons, and almost anything else they desired, enabling them to range out from a home base and bring things back for others to share. Some anthropologists believe that the social advantages of carrying and sharing may actually account for our bipedalism.

Biological processes have led to another important human characteristic, the development of a large and complex brain. The human brain is capable of holding an enormous inventory of information. With it, we can classify the parts of our environment and retain instructions for complex ways to deal with the things in our world. Because we can communicate our knowledge symbolically through language, we are able to teach one another. Instead of a genetic code that directs behavior automatically, we operate with a learned cultural code. Culture gives us the ability to behave in a much wider variety of ways, and to change rapidly in new situations. With culture, people have been able to live successfully in almost every part of the world.

Cultural ecology is the way people use their culture to adapt to particular environments. All people live in a *physical environment,* the world they can experience through their senses, but they will conceive of it in terms that seem most important to their adaptive needs and cultural perspective. We call this perspective the *cultural environment.*

All human societies must provide for the material needs of their members. People everywhere have to eat, clothe themselves, provide shelter against the elements, and take care of social requirements such as hospitality, gift giving, and proper dress.

Societies employ several different strategies to meet their material needs, strategies that affect their complexity and internal organization as well as relationships to the natural environment and to other human groups. Anthropologists often use these *subsistence strategies* to classify different groups into five types: hunter-gatherers, horticulturalists, pastoralists, agriculturalists, and industrialists. Let us look briefly at each of these.

Hunter-gatherers depend for subsistence on wild plants and animals. They forage for food, moving to different parts of their territories as supplies of plants, animals, and water grow scarce. They live in small bands of from 10 to 50 people and are typically egalitarian, leading a life marked by sharing and cooperation. Because hunter-gatherer bands are so small, they tend to lack formal political, legal, and religious structure, although members have regular ways to make group decisions, settle disputes, and deal ritually with the questions of death, adversity, social value, and world identification.

Hunter-gatherers tend to see themselves as part of the environment, not masters of it. This view shapes a religious ritual aimed at the maintenance and restoration of environmental harmony. All people lived as hunter-gatherers until about ten thousand years ago, when the first human groups began to farm and dwell in more permanent settlements. Today few hunter-gatherers survive. Most have lost their habitats to more powerful groups bent on economic and political exploitation.

Horticulture represents the earliest farming strategy, one that continues on a diminishing basis among many groups today. Horticulturalists garden. They often use a technique called *slash-and-burn agriculture,* which requires them to clear and burn over wild land and, with the aid of a digging stick, sow seeds in the ashes. When fields lose their fertility after a few years, they are abandoned and new land is cleared. Although horticulturalists farm, they often continue to forage for wild foods and still feel closely related to the natural environment.

Horticulture requires a substantial amount of undeveloped land, so overall population densities must remain fairly low. But the strategy permits higher population densities than hunting and gathering, so horticulturalists tend to live in larger permanent settlements numbering from 50 to 250 individuals. (Some horticultural societies have produced chiefdomships with much larger administrative and religious town centers.) Although they are still small by our standards, horticultural communities are large enough to require more complex organizational strategies. They often display more elaborate kinship systems based on descent, political structures that include headmen or chiefs, political alliances, religions characterized by belief in a variety of supernatural beings, and the beginnings of social inequality. Many of today's so-called tribal peoples are horticulturalists.

Pastoralists follow a subsistence strategy based on the herding of domesticated animals such as cattle, goats, sheep, and camels. Although herding strategies vary from one environment to another, pastoralists share some general attributes. They move on a regular basis during the year to take advantage of fresh sources of water and fodder for their animals. They usually congregate in large encampments for part of the year when food and water are plentiful, then divide into smaller groups when these resources become scarce. Pastoralists often display a strong sense of group identity and pride, a fierce independence, and skill at war and raiding. Despite attempts by modern governments to place them in permanent settlements, many pastoral groups in Africa and Asia continue their nomadic lifestyle.

Agriculture is still a common subsistence strategy in many parts of the world. Agriculture refers to a kind of farming based on the intensive cultivation of permanent land holdings. Agriculturalists usually use plows and organic fertilizers and may irrigate their fields in dry conditions.

Agrarian societies are marked by a high degree of social complexity. They are often organized as nation-states with armies and bureaucracies, social stratification, markets, extended families and kin groups, and some occupational specialization. Religion takes on a formal structure and is organized as a separate institution.

The term *industrialism* labels the final kind of subsistence strategy. Ours is an industrial society, as is much of the Western, and more recently, the Asian world. Industrial nations are highly complex; they display an extensive variety of subgroups and social statuses. Industrial societies tend to be dominated by market economies in which goods and services are exchanged on the basis of price, supply, and demand. There is a high degree of economic specialization, and mass marketing may lead to a depersonalization of human relations. Religious, legal, political, and economic systems find expression as separate institutions in a way that might look disjointed to hunter-gatherers or others from smaller, more integrated societies.

The study of cultural ecology involves more than an understanding of people's basic subsistence strategies. Each society exists in a distinctive environment. Although a group may share many subsistence methods with other societies, there are always special environmental needs that shape productive techniques. Andean farmers, for example, have developed approximately three thousand varieties of potatoes to meet the demands of growing conditions at different elevations in their mountain habitat. Bhil farmers in India have learned to create fields by damming up small streams in their rugged Aravalli hill villages. Otherwise they would find it difficult to cultivate there at all. American farmers learned to "contour-plow" parallel to slopes in response to water erosion and now increasingly use plowless farming to prevent the wind from carrying away precious topsoil.

No matter how successful are their microenvironmental adjustments, most groups in the world now face more serious adaptive challenges. One difficulty is the exploitation of their lands by outsiders, who are often unconstrained by adaptive necessity. A second is the need to overexploit the environment to meet market demand (See Part V for articles on market pressures). In either case, many local peoples find that their traditional subsistence techniques no longer work. They have lost control of their own environmental adjustment and must struggle to adapt to outsiders and what is left of their habitat.

The !Kung, described by Richard Lee in the first selection, provide an excellent example of a traditional foraging lifestyle. But today, the same bands of people who once lived on wild foods in the Kalahari find themselves confined to small government-mandated settlements. Cattle herders tend their animals on the desert lands once occupied by the !Kung. The second article, by Richard Reed, is a sobering reminder of what can happen to a horticultural people who once subsisted in harmony with their tropical forest habitat, but who now find themselves being displaced by colonists. These outsiders have stripped the forest bare. The third selection, by Warren Hern, details the effects of high fertility and population growth on the health and welfare of Shipibo Indians. Finally, the classic article on India's sacred cattle by Marvin Harris demonstrates that even religious beliefs may be used to facilitate adaptation to a group's subsistence requirements.

KEY TERMS

ecology	horticulture
cultural ecology	slash-and-burn agriculture
physical environment	pastoralism
cultural environment	agriculture
subsistence strategies	industrialism
hunting and gathering	

READINGS IN THIS SECTION

9

The Hunters:
Scarce Resources in the Kalahari

Richard Borshay Lee

*Peoples who hunt and gather wild foods experience an intimate rela-
tionship with their natural environments. A band's size and structure, the breadth of its territory, and the frequency and pattern of its
movement depend on the abundance of vegetable foods, game, and
water. For many Western anthropologists, the life of hunter-gatherers
seems precarious and fraught with hardship. Yet, according to
Richard Lee, this picture is largely inaccurate. In this article he points
out that the !Kung Bushmen who live in the Kalahari Desert of South
Africa survive well in what Westerners would consider a marginal
habitat. Depending, like most hunter-gatherers, on vegetable foods for
their sustenance, the !Kung actually spend little time in food collecting, yet they live long and fruitful lives in their desert home.[1]*

Reprinted by permission from Richard Lee and Irvin Devore, editors, *Man the Hunter*
(Hawthorne, NY: Aldine Publishing Company); copyright © 1968 Wenner-Gren Foundation
for Anthropological Research, Inc.

[1] Research for this article was conducted for an extended period of time over 25 years ago.
Since then, the !Kung, as well as most of the world's foraging groups have had their lives disrupted by government intervention and the encroachment of colonists. (An account of this
worldwide process is contained in the selection by John Bodely in Part X of this book.) Most
!Kung now live as poor squatters in more permanent government-initiated settlements. Research on the !Kung nevertheless remains one of the best sources of information on the
hunter-gatherer lifestyle, a subsistence strategy shared by all people only 12,000 years ago.

T he current anthropological view of hunter-gatherer subsistence
rests on two questionable assumptions. First is the notion that these
people are primarily dependent on the hunting of game animals, and second is the assumption that their way of life is generally a precarious and
arduous struggle for existence.

Recent data on living hunter-gatherers show a radically different picture. We have learned that in many societies, plant and marine resources
are far more important than are game animals in the diet. More important,
it is becoming clear that, with few conspicuous exceptions, the hunter-
gatherer subsistence base is at least routine and reliable and at best surprisingly abundant. Anthropologists have consistently tended to underes-
timate the viability of even those "marginal isolates" of hunting peoples
that have been available to ethnographers.

The purpose of this paper is to analyze the food-getting activities of
one such "marginal" people, the !Kung Bushmen of the Kalahari Desert.
Three related questions are posed: How do the Bushmen make a living?
How easy or difficult is it for them to do this? What kinds of evidence are
necessary to measure and evaluate the precariousness or security of a way
of life? And after the relevant data are presented, two further questions are
asked: What makes this security of life possible? To what extent are the
Bushmen typical of hunter-gatherers in general?

BUSHMAN SUBSISTENCE

The !Kung Bushmen of Botswana are an apt case for analysis. They inhabit
the semi-arid northwest region of the Kalahari Desert. With only six to
nine inches of rainfall per year, this is, by any account, a marginal environment for human habitation. In fact, it is precisely the unattractiveness
of their homeland that has kept the !Kung isolated from extensive contact
with their agricultural and pastoral neighbors.

Fieldwork was carried out in the Dobe area, a line of eight permanent
waterholes near the South-West Africa border and 125 miles south of the
Okavango River. The population of the Dobe area consists of 466 Bushmen, including 379 permanent residents living in independent camps or
associated with Bantu cattle posts, as well as 87 seasonal visitors. The
Bushmen share the area with some 340 Bantu pastoralists largely of the
Herero and Tswana tribes. The ethnographic present refers to the period
of fieldwork: October 1963 to January 1965.

The Bushmen living in independent camps lack firearms, livestock,
and agriculture. Apart from occasional visits to the Herero for milk, these
!Kung are entirely dependent upon hunting and gathering for their subsistence. Politically they are under the nominal authority of the Tswana
headman, although they pay no taxes and receive very few government
services. European presence amounts to one overnight government patrol

every six to eight weeks. Although Dobe-area !Kung have had some contact with outsiders since the 1880s, the majority of them continue to hunt and gather because there is no viable alternative locally available to them.

Each of the fourteen independent camps is associated with one of the permanent waterholes. During the dry season (May–October) the entire population is clustered around these wells. Table I shows the numbers at each well at the end of the 1964 dry season. Two wells had no camp resident and one large well supported five camps. The number of camps at each well and the size of each camp changed frequently during the course of the year. The "camp" is an open aggregate of cooperating persons which changes in size and composition from day to day. Therefore, I have avoided the term "band" in describing the !Kung Bushman living groups.

Each waterhole has a hinterland lying within a six-mile radius that is regularly exploited for vegetable and animal foods. These areas are not territories in the zoological sense, since they are not defended against outsiders. Rather, they constitute the resources that lie within a convenient walking distance of a waterhole. The camp is a self-sufficient subsistence unit. The members move out each day to hunt and gather, and return in the evening to pool the collected foods in such a way that every person present receives an equitable share. Trade in foodstuffs between camps is minimal; personnel do move freely from camp to camp, however. The net effect is of a population constantly in motion. On the average, an individual spends a third of his time living only with close relatives, a third visiting other camps, and a third entertaining visitors from other camps.

Because of the strong emphasis on sharing, and the frequency of movement, surplus accumulation of storable plant foods and dried meat is kept to a minimum. There is rarely more than two or three days' supply of food on hand in a camp at any time. The result of this lack of surplus is that a constant subsistence effort must be maintained throughout the year.

Table I Numbers and Distribution of Resident Bushmen and Bantu by Waterhole*

Name of Waterhole	No. of Camps	Population of Camps	Other Bushmen	Total Bushmen	Bantu
Dobe	2	37	—	37	—
!angwa	1	16	23	39	84
Bate	2	30	12	42	21
!ubi	1	19	—	19	65
!gose	3	52	9	61	18
/ai/ai	5	94	13	107	67
!xabe	—	—	8	8	12
Mahopa	—	—	23	23	73
Total	14	248	88	336	340

*Figures do not include 130 Bushmen outside area on the date of census.

Unlike agriculturalists, who work hard during the planting and harvesting seasons and undergo "seasonal unemployment" for several months, the Bushmen hunter-gatherers collect food every third or fourth day throughout the year.

Vegetable foods comprise from 60 to 80 percent of the total diet by weight, and collecting involves two or three days of work per woman per week. The men also collect plants and small animals, but their major contribution to the diet is the hunting of medium and large game. The men are conscientious but not particularly successful hunters; although men's and women's work input is roughly equivalent in terms of man-day of effort, the women provide two to three times as much food by weight as the men.

Table II summarizes the seasonal activity cycle observed among the Dobe-area !Kung in 1964. For the greater part of the year, food is locally abundant and easily collected. It is only during the end of the dry season in September and October, when desirable foods have been eaten out in the immediate vicinity of the waterholes, that the people have to plan longer hikes of 10 to 15 miles and carry their own water to those areas where the mongongo nut is still available. The important point is that food is a constant, but distance required to reach food is a variable; it is short in the summer, fall, and early winter, and reaches its maximum in the spring.

This analysis attempts to provide quantitative measures of subsistence status, including data on the following topics: abundance and variety of resources, diet selectivity, range size and population density, the composition of the work force, the ratio of work to leisure time, and the caloric and protein levels in the diet. The value of quantitative data is that they can be used comparatively and also may be useful in archeological reconstruction. In addition, one can avoid the pitfalls of subjective and qualitative impressions; for example, statements about food "anxiety" have proven to be difficult to generalize across cultures.

Abundance and Variety of Resources

It is impossible to define "abundance" of resources absolutely. However, one index of *relative* abundance is whether or not a population exhausts all the food available from a given area. By this criterion, the habitat of the Dobe-area Bushmen is abundant in naturally occurring foods. By far the most important food is the mongongo (mangetti) nut (*Ricinodendron rautanenii* Schinz). Although tens of thousands of pounds of these nuts are harvested and eaten each year, thousands more rot on the ground each year for want of picking.

The mongongo nut, because of its abundance and reliability, alone accounts for 50 percent of the vegetable diet by weight. In this respect it resembles a cultivated staple crop such as maize or rice. Nutritionally it is even more remarkable, for it contains five times the calories and ten times the proteins per cooked unit of the cereal crops. The average daily per-

Table II The Bushman Annual Round

	Jan.	Feb.	Mar.	April	May	June	July	Aug.	Sept.	Oct.	Nov.	Dec.
Season		Summer Rains		Autumn Dry			Winter Dry			Spring Dry		First Rains
Availability of water	Temporary summer pools everywhere			Large summer pools				Permanent waterholes only				Summer pools developing
Group moves	Widely dispersed at summer pools			At large summer pools				All population restricted to permanent waterholes				Moving out to summer pools
Men's subsistence activities	1. Hunting with bow, arrows, and dogs (year-round) 2. Running down immatures 3. Some gathering (year-round)						Trapping small game in snares				Running down newborn animals	
Women's subsistence activities	1. Gathering of mongongo nuts (year-round) 2. Fruits, berries, melons						Roots, bulbs, resins				Roots, leafy greens	
Ritual activities	Dancing, trance performances, and ritual curing (year-round)				Boys' initiation*						+	
Relative subsistence hardship			Water-food distance minimal				Increasing distance from water to food				Water-food distance minimal	

* Held once every five years; none in 1963–64.

† New Year's: Bushmen join the celebrations of their missionized Bantu neighbors.

115

capita consumption of 300 nuts yields about 1,260 calories and 56 grams of protein. This modest portion, weighing only about 7.5 ounces, contains the caloric equivalent of 2.5 pounds of cooked rice and the protein equivalent of 14 ounces of lean beef.

Furthermore, the mongongo nut is drought resistant, and it will still be abundant in the dry years when cultivated crops may fail. The extremely hard outer shell protects the inner kernel from rot and allows the nuts to be harvested for up to twelve months after they have fallen to the ground. A diet based on mongongo nuts is in fact more reliable than one based on cultivated foods, and it is not surprising, therefore, that when a Bushman was asked why he hadn't taken to agriculture, he replied: "Why should we plant, when there are so many mongongo nuts in the world?"

Apart from the mongongo, the Bushmen have available eighty-four other species of edible food plants, including twenty-nine species of fruits, berries, and melons and thirty species of roots and bulbs. The existence of this variety allows for a wide range of alternatives in subsistence strategy. During the summer months the Bushmen have no problem other than to choose among the tastiest and most easily collected foods. Many species, which are quite edible but less attractive, are bypassed, so that gathering never exhausts *all* the available plant foods of an area. During the dry season the diet becomes much more eclectic and the many species of roots, bulbs, and edible resins make an important contribution. It is this broad base that provides an essential margin of safety during the end of the dry season, when the mongongo nut forests are difficult to reach. In addition, it is likely that these rarely utilized species provide important nutritional and mineral trace elements that may be lacking in the more popular foods.

Diet Selectivity

If the Bushmen were living close to the "starvation" level, then one would expect them to exploit every available source of nutrition. That their life is well above this level is indicated by the data in Table III. Here all the edible plant species are arranged in classes according to the frequency with which they were observed to be eaten. It should be noted that although there are some eighty-five species available, about 90 percent of the vegetable diet by weight is drawn from only twenty-three species. In other words, 75 percent of the listed species provide only 10 percent of the food value.

In their meat-eating habits, the Bushmen show a similar selectivity. Of the 223 local species of animals known and named by the Bushmen, 54 species are classified as edible, and of these only 17 species were hunted on a regular basis. Only a handful of the dozens of edible species of small mammals, birds, reptiles, and insects that occur locally are regarded as food. Such animals as rodents, snakes, lizards, termites, and grasshoppers, which in the literature are included in the Bushman diet, are despised by the Bushmen of the Dobe area.

Table III !Kung Bushman Plant Foods

Food Class	Part Eaten								Total Number of Species in Class	Totals (percentages)	
	Fruit and Nut	Bean and Root	Fruit and Stalk	Root, Bulb	Fruit, Berry, Melon	Resin	Leaves	Seed, Bean		Estimated Contribution by Weight to Vegetable Diet	Estimated Contribution of Each Species
I. Primary Eaten daily throughout year (mongongo nut)	1	—	—	—	—	—	—	—	1	c. 50	c. 50*
II. Major Eaten daily in season	1	1	1	1	4	—	—	—	8	c. 25	c. 3†
III. Minor Eaten several times per week in season	—	—	—	7	3	2	2	—	14	c. 15	c. 1
IV. Supplementary Eaten when classes I–III locally unavailable	—	—	—	9	12	10	1	—	32	c. 7	c. 0.2
V. Rare Eaten several times per year	—	—	—	9	4	—	—	—	13	c. 3	c. 0.1‡
VI. Problematic Edible but not observed to be eaten	—	—	—	4	6	4	1	2	17	nil	nil
Total Species	2	1	1	30	29	16	4	2	85	100	—

* 1 species constitutes 50 percent of the vegetable diet by weight.
† 23 species constitute 90 percent of the vegetable diet by weight.
‡ 62 species constitute the remaining 10 percent of the diet.

Range Size and Population Density

The necessity to travel long distances, the high frequency of moves, and the maintenance of populations at low densities are also features commonly associated with the hunting and gathering way of life. Density estimates for hunters in western North America and Australia have ranged from 3 persons/square mile to as low as 1 person/100 square miles. In 1963–65, the resident and visiting Bushmen were observed to utilize an area of about 1,000 square miles during the course of the annual round for an effective population density of 41 person/100 square miles. Within this area, however, the amount of ground covered by members of an individual camp was surprisingly small. A day's round-trip of twelve miles serves to define a "core" area six miles in radius surrounding each water point. By fanning out in all directions from their well, the members of a camp can gain access to the food resources of well over 100 square miles of territory within a two-hour hike. Except for a few weeks each year, areas lying beyond this six-mile radius are rarely utilized, even though they are no less rich in plants and game than are the core areas.

Although the Bushmen move their camps frequently (five or six times a year), they do not move them very far. A rainy season camp in the nut forests is rarely more than ten or twelve miles from the home waterhole, and often new campsites are occupied only a few hundred yards away from the previous one. By these criteria, the Bushmen do not lead a free-ranging nomadic way of life. For example, they do not undertake long marches of 30 to 100 miles to get food, since this task can be readily fulfilled within a day's walk of home base. When such long marches do occur they are invariably for visiting, trading, and marriage arrangements, and should not be confused with the normal routine of subsistence.

Demographic Factors

Another indicator of the harshness of a way of life is the age at which people die. Ever since Hobbes characterized life in the state of nature as "nasty, brutish and short," the assumption has been that hunting and gathering is so rigorous that members of such societies are rapidly worn out and meet an early death. Silberbauer, for example, says of the Gwi Bushmen of the central Kalahari that "life expectancy . . . is difficult to calculate, but I do not believe that many live beyond 45." And Coon has said of hunters in general:

> The practice of abandoning the hopelessly ill and aged has been observed in many parts of the world. It is always done by people living in poor environments where it is necessary to move about frequently to obtain food, where food is scarce, and transportation difficult. . . . Among peoples who are forced to live in this way the oldest generation, the generation of individuals who have passed their physical peak, is reduced in numbers and influence. There is no body of elders to hand on tradition and control the affairs of younger men and women, and no formal system of age grading.

The !Kung Bushmen of the Dobe area flatly contradict this view. In a total population of 466, no fewer than 46 individuals (17 men and 29 women) were determined to be over sixty years of age, a proportion that compares favorably to the percentage of elderly in industrialized populations.

The aged hold a respected position in Bushmen society and are the effective leaders of the camps. Senilicide is extremely rare. Long after their productive years have passed, the old people are fed and cared for by their children and grandchildren. The blind, the senile, and the crippled are respected for the special ritual and technical skills they possess. For instance, the four elders at !gose waterhole were totally or partially blind, but this handicap did not prevent their active participation in decision making and ritual curing.

Another significant feature of the composition of the work force is the late assumption of adult responsibility by the adolescents. Young people are not expected to provide food regularly until they are married. Girls typically marry between the ages of fifteen and twenty, and boys about five years later, so that it is not unusual to find healthy, active teenagers visiting from camp to camp while their older relatives provide food for them.

As a result, the people in the twenty to sixty age group support a surprisingly large percentage of nonproductive young and old people. About 40 percent of the population in camps contributes little to the food supplies. This allocation of work to young and middle-aged adults allows for a relatively carefree childhood and adolescence and a relatively unstrenuous old age.

Leisure and Work

Another important index of ease or difficulty of subsistence is the amount of time devoted to the food quest. Hunting has usually been regarded by social scientists as a way of life in which merely keeping alive is so formidable a task that members of such societies lack the leisure time necessary to "build culture." The !Kung Bushmen would appear to conform to the rule, for as Lorna Marshall says:

> It is vividly apparent that among the !Kung Bushmen, ethos, or "the spirit which actuates manners and customs," is survival. Their time and energies are almost wholly given to this task, for life in their environment requires that they spend their days mainly in procuring food.

It is certainly true that getting food is the most important single activity in Bushman life. However, this statement would apply equally well to small-scale agricultural and pastoral societies too. How much time is *actually* devoted to the food quest is fortunately an empirical question. And an analysis of the work effort of the Dobe Bushmen shows some unexpected results. From July 6 to August 2, 1964, I recorded all the daily activities of the Bushmen living at the Dobe waterhole. Because of the coming and going of visitors, the camp population fluctuated in size day by day, from a low of 23 to a high of 40, with a mean of 31.8 persons. Each day some of the adult members of the camp went out to hunt and/or gather while others stayed home or went visiting. The daily recording of all personnel on hand made it possible to calculate the number of man-days of work as a percentage of total number of man-days of consumption.

Although the Bushmen do not organize their activities on the basis of a seven-day week, I have divided the data this way to make them more intelligible. The workweek was calculated to show how many days out of seven each adult spent in subsistence activities (Table IV, Column 7). Week II has been eliminated from the totals since the investigator contributed food. In week I, the people spent an average of 2.3 days in subsistence activities, in week II, 1.9 days, and in week IV, 3.2 days. In all, the adults of the Dobe camp worked about two and a half days a week. Since the average working day was about six hours long, the fact emerges that !Kung Bushmen of Dobe, despite their harsh environment, devote from twelve to nineteen hours a week to getting food. Even the hardest-working individual in the camp, a man named ≠oma who went out hunting on sixteen of the twenty-eight days, spent a maximum of thirty-two hours a week in the food quest.

Because the Bushmen do not amass a surplus of foods, there are no seasons of exceptionally intensive activities such as planting and harvesting, and no seasons of unemployment. The level of work observed is an accurate reflection of the effort required to meet the immediate caloric needs of the group. This work diary covers the midwinter dry season, a period when food is neither at its most plentiful nor at its scarcest levels, and the diary documents the transition from better to worse conditions (see Table II). During the fourth week the gatherers were making overnight trips to camps in the mongongo nut forests seven to ten miles distant from the waterhole. These longer trips account for the rise in the level of work, from twelve or thirteen to nineteen hours per week.

If food getting occupies such a small proportion of a Bushman's waking hours, then how *do* people allocate their time? A woman gathers on one day enough food to feed her family for three days, and spends the rest of her time resting in camp, doing embroidery, visiting other camps, or entertaining visitors from other camps. For each day at home, kitchen routines, such as cooking, nut cracking, collecting firewood, and fetching water, occupy one to three hours of her time. This rhythm of steady work and steady leisure is maintained throughout the year.

The hunters tend to work more frequently than the women, but their schedule is uneven. It is not unusual for a man to hunt avidly for a week and then do nothing at all for two or three weeks. Since hunting is an unpredictable business and subject to magical control, hunters sometimes experience a run of bad luck and stop hunting for a month or longer. During these periods, visiting, entertaining, and especially dancing are the primary activities of men. (Unlike the Hadza, gambling is only a minor leisure activity.)

Table IV Summary of Dobe Work Diary

Week	(1) Mean Group Size	(2) Adult-Days	(3) Child-Days	(4) Total Man-Days of Consumption	(5) Man-Days of Work	(6) Meat (lbs.)	(7) Average Workweek/ Adult	(8) Index of Subsistence Effort
I (July 6–12)	25.6 (23–29)	114	65	179	37	104	2.3	.21
II (July 13–19)	28.3 (23–27)	125	73	198	22	80	1.2	.11
III (July 20–26)	34.3 (29–40)	156	84	240	42	177	1.9	.18
IV (July 27–Aug. 2)	35.6 (32–40)	167	82	249	77	129	3.2	.31
4-wk. total	30.9	562	304	866	178	490	2.2	.21
Adjusted total*	31.8	437	231	668	156	410	2.5	.23

*See text

Key: Column 1: Mean group size = $\dfrac{\text{total man-days of consumption}}{7}$

Column 7: Workweek = the number of workdays per adult per week.

Column 8: Index of subsistence effort = $\dfrac{\text{man-days of work}}{\text{man-days of consumption}}$ (e.g., in Week I, the value of "S" = 21, i.e., 21 days of work/100 days of consumption or 1 workday produces food for 5 consumption days).

The trance dance is the focus of Bushman ritual life; over 50 percent of the men have trained as trance-performers and regularly enter trance during the course of the all-night dances. At some camps, trance dances occur as frequently as two or three times a week, and those who have entered trances the night before rarely go out hunting the following day. . . . In a camp with five or more hunters, there are usually two or three who are actively hunting and several others who are inactive. The net effect is to phase the hunting and non-hunting so that a fairly steady supply of meat is brought into camp.

Caloric Returns

Is the modest work effort of the Bushmen sufficient to provide the calories necessary to maintain the health of the population? Or have the !Kung, in common with some agricultural peoples, adjusted to a permanently substandard nutritional level?

During my fieldwork I did not encounter any cases of kwashiorkor, the most common nutritional disease in the children of African agricultural societies. However, without medical examinations, it is impossible to exclude the possibility that subclinical signs of malnutrition existed.

Another measure of nutritional adequacy is the average consumption of calories and proteins per person per day. The estimate for the Bushmen is based on observations of the weights of foods of known composition that were brought into Dobe camp on each day of the study period. The per-capita figure is obtained by dividing the total weight of foodstuffs by the total number of persons in the camp. These results are set out in detail elsewhere and can only be summarized here. During the study period 410 pounds of meat were brought in by the hunters of the Dobe camp, for a daily share of nine ounces of meat per person. About 700 pounds of vegetables were gathered and consumed during the same period. Table V sets

Table V Caloric and Protein Levels in the !Kung Bushman Diet, July–August, 1964

| | | Per-Capita Consumption | | | Percentage |
Class of Food	Percentage Contribution to Diet by Weight	Weight in Grams	Protein in Grams	Calories per Person per Day	Caloric Contribution of Meat and Vegetables
Meat	37	230	34.5	690	33
Mongongo nuts	33	210	56.7	1,260	67
Other vegetable foods	30	190	1.9	190	
Total all sources	100	630	93.1	2,140	100

out the calories and proteins available per capita in the !Kung Bushman diet from meat, mongongo nuts, and other vegetable sources.

This output of 2,140 calories and 93.1 grams of protein per person per day may be compared with the Recommended Daily Allowances (RDA) for persons of the small size and stature but vigorous activity regime of the !Kung Bushmen. The RDA for Bushmen can be estimated at 1,975 calories and 60 grams of protein per person per day. Thus it is apparent that food output exceeds energy requirements by 165 calories and 33 grams of protein. One can tentatively conclude that even a modest subsistence effort of two or three days' work per week is enough to provide an adequate diet for the !Kung Bushmen.

THE SECURITY OF BUSHMAN LIFE

I have attempted to evaluate the subsistence base of one contemporary hunter-gatherer society living in a marginal environment. The !Kung Bushmen have available to them some relatively abundant high-quality foods, and they do not have to walk very far or work very hard to get them. Furthermore, this modest work effort provides sufficient calories to support not only active adults, but also a large number of middle-aged and elderly people. The Bushmen do not have to press their youngsters into the service of the food quest, nor do they have to dispose of the oldsters after they have ceased to be productive.

The evidence presented assumes an added significance because this security of life was observed during the third year of one of the most severe droughts in South Africa's history. Most of the 576,000 people of Botswana are pastoralists and agriculturalists. After the crops had failed three years in succession and over 100,000 head of cattle had died on the range for lack of water, the World Food Program of the United Nations instituted a famine relief program which has grown to include 180,000 people, over 30 percent of the population. This program did not touch the Dobe area in the isolated northwest corner of the country, and the Herero and Tswana women there were able to feed their families only by joining the Bushman women to forage for wild foods. Thus the natural plant resources of the Dobe area were carrying a higher proportion of population than would be the case in years when the Bantu harvested crops. Yet this added pressure on the land did not seem to adversely affect the Bushmen.

In one sense it was unfortunate that the period of my fieldwork happened to coincide with the drought, since I was unable to witness a "typical" annual subsistence cycle. However, in another sense, the coincidence was a lucky one, for the drought put the Bushmen and their subsistence system to the acid test and, in terms of adaptation to scarce resources, they passed with flying colors. One can postulate that their subsistence base would be even more substantial during years of higher rainfall.

What are the crucial factors that make this way of life possible? I suggest that the primary factor is the Bushmen's strong emphasis on vegetable food sources. Although hunting involves a great deal of effort and prestige, plant foods provide from 60 to 80 percent of the annual diet by weight. Meat has come to be regarded as a special treat; when available, it is welcomed as a break from the routine of vegetable foods, but it is never depended upon as a staple. No one ever goes hungry when hunting fails.

The reason for this emphasis is not hard to find. Vegetable foods are abundant, sedentary, and predictable. They grow in the same place year after year, and the gatherer is guaranteed a day's return of food for a day's expenditure of energy. Game animals, by contrast, are scarce, mobile, unpredictable, and difficult to catch. A hunter has no guarantee of success and may in fact go for days or weeks without killing a large mammal. During the study period, there were eleven men in the Dobe camp, of whom four did no hunting at all. The seven active men spent a total of 78 mandays hunting, and this work input yielded eighteen animals killed, or one kill for every four man-days of hunting. The probability of any one hunter making a kill on a given day was 0.23. By contrast, the probability of a woman finding plant food on a given day was 1.00. In other words, hunting and gathering are not equally felicitous subsistence alternatives.

Consider the productivity per man-hour of the two kinds of subsistence activities. One man-hour of hunting produces about 100 edible calories, and of gathering, 240 calories. Gathering is thus seen to be 2.4 times more productive than hunting. In short, hunting is a *high-risk, low-return* subsistence activity, while gathering is a low-risk, high-return subsistence activity.

It is not at all contradictory that the hunting complex holds a central place in the Bushmen ethos and that meat is valued more highly than vegetable foods. Analogously, steak is valued more highly than potatoes in the food preferences of our own society. In both situations the meat is more "costly" than the vegetable food. In the Bushman case, the cost of food can be measured in terms of time and energy expended. By this standard, 1,000 calories of meat "costs" ten man-hours, while the "cost" of 1,000 calories of vegetable foods is only four man-hours. Further, it is to be expected that the less predictable, more expensive food source would have a greater accretion of myth and ritual built up around it than would the routine staples of life, which rarely if ever fail.

CONCLUSIONS

Three points ought to be stressed. First, life in the state of nature is not necessarily nasty, brutish, and short. The Dobe-area Bushmen live well today on wild plants and meat, in spite of the fact that they are confined to the least productive portion of the range in which Bushman peoples were formerly found. It is likely that an even more substantial subsistence would have been characteristic of these hunters and gatherers in the past, when they had the pick of African habitats to choose from.

Second, the basis of Bushman diet is derived from sources other than meat. This emphasis makes good ecological sense to the !Kung Bushmen and appears to be a common feature among hunters and gatherers in general. Since a 30 to 40 percent input of meat is such a consistent target for modern hunters in a variety of habitats, is it not reasonable to postulate a similar percentage for prehistoric hunters? Certainly the absence of plant remains on archeological sites is by itself not sufficient evidence for the absence of gathering. Recently abandoned Bushman campsites show a similar absence of vegetable remains, although this paper has clearly shown that plant foods comprise over 60 percent of the actual diet.

Finally, one gets the impression that hunting societies have been chosen by ethnologists to illustrate a dominant theme, such as the extreme importance of environment in the molding of certain cultures. Such a theme can best be exemplified by cases in which the technology is simple and/or the environment is harsh. This emphasis on the dramatic may have been pedagogically useful, but unfortunately it has led to the assumption that a precarious hunting subsistence base was characteristic of all cultures in the Pleistocene. This view of both modern and ancient hunters ought to be reconsidered. Specifically I am suggesting a shift in focus away from the dramatic and unusual cases, and toward a consideration of hunting and gathering as a persistent and well-adapted way of life.

REVIEW QUESTIONS

1. How does Lee assess the day-to-day quality of !Kung life? How does his view compare with the stereotype of hunter-gatherers?
2. Give the evidence that supports Lee's viewpoint about the !Kung.
3. According to Lee, !Kung children are not expected to work until after they are married; old people are supported and respected. How does this arrangement differ from behavior in our own society, and what might explain the difference?
4. What is the key to successful subsistence for the !Kung and other hunter-gatherers?

10

Cultivating the Tropical Forest

Richard K. Reed

*To most industrialized peoples, the practice of slash-and-burn agri-
culture seems especially wasteful. The horticulturalists who manifest such practices must often laboriously cut and burn thick forest
cover, then plant in the ashes. Because clearing is difficult and fields
are left fallow for many years to recover from agricultural use, most
land lies dormant. For people used to thinking of agriculture as a
source of income, horticultural practices seem to epitomize "underdevelopment." In this article, Richard Reed challenges this simplis-
tic notion. Describing the subsistence practices of the Guarani Indians living in the tropical forests of Paraguay, he shows that Indian
slash-and-burn agriculture combined with foraging for wild game
and plants represents the optimal use of the forest and a model for
modern forest management programs.*

The world's great tropical forests, which once seemed so forbidding
and impenetrable, are now prime targets for economic exploitation.
Developers and colonists, from Brazil to Indonesia, flock to the jungle
frontiers armed with chain saws and bulldozers. They build roads, clear-

cut timber, and denude the land of foliage, often burning the trees and brush as they go. The scope of this human invasion staggers the mind. Development destroys hundreds of square miles of virgin tropical forest each day. In the Amazon alone, an area the size of Louisiana is cleared every year. At this rate, authorities predict that the forests will be gone by the year 2000.

Damage to the forest has not gone unnoticed. Publicized by newscasters, environmentalists, rock stars, and a host of others, the plight of rain forests is now familiar to many Americans. Concern has centered most on the consequences of deforestation for the world ecosystem. Forests are the "lungs of the earth," producing crucial oxygen. Burning them not only reduces world oxygen production, it releases large amounts of carbon dioxide, a greenhouse gas, into the atmosphere. A warmer world is the likely result.

Many authorities have also warned about the impact of deforestation on the survival of wildlife. Tropical forests contain the world's richest variety of animals and plants. As the trees disappear, so do countless irreplaceable species.

Curiously, there is less said about the plight of people who are native to the forests. In South America, for example, up to six million Indians once lived scattered across the vast lowland forests. Only a tenth of that population remains today, the rest having fallen victim to the colonial advance over the past 400 years. Each year, these survivors find it increasingly difficult to maintain their populations and communities.

The damage being done to these Indian societies is particularly distressing because they are the only humans who have managed to subsist in the forest without causing permanent harm. By employing a subsistence strategy that combines horticulture, gathering, and hunting, these indigenous peoples have managed to live in harmony with the forest environment for centuries.

We may ask what accounts for this successful adaptation. Is there a special genius to the social organization of indigenous peoples? What subsistence strategies permit them to live amicably with the forest? What happens to them when they are overtaken by settlers and commercial development? Can such people provide a model for successful tropical forest management? Let's look at these questions in the context of one group living in the South American forest, the Guarani of eastern Paraguay.

THE GUARANI

The Guarani Indians provide an excellent example of a group well adapted to the forest environment. Like most horticulturalists, they live in small, widely scattered communities. Because their population densities are low, and because they practice a mixture of slash-and-burn agriculture and foraging, they place a light demand on forest resources. Small size also means a more personal social organization and an emphasis on cooperation and sharing. Although of greater size and complexity than hunter-gatherer bands, Guarani villages contain many of the cultural values found in these nomadic societies.

I have conducted ethnographic fieldwork among the Guarani for the past ten years, mostly in the village of Itanarami, located in eastern Paraguay. The residents of Itanarami are among the last of the Guarani Indians still living in the forests of southern South America. They are the remnants of an ethnic group that once dominated southern Brazil and Paraguay from the Atlantic Ocean to the Andes. The Guarani have suffered as their forests have fallen to development. Today, only 15,500 Guarani remain in Paraguay in isolated settlements where the tropical forest survives.

The forests surrounding Itanarami are characterized by high canopies that shade thick undergrowth and shelter both animal and human populations. From the air, the dense expanse of trees is broken only by streams and rivers that drain westward to the broad, marshy valley of the Parana River. Viewed from the ground, the density of the forest growth is matched only by the diversity of plant species.

Itanarami itself is built along a small stream that gives the settlement its name. To the uninformed observer, it is difficult to recognize the existence of a village at all. Homesteads, which consist of a clearing, a thatched hut, and one or two nearby fields, lie scattered in the forest, often out of sight of one another. Yet a closer look reveals the pathways through the deep forest that connect houses to each other and to a slightly larger homestead, that of the *tamoi* (literally grandfather), the group's religious leader. As in many small societies, households are tied together by kinship; people live only a short distance from close relatives. Kinship networks tie all members of the community together, weaving a tapestry of relations that organize social affairs and link Itanarami to other Guarani communities.

The Guarani emphasize sharing and cooperation. Sisters often share fieldwork and child care. Brothers usually hunt together. Food is distributed among members of the extended family, including cousins, aunts, and uncles. People emphasize the general welfare, not personal wealth.

The *tamoi*, although in no sense a leader with formal authority, commands considerable respect in the community. He settles disputes, chastises errant juniors, and leads the entire community in evening religious ceremonies where people drink *kanguijy* (fermented corn), dance, and sing to the gods.

The people of Itanarami not only live in the forest, they see themselves as part of it. The forest is basic to indigenous cosmology. The people refer to themselves as *ka'aguygua*, or "people of the forest." Villagers often name their children after the numerous varieties of forest song birds, symbolizing their close personal ties to the environment.

SUBSISTENCE

The Guarani have lived in their present locale for centuries and have dwelled throughout the tropical forests of lowland South America for thousands of years. During all this time, they have exploited flora, fauna, and soils of the forests without doing permanent harm. The secret of their success is in their production strategy. The Indians mix agriculture with gathering, hunting, and fishing in a way that permits environmental recovery. They even collect forest products for sale to outsiders, again without causing environmental damage.

Guarani farming is well-suited to forest maintenance. Using a form of shifting agriculture called slash-and-burn farming, the Indians permit the forest to recover from the damage of field clearing. The way Veraju, the *tamoi* of Itanarami, and his wife, Kitu, farm provides a typical example. When the family needs to prepare a new field, it is Veraju who does the heavy work. He cuts the trees and undergrowth to make a half-acre clearing near his house. Then he, Kitu, and some of their five children burn the fallen trees and brush, creating an ash that provides a natural fertilizer on top of the thin forest soils. When the field is prepared, Kitu uses a digging stick fashioned from a sapling to poke small holes in the ground, and plants the three staple Guarani crops, corn, beans, and manioc root (from which tapioca is made). When the crops mature, it is Kitu and her daughters who will harvest them.

The secret to successful slash-and-burn agriculture is field "shifting" or rotation. Crops flourish the first year and are plentiful the next, but the sun and rain soon take their toll on the exposed soil. The thin loam layer, so typical of tropical forests, degenerates rapidly to sand and clay. By the third year, the poor soils are thick with weeds and grow only a sparse corn crop and a few small manioc roots. Rather than replant a fourth time, Veraju and Kitu will clear a new field nearby where soils are naturally more fertile and the forest can be burned for additional ash fertilizer. The surrounding forest quickly reclaims the old field, reconstituting and strengthening the depleted soil. In this way, the forest produces a sustained yield without degrading the natural ecosystem.

The forest recovers sufficiently fast for the same plot to be cleared and planted within ten or fifteen years. This "swidden" agricultural system results in the cyclic use of a large area of forest, with a part under cultivation and a much larger portion lying fallow in various stages of decomposition.

If farming formed the only subsistence base, the Guarani would probably have to clear more land than the forest could rejuvenate. But they also turn to other forest resources—game, fish, and forest products—to meet their needs for food and material items. Guarani men often form small groups to hunt large animals, such as deer, tapir, and peccary, with guns purchased from outsiders or with the more traditional bows and arrows they make themselves. A successful hunt will provide enough meat to share liberally with kin and friends. Men also trap smaller mammals, such as armadillo and paca (a large rodent). They fashion snares and deadfall traps from saplings, tree trunks, and cactus fiber twine. These are set near homesteads, along stream banks, and at the edges of gardens. Traps not only catch small game for meat, they kill animals that would otherwise enter the fields to eat the crops.

Fish also supply protein in the Guarani diet and reduce dependence on agricultural produce. Many rivers and streams flow near Itanarami on flat bottom land. These water courses meander in broad loops that may be cut off when the river or stream changes course during a flood. Meanders, called ox-bow lakes, make ideal fishing spots. In addition to hook and line, men capture the fish by using a poison extracted from the bark of a particular vine. Floated over the surface of the water, the poison stuns the fish and allows the men to catch them by hand.

The forest also supplies a variety of useful products for the Guarani. They make houses from tree trunks and bamboo stalks; rhododendron vines secure the thatched roofs. Villagers collect wild honey and fruit to add sweetness to their diets. Wild tubers replace manioc as a principal food source when crops fail in the gardens. Even several species of insect larva and ants are collected as tasty and nutritious supplements to the daily meal. Finally, the Indians know about a wide variety of medicinal plants. They process several different kinds of roots, leaves, flowers, and seeds to release powerful alkaloids and to make teas and poultices for the sick and injured.

White traders have entered the forests of the Guarani and give the Indians access to manufactured goods. The Guarani continue to produce for most of their needs, but items such as machetes, hooks, soap, and salt are more easily bought than manufactured or collected. As they do with farming and hunting, the Guarani turn to the forest to meet such economic needs. They regularly collect two forest products, *yerba mate* (a caffeinated tea) and oil extract from wild orange trees, used for flavorings and perfumes, to raise the necessary funds.

It is important to note the special Guarani knowledge and values associated with subsistence activities. Because they have lived in the forest for such a long time, and because they would have nowhere to turn if their own resources disappeared, they treat the rain forest with special respect. They can do so, however, only by using a special and complex knowledge of how the forest works and how it can be used.

For example, Guarani, such as Veraju, distinguish among a variety of "ecozones," each with a unique combination of soil, flora, and fauna. They recognize obvious differences, such as those among the high forests that grow on the hills, the deep swamps that cover the flood plains by the rivers, and the grassy savannahs of the high plains. But they make more subtle distinctions within these larger regions. For example, they call the low scrub bordering rivers, *ca'ati.* Flooded each year during the rainy season, this zone supports bamboo groves that harbor small animals for trapping and material for house construction. The forests immediately above the flood plain look like an extension of the *ca'ati,* but to the Guarani they differ in important ways. This ecozone supports varieties of bamboo that are useless for house construction but that attract larger animals, such as peccary and deer, that can be hunted. In all, the Guarani distinguish among nine resource zones, each with distinctive soils, flora, fauna, and uses. These subtle distinctions between ecozones enable the Guarani to use the forest to greatest benefit. By shifting their subsistence efforts from one zone to another, just as they shift their fields from one spot to the next, the Guarani assure that their forest environment, with its rich variety of life, will always be able to renew itself.

THE IMPACT OF DEVELOPMENT

In the last few years, intensive commercial development has come to the region in which Itanarami lies. The spectre of complete ecological destruction stalks the forest. White *colonos* (settlers), armed with chain saws and earth movers, attack the trees. They vandalize the land without concern for the carefully integrated ecozones. As the trees fall, the forest products, such as *yerba mate,* disappear. So do the mammals and fish, the bamboo and the rhododendron vines, the honey and the fruits, and the reconstituting fields. As these resources disappear, so does the economy of the once self-sufficient Guarani. Without their traditional mode of subsistence, their kin-organized society, the influence of the *tamoi,* and the willingness to share, their independence as a people becomes impossible. Indian communities are destroyed by poverty and disease, and the members who remain join the legions of poor laborers who form the lowest class of the national society.

Recent intensive development began near Itanarami in 1974, when *colonos* cut a road into the jungle located within two hours' walk of the village. Through this gash in the forest moved logging trucks, bulldozers, farm equipment, and buses. Accompanying the machinery of development were farmers, ranchers, and speculators, hoping to make a quick profit from the verdant land. They descended from their vehicles onto the muddy streets of a newly built frontier town. They cleared land for general stores and bars, which were soon filled with merchandise and warm beer. By day, the air in the town was fouled by truck noise and exhaust fumes; by night it was infused with the glare of electric lights and the noise of blaring tape players.

Soon the settlers began to fell the forest near the town and road, creating fields for cotton and soybeans, and pasture. Surveying teams demarcated boundaries and drew maps. Lumber companies invaded the forests, clear-cutting vast tracts of trees. Valuable timber was hauled off to newly established lumber mills; remaining brush was piled and burned. Heavy machinery created expanses of sunlight in the previously unbroken forest.

Within months, grass, cotton, and soybeans sprouted in the exposed soils. Where once the land had been home for game, it now provided for cattle. Cattle herds often clogged the roads, blocking the path of trucks hauling cotton to market and chewing deep ruts in the soft forest soils. Settlers fenced in the fields and cut lanes through the forest to mark off portions that would be "private property," off-limits to Indians.

Guarani communities nearest the road suffered first from development. The forests they once used for farming and hunting disappeared before the onslaught of chain saws and bulldozers. The paths that previously connected homesteads became sandy jeep tracks across unbroken expanses of open fields. Within a few years, the Guarani of these villages had little left but their homesteads.

Moreover, by destroying the forest resources surrounding Indian villages, the *colonos* set in motion a process that destroyed the native culture and society. Guarani communities became small islands of forest surrounded by a sea of pastures and farm fields. Although the Indians retained some land for agriculture, they lost the forest resources needed to sustain their original mode of subsistence, which depended on hunting, fishing, and gathering in the forest as well as farming. These economic changes forced alterations in the Indian community.

First, without the forest to provide game, fish, and other products, the Guarani became dependent on farming alone for their survival. Without wild foods, they had to clear and farm fields three times larger than the original ones. Without the forest production of *yerba mate* leaves to collect for sale, they were forced to plant cash crops, such as cotton and tobacco. These two new crops demanded large, clean fields.

While the loss of the forest for hunting and gathering increased their dependence on agriculture, the fences and land titles of the new settlers reduced the land available to the Indians for cultivation. Families soon cleared the last of the remaining high forests that they controlled. Even the once forested stream banks were denuded.

After they had cleared their communities' remaining forest, Indian farmers were forced to replant fields without allowing sufficient fallow time for the soils to rejuvenate. Crops suffered from lack of nutrients and yields declined despite additional effort devoted to clearing and weeding. As production suffered, the Indians cleared and farmed even larger areas. The resulting spiral of poor harvests and enlarged farms outstripped the soil's capacity to produce and the Guarani's ability to care for the crops. Food in the Indian communities grew scarce. The Indian diet was increasingly restricted to non-nutritious manioc as a dietary staple, because it was the only plant that could survive in the exhausted soils.

The Guarani felt the decline in their subsistence base in other ways. The loss of game and poor crop yields exacerbated health problems. Settlers brought new diseases into the forest, such as colds and flu. The Guarani had no inherited resistance to these illnesses and poor nutrition reduced their defenses even further. Disease not only sapped the adults' energy for farming and child care, it increased death rates at all ages. Tuberculosis, which well-fed Guarani rarely contract, became the major killer in the community.

Deforestation also disrupted social institutions. Without their subsistence base, many Guarani needed additional cash to buy food and goods. Indian men were forced to seek work as farm hands, planting pasture and picking cotton on land where they once hunted. Women stayed at home to tend children and till the deteriorating soils of the family farms.

The search for wage labor eventually forced whole Guarani families to move. Many jobs were available on farms located over a day's walk from their villages. Entire families left home for hovels they constructed on the farms of their employers. From independent farmers and gatherers, they became tenants of *patrones* (landowners). *Patrones* prohibited the Guarani farmhands from planting gardens of their own, so the displaced Indians were forced to buy all their food, usually from the *patrones* themselves. Worse, *patrones* set their own inflated prices on the food and goods sold to Indians. Dependence on the white *patrones* displaced the mutual interdependence of traditional Guarani social organization.

As individuals and families left the Guarani villages in search of work on surrounding farms and ranches, *tamoi* leaders lost influence. It became impossible to gather relatives and friends together from disparate work places for religious ritual. The distances were too great for the elders' nieces and nephews to seek out counsel and medicines. Moreover, the diseases and problems suffered by the people were increasingly caused by people and powers outside the forest. The *tamoi* could neither control nor explain the changing world.

Finally, as the forest disappeared, so did its power to symbolize Guarani identity. No longer did young Indians see themselves as "people of the forest."

Today, many of the Guarani of eastern Paraguay remain in small but impoverished communities in the midst of a frontier society based on soybean farming and cattle ranching. The households that previously were isolated in individual plots are now concentrated in one small area without forest for fallow or privacy. The traditional *tamoi* continue to be the center of the social and religious life of the community, but no longer exert influence over village decisions, which are increasingly dominated by affairs external to the local community.

DEVELOPMENT AND ECOLOGY

Some people might argue that the plight of the Guarani is inevitable and that in the long run, the Indians will be absorbed in a more modern, prosperous society. The forest, they claim, provides a rich, nearly unlimited re-

source for development. Its exploitation, although painful for a few indigenous Indians, will provide an unequaled opportunity for the poor of
Latin America.

Unfortunately, this argument makes forest development appear to be
socially responsible. Yet, the long-run implications of forest clearing are
disastrous, not simply for the Guarani and other Indians, but for settlers
and developers as well. The tropical forest ecosystem is extremely fragile.
When the vegetable cover is destroyed, the soil quickly disappears. Erosion clogs rivers with silt, and the soils left behind are baked to a hardpan
on which few plants can survive. Rainwater previously captured by foliage and soil is quickly lost to runoff, drying the winds that feed the regional rain systems. Although first harvests in frontier areas seem bounti-
ful, long-term farming and ranching are unprofitable as the soils, deprived
of moisture and the rejuvenating forces of the original forest, are reduced
to a "red desert." And even worse, leaving the cleared land fallow does not
restore it. Once destroyed, the forest cannot reclaim the hardpan left by
modern development.

Nor have developers been interested in husbanding the land. The
colonos who clear the forests are concerned with short-term profit. Entrepreneurs and peasant farmers maximize immediate returns on their labor
and investment. When the trees and soils of one area are exhausted, the
farmers, ranchers, and loggers move farther into the virgin forest in search
of new resources. The process creates a development frontier that moves
through fertile forest leaving destruction in its wake. Unlike the Guarani,
developers are not forced to contend with the environmental destruction
caused by their activities.

CONSERVATION

International agencies and national governments have begun to recognize
the damage caused by uncontrolled rain forest development. Although
deforestation continues unchecked in many regions of the Amazon Basin,
forest conservation programs are being established in some areas, based
on the experience of indigenous Indians and often formulated with the
help of anthropologists. In one innovative approach, biosphere reserves
are being created, which restrict development but permit Indians to practice their traditional subsistence activities.

Such is the case in eastern Paraguay where a program is now being im-
plemented to preserve the remaining tropical forests. Itanarami, so recently threatened by encroaching development, stands to benefit from this
plan. The natural forests near the community are the last remaining undisturbed subtropical forest in eastern Paraguay. Although small, this area of
280 square miles is being set aside as a biosphere reserve. The Nature
Conservancy, an international conservation agency, is working with the
World Bank and the Paraguayan government to preserve the forest.

If the project is successful, Itanarami and its way of life will be preserved. Veraju, Kitu, and their compatriots will be able to continue trapping, hunting, fishing, and gathering on the land. Recognizing that Indian production does not destroy the land, planners are providing the Indians with the right to continue indigenous production, enabling the Guarani to maintain their traditional social organization and ethnic identity.

Furthermore, aided by anthropologists who have made detailed studies of Indian subsistence techniques, planners are integrating the Indians' own models of agro-forestry into an alternative design for tropical forest use. Guarani techniques of commercial extraction have been of special interest, particularly the harvest of *yerba mate* and fragrant oils. Guarani collect these products by trimming the foliage. They allow the trees to regrow so they will produce again. Planners believe that this use of the forest will economically outperform the proceeds gained from destructive farming in the long run, and they have adopted the Guarani model for implementation in other forested areas. Far from being backward and inefficient, the mixed horticultural subsistence strategies of indigenous forest groups have turned out to be the most practical way to manage the fragile tropical forest environment.

REVIEW QUESTIONS

1. Anthropologists claim that subsistence strategies affect a society's social organization and ideology. Evaluate this assertion in light of reading about the way the Guarani live in their rain forest environment.
2. Why is horticulture more environmentally sensible than intensive agricultural and pastoral exploitation of the Amazonian rain forest?
3. Guarani Indians are largely subsistence farmers and foragers. How do they use their forest environment without destroying it?
4. How have *colonos* disrupted the lives of Guarani villagers? What does this tell us about the relationship between subsistence and social structure?
5. How can the Guarani use their rain forest habitat to make money, and what does their experience suggest as a way to integrate forest exploitation into a market economy without environmental destruction?

11

Polygyny and Fertility in the Amazon

Warren M. Hern

In the previous article, we encountered a dramatic example of what happens to horticulturalists when their tropical forest is invaded by colonists. In this selection by Warren Hern, we look at a root cause of environmental and cultural degradation: overpopulation. During 29 years of fieldwork among the Shipibo of the Peruvian Amazon, Hern discovered that traditional Indian controls on fertility, especially the marriage custom of polygyny (marriage of one man to more than one wife at the same time), have been eliminated by outsiders. The resulting population explosion, along with an inability to survive by fishing and horticulture, has created severe health problems, poverty, and cultural dislocation for the struggling Indians.

"**W**hen you come back, don't forget to bring *toötimarau*," Chomoshico called to me. I was leaving the Shipibo Indian village of Manco Capac, on the banks of the Pisqui River in the Peruvian Amazon, where I had been doing medical research. Chomoshico was

Originally published as "Family Planning Amazon Style." With permission from *Natural History*, January 1993. Copyright © the American Museum of Natural History, 1993.

nearing the end of her eleventh pregnancy. She already had seven living children. Neither she nor her husband wants more. "Enough. Clothes cost," they told me. "I'm tired of having children," she said. "I almost died with the last one." Her husband has tuberculosis.

Toötimarau means "medicine to keep from being pregnant"—birth control. I knew I could promise Chomoshico worm medicine for her children's parasites, and I might be able to bring her vitamins and iron for her pregnancy, even medicine for tuberculosis. But while I could informally provide other kinds of medical care, I could not arrange to bring her birth control without risking reprisals from politicians who are against it. The Shipibo have been asking me for *toötimarau* for more than twenty-five years, but I haven't been able to arrange any yet. I can only refer them to a Peruvian doctor in Pucallpa, many days away by canoe. Most can never get there. The men even pull me aside to ask if I know about an operation to "fix" men—vasectomy—and, again, I tell them the name of my medical colleague in Pucallpa.

In the same village, a few weeks before, a young girl had died on her thirteenth birthday trying to give birth to twins. And in that girl's natal village, just up the river, I had just seen my first case of frank starvation among the Shipibo Indians, with whom I had worked as a physician and scientist since 1964. The starving man had tuberculosis. His family, which would normally have taken care of someone so ill, was away working for a logging company.

Chomoshico's desperate request for birth control, the death of the thirteen-year-old girl, and the plight of the starving man are all related. The Shipibo's own high fertility, uncontrolled by any effective means, is compounding the problem of the population pressure created by an influx of outsiders, who are moving into Shipibo territory and destroying the natural resources.

The Shipibo Indians who live along the Ucayali River and its tributaries, such as the Pisqui, notice that the fish are getting smaller and harder to find, and that the game animals they rely on during the rainy season—when fish are almost impossible to catch—are more elusive than in the past. Palm leaves for thatching roofs seem scarcer, and people have to trek long distances, sometimes a mile or more, to gather firewood, once available a few steps away. People are aware that their own village is growing, that they do not know all its inhabitants, that the village school is crowded. Sometimes they have to go all day without eating fish. The Shipibo word for fish, *piti,* is also their word for food: a Shipibo without fish is truly poor.

In this crisis, the Shipibo are not alone. The Peruvian government has urged desperate people from the crowded coastal cities and Andean communities to settle and live in the jungle "paradise." They have. Pucallpa, the major port on the Ucayali, the "highway" river that becomes the Amazon, was probably an aboriginal Shipibo settlement (its Shipibo name means "red earth"). In the 1940s, just before the trans-Andes highway was put through to Pucallpa from Lima, the settlement's population was about 2,500. When I first visited Pucallpa in 1964, the population had grown to about 25,000. It was a raw, dusty, frontier town with dirt streets and Saturday night gunfights. More than 250,000 people live there now—a hundredfold increase in fifty years.

With the local waters already depleted, fishing boats from Pucallpa speed downstream more than 150 miles, where they take all fish more than two inches long with drift nets, pack the fish in ice, and start back up the river. The smaller fish are discarded to rot. There is not much left for the Shipibo, for the mestizo colonists from elsewhere in Peru, for the large fish, for the alligators, or for the wading birds that used to line the shores of the Ucayali. Areas around Pucallpa that were covered by canopy rain forest in 1964 now look like Oklahoma. The hundreds of bird species that enlivened the forest have been replaced by emaciated cows. Swamps filled with fish are replaced by causeways carrying buses and motorcycles. Twenty years ago, a traveler camped on the beach of the Ucayali River could not sleep for the sounds of fish splashing and alligators hunting them. There aren't enough fish to keep one awake now; the traveler is kept awake by the whine of fishermen's outboard motors.

Instead of living by subsistence fishing and horticulture, as the Shipibo principally do, their new neighbors exploit the environment to make money. First come the timber cutters, followed by cattle ranchers, commercial fishermen, and the farmers of bananas, rice, and other cash crops. The resultant deforestation and flooding have eliminated some crops and game animals that were sources of food for the Shipibo in the rainy season. The Shipibo themselves are drawn into the money economy and sometimes sell products from scarce animals (such as water turtle eggs) in order to get cash.

The Shipibo painfully admit that, although they work much harder than before, they don't have enough money for clothes (which they used to make by hand from woven cloth) and schoolbooks for their children (not a factor thirty years ago). They now have to buy food at times, even though it was previously plentiful.

The Shipibo (and the closely related Conibo) are the dominant indigenous people of the upper Peruvian Amazon. They have survived there for about a thousand years, but only by battling fiercely with other tribes and exhibiting a pragmatic tenacity in the face of colonization. Before the European conquest, they may have numbered more than 50,000. By the early twentieth century, fewer than 3,000 remained. Somehow they escaped the further decimation or complete extinction that befell many other Amazon tribes exposed to European diseases, enslavement, intertribal warfare sponsored by rubber tappers, and other openly genocidal attempts to rid the Amazon of its native inhabitants. Their population is now about 30,000 and growing.

The last smallpox epidemic was in 1964. But now, in addition to the modern plagues of tuberculosis and cholera, the Shipibo have a new health problem: high fertility, which places pressure on resources and takes a heavy toll among Shipibo women.

In the past the Shipibo controlled their birth rate and population growth in a variety of ways: by sexual abstinence, by abortion (using pressure on the uterus), by infanticide, and by the use of herbal contraceptives. Knowledge of these contraceptives was passed down through the generations from mother to daughter, from grandmother to granddaughter. But several things happened to interrupt this tradition. The horrifying epidemics that wiped out whole villages following European contact prompted shamans in related tribes to forbid the practices of infanticide and abortion. The Shipibo shamans may also have taken this step, but more likely, Christian missionaries played a role in disrupting the cultural traditions that controlled fertility. In 1697, the Shipibo massacred a group of Franciscans who were insisting that the Shipibo give up polygyny (multiple wives). Today, the custom remains strong in some parts of the Shipibo culture area but is declining in villages close to centers of Western influence.

Even though polygyny allows some men to have more offspring than others, it permits women to have fewer children with longer intervals between births. This arrangement has several important effects: it allows women to recover from each pregnancy; it allows children to gain maturity before being weaned and placed on a diet of all solid foods; and it reduces the total number of children borne by individual women. The result for the group is that women have a better chance of recovering from pregnancy and therefore of living longer, and child survival is better.

These advantages of polygyny are often cited by members of traditional societies, whose strategy is, not to have as many children as possible, but to have as many as possible that survive to adulthood. A final result of polygyny, paradoxically, is that community fertility could be restrained.

My acquaintance with Shipibo methods of controlling fertility began in 1964, when I was a third-year medical student from the University of Colorado. I had just finished working intensively for several months at the Hospital Amazonico "Albert Schweitzer" near Pucallpa, and had traveled to the Shipibo village of Paococha to learn about native ideas concerning the nature, treatment, and control of disease. A Shipibo friend who was helping me, Ambrosio, came to me one day to tell me that his wife was bleeding to death: she had just had a baby. Ambrosio asked me to see her, and I treated his wife for retained membranes and postpartum uterine atony (relaxation of the uterus). She recovered, and he asked me what he could do for me. I told him I would like to learn about medicines that women use to control pregnancy. His aunt Julia was the local expert.

From Julia I learned that Shipibo women have several such herbal preparations. One of the most common is called *toötimahuaste* (*toöti* means "pregnancy," *ma* means "not," and *huaste* means "herb"). Taken as a tea during three successive menstrual periods, it is supposed to cause sterility.

In 1969, for my master of public health thesis, I returned to the village to conduct a more formal census and collect the inhabitants' reproductive histories. I asked the Shipibo women in my survey if they knew about these medicines and if they used them. They roared with laughter at the idea of a male gringo asking these intimate questions in their language. Then they usually told me that they knew about them; many had used them. Some of the women had seriously harmed themselves by using highly toxic natural substances in a desperate attempt to control fertility.

At first I was puzzled to find that women who had used the herbal contraceptives had more children, on the average, than those who hadn't. This turned out to be because older women, who had already had many children, were more likely to have used the herbal contraceptives. But my doubts about the effectiveness of the traditional contraceptives were renewed when I analyzed the results of my two population studies in 1964 and 1969. The Shipibo in Paococha turned out to have the highest fertility ever recorded for a human group, with a woman having an average of ten births during her reproductive life.

Moreover, their rate of population growth was nearly 4.9 percent per year, with the population doubling every 14.5 years. Such a population explosion had to be fairly recent, for if such a rate had been in effect for very long the population would have been huge. The phenomenon could not be completely explained by better medical care (some of which I had provided) and a declining death rate. Either the herbal contraceptives didn't work, or I wasn't getting all the information.

There were two other factors. By 1969, a large extended family from down the Ucayali river, at the periphery of the Shipibo territory, moved into Paococha. Several of the men had multiple wives. (The local, "downtown" Shipibo assured me that, unlike themselves, the new family was composed of *salvajes*—savages—and that they practiced the old ways, including polygyny.) Because missionaries and schoolteachers discouraged it, this family structure was becoming rare.

The second factor was suggested to me when I remembered that the Shipibo always observed certain taboos, including "dieting," when taking medications of any kind. I asked the women what they did when they took *toötimahuaste*. They replied that one cannot eat salt, honey from the forest or other sweets, ripe bananas, and certain kinds of fish. And a woman taking *toötimahuaste* may not have sex. This would mean an abstinence of three months or more. Right away, I suspected what epidemiologists call a "secondary noncausal association" between the use of herbal contraceptives and fewer pregnancies.

Postpartum sexual abstinence is often linked with polygyny in tribal societies. The woman who has just given birth may not sleep with her husband for a period of time, which may be from three months to three years. During that time her husband sleeps with one of the other wives. In Shipibo tradition, it is not uncommon for a man to have two or three wives. Because women in polygynous marriages might be better able to observe the sexual abstinence associated with herbal contraceptives, and because this might help these women have longer birth intervals, I speculated that a decline in the practice of polygyny could be contributing to the community's high fertility.

To be sure of this, I had to determine that, on average, the birth intervals were indeed longer for women in polygynous marriages than for women in monogamous marriages and that fertility was actually lower for the former than for the latter. Further, I wanted to determine if the rates of polygyny differed among the villages, and if so, whether less polygyny is associated with lower or higher community fertility. By studying Shipibo villages that were separated by long distances and had different levels of cultural contact with Western society, I could compare the relationship between polygyny and fertility.

Up on the Pisqui River, Shipibo lives are more traditional than in the Shipibo villages lining the Ucayali. The Pisqui is much smaller and fluctuates more quickly than the Ucayali. It contains fewer fish and other edible wildlife. The Pisqui Shipibo live more by hunting and gathering than their Ucayali brethren. They are more isolated from outside influences, and have been since at least early colonial times.

In 1983 and 1984, I studied eight Shipibo villages in different states of cultural transition. Six of the villages were as much as sixty miles up the Pisqui. The results of the study showed that polygyny is generally more common on the Pisqui, and that longer birth intervals occur in the polygynous unions there. In some Pisqui villages, 45 percent of the women were in polygynous marriages, whereas in Paoyhän, a new Shipibo village on the Ucayali, only about 5 percent of the women were in this kind of union.

Comparing the birth interval lengths and fertility of all women, regardless of their villages, I found that, on average, the birth intervals for women in polygynous marriages were thirty-four months—four months longer than those of women in monogamous marriages. And most significant, women in monogamous marriages had 1.3 more children during their reproductive lives than women in polygynous marriages. Accordingly, in villages where polygyny was more common, the average intervals between births were longer and community fertility rates were lower.

The most acute health problem for the Shipibo, as both they and I see it, is epidemic disease—tuberculosis, cholera, and influenza, to mention a few. These diseases carry off the older people who know the cultural traditions, and they carry off many children. But the long-term problem is high fertility, which is placing pressure on the diminishing resources. Weakened by increasingly poor nutrition, the Shipibo are more vulnerable to epidemics. In their case, population growth means poverty and disease.

For Shipibo women, high fertility means sickness and death. They have an extremely high rate of cervical cancer, which is probably related, among other things, to early childbearing and many pregnancies. I estimate that the maternal mortality ratio—the proportion of women who die from pregnancy and childbirth—is roughly one for every hundred live births, one hundred times higher than in the United States.

A larger question raised by studies such as mine is whether we really understand how fast the world's population is growing and will grow in the future. The Shipibo are essentially not counted in the Peruvian census, and neither are their mestizo and other Shipibo neighbors. Numbers sent to the government offices are highly inaccurate (but then I, for one, never received a U.S. census form in 1990).

From my experiences in Latin America, I would speculate that official census counts are missing at least one in ten people and perhaps every fourth person. Some of those groups excluded appear to have population growth rates of more than 3.5 percent. If this is true—and if it is similarly true in other parts of the developing world—world population growth rates may not only be higher than official estimates but may also grow higher as traditional societies like the Shipibo experience rapid cultural change.

Human population growth is not new. But there was a time, long past, when it took 100,000 years for world population to double. Soon after agriculture was invented, the doubling time dropped to 700 years. Now our population is doubling every 35 to 40 years. What happened?

While there are many answers, one emerges from this study and others like it: many human societies that controlled their fertility in the past have lost the tradition of doing so in the frenzy of modern cultural change. The old methods that reduced births have not yet been replaced by the new technologies of fertility control. The result is chaos, suffering, more cultural change, and in some cases, even more rapid population growth. Where will it stop?

For the Shipibo it stops when the beloved *yoshanshico* (grandmother) dies of tuberculosis and takes with her the ancient Amazon traditions of pottery making and weaving and knowledge of the plants and seasons. It stops with the loss of half the village's children to a measles epidemic. It stops with the death of a beautiful thirteen-year-old girl in childbirth. It stops when the village chief, a vigorous and intelligent young man, dies of cholera. It stops when the legendary hunter of *piache*, a giant fish once commonly found in Amazon lakes, returns after three days in the bush with his canoe empty and his harpoon unused. His family gets by on another meal of banana porridge.

It stops when the bright but superfluous young men and women of the village leave for the city, where they can get low-level jobs and survive. Their village education, which kept them from the forest and from learning their environment and own culture, has given them only minimal skills for life in town, where they sometimes conceal their cultural identity to get jobs.

It stopped for Ambrosio's wife when she died, exhausted, trying to give birth the next time, at the end of her twelfth pregnancy. The previous child proved to be mentally retarded, probably the result of a two-day labor and difficult delivery. For Ambrosio, a friendly man with a mischievous smile and quick wit, it stopped when he died from tetanus two years later. For Julia, who became one of my dearest friends in life, a woman who had outlived two husbands and thrown out several others, who was fiercely independent and could hunt and fish with the men, who was a skilled artist and walking library of Shipibo culture, it stopped when she started coughing blood and bled to death in a few minutes in front of her horrified family. The Shipibo are being forced to choose between buying tuberculosis medicine for people like Julia and building schools for their children.

For me, there are few things as delightful as the sound of Shipibo children laughing. The Shipibo love their children, and it shows. But what is ahead for people like Chomoshico and her husband and children? The inexorable arithmetic of population growth is upon them, and the consequences for their environment and families are plain to see. As a public health physician, I cannot help noticing that the Shipibo's fertility problems are inseparable from their other health problems and the changes going on around them. I also cannot help noticing that each family, with few exceptions, wants to limit its fertility but has no safe, effective means of doing so. That is not a scientific issue, but a political problem that neither I nor the Shipibo can solve.

REVIEW QUESTIONS

1. What accounts for the population explosion documented for the Shipibo Indians of the Peruvian Amazon?
2. How does the custom of polygyny limit fertility among the Shipibo?
3. What are the effects of high fertility on the health and welfare of the Shipibo?
4. How have the Shipibo tried to cope with their high fertility rate and its consequences for their health and economic security?
5. How has the high fertility rate affected the lives of Shipibo women?

12

India's Sacred Cow

Marvin Harris

Other people's religious practices and beliefs may often appear to be wasteful. They seem to involve a large expenditure of scarce resources on ritual; they contain taboos that restrict the use of apparently useful materials. Their existence seems irrational in the face of ecological needs. One example that many cite in support of this viewpoint is the religious proscription on the slaughter of cattle in India. How can people permit millions of cattle to roam about eating, but uneaten, in a land so continuously threatened by food shortages and starvation? In this article, Marvin Harris challenges the view that religious value is ecologically irrational. Dealing with the Indian case, he argues that Indian cattle, far from being useless, are an essential part of Indian's productive base. Religious restrictions on killing cattle are ecologically sensible; they have developed and persisted to ensure a continuous supply of these valuable animals.

N ews photographs that came out of India during the famine of the late 1960s showed starving people stretching out bony hands to beg for food while sacred cattle strolled behind them undisturbed. The Hindu, it seems, would rather starve to death than eat his cow or even deprive it of food. The cattle appear to browse unhindered through urban markets eating an orange here, a mango there, competing with people for meager supplies of food.

By Western standards, spiritual values seem more important to Indians than life itself. Specialists in food habits around the world like Fred Simoons at the University of California at Davis consider Hinduism an irrational ideology that compels people to overlook abundant, nutritious foods for scarcer, less healthful foods.

What seems to be an absurd devotion to the mother cow pervades Indian life. Indian wall calendars portray beautiful young women with bodies of fat white cows, often with milk jetting from their teats into sacred shrines.

Cow worship even carries over into politics. In 1966 a crowd of 120,000 people, led by holy men, demonstrated in front of the Indian House of Parliament in support of the All-Party Cow Protection Campaign Committee. In Nepal, the only contemporary Hindu kingdom, cow slaughter is severely punished. As one story goes, the car driven by an official of a United States agency struck and killed a cow. In order to avoid the international incident that would have occurred when the official was arrested for murder, the Nepalese magistrate concluded that the cow had committed suicide.

Many Indians agree with Western assessments of the Hindu reverence for their cattle, the zebu, or *Bos indicus*, a large-humped species prevalent in Asia and Africa. M. N. Srinivas, an Indian anthropologist states: "Orthodox Hindu opinion regards the killing of cattle with abhorrence, even though the refusal to kill the vast number of useless cattle which exists in India today is detrimental to the nation." Even the Indian Ministry of Information formerly maintained that "the large animal population is more a liability than an asset in view of our land resources." Accounts from many different sources point to the same conclusion: India, one of the world's great civilizations, is being strangled by its love for the cow.

The easy explanation for India's devotion to the cow, the one most Westerners and Indians would offer, is that cow worship is an integral part of Hinduism. Religion is somehow good for the soul, even if it sometimes fails the body. Religion orders the cosmos and explains our place in the universe. Religious beliefs, many would claim, have existed for thousands of years and have a life of their own. They are not understandable in scientific terms.

But all this ignores history. There is more to be said for cow worship than is immediately apparent. The earliest Vedas, the Hindu sacred texts from the Second Millennium B.C., do not prohibit the slaughter of cattle. Instead, they ordain it as a part of sacrificial rites. The early Hindus did not avoid the flesh of cows and bulls; they ate it at ceremonial feasts presided over by Brahman priests. Cow worship is a relatively recent development in India; it evolved as the Hindu religion developed and changed.

This evolution is recorded in royal edicts and religious texts written during the last 3,000 years of Indian history. The Vedas from the First Millennium B.C. contain contradictory passages, some referring to ritual slaughter and others to a strict taboo on beef consumption. A. N. Bose, in *Social and Rural Economy of Northern India, 600 B.C.–200 A.D.*, concludes that many of the sacred-cow passages were incorporated into the texts by priests of a later period.

By 200 A.D. the status of Indian cattle had undergone a spiritual transformation. The Brahman priesthood exhorted the population to venerate the cow and forbade them to abuse it or to feed on it. Religious feasts involving the ritual slaughter and consumption of livestock were eliminated and meat eating was restricted to the nobility.

By 1000 A.D., all Hindus were forbidden to eat beef. Ahimsa, the Hindu belief in the unity of all life, was the spiritual justification for this restriction. But it is difficult to ascertain exactly when this change occurred. An important event that helped to shape the modern complex was the Islamic invasion, which took place in the Eighth Century A.D. Hindus may have found it politically expedient to set themselves off from the invaders, who were beefeaters, by emphasizing the need to prevent the slaughter of their sacred animals. Thereafter, the cow taboo assumed its modern form and began to function much as it does today.

The place of the cow in modern India is every place—on posters, in the movies, in brass figures, in stone and wood carvings, on the streets, in the fields. The cow is a symbol of health and abundance. It provides the milk that Indians consume in the form of yogurt and ghee (clarified butter), which contribute subtle flavors to much spicy Indian food.

This, perhaps, is the practical role of the cow, but cows provide less than half the milk produced in India. Most cows in India are not dairy breeds. In most regions, when an Indian farmer wants a steady, high-quality source of milk he usually invests in a female water buffalo. In India the water buffalo is the specialized diary breed because its milk has a higher butterfat content than zebu milk. Although the farmer milks his zebu cows, the milk is merely a by-product.

More vital than zebu milk to South Asian farmers are zebu calves. Male calves are especially valued because from bulls come oxen, which are the mainstay of the Indian agricultural system.

Small, fast oxen drag wooden plows through late-spring fields when monsoons have dampened the dry, cracked earth. After harvest, the oxen break the grain from the stalk by stomping through mounds of cut wheat and rice. For rice cultivation in irrigated fields, the male water buffalo is preferred (it pulls better in deep mud), but for most other crops, including rainfall rice, wheat, sorghum, and millet, and for transporting goods and people to and from town, a team of oxen is preferred. The ox is the Indian peasant's tractor, thresher, and family car combined; the cow is the factory that produces the ox.

If draft animals instead of cows are counted, India appears to have too few domesticated ruminants, not too many. Since each of the 70 million farms in India requires a draft team, it follows that Indian peasants should use 140 million animals in the fields. But there are only 83 million oxen and male water buffalo on the subcontinent, a shortage of 30 million draft teams.

In other regions of the world, joint ownership of draft animals might overcome a shortage, but Indian agriculture is closely tied to the monsoon rains of late spring and summer. Field preparation and planting must coincide with the rain, and a farmer must have his animals ready to plow when the weather is right. When the farmer without a draft team needs bullocks most, his neighbors are all using theirs. Any delay in turning the soil drastically lowers production.

Because of this dependence on draft animals, loss of the family oxen is devastating. If a beast dies, the farmer must borrow money to buy or rent an ox at interest rates so high that he ultimately loses his land. Every year foreclosures force thousands of poverty-stricken peasants to abandon the countryside for the overcrowded cities.

If a family is fortunate enough to own a fertile cow, it will be able to rear replacements for a lost team and thus survive until life returns to normal. If, as sometimes happens, famine leads a family to sell its cow and ox team, all ties to agriculture are cut. Even if the family survives, it has no way to farm the land, no oxen to work the land, and no cows to produce oxen.

The prohibition against eating meat applies to the flesh of cows, bulls, and oxen, but the cow is the most sacred because it can produce the other two. The peasant whose cow dies is not only crying over a spiritual loss but over the loss of his farm as well.

Religious laws that forbid the slaughter of cattle promote the recovery of the agricultural system from the dry Indian winter and from periods of drought. The monsoon, on which all agriculture depends, is erratic. Sometimes it arrives early, sometimes late, sometimes not at all. Drought has struck large portions of India time and again in this century, and Indian farmers and the zebus are accustomed to these natural disasters. Zebus can pass weeks on end with little or no food and water. Like camels, they store both in their humps and recuperate quickly with only a little nourishment.

During droughts the cows often stop lactating and become barren. In some cases the condition is permanent but often it is only temporary. If barren animals were summarily eliminated, as Western experts in animal husbandry have suggested, cows capable of recovery would be lost along with those entirely debilitated. By keeping alive the cows that can later produce oxen, religious laws against cow slaughter assure the recovery of the agricultural system from the greatest challenge it faces—the failure of the monsoon.

The local Indian governments aid the process of recovery by maintaining homes for barren cows. Farmers reclaim any animal that calves or begins to lactate. One police station in Madras collects strays and pastures them in a field adjacent to the station. After a small fine is paid, a cow is returned to its rightful owner when the owner thinks the cow shows signs of being able to reproduce.

During the hot, dry spring months most of India is like a desert. Indian farmers often complain they cannot feed their livestock during this period. They maintain the cattle by letting them scavenge on the sparse grass along the roads. In the cities cattle are encouraged to scavenge near food stalls to supplement their scant diet. These are the wandering cattle tourists report seeing throughout India.

Westerners expect shopkeepers to respond to these intrusions with the deference due a sacred animal; instead, their response is a string of curses and the crack of a long bamboo pole across the beast's back or a poke at its genitals. Mahatma Gandhi was well aware of the treatment sacred cows (and bulls and oxen) received in India. "How we bleed her to take the last drop of milk from her. How we starve her to emaciation, how we ill-treat the calves, how we deprive them of their portion of milk, how cruelly we treat the oxen, how we castrate them, how we beat them, how we overload them."

Oxen generally receive better treatment than cows. When food is in short supply, thrifty Indian peasants feed their working bullocks and ignore their cows, but rarely do they abandon the cows to die. When cows are sick, farmers worry over them as they would over members of the family and nurse them as if they were children. When the rains return and when the fields are harvested, the farmers again feed their cows regularly and reclaim their abandoned animals. The prohibition against beef consumption is a form of disaster insurance for all India.

Western agronomists and economists are quick to protest that all the functions of the zebu cattle can be improved with organized breeding programs, cultivated pastures, and silage. Because stronger oxen would pull the plow faster, they could work multiple plots of land, allowing farmers to share their animals. Fewer healthy, well-fed cows could provide Indians with more milk. But pastures and silage require arable land, land needed to produce wheat and rice.

A look at Western cattle farming makes plain the cost of adopting advanced technology in Indian agriculture. In a study of livestock production in the United States, David Pimentel of the College of Agriculture and Life Sciences at Cornell University found that 91 percent of the cereal, legume, and vegetable protein suitable for human consumption is consumed by livestock. Approximately three quarters of the arable land in the United States is devoted to growing food for livestock. In the production of meat and milk, American ranchers use enough fossil fuel to equal more than 82 million barrels of oil annually. (See Figure I.)

Figure I
American cattle: Energy consumption and production.

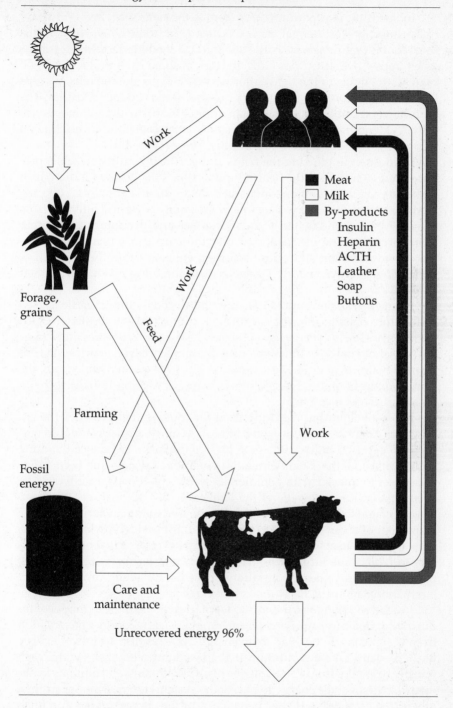

Work

Meat
Milk
By-products
  Insulin
  Heparin
  ACTH
  Leather
  Soap
  Buttons

Forage,
grains

Work

Feed

Work

Farming

Work

Fossil
energy

Care and
maintenance

Unrecovered energy 96%

Indian cattle do not drain the system in the same way. In a 1971 study of livestock in West Bengal, Stewart Odend'hal of the University of Missouri found that Bengalese cattle ate only the inedible remains of subsistence crops—rice straw, rice hulls, the tops of sugar cane, and mustard-oil cake. Cattle graze in the fields after harvest and eat the remains of crops left on the ground; they forage for grass and weeds on the roadsides. The food for zebu cattle costs the human population virtually nothing. "Basically," Odend'hal says, "the cattle convert items of little direct human value into products of immediate utility." (See Figure II.)

In addition to plowing the fields and producing milk, the zebus produce dung, which fires the hearths and fertilizes the fields of India. Much of the estimated 800 million tons of manure produced annually is collected by the farmers' children as they follow the family cows and bullocks from place to place. And when the children see the droppings of another farmer's cattle along the road, they pick those up also. Odend'hal reports that the system operates with such high efficiency that the children of West Bengal recover nearly 100 percent of the dung produced by their livestock.

From 40 to 70 percent of all manure produced by Indian cattle is used as fuel for cooking; the rest is returned to the fields as fertilizer. Dried dung burns slowly, cleanly, and with low heat—characteristics that satisfy the household needs of Indian women. Staples like curry and rice can simmer for hours. While the meal slowly cooks over an unattended fire, the women of the household can do other chores. Cow chips, unlike firewood, do not scorch as they burn.

It is estimated that the dung used for cooking fuel provides the energy-equivalent of 43 million tons of coal. At current prices, it would cost India an extra 1.5 billion dollars in foreign exchange to replace the dung with coal. And if the 350 million tons of manure that are being used as fertilizer were replaced with commercial fertilizers, the expense would be even greater. Roger Revelle of the University of California at San Diego has calculated that 89 percent of the energy used in Indian agriculture (the equivalent of about 140 million tons of coal) is provided by local sources. Even if foreign loans were to provide the money, the capital outlay necessary to replace the Indian cow with tractors and fertilizers for the fields, coal for the fires, and transportation for the family would probably warp international financial institutions for years.

Instead of asking the Indians to learn from the American model of industrial agriculture, American farmers might learn energy conservation from the Indians. Every step in an energy cycle results in a loss of energy to the system. Like a pendulum that slows a bit with each swing, each transfer of energy from sun to plants, plants to animals, and animals to human beings involves energy losses. Some systems are more efficient than others; they provide a higher percentage of the energy inputs in a final, useful form. Seventeen percent of all energy zebus consume is returned in

Figure II
Indian cattle: Energy consumption and production.

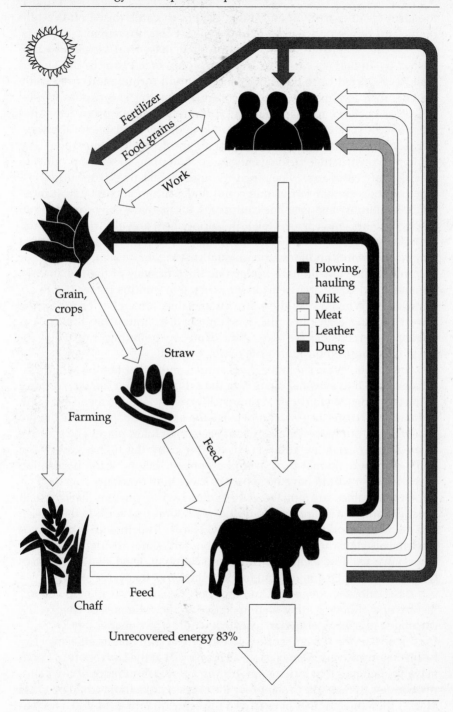

Fertilizer

Food grains

Work

Grain, crops

Farming

Straw

Feed

Plowing, hauling
Milk
Meat
Leather
Dung

Chaff

Feed

Unrecovered energy 83%

the form of milk, traction and dung. American cattle raised on Western range land return only 4 percent of the energy they consume.

But the American system is improving. Based on techniques pioneered by Indian scientists, at least one commercial firm in the United States is reported to be building plants that will turn manure from cattle feedlots into combustible gas. When organic matter is broken down by anaerobic bacteria, methane gas and carbon dioxide are produced. After the methane is cleansed of the carbon dioxide, it is available for the same purposes as natural gas—cooking, heating, electricity generation. The company constructing the biogasification plant plans to sell its product to a gas-supply company, to be piped through the existing distribution system. Schemes similar to this one could make cattle ranches almost independent of utility and gasoline companies, for methane can be used to run trucks, tractors, and cars as well as to supply heat and electricity. The relative energy self-sufficiency that the Indian peasant has achieved is a goal American farmers and industry are now striving for.

Studies like Odend'hal's understate the efficiency of the Indian cow, because dead cows are used for purposes that Hindus prefer not to acknowledge. When a cow dies, an Untouchable, a member of one of the lowest ranking castes in India, is summoned to haul away the carcass. Higher castes consider the body of the dead cow polluting; if they do handle it, they must go through a rite of purification.

Untouchables first skin the dead animal and either tan the skin themselves or sell it to a leather factory. In the privacy of their homes, contrary to the teachings of Hinduism, untouchable castes cook the meat and eat it. Indians of all castes rarely acknowledge the existence of these practices to non-Hindus, but more are aware that beefeating takes place. The prohibition against beefeating restricts consumption by the higher castes and helps distribute animal protein to the poorest sectors of the population that otherwise would have no source of these vital nutrients.

Untouchables are not the only Indians who consume beef. Indian Muslims and Christians are under no restriction that forbids them beef, and its consumption is legal in many places. The Indian ban on cow slaughter is state, not national, law and not all states restrict it. In many cities, such as New Delhi, Calcutta, and Bombay, legal slaughterhouses sell beef to retail customers and to the restaurants that serve steak.

If the caloric value of beef and the energy costs involved in the manufacture of synthetic leather were included in the estimates of energy, the calculated efficiency of Indian livestock would rise considerably.

As well as the system works, experts often claim that its efficiency can be further improved. Alan Heston, an economist at the University of Pennsylvania, believes that Indians suffer from an overabundance of cows simply because they refuse to slaughter the excess cattle. India could produce at least the same number of oxen and the same quantities of milk and manure with 30 million fewer cows. Heston calculates that only 40 cows are necessary to maintain a population of 100 bulls and oxen. Since India averages 70 cows for every 100 bullocks, the difference, 30 million cows, is expendable.

What Heston fails to note is that sex ratios among cattle in different regions of India vary tremendously, indicating that adjustments in the cow population do take place. Along the Ganges River, one of the holiest shrines of Hinduism, the ratio drops to 47 cows for every 100 male animals. This ratio reflects the preference for dairy buffalo in the irrigated sectors of the Gangetic Plains. In nearby Pakistan, in contrast, where cow slaughter is permitted, the sex ratio is 60 cows to 100 oxen.

Since the sex ratios among cattle differ greatly from region to region and do not even approximate the balance that would be expected if no females were killed, we can assume that some culling of herds does take place; Indians do adjust their religious restrictions to accommodate ecological realities.

They cannot kill a cow but they can tether an old or unhealthy animal until it has starved to death. They cannot slaughter a calf but they can yoke it with a large wooden triangle so that when it nurses it irritates the mother's udder and gets kicked to death. They cannot ship their animals to the slaughterhouse but they can sell them to Muslims, closing their eyes to the fact that the Muslims will take the cattle to the slaughterhouse.

These violations of the prohibition against cattle slaughter strengthen the premise that cow worship is a vital part of Indian culture. The practice arose to prevent the population from consuming the animal on which Indian agriculture depends. During the First Millennium B.C., the Ganges Valley became one of the most densely populated regions of the world.

Where previously there had been only scattered villages, many towns and cities arose and peasants farmed every available acre of land. Kingsley Davis, a population expert at the University of California at Berkeley, estimates that by 300 B.C. between 50 million and 100 million people were living in India. The forested Ganges Valley became a windswept semi-desert and signs of ecological collapse appeared; droughts and floods became commonplace, erosion took away the rich topsoil, farms shrank as population increased, and domesticated animals became harder and harder to maintain.

It is probable that the elimination of meat eating came about in a slow, practical manner. The farmers who decided not to eat their cows, who saved them for procreation to produce oxen, were the ones who survived the natural disasters. Those who ate beef lost the tools with which to farm. Over a period of centuries, more and more farmers probably avoided beef until an unwritten taboo came into existence.

Only later was the practice codified by the priesthood. While Indian peasants were probably aware of the role of cattle in their society, strong sanctions were necessary to protect zebus from a population faced with starvation. To remove temptation, the flesh of cattle became taboo and the cow became sacred.

The sacredness of the cow is not just an ignorant belief that stands in the way of progress. Like all concepts of the sacred and the profane, this one affects the physical world; it defines the relationships that are important for the maintenance of Indian society.

Indians have the sacred cow; we have the "sacred" car and the "sacred" dog. It would not occur to us to propose the elimination of automobiles and dogs from our society without carefully considering the consequences, and we should not propose the elimination of zebu cattle without first understanding their place in the social order of India.

Human society is neither random nor capricious. The regularities of thought and behavior called culture are the principal mechanisms by which we human beings adapt to the world around us. Practices and beliefs can be rational or irrational, but a society that fails to adapt to its environment is doomed to extinction. Only those societies that draw the necessities of life from their surroundings, without destroying those surroundings, inherit the earth. The West has much to learn from the great antiquity of Indian civilization, and the sacred cow is an important part of that lesson.

REVIEW QUESTIONS

1. A friend asks, "Why don't Indians eat the millions of cattle that roam loose over their country?" Based on the information in this article, how would you answer?
2. What are the main uses and products of cattle in India? What is most important about cattle for continued human material welfare?
3. How does Harris explain the rise of cattle protection in India?
4. Clearly Indians need bulls and bullocks to plow, but why can't they limit the number of cows to a level just sufficient for breeding?
5. Some anthropologists argue that the sacredness of Indian cattle evolved as part of the religious system, apart from practical considerations. How would Harris respond to this assertion?

ECONOMIC SYSTEMS

People everywhere experience wants that can be satisfied only by the acquisition and use of material goods and the services of others. To meet such wants, humans rely on an aspect of their cultural inventory, the *economic system*, which we will define as the provision of goods and services to meet biological and social wants.

The meaning of the term *want* can be confusing. It can refer to what humans *need* for their survival. We must eat, drink, maintain a constant body temperature, defend ourselves, and deal with injury and illness. The economic system meets these needs by providing food, water, clothing, shelter, weapons, medicines, and the cooperative services of others.

But material goods serve more than just our survival needs: they meet our culturally defined *wants* as well. We need clothes to stay warm, but we want garments of a particular style, cut, and fabric to signal our status, rank, or anything else we wish to communicate socially. We need food to sustain life, but we want particular foods prepared in special ways to fill our aesthetic and social desires. Services and goods may also be exchanged to strengthen ties between people or groups. Birthday presents may not always meet physical needs, but they clearly function to strengthen the ties between the parties to the exchange.

Part of the economic system is concerned with *production*, which means rendering material items useful and available for human consumption. Production systems must designate ways to allocate resources. The *allocation of resources* refers to the cultural rules people use to assign rights to the ownership and use of resources. Production systems must also include technologies. Americans usually associate technology with the tools and machines used for manufacturing, rather than with the knowledge for doing it. But many anthropologists link the concept directly to culture. Here we will define *technology* as the cultural knowledge for making and using tools and extracting and refining raw materials.

Production systems also include a *division of labor,* which refers to the rules that govern the assignment of jobs to people. In hunting and gathering societies, labor is most often divided along the lines of gender, and sometimes age. In these societies, almost everyone knows how to produce, use, and collect the necessary material goods. In industrial society, however, jobs are highly specialized, and labor is divided, at least ideally, on the basis of skill and experience. It is rarely that we know how to do someone else's job in our complex society.

The *unit of production,* meaning the persons or groups responsible for producing goods, follows a pattern similar to the way labor is divided in various societies. Among hunter-gatherers, there is little specialization; individuals, families, groups of friends, or sometimes bands form the units of production. But in our own complex society, we are surrounded by groups specially organized to manufacture, transport, and sell goods.

Another part of the economic system is *distribution.* There are three basic modes of distribution: market exchange, reciprocal exchange, and redistribution.

We are most conscious of market exchange because it lies at the heart of our capitalist system. *Market exchange* is the transfer of goods and services based on price, supply, and demand. Every time we enter a store and pay for something, we engage in market exchange. The price of an item may change with the supply. For example, a discount store may lower the price of a television set because it has too many of the appliances on hand. Prices may go up, however, if everyone wants the sets when there are few to sell. Money is often used in market systems; it enables people to exchange a large variety of items easily. Barter involves the trading of goods, not money, but it, too, is a form of market exchange because the number of items exchanged may also vary with supply and demand. Market exchange appears in human history when societies become larger and more complex. It is well suited for exchange between the strangers who make up these larger groups.

Although we are not so aware of it, we also engage in reciprocal exchange. *Reciprocal exchange* involves the transfer of goods and services between two people or groups based on role obligations. Birthday and holiday gift giving is a fine example of reciprocity. On these occasions we exchange goods not because we necessarily need or want them, but because we are expected to do so as part of our status and role. Parents should give gifts to their children, for example; children should reciprocate. If we fail in our reciprocal obligations, we signal an unwillingness to continue the relationship. Small, simply organized societies, such as the !Kung described earlier, base their exchange systems on reciprocity. Complex ones like ours, although largely organized around the market or redistribution, still manifest reciprocity between kin and close friends.

Finally, there is *redistribution,* the transfer of goods and services between a central collecting source and a group of individuals. Like reciprocity, redistribution is based on role obligation. Taxes typify this sort of exchange in the United States. We must pay our taxes because we are citizens, not because we are buying something. We receive goods and services back—education, transportation, roads, defense—but not necessarily in proportion to the amount we contribute. Redistribution may be the predominant mode of exchange in socialist societies.

Anthropologists also frequently talk about two kinds of economies. In the past, many of the world's societies had *subsistence economies* organized around the need to meet material necessities and social obligations. Subsistence economies are typically associated with smaller groups. They occur at a local level. Such economies depend most on the non-market-exchange mechanisms: reciprocity and redistribution. Their members are occupational generalists. Most people can do most jobs, although there may be distinctions on the basis of gender and age. The !Kung described by Richard Lee in Parts II and IV of this book had subsistence economies as do most horticulturalists.

Market economies differ from subsistence economies in their size and motive for production. Although reciprocity and redistribution exist in market economies, market exchange drives production and consumption. Market economies are larger (indeed, there is a growing world market economy that includes almost everyone) and are characterized by high economic specialization, as well as impersonality. The American economy is market-driven as are most national systems. If they have not been already, most subsistence economies will, in the near future, be absorbed into national market systems.

The selections in this section illustrate several of the concepts discussed above. In the first article, Lee Cronk looks at gift giving, a classic example of reciprocity. He finds that gifts can cement relationships, confer prestige, and obligate subordinates. Lynn Bolles looks at a different topic in the second selection. She details how poor and working-class third-world women have managed to survive in changing, increasingly market-dominated economies. The third article, by Bernard Nietschmann, details the impact of the international market system on a local subsistence economy. Motivated by money, Miskito Indians came to be dependent on outsiders for food and found themselves unable to meet their traditional reciprocal obligations. Readers should note that most Miskito Indians were displaced from their traditional communities and occupations by the Sandanista government of Nicaragua after this article was written. Jack Weatherford also deals with the impact of the world economy in the final article. He shows that the Western demand for cocaine has had devastating consequences for the indigenous people of Peru, Bolivia, and Colombia who grow coca and prepare the drug for market.

KEY TERMS

economic system   distribution
production   market exchange
allocation of resources   reciprocal exchange
technology   redistribution
division of labor   subsistence economies
unit of production   market economies

READINGS IN THIS SECTION

13

Reciprocity and the Power of Giving

Lee Cronk

As we saw in the introduction to Part V, reciprocity constitutes an important exchange system in every society. At the heart of reciprocal exchange is the idea of giving. In this article, Lee Cronk explores the functions of giving using a variety of examples from societies around the world. Giving may be benevolent. It may be used to strengthen existing relationships or to form new ones. Gifts may also be used aggressively to "fight" people, to "flatten" them with generosity. Givers often gain position and prestige in this way. Gifts may also be used to place others in debt so that one can control them and require their loyalty. Cronk shows that, in every society, from !Kung hxaro exchange to American foreign aid, there are "strings attached" to giving that affect how people and groups relate to each other.

During a trek through the Rockies in the 1830s, Captain Benjamin Louis E. de Bonneville received a gift of a fine young horse from a Nez Percé chief. According to Washington Irving's account of the incident,

---

the American explorer was aware that "a parting pledge was necessary on his own part, to prove that this friendship was reciprocated." Accordingly, he "placed a handsome rifle in the hands of the venerable chief; whose benevolent heart was evidently touched and gratified by this outward and visible sign of amity."

Even the earliest white settlers in New England understood that presents from natives required reciprocity, and by 1764, "Indian gift" was so common a phrase that the Massachusetts colonial historian Thomas Hutchinson identified it as "a proverbial expression, signifying a present for which an equivalent return is expected." Then, over time, the custom's meaning was lost. Indeed, the phrase now is used derisively, to refer to one who demands the return of a gift. How this cross-cultural misunderstanding occurred is unclear, but the poet Lewis Hyde, in his book *The Gift*, has imagined a scenario that probably approaches the truth.

Say that an Englishman newly arrived in America is welcomed to an Indian lodge with the present of a pipe. Thinking the pipe a wonderful artifact, he takes it home and sets it on his mantelpiece. When he later learns that the Indians expect to have the pipe back, as a gesture of goodwill, he is shocked by what he views as their short-lived generosity. The newcomer did not realize that, to the natives, the point of the gift was not to provide an interesting trinket but to inaugurate a friendly relationship that would be maintained through a series of mutual exchanges. Thus, his failure to reciprocate appeared not only rude and thoughtless but downright hostile. "White man keeping" was as offensive to native Americans as "Indian giving" was to settlers.

In fact, the Indians' tradition of gift giving is much more common than our own. Like our European ancestors, we think that presents ought to be offered freely, without strings attached. But through most of the world, the strings themselves are the main consideration. In some societies, gift giving is a tie between friends, a way of maintaining good relationships, whereas in others it has developed into an elaborate, expensive, and antagonistic ritual designed to humiliate rivals by showering them with wealth and obligating them to give more in return.

In truth, the dichotomy between the two traditions of gift giving is less behavioral than rhetorical: our generosity is not as unconditional as we would like to believe. Like European colonists, most modern Westerners are blind to the purpose of reciprocal gift giving, not only in non-Western societies but also, to some extent, in our own. Public declarations to the contrary, we, too, use gifts to nurture long-term relationships of mutual obligation, as well as to embarrass our rivals and to foster feelings of indebtedness. And this ethic touches all aspects of contemporary life, from the behavior of scientists in research networks to superpower diplomacy. Failing to acknowledge this fact, especially as we give money, machines, and technical advice to peoples around the world, we run the risk of being misinterpreted and, worse, of causing harm.

Much of what we know about the ethics of gift giving comes from tempts of anthropologists to give things to the people they are stu Richard Lee, of the University of Toronto, learned a difficult lesson from the !Kung hunter-gatherers, of the Kalahari desert, when, as a token of goodwill, he gave them an ox to slaughter at Christmas. Expecting grati- tude, he was shocked when the !Kung complained about having to make do with such a scrawny "bag of bones." Only later did Lee learn, with re- lief, that the !Kung belittle all gifts. In their eyes, no act is completely gen- erous, or free of calculation; ridiculing gifts is their way of diminishing the expected return and of enforcing humility on those who would use gifts to raise their own status within the group.

Rada Dyson-Hudson, of Cornell University, had a similar experience among the Turkana, a pastoral people of northwestern Kenya. To compensate her informants for their help, Dyson-Hudson gave away pots, maize meal, tobacco, and other items. The Turkana reaction was less than heartwarming. A typical response to a gift of a pot, for example, might be, "Where is the maize meal to go in this pot?" or, "Don't you have a bigger one to give me?" To the Turkana, these are legitimate and ex- pected questions.

The Mukogodo, another group of Kenyan natives, responded in a sim- ilar way to gifts Beth Leech and I presented to them during our fieldwork in 1986. Clothing was never nice enough, containers never big enough, to- bacco and candies never plentiful enough. Every gift horse was examined carefully, in the mouth and elsewhere. Like the !Kung, the Mukogodo be- lieve that all gifts have an element of calculation, and they were right to think that ours were no exception. We needed their help, and their efforts to diminish our expectations and lessen their obligations to repay were as fair as our attempts to get on their good side.

The idea that gifts carry obligations is instilled early in life. When we gave Mukogodo children candies after visiting their villages, their moth- ers reminded them of the tie: "Remember these white people? They are the ones who gave you candy." They also reinforced the notion that gifts are meant to circulate, by asking their children to part with their precious can- dies, already in their mouths. Most of the youngsters reluctantly surren- dered their sweets, only to have them immediately returned. A mother might take, at most, a symbolic nibble from her child's candy, just to drive home the lesson.

The way food, utensils, and other goods are received in many societies is only the first stage of the behavior surrounding gift giving. Although re- payment is expected, it is crucial that it be deferred. To reciprocate at once indicates a desire to end the relationship, to cut the strings; delayed re- payment makes the strings longer and stronger. This is especially clear on the Truk Islands, of Micronesia, where a special word—*niffag*—is used to designate objects moving through the island's exchange network. From the Trukese viewpoint, to return niffag on the same day it is received alters its nature from that of a gift to that of a sale, in which all that matters is material gain.

After deciding the proper time for response, a recipient must consider how to make repayment, and that is dictated largely by the motive behind the gift. Some exchange customs are designed solely to preserve a relationship. The !Kung have a system, called *hxaro,* in which little attention is paid to whether the items exchanged are equivalent. Richard Lee's informant !Xoma explained to him that "Hxaro is when I take a thing of value and give it to you. Later, much later, when you find some good thing, you give it back to me. When I find something good I will give it to you, and so we will pass the years together." When Lee tried to determine the exact exchange values of various items (Is a spear worth three strings of beads, two strings, or one?), !Xoma explained that any return would be all right: "You see, we don't trade with things, we trade with people!"

One of the most elaborate systems of reciprocal gift giving, known as *kula,* exists in a ring of islands off New Guinea. Kula gifts are limited largely to shell necklaces, called *soulava,* and armbands, called *mwali.* A necklace given at one time is answered months or years later with an armband, the necklaces usually circulating clockwise, and the armbands counterclockwise, through the archipelago. Kula shells vary in quality and value, and men gain fame and prestige by having their names associated with noteworthy necklaces or armbands. The shells also gain value from their association with famous and successful kula partners.

Although the act of giving gifts seems intrinsically benevolent, a gift's power to embarrass the recipient and to force repayment has, in some societies, made it attractive as a weapon. Such antagonistic generosity reached its most elaborate expression, during the late nineteenth century, among the Kwakiutl, of British Columbia.

The Kwakiutl were acutely conscious of status, and every tribal division, clan, and individual had a specific rank. Disputes about status were resolved by means of enormous ceremonies (which outsiders usually refer to by the Chinook Indian term *potlatch*), at which rivals competed for the honor and prestige of giving away the greatest amount of property. Although nearly everything of value was fair game—blankets, canoes, food, pots, and, until the mid-nineteenth century, even slaves—the most highly prized items were decorated sheets of beaten copper, shaped like shields and etched with designs in the distinctive style of the Northwest Coast Indians.

As with the kula necklaces and armbands, the value of a copper sheet was determined by its history—by where it had been and who had owned it—and a single sheet could be worth thousands of blankets, a fact often reflected in its name. One was called "Drawing All Property from the House," and another, "About Whose Possession All Are Quarreling." After the Kwakiutl began to acquire trade goods from the Hudson's Bay Company's Fort Rupert post, in 1849, the potlatches underwent a period of extreme inflation, and by the 1920s, when items of exchange included sewing machines and pool tables, tens of thousands of Hudson's Bay blankets might be given away during a single ceremony.

In the 1880s, after the Canadian government began to suppress warfare between tribes, potlatching also became a substitute for battle. As a Kwakiutl man once said to the anthropologist Franz Boas, "The time of fighting is past. . . . We do not fight now with weapons: we fight with property." The usual Kwakiutl word for potlatch was *p!Esa*, meaning to flatten (as when one flattens a rival under a pile of blankets), and the prospect of being given a large gift engendered real fear. Still, the Kwakiutl seemed to prefer the new "war of wealth" to the old "war of blood."

Gift giving has served as a substitute for war in other societies, as well. Among the Siuai, of the Solomon Islands, guests at feasts are referred to as attackers, while hosts are defenders, and invitations to feasts are given on short notice in the manner of "surprise attacks." And like the Kwakiutl of British Columbia, the Mount Hagen tribes of New Guinea use a system of gift giving called *moka* as a way of gaining prestige and shaming rivals. The goal is to become a tribal leader, a "big-man." One moka gift in the 1970s consisted of several hundred pigs, thousands of dollars in cash, some cows and wild birds, a truck, and a motorbike. The donor, quite pleased with himself, said to the recipient, "I have won. I have knocked you down by giving so much."

Although we tend not to recognize it as such, the ethic of reciprocal gift giving manifests itself throughout our own society, as well. We, too, often expect something, even if only gratitude and a sense of indebtedness, in exchange for gifts, and we use gifts to establish friendships and to manipulate our positions in society. As in non-Western societies, gift giving in America sometimes takes a benevolent and helpful form; at other times, the power of gifts to create obligations is used in a hostile way.

The Duke University anthropologist Carol Stack found a robust tradition of benevolent exchange in an Illinois ghetto known as the Flats, where poor blacks engage in a practice called swapping. Among residents of the Flats, wealth comes in spurts; hard times are frequent and unpredictable. Swapping, of clothes, food, furniture, and the like, is a way of guaranteeing security, of making sure that someone will be there to help out when one is in need and that one will get a share of any windfalls that come along.

Such networks of exchange are not limited to the poor, nor do they always involve objects. Just as the exchange of clothes creates a gift community in the Flats, so the swapping of knowledge may create one among scientists. Warren Hagstrom, a sociologist at the University of Wisconsin, in Madison, has pointed out that papers submitted to scientific journals often are called contributions, and, because no payment is received for them, they truly are gifts. In contrast, articles written for profit—such as this one—often are held in low esteem: scientific status can be achieved only through *giving* gifts of knowledge.

Recognition also can be traded upon, with scientists building up their gift-giving networks by paying careful attention to citations and acknowledgments. Like participants in kula exchange, they try to associate themselves with renowned and prestigious articles, books, and institutions. A desire for recognition, however, cannot be openly acknowledged as a motivation for research, and it is a rare scientist who is able to discuss such desires candidly. Hagstrom was able to find just one mathematician (whom he described as "something of a social isolate") to confirm that "junior mathematicians want recognition from big shots and, consequently, work in areas prized by them."

Hagstrom also points out that the inability of scientists to acknowledge a desire for recognition does not mean that such recognition is not expected by those who offer gifts of knowledge, any more than a kula trader believes it is all right if his trading partner does not answer his gift of a necklace with an armband. While failure to reciprocate in New Guinean society might once have meant warfare, among scientists it may cause factionalism and the creation of rivalries.

Whether in the Flats of Illinois or in the halls of academia, swapping is, for the most part, benign. But manipulative gift giving exists in modern societies, too—particularly in paternalistic government practices. The technique is to offer a present that cannot be repaid, coupled with a claim of beneficence and omniscience. The Johns Hopkins University anthropologist Grace Goodell documented one example in Iran's Khūzestān Province, which, because it contains most of the country's oil fields and is next door to Iraq, is a strategically sensitive area. Goodell focused on the World Bank–funded Dez irrigation project, a showpiece of the shah's ambitious "white revolution" development plan. The scheme involved the irrigation of tens of thousands of acres and the forced relocation of people from their villages to new, model towns. According to Goodell, the purpose behind dismantling local institutions was to enhance central government control of the region. Before development, each Khūzestāni village had been a miniature city-state, managing its own internal affairs and determining its own relations with outsiders. In the new settlements, decisions were made by government bureaucrats, not townsmen, whose autonomy was crushed under the weight of a large and strategically placed gift.

On a global scale, both the benevolent and aggressive dimensions of gift giving are at work in superpower diplomacy. Just as the Kwakiutl were left only with blankets with which to fight after warfare was banned, the United States and the Soviet Union now find, with war out of the question, that they are left only with gifts—called concessions—with which to do battle. Offers of military cutbacks are easy ways to score points in the public arena of international opinion and to shame rivals, and failure either to accept such offers or to respond with even more extreme proposals may be seen as cowardice or as bellicosity. Mikhail Gorbachev is a virtuoso, a master potlatcher, in this new kind of competition, and, predictably,

Americans often see his offers of disarmament and openness as gifts with long strings attached. One reason U.S. officials were buoyed last December, when, for the first time since the Second World War, the Soviet Union accepted American assistance, in the aftermath of the Armenian earthquake, is that it seemed to signal a wish for reciprocity rather than dominance—an unspoken understanding of the power of gifts to bind people together.

Japan, faced with a similar desire to expand its influence, also has begun to exploit gift giving in its international relations. In 1989, it will spend more than ten billion dollars on foreign aid, putting it ahead of the United States for the second consecutive year as the world's greatest donor nation. Although this move was publicly welcomed in the United States as the sharing of a burden, fears, too, were expressed that the resultant blow to American prestige might cause a further slip in our international status. Third World leaders also have complained that too much Japanese aid is targeted at countries in which Japan has an economic stake and that too much is restricted to the purchase of Japanese goods—that Japan's generosity has less to do with addressing the problems of underdeveloped countries than with exploiting those problems to its own advantage.

The danger in all of this is that wealthy nations may be competing for the prestige that comes from giving gifts at the expense of Third World nations. With assistance sometimes being given with more regard to the donors' status than to the recipients' welfare, it is no surprise that, in recent years, development aid often has been more effective in creating relationships of dependency, as in the case of Iran's Khūzestān irrigation scheme, than in producing real development. Nor that, given the fine line between donation and domination, offers of help are sometimes met with resistance, apprehension and, in extreme cases, such as the Iranian revolution, even violence.

The Indians understood a gift's ambivalent power to unify, antagonize, or subjugate. We, too, would do well to remember that a present can be a surprisingly potent thing, as dangerous in the hands of the ignorant as it is useful in the hands of the wise

REVIEW QUESTIONS

1. What does Cronk mean by *reciprocity?* What is the social outcome of reciprocal gift giving.
2. According to Cronk, what are some examples of benevolent gift giving?
3. How can giving be used to intimidate other people or groups? Give some examples cited by Cronk, and think of some from your own experience.
4. How does Cronk classify gift-giving strategies such as government foreign aid? Can you think of other examples of the use of exchange as a political device?

14

Women's Work in the Third World

A. Lynn Bolles

Division of labor by sex is a feature of societies everywhere. Among foragers, for example, women traditionally collect plant foods while men hunt (see the article by Ernestine Friedl in Part VII). Among horticulturalists, women are likely to concentrate on agricultural work while men clear the forest for gardens and hunt wild game. Conditions today describe a different arrangement, especially in the third world, according to Lynn Bolles in this article. Third-world national economies define two sectors, one formal, the other informal. Poor and working-class women lack the education, training, freedom, and opportunity to enter the formal sector in great numbers. Yet because of the shift to a cash economy and the relative poverty into which they are born, poor women need to work. The result is a creative entrance into the informal economic sector, where women often make money as vendors, small importers, domestics, and prostitutes, and in a variety of other jobs that allow them the freedom to survive.

In "The Poets in the Kitchen," Paule Marshall tells stories from her childhood in the late 1930s and early '40s that reflect what it means to be an immigrant, a West Indian, a black in a racist society, a mother, a wife, a woman in a male-dominated culture, and a worker near the bottom of the economic ladder. Marshall's mother and her mother's women friends had all immigrated from Barbados. After a long day toiling as domestics or in other low-paid jobs, and before going home to their families and their own household chores, they would gather in Marshall's mother's kitchen. There, the "soully-gals," a self-reflexive term implying both spirit and the visible self, took the time to drink a cup of tea or cocoa, relax, and comment on their day, their lives, and their jobs. In Marshall's retelling, their humorous stories are philosophical treatises on "living in this man country," as they called the United States. These women strive to make a living, save money as best as they can, and "see the children through."

The poets in the Marshall kitchen are not alone in the way they struggle for survival under inequitable situations. The poets and their poor and working-class sisters from around the world strive to fulfill their obligations as mothers, wives, and kinswomen.

In the Third World, even more than elsewhere, only a few people hold well-paying, high-status jobs. Many more workers find themselves in the informal sector, where jobs range from traditional ones—transferred to cities from rural areas—to producing technologically advanced goods for export. These jobs share the fact that they are unprotected and unregulated.

Because women are discriminated against in both education and the labor market, they are heavily represented in the informal sector. Lacking the educational, political, or social qualifications to find jobs in the formal sector, women create alternative openings for themselves—as street vendors, traders, small shop operators, domestic workers, prostitutes, and so on.

This is true of indigenous women and of poor Third World women in general. Jamaican market women continue to trade as their ancestors did during slavery—a female enterprise that survived the middle passage. Driven off traditional community lands, Peruvian Indian women come to Lima to find employment in the homes of the middle and upper classes. And in Kenya, an oral history recounts how Kikuyu girls were recruited for brothels in Nairobi.

That women in many cultures utilize similar survival strategies suggests the presence of a global common ground of creativity among Third World women, particularly if they are members of oppressed indigenous groups or of poor and working-class origins and denied access to their society's resources for human development. Poor and working-class women fight for daily survival—and for the future of themselves and their families. These women are choosers and doers, not passive reactors.

TRADING AND STREET VENDING

Trading has a long history in the Caribbean. Its heritage begins in West Africa, where trading was an important role for women. According to noted anthropologist Sidney Mintz, West Africans brought the concept of woman-as-trader to their enslavement in the Americas.

In Jamaica, slaves grew enough food in house gardens to sell some of it to other slaves and white masters. In vibrant Sunday markets, a West African tradition became a part of Jamaican culture—and stayed the domain of women. Over the next 130 years, notes Jamaican sociologist Elsie Le Franc, "higglering," as it is called, changed little. After emancipation in 1838, as peasant holdings and small farms grew, the trading in produce became entrenched. Today, small farmers produce 90 percent of Jamaica's food, and higglers distribute 80 percent of it.

Recently, a new type of higgler has emerged—the informal commercial importer. These women import goods from Panama, Haiti, Curaçao, the United States, and other countries to sell in Kingston. Informal importing expanded in the late 1970s, when scarcity and high prices in Jamaica's formal economy brought the traders high profits.

Despite this connection between the formal and informal sectors, Le Franc argues, the higglers' main goal is to be independent, as individuals and workers. A higgler determines her own timetable and marketing strategy, uses her own access to capital, makes personnel decisions, and manages her own investments.

Similarly drawing on historical roots is the inter-island trade in the Eastern Caribbean, which serves a different function than Jamaica's importers. Ecological differences have fostered a brisk trade in fruit and vegetables from St. Vincent, Dominica, and Grenada to Barbados to Antigua, St. Kitts, Guadeloupe, and the smaller French islands, and from both St. Lucia and Dominica to the Virgin Islands. Small ships carry women traders to nearby islands. Some women specialize in one port, while others diversify.

As Charles Carnegie, a Jamaican anthropologist, explains, the "speculators" of St. Lucia bring both locally made goods and imported items to Martinique and buy other consumer goods in a variety of markets to sell in St. Lucia. Each speculator works on her own or with one or two others, coordinates her crew, and arranges transportation. No one knows how many speculators—called traffickers in St. Vincent and hucksters in Dominica—there are, but it is one of the few occupations a rapidly growing, unskilled population can enter.

In Peru, rural Indian women migrate to Lima and initially work as maids, but many move on to street vending as soon as their first child is born. According to Ximena Bunster, a Chilean anthropologist, and Elsa Chaney, her American coresearcher, the vendors—*ambulantes*—take up street hawking for two reasons: women can keep children with them, and vendors have "a feeling of 'independence' and/or greater flexibility than either a factory or domestic work situation allowed." *Ambulantes* recognize that their lack of skills, education, and training preclude other ways for them to earn a living.

Women are relatively recent participants in trading in sub-Saharan Africa. Ilsa Schuster describes the situation of poor women in Lusaka, Zambia, who can no longer subsist on farms. With the emphasis on cash earnings, trading has replaced farming as an important female enterprise. Much the same transition took place in Zambia, says Maud Shimway Muntemba. British colonialism undermined their agricultural role, so women moved to towns to become traders, sell food, and take on other roles in the informal economy.

Women dominate other areas of trade as well. Outside Davao City in the Philippines, *sari-sari* stores link producers and consumers. In every neighborhood—poor and wealthy alike—*sari-sari* stores provide a way for a working-class woman with some capital to become an entrepreneur in her own right. Although the government licenses *sari-sari* stores, most owners operate without official sanction. However, they are free from police harassment, unlike street peddlers, because a number of them do have licenses.

The links between time-honored women's economic activities—such as between West African trading and its Caribbean variants—have contemporary consequences. Traders must have management skills and access to credit to compete for their market-share of goods and services. The women who own *sari-saris* know their low profit margin is a consequence of the goods they sell and their business's size, as well as its location close to home so they can tend to children.

A LONG HISTORY

Perhaps women's most common informal-sector job is domestic service, which ranks very low, often lowest, in prestige and pay. In the Philippines, notes sociologist Marilou Palabrica-Costello, servants rank so low that it only attracts people with little chance of finding any other job.

In Latin America, the institution of domestic service can reinforce the sense of social superiority one group feels over another based on class, racial, or ethnic divisions. Bunster and Chaney note that having a servant is the badge of a lower-middle-class family's upward mobility and the sign that a middle-class family is maintaining its status.

While much domestic work resembles other wage work, it is "fraught with contradictions," anthropologist Shellee Colen suggests, "between its status as wage labor and very personalized relations . . . and its own peculiar form of exploitation, depersonalization, and dehumanization." The West Indian domestics she has studied call the lack of esteem for housework and those who perform it "the worst part" of their jobs. On the other hand, Bunster and Chaney found that many domestic servants in Lima say that a good thing about the work is their personal relation to a *patrona*—a good mistress. The servants recognize that changing situations wouldn't necessarily alleviate harsh working conditions, but the women do change their jobs until they find a *patrona*. In fact, an agreeable employer is one of the few job-related variables that servants can sometimes control.

Perhaps even lower on the status scale is another informal-sector job with a long history: prostitution. The reasons why women enter this occupation are many: some are recruited and others enlist voluntarily, some seek the income and others excitement. Alternatives to unemployment, lack of opportunity for marriage, lack of education, and severe economic need are all common motivations.

In colonial Kenya, the choice sometimes derived from government restrictions on women's traditional economic activities coupled with new opportunities for men, such as railroad construction work in the 1920s. According to Margaret Strobel's history of women in Mombasa, Kenya's second largest city, population imbalances, all-male work camps, and few economic avenues for women after the outlawing of slavery fostered prostitution.

Historian Claire Robertson provides a case study of an elderly woman named Murithi, who was a prostitute in her youth in the 1920s and 1930s. An abused wife, Murithi and another divorced woman moved to Nairobi, Kenya's capital. In addition to her native Swahili, Murithi learned English by attending night classes that a church missionary society gave for Christian converts. She and her friend rented a downtown room and began street walking. The clients were Europeans, Indians, and affluent Africans. Eventually, Murithi built a six-room house in Nairobi and recruited Kikuyu girls into the "business." She no longer walked the streets herself but maintained a list of old clients. In her old age, she lived on the income of her house.

Murithi's trade let her assume family obligations. She built her parents a stone house and made the marriage payment for two of her brothers' wives. In 1948, when Africans won the right to produce coffee, she bought coffee trees for her parents, and she continued to subsidize her family over the years.

According to Audrey Wipper, the many prostitutes' associations in West and Central Africa act as mutual-aid organizations, affording protection usually provided by relatives. The most prestigious voluntary associations are composed of successful "courtesans," whose clientele includes high-level civil servants, businessmen, and professionals. The higher-status associations organize festivals and deliver mutual aid; those formed by ordinary women emphasize "bread-and-butter" issues and provide psychological support.

In Southeast Asia, as tourism in general has grown, so have prostitution and controversy over sex tourism, one component of the global trade in sexuality. "Sex-tour" ads mix images of graceful, docile women with those of sexual temptresses, while the proximity of huge military bases means that prostitution as a line of work is ever-present. According to Pasuk Phongpaichit, who has studied Thai *aarb obnuad*—massage parlors—only wealthy men could afford to indulge in the trade of female sexuality in the "old days." "Now any man in Bangkok can get himself a 10-baht massage at the end of the day."

Prostitution is illegal in Thailand, but the *aarb obnuad* provides a way to thinly disguise it. In a massage parlor, women work in a safe and comfortable manner, in contrast to other forms of prostitution. Two-thirds of the women Phongpaichit studied came to town to be masseuses, while the rest turned to prostitution after other jobs delivered too little income. "A pretty girl who works in a massage parlor can earn seven to eight times what she can earn as a salesgirl," notes Phongpaichit, "and more than ten times what she can earn as an inexperienced housemaid."

The cost is high. Virtually all the women Phongpaichit spoke with wanted to quit the massage parlor. Many confessed to substance abuse and depression. A number of them were afflicted with venereal disease or had had abortions. Many of their young friends in the trade had died from abortion-related complications.

A HIDDEN WORKFORCE

One realm of the informal sector is a reincarnation of sorts. In its latest form, homework production is industrial homework—what was known in eighteenth-century England as the "putting out system." However, Third World manufacturing adds a new aspect, in that the women working out of their homes are actually subcontractors—that is, their work forms a "neo-putting out" system. Unless it is a garment, the women rarely make a whole product but rather a component for a product that is assembled elsewhere. Most types of industrial homework involve simple, deskilled, labor-intensive tasks that require little capital and few tools. Work is unstable and offers no security.

Economist Lourdes Beneria and Martha Roldan, an Argentinean sociologist, have made one of the most comprehensive studies of neo-putting out systems. They show that the differences between the formal and informal sectors in Mexico City arise because production in the latter case is by definition underground. Homework means sharply lowered wages, and the lack of labor regulations means a major decline in working conditions.

The workers Beneria and Roldan interviewed listed many motives for the predominance of women in homework: illiteracy, domestic chores, child-care responsibilities, and no alternatives. In other words, industrial homework provides jobs for those the formal labor force doesn't incorporate. Women's willingness to engage in this type of work shows their need to generate income, regardless of exploitation.

In the case of industrial jobs, informal workers are a disguised proletariat: seemingly self-employed workers actually work for others. In other cases, home production may be a family business or part of a coop, which are more lucrative but require capital or outside support. Either way, the informal economy provides wage opportunities when women are unskilled, untrained, and illiterate.

MAKING A LIVING

Traders, shop keepers, domestic servants, prostitutes, and industrial homeworkers all speak of similar problems. Survival must be paid in cash, while gender hierarchies, aggravated by ethnicity and class, mean that women have less access to marketable skills and resources.

Despite their limited opportunities, women choose to survive. Wives whose husbands have migrated sell food in the streets to provide the only wage for their families. Young girls sell sexuality to provide for themselves and for families in rural areas. Domestics change jobs to find decent patronage. These women are active agents who channel resources to cope on a daily basis and plan for the future. The varied ways poor and working-class women cope, manage, and survive show that creativity is not in short supply.

Increasingly, women are coming to understand the sources of their exploitation and have begun to challenge them. This is happening throughout the world through new forms of social movements. Battered women's shelters, cooperatives that make and distribute farm products, and literacy campaigns are just a few examples. These organizations are not waiting for governments to deal with these local issues but take steps on their own behalf.

These women's experiences demand that policy makers include the perspectives of poor and working-class women, who are looking for new directions. How can women's survival strategies in the informal sector become vehicles for social transformation, rather than supports for the status quo?

REVIEW QUESTIONS

1. According to Bolles, what is the difference between the formal and informal sectors of third-world economies?
2. What are the main conditions that determine the kinds of jobs women can hold in third-world economies?
3. What are the usual kinds of jobs held by poor and working-class women in the third world?
4. What effect do you think the entrance of poor third-world women into local and national economies will have on their domestic lives, relations to kin, and prestige? Why?

15

Subsistence and Market:
When the Turtle Collapses

Bernard Nietschmann

Subsistence economies were once common in the world. People hunted and gathered or farmed largely for their own needs. But the world market economy has penetrated even the most remote areas and has brought with it a change from subsistence economies to production for money. In this article, Bernard Nietschmann traces the disturbing effect of the international market for green sea turtles on the Miskito Indians, who once harpooned the large sea reptiles only for food. Trapped in a vicious circle, Indians began to catch the turtles to sell rather than to eat. With no turtle meat to eat came a need for money to buy food. Money came only from catching and selling more turtles. The need for cash also reduced the Indians' ability to perform reciprocal economic obligations. In the end, the new economy began to disappear because of the diminished catch of overexploited turtles, leaving the Miskito without even their original

In the half-light of dawn, a sailing canoe approaches a shoal where nets have been set the day before. A Miskito turtleman stands in the bow and points to a distant splash that breaks the gray sheen of the Caribbean waters. Even from a hundred yards, he can tell that a green turtle has been caught in one of the nets. His two companions quickly bring the craft alongside the turtle, and as they pull it from the sea, its glistening shell reflects the first rays of the rising sun. As two men work to remove the heavy reptile from the net, the third keeps the canoe headed into the swells and beside the anchored net. After its fins have been pierced and lashed with bark fiber cord, the 250-pound turtle is placed on its back in the bottom of the canoe. The turtlemen are happy. Perhaps their luck will be good today and their other nets will also yield many turtles.

These green turtles, caught by Miskito Indian turtlemen off the eastern coast of Nicaragua, are destined for distant markets. Their butchered bodies will pass through many hands, local and foreign, eventually ending up in tins, bottles, and freezers far away. Their meat, leather, shell, oil, and calipee, a gelatinous substance that is the base for turtle soup, will be used to produce goods consumed in more affluent parts of the world.

The coastal Miskito Indians are very dependent on green turtles. Their culture has long been adapted to utilizing the once vast populations that inhabited the largest sea turtle feeding grounds in the Western Hemisphere. As the most important link between livelihood, social interaction, and environment, green turtles were the pivotal resource around which traditional Miskito Indian society revolved. These large reptiles also provided the major source of protein for Miskito subsistence. Now this priceless and limited resource has become a prized commodity that is being exploited almost entirely for economic reasons.

In the past, turtles fulfilled the nutritional needs as well as the social responsibilities of Miskito society. Today, however, the Miskito depend mainly on the sale of turtles to provide them with the money they need to purchase household goods and other necessities. But turtles are a declining resource; overdependence on them is leading the Miskito into an ecological blind alley. The cultural control mechanisms that once adapted the Miskito to their environment and faunal resources are now circumvented or inoperative, and they are caught up in a system of continued intensification of turtle fishing, which threatens to provide neither cash nor subsistence.

I have been studying this situation for several years, unraveling its historical context and piecing together its past and future effect on Miskito society, economy, and diet, and on the turtle population.

The coastal Miskito Indians are among the world's most adept small-craft seamen and turtlemen. Their traditional subsistence system provided dependable yields from the judicious scheduling of resource procurement activities. Agriculture, hunting, fishing, and gathering were organized in accordance with seasonal fluctuations in weather and resource availability and provided adequate amounts of food and materials without over-exploiting any one species or site. Women cultivated the crops while men hunted and fished. Turtle fishing was the backbone of subsistence, providing meat throughout the year.

Miskito society and economy were interdependent. There was no economic activity without a social context and every social act had a reciprocal economic aspect. To the Miskito, meat, especially turtle meat, was the most esteemed and valuable resource, for it was not only a mainstay of subsistence, it was the item most commonly distributed to relatives and friends. Meat shared in this way satisfied mutual obligations and responsibilities and smoothed out daily and seasonal differences in the acquisition of animal protein. In this way, those too young, old, sick, or otherwise unable to secure meat received their share, and a certain balance in the village was achieved: minimal food requirements were met, meat surplus was disposed of to others, and social responsibilities were satisfied.

Today, the older Miskito recall that when meat was scarce in the village, a few turtlemen would put out to sea in their dugout canoes for a day's harpooning on the turtle feeding grounds. In the afternoon, the men would return, sailing before the northeast trade wind, bringing meat for all. Gathered on the beach, the villagers helped drag the canoes into thatched storage sheds. After the turtles were butchered and the meat distributed, everyone returned home to the cooking fires.

Historical circumstances and a series of boom-bust economic cycles disrupted the Miskito's society and environment. In the seventeenth and eighteenth centuries, intermittent trade with English and French buccaneers—based on the exchange of forest and marine resources for metal tools and utensils, rum, and firearms—prompted the Miskito to extend hunting, fishing, and gathering beyond subsistence needs to exploitative enterprises.

During the nineteenth and early twentieth centuries, foreign-owned companies operating in eastern Nicaragua exported rubber, lumber, and gold, and initiated commercial banana production. As alien economic and ecological influences were intensified, contract wage labor replaced seasonal, short-term economic relationships; company commissaries replaced limited trade goods; and large-scale exploitation of natural resources replaced sporadic, selective extraction. During economic boom periods the relationship between resources, subsistence, and environment was drastically altered for the Miskito. Resources became a commodity with a price tag, market exploitation a livelihood, and foreign wages and goods a necessity.

For more than two hundred years, relations between the coastal Miskito and the English were based on sea turtles. It was from the Miskito that the English learned the art of turtling, which they then organized into intensive commercial exploitation of Caribbean turtle grounds and nesting beaches. Sea turtles were among the first resources involved in trade relations and foreign commerce in the Caribbean. Zoologist Archie Carr, an authority on sea turtles, has remarked that "more than any other dietary factor, the green turtle supported the opening up of the Caribbean." The once abundant turtle populations provided sustenance to ships' crews and to the new settlers and plantation laborers.

The Cayman Islands, settled by the English, became in the seventeenth and eighteenth centuries the center of commercial turtle fishing in the Caribbean. By the early nineteenth century, pressure on the Cayman turtle grounds and nesting beaches to supply meat to Caribbean and European markets became so great that the turtle population was decimated. The Cayman Islanders were forced to shift to other turtle areas off Cuba, the Gulf of Honduras, and the coast of eastern Nicaragua. They made annual expeditions, lasting four to seven weeks, to the Miskito turtle grounds to net green turtles, occasionally purchasing live ones, dried calipee, and the shells of hawksbill turtles (*Eretmochelys imbricata*) from the Miskito Indians. Reported catches of green turtles by the Cayman turtlers generally ranged between two thousand and three thousand a year up to the early 1960s, when the Nicaraguan government failed to renew the islanders' fishing privileges.

Intensive resource extraction by foreign companies led to seriously depleted and altered environments. By the 1940s, many of the economic booms had turned to busts. As the resources ran out and operating costs mounted, companies shut down production and moved to other areas in Central America. Thus, the economic mainstays that had helped provide the Miskito with jobs, currency, markets, and foreign goods were gone. The company supply ships and commissaries disappeared, money became scarce, and store-bought items expensive.

In the backwater of the passing golden boom period, the Miskito were left with an ethic of poverty, but they still had the subsistence skills that had maintained their culture for hundreds of years. Their land and water environment was still capable of providing reliable resources for local consumption. As it had been in the past, turtle fishing became a way of life, a provider of life itself. But traditional subsistence culture could no longer integrate Miskito society and environment in a state of equilibrium. Resources were now viewed as having a value and labor a price tag. All that was needed was a market.

Recently, two foreign turtle companies began operations along the east coast of Nicaragua. One was built in Puerto Cabezas in late 1968, and another was completed in Bluefields in 1969. Both companies were capable of processing and shipping large amounts of green turtle meat and by-products to markets in North America and Europe. Turtles were acquired by purchase from the Miskito. Each week company boats visited coastal Miskito communities and offshore island turtle camps to buy green turtles. The "company" was back, money was again available, and the Miskito were expert in securing the desired commodity. Another economic boom period was at hand. But the significant difference between this boom and previous ones was that the Miskito were now selling a subsistence resource.

As a result, the last large surviving green turtle population in the Caribbean was opened to intensive, almost year-round exploitation. Paradoxically, it would be the Miskito Indians, who once caught only what they needed for food, who would conduct the assault on the remaining turtle population. . . .

Green turtles, *Chelonia mydas,* are large, air-breathing, herbivorous marine reptiles. They congregate in large populations and graze on underwater beds of vegetation in relatively clear, shallow, tropical waters. A mature turtle can weigh two hundred fifty pounds or more and when caught, can live indefinitely in a saltwater enclosure or for a couple of weeks if kept in shade on land. Green turtles have at least six behavioral characteristics that are important in their exploitation: they occur in large numbers in localized areas; they are air breathing, so they have to surface; they are mass social nesters; they have an acute location-finding ability; when mature, they migrate seasonally on an overlapping two- or three-year cycle for mating and nesting; and they exhibit predictable local distributional patterns.

The extensive shallow shelf off eastern Nicaragua is dotted with numerous small coral islands, thousands of reefs, and vast underwater pastures of marine vegetation called "turtle banks." During the day, a large group of turtles may be found feeding at one of the many turtle banks, while adjacent marine pastures may have only a few turtles. They graze on the vegetation, rising periodically to the surface for air and to float for a while before diving again. In the late afternoon, groups of turtles will leave the feeding areas and swim to shoals, some up to four or five miles away, to spend the night. By five the next morning, they gather to depart again for the banks. The turtles' precise, commuterlike behavior between sleeping and feeding areas is well known to the Miskito and helps insure good turtling.

Each coastal turtling village exploits an immense sea area, containing many turtle banks and shoals. For example, the Miskito of Tasbapauni utilize a marine area of approximately six hundred square miles, with twenty major turtle banks and almost forty important shoals.

Having rather predictable patterns of movement and habitat preference, green turtles are commonly caught by the Miskito in three ways: on the turtle banks with harpoons; along the shoal-to-feeding area route with harpoons; and on the shoals using nets, which entangle the turtles when they surface for air.

The Miskito's traditional means of taking turtles was by harpoon—an eight- to ten-foot shaft fitted with a detachable short point tied to a strong line. The simple technology pitted two turtlemen in a small, seagoing canoe against the elusive turtles. Successful turtling with harpoons requires an extensive knowledge of turtle behavior and habits and tremendous skill and experience in handling a small canoe in what can be very rough seas. Turtlemen work in partnerships: a "strikerman" in the bow; the "captain" in the stern. Together, they make a single unit engaged in the delicate and almost silent pursuit of a wary prey, their movements coordinated by experience and rewarded by proficiency. Turtlemen have mental maps of all the banks and shoals in their area, each one named and located through a complex system of celestial navigation, distance reckoning, wind and current direction, and the individual surface-swell motion over each site. Traditionally, not all Miskito were sufficiently expert in seamanship and turtle lore to become respected "strikermen," capable of securing turtles even during hazardous sea conditions. Theirs was a very specialized calling. Harpooning restrained possible overexploitation since turtles were taken one at a time by two men directly involved in the chase, and there were only a limited number of really proficient "strikermen" in each village.

Those who still use harpoons must leave early to take advantage of the land breeze and to have enough time to reach the distant offshore turtle grounds by first light. Turtlemen who are going for the day, or for several days, will meet on the beach by 2:00 A.M. They drag the canoes on bamboo rollers from beachfront sheds to the water's edge. There, in the swash of spent breakers, food, water, paddles, lines, harpoons, and sails are loaded and secured. Using a long pole, the standing bowman propels the canoe through the foaming surf while the captain in the stern keeps the craft running straight with a six-foot mahogany paddle. Once past the inside break, the men count the dark rolling seas building outside until there is a momentary pause in the sets; then with paddles digging deep, they drive the narrow, twenty-foot canoe over the cresting swells, rising precipitously on each wave face and then plunging down the far side as the sea and sky seesaw into view. Once past the breakers, they rig the sail and, running with the land breeze, point the canoe toward a star in the eastern sky.

A course is set by star fix and by backsight on a prominent coconut palm on the mainland horizon. Course alterations are made to correct for the direction and intensity of winds and currents. After two or three hours of sailing the men reach a distant spot located between a turtle sleeping shoal and feeding bank. There they intercept and follow the turtles as they leave for specific banks.

On the banks the turtlemen paddle quietly, listening for the sound of a "blowing" turtle. When a turtle surfaces for air it emits a hissing sound audible for fifty yards or more on a calm day. Since a turtle will stay near the surface for only a minute or two before diving to feed, the men must approach quickly and silently, maneuvering the canoe directly in front of or behind the turtle. These are its blind spots. Once harpooned, a turtle explodes into a frenzy of action, pulling the canoe along at high speeds in its hopeless, underwater dash for escape until it tires and can be pulled alongside the canoe.

But turtle harpooning is a dying art. The dominant method of turtling today is the use of nets. Since their introduction, the widespread use of turtle nets has drastically altered turtling strategy and productivity. Originally brought to the Miskito by the Cayman Islanders, nets are now extensively distributed on credit by the turtle companies. This simple technological change, along with a market demand for turtles, has resulted in intensified pressure on green turtle populations.

Buoyed by wooden floats and anchored to the bottom by a single line, the fifty-foot-long by fourteen-foot-wide nets hang from the surface like underwater flags, shifting direction with the current. Nets are set in place during midday when the turtlemen can see the dark shoal areas. Two Miskito will set five to thirty nets from one canoe, often completely saturating a small shoal. In the late afternoon, green turtles return to their shoals to spend the night. There they will sleep beside or beneath a coral outcrop, periodically surfacing for air where a canopy of nets awaits them.

Catching turtles with nets requires little skill; anyone with a canoe can now be a turtleman. The Miskito set thousands of nets daily, providing continuous coverage in densely populated nocturnal habitats. Younger Miskito can become turtlemen almost overnight simply by following more experienced men to the shoal areas, thus circumventing the need for years of accumulated skill and knowledge that once were the domain of the "strikermen." All one has to do is learn where to set the nets, retire for the night, remove the entangled turtles the next morning, and reset the nets. The outcome is predictable: more turtlemen, using more effective methods, catch more turtles.

With an assured market for turtles, the Miskito devote more time to catching turtles, traveling farther and staying at sea longer. Increased dependence on turtles as a source of income and greater time inputs have meant disruption of subsistence agriculture and hunting and fishing. The Miskito no longer produce foodstuffs for themselves; they buy imported foods with money gained from the sale of turtles. Caught between contradictory priorities—their traditional subsistence system and the market economy—the Miskito are opting for cash.

The Miskito are now enveloped in a positive feedback system where change spawns change. Coastal villages rely on turtles for a livelihood. Decline of subsistence provisioning has led to the need to secure food from local shopkeepers on credit to feed the families in the villages and the men during their turtling expeditions. Initial high catches of turtles encouraged more Miskito to participate, and by 1972 the per-person and per-day catch began to decline noticeably.

In late 1972, several months after I had returned to Michigan, I received a letter from an old turtleman, who wrote: "Turtle is getting scarce,

Mr. Barney. You said it would happen in five or ten years but it is happening now."

Burdened by an overdependence on an endangered species and with accumulating debts for food and nets, the Miskito are finding it increasingly difficult to break even, much less secure a profit. With few other economic alternatives, the inevitable step is to use more nets and stay out at sea longer.

The turtle companies encourage the Miskito to expand turtling activities by providing them with building materials so that they can construct houses on offshore cays, thereby eliminating the need to return to the mainland during rough weather. On their weekly runs up and down the coast, company boats bring food, turtle gear, and cash for turtles to fishing camps from the Miskito Cays to the Set Net Cays. Frequent visits keep the Miskito from becoming discouraged and returning to their villages with the turtles. On Saturdays, villagers look to sea, watching for returning canoes. A few men will bring turtle for their families; the majority will bring only money. Many return with neither.

Most Miskito prefer to be home on Sunday to visit with friends and for religious reasons. (There are Moravian, Anglican, and Catholic mission churches in many of the villages.) But more and more, turtlemen are staying out for two to four weeks. The church may promise salvation, but only the turtle companies can provide money.

Returning to their villages, turtlemen are confronted with a complex dilemma: how to satisfy both social and economic demands with a limited resource. Traditional Miskito social rules stipulate that turtle meat should be shared among kin, but the new economic system requires that turtles be sold for personal economic gain. Kin expect gifts of meat, and friends expect to be sold meat. Turtlemen are besieged with requests forcing them to decide between who will or will not receive meat. This is contrary to the traditional Miskito ethic, which is based on generosity and mutual concern for the well-being of others. The older Miskito ask why the turtlemen should have to allocate a food that was once abundant and available to all. Turtlemen sell and give to other turtlemen, thereby ensuring reciprocal treatment for themselves, but there simply are not enough turtles to accommodate other economic and social requirements. In order to have enough turtles to sell, fewer are butchered in the villages. This means that less meat is being consumed than before the turtle companies began operations. The Miskito presently sell 70 to 90 percent of the turtles they catch; in the near future they will sell even more and eat less. . . .

Social tension and friction are growing in the villages. Kinship relationships are being strained by what some villagers interpret as preferential and stingy meat distribution. Rather than endure the trauma caused by having to ration a limited item to fellow villagers, many turtlemen prefer to sell all their turtles to the company and return with money, which does not have to be shared. However, if a Miskito sells out to the company, he will probably be unable to acquire meat for himself in the village, regardless of kinship or purchasing power. I overheard an elderly turtleman muttering to himself as he butchered a turtle: "I no going to sell, neither give dem meat. Let dem eat de money."

The situation is bad and getting worse. Individuals too old or sick to provide for themselves often receive little meat or money from relatives. Families without turtlemen are families without money or access to meat. The trend is toward the individualization of nuclear families, operating for their own economic ends. Miskito villages are becoming neighborhoods rather than communities.

The Miskito diet has suffered in quality and quantity. Less protein and fewer diverse vegetables and fruits are consumed. Present dietary staples—rice, white flour, beans, sugar, and coffee—come from the store. In one Miskito village, 65 percent of all food eaten in a year was purchased.

Besides the nutritional significance of what is becoming a largely carbohydrate diet, dependence on purchased foods has also had major economic reverberations. Generated by national and international scarcities, inflationary fallout has hit the Miskito. Most of their purchased foods are imported, much coming from the United States. In the last five years prices for staples have increased 100 to 150 percent. This has had an overwhelming impact on the Miskito, who spend 50 to 75 percent of their income for food. Consequently, their entry into the market by selling a subsistence resource, diverting labor from agriculture, and intensifying exploitation of a vanishing species has resulted in their living off poorer-quality, higher-priced foods.

The Miskito now depend on outside systems to supply them with money and materials that are subject to world market fluctuations. They have lost their autonomy and their adaptive relationship with their environment. Life is no longer socially rewarding, nor is their diet satisfying. The coastal Miskito have become a specialized and highly vulnerable sector of the global market economy.

Loss of turtle markets would be a serious economic blow to the Miskito, who have almost no other means of securing cash for what have now become necessities. Nevertheless, continued exploitation will surely reduce the turtle population to a critical level.

National and international legislation is urgently needed. At the very least, commercial turtle fishing must be curtailed for several years until the *Chelonia* population can rebound and exploitation quotas can be set. While turtle fishing for subsistence should be permitted, exportation of sea turtle products used in the gourmet, cosmetic, or jewelry trade should be banned.

Restrictive environmental legislation, however, is not a popular subject in Nicaragua, a country that has recently been torn by earthquakes, volcanic eruption, and hurricanes. A program for sea turtle conservation submitted to the Nicaraguan government for consideration ended up in a pile of rubble during the earthquake that devastated Managua in December 1972, adding a sad footnote to the Miskito–sea turtle situation. With other problems to face, the government has not yet reviewed what is happening on the distant east coast, separated from the capital by more than two hundred miles of rain forest—and years of neglect.

As it is now, the turtles are going down and, along with them, the Miskito—seemingly a small problem in terms of the scale of ongoing ecological and cultural change in the world. But each localized situation involves species and societies with long histories and, perhaps, short futures. They are weathervanes in the conflicting winds of economic and environmental priorities. As Bob Dylan sang: "You don't need a weatherman to tell which way the wind blows."

REVIEW QUESTIONS

1. What does Nietschmann mean by *subsistence economy?*
2. How has the Miskito Indians' exploitation of the green sea turtle affected their economy?
3. What does Nietschmann mean when he says that the Miskito Indian economy is "enveloped in a positive feedback system"?
4. How has the world market affected the Miskito economy?

16

Cocaine and the Economic Deterioration of Bolivia

Jack McIver Weatherford

The demands of the world market have eroded local subsistence economies for centuries. Lands once farmed by individual families to meet their own needs now grow sugarcane, cotton, grain, or vegetables for market. Deprived of their access to land, householders must work as day laborers or migrate to cities to find jobs. Villages are denuded of the men, who have gone elsewhere for work, leaving women to farm and manage the family. The rhythm and structure of daily village life are altered dramatically. In this article, Jack Weatherford describes the impact of a new world market for cocaine on the structure and lives of rural Bolivians. Fed by an insatiable demand in Europe and the United States, the Bolivian cocaine trade has drawn males from the countryside, disrupted communications, destroyed families, unbalanced the local diet, and upset traditional

"They say you Americans can do anything. So, why can't you make your own cocaine and let our children come home from the coca plantations in the Chapare?" The Indian woman asked the question with confused resignation. In the silence that followed, I could hear only the rats scurrying around in the thatched roof. We continued shelling corn in the dark. The large house around us had once been home to an extended clan but was now nearly empty.

There was no answer to give her. Yet it was becoming increasingly obvious that the traditional Andean system of production and distribution built over thousands of years was now crumbling. Accompanying the destruction of the economic system was a marked distortion of the social and cultural patterns of the Quechua Indians. Since early in Inca history, the village of Pocona where I was working had been a trading village connecting the highlands, which produced potatoes, with the lowlands, which produced coca, a mildly narcotic plant used by the Incas. Over the past decade, however, new market demands from Europe and the United States have warped this system. Now the commodity is cocaine rather than the coca leaves, and the trade route bypasses the village of Pocona.

Bolivian subsistence patterns range from hunting and gathering in the jungle to intensive farming in the highlands, and since Inca times many parts of the country have depended heavily on mining. In the 1980s all of these patterns have been disrupted by the Western fad for one particular drug. Adoption of cocaine as the "drug of choice" by the urban elite of Europe and America has opened up new jungle lands and brought new Indian groups into Western economic systems. At the same time, the cocaine trade has cut off many communities such as Pocona from their traditional role in the national economy. Denied participation in the legal economy, they have been driven back into a world of barter and renewed isolation.

The vagaries of Western consumerism produce extensive and profound effects on Third World countries. It makes little difference whether the demand is for legitimate products such as coffee, tungsten, rubber, and furs marketed through legal corporations, or for illegal commodities such as opium, marijuana, cocaine, and heroin handled through criminal corporations. The same economic principles that govern the open, legal market also govern the clandestine, illegal markets, and the effects of both are frequently brutal.

Before coming to this Bolivian village, I assumed that if Americans and Europeans wanted to waste their money on cocaine, it was probably good that some of the poor countries such as Bolivia profit from it. In Cochabamba, the city in the heart of the cocaine-producing area, I had seen the benefits of this trade among the *narco chic* who lived in a new suburb of houses styled to look like Swiss chalets, Spanish haciendas, and English country homes. All these homes were surrounded by large wrought-iron fences, walls with broken glass set in the tops, and with large dogs that barked loudly and frequently. Such homes cost up to a hundred thousand dollars, an astronomical sum for Bolivia. I had also seen the narco elite of Cochabamba wearing gold chains and the latest Miami fashions and driving Nissans, Audis, Ford Broncos, an occasional BMW, or even a Mercedes through the muddy streets of the city. Some of their children attended the expensive English-speaking school; much of Cochabamba's meager nightlife catered to the elite. But as affluent as they may be in Bolivia, this elite would probably not earn as much as working-class families in such cities as Detroit, Frankfurt, or Tokyo.

Traveling outside of Cochabamba for six hours on the back of a truck, fording the same river three times, and following a rugged path for the last twenty-five kilometers, I reached Pocona and saw a different face of the cocaine trade. Located in a valley a mile and a half above sea level, Pocona is much too high to grow the coca bush. Coca grows best below six thousand feet, in the lush area called the Chapare where the eastern Andes meet the western edge of the Amazon basin and rain forest.

Like the woman with whom I was shelling corn, most of the people of Pocona are older, and community life is dominated by women together with their children who are still too young to leave. This particular woman had already lost both of her sons to the Chapare. She did not know it at the time, but within a few months, she was to lose her husband to the same work as well. With so few men, the women are left alone to plant, work, and harvest the fields of potatoes, corn, and fava beans, but with most of the work force missing, the productivity of Pocona has declined substantially.

In what was once a moderately fertile valley, hunger is now a part of life. The daily diet consists almost exclusively of bread, potato soup, boiled potatoes, corn, and tea. The majority of their daily calories comes from the potatoes and from the sugar that they put in their tea. They have virtually no meat or dairy products and very few fresh vegetables. These products are now sent to the Chapare to feed the workers in the coca fields, and the people of Pocona cannot compete against them. The crops that the people of Pocona produce are now difficult to sell because truck drivers find it much more profitable to take goods in and out of the Chapare rather than face the long and unprofitable trip to reach such remote villages as Pocona.

Despite all the hardships caused by so many people being away from the village, one might assume that more cash should be flowing into Pocona from the Chapare, where young men easily earn three dollars a day—three times the average daily wage of porters or laborers in Cochabamba. But this assumption was contradicted by the evidence of Pocona. As one widowed Indian mother of four explained, the first time her sixteen-year-old son came home, he brought bags of food, presents, and money for her and the younger children. She was very glad that he was working in the Chapare. On the second visit home he brought only a plastic bag of white powder for himself, and instead of bringing food, he took away as much as he could carry on the two-day trip back into the Chapare.

The third time, he told his mother that he could not find enough work in the Chapare. As a way to earn more money he made his mother bake as much bread as she could, and he took Mariana, his ten-year-old sister, with him to sell the bread to the workers in the Chapare. According to the mother, he beat the little girl and abused her repeatedly. Moreover, the money she made disappeared. On one of Mariana's trips home to get more bread, the mother had no more wheat or corn flour to supply her son. So, she sent Mariana away to Cochabamba to work as a maid. The enraged son found where Mariana was working and went to the home to demand that she be returned to him. When the family refused, he tried but failed to have her wages paid to him rather than to his mother. Mariana was separated from her family and community, but at least she was not going to be one more of the prostitutes in the Chapare, and for her mother that was more important.

The standard of living in Pocona was never very high, but with the advent of the cocaine boom in Bolivia, the standard has declined. Ten years ago, Pocona's gasoline-powered generator furnished the homes with a few hours of electric light each night. The electricity also allowed a few families to purchase radios, and occasionally someone brought in a movie projector to show a film in a large adobe building on the main square. For the past two years, the people of Pocona have not been able to buy gasoline for their generator. This has left the village not only without electricity but without entertainment and radio or film contact with the outside world. A few boys have bought portable radios with their earnings from the Chapare, but their families were unable to replace the batteries. Nights in Pocona are now both dark and silent.

In recent years the national economy of Bolivia has been virtually destroyed, and peasants in communities such as Pocona are reverting to barter as the only means of exchange. The value of the peso may rise or fall by as much as 30 percent in a day; the peasants cannot take a chance on trading their crops for money that may be worth nothing in a week. Cocaine alone has not been responsible for the destruction of the Bolivian economy, but it has been a major contributor. It is not mere coincidence that the world's largest producer of coca is also the country with the world's worst inflation.

During part of 1986, inflation in Bolivia varied at a rate between 2,000 and 13,000 percent, if calculated on a yearly basis. Prices in the cities changed by the hour, and on some days the dollar would rise at the rate of more than 1 percent per hour. A piece of bread cost 150,000 pesos, and an American dollar bought between two and three million pesos on the black market. Large items such as airplane tickets were calculated in the billions of pesos, and on one occasion I helped a man carry a large box of money to pay for such a ticket. It took two professional counters half an hour to count the bills. Workers were paid in stacks of bills that were often half a meter high. Because Bolivia is too undeveloped to print its money, the importation of its own bills printed in West Germany and Brazil was one of the leading imports in the mid-1980s.

Ironically, by no longer being able to participate fully in the money economy, the villagers of Pocona who have chewed coca leaves for centuries now find it difficult to afford the leaves. The narcotics industry pays such a high price that the people of Pocona can afford only the rejected trash from the cocaine industry. Whether chewed or made into a tea, the coca produces a mild lift somewhat like a cup of coffee but without the jagged comedown that follows a coffee high. Coca also reduces hunger, thirst, headaches, stomach pains, and the type of altitude sickness known as *sorroche*.

Were this all, coca use might be viewed as merely a bad habit somewhat like drinking coffee, smoking cigarettes, or overindulging in chocolates, but unlike these practices coca actually has a number of marked health benefits. The coca leaf is very high in calcium. In a population with widespread lactose intolerance and in a country without a national system of milk distribution, this calcium source is very important. The calcium also severely reduces cavities in a population with virtually no dental services outside the city. Coca also contains large amounts of vitamins A, C, and D, which are often lacking in the starchy diets of the mountain peasants.

Without coca, and with an excess of corn that they cannot get to market, the people of Pocona now make more *chicha,* a form of home-fermented corn beer that tastes somewhat like the silage that American dairymen feed their cows. It is ironic that as an affluent generation of Americans are decreasing their consumption of alcohol in favor of drugs such as cocaine, the people of Pocona are drinking more alcohol to replace their traditional coca. *Chicha,* like most beers, is more nutritious than other kinds of distilled spirits but lacks the health benefits of the coca leaves. It also produces intoxication, something that no amount of coca leaves can do. Coca chewing is such a slow process and produces such a mild effect that a user would have to chew a bushel of leaves to equal the impact of one mixed drink or one snort of cocaine.

In many ways, the problems and complaints of Pocona echo those of any Third World country with a cash crop, particularly those caught in the boom-and-bust cycle characteristic of capitalist systems. Whether it is the sisal boom of the Yucatán, the banana boom of Central America, the rubber boom of Brazil, or the cocaine boom in Bolivia, the same pattern develops. Rural villages are depleted of their work forces. Family and traditional cultural patterns disintegrate. And the people are no longer able to afford certain local products that suddenly become valued in the West. This is what happened to Pocona.

Frequently, the part of a country that produces the boom crop benefits greatly, while other areas suffer greatly. If this were true in Bolivia, benefits accruing in the coca-producing area of the Chapare would outweigh the adjustment problems of such villages as Pocona. As it turns out, however, the Chapare has been even more adversely affected.

Most of the young men who go to the Chapare do not actually work in the coca fields. The coca bush originated in this area and does not require extensive care. One hectare can easily produce eight hundred kilograms of coca leaves in a year, but not much labor is needed to pick them. After harvesting, the leaves are dried in the sun for three to four days. Most of these tasks can easily be done by the farmer and his family. Wherever one goes in the Chapare one sees coca leaves spread out on large drying cloths. Old people or young children walk up and down these cloths, turning the drying leaves with their whisk brooms.

The need for labor, especially the labor of strong young men, comes in the first stage of cocaine production, in the reduction of large piles of leaves into a small quantity of *pasta,* or coca paste from which the active ingredient, cocaine, can then be refined. Three hundred to five hundred kilograms of leaves must be used to make one kilogram of pure cocaine. The leaves are made into *pasta* by soaking them in vats of kerosene and by applying salt, acetone, and sulfuric acid. To make the chemical reaction occur, someone must trample on the leaves for several days—a process very much like tromping on grapes to make wine, only longer. Because the corrosive mixture dissolves shoes or boots, the young men walk barefooted. These men are called *pisacocas* and usually work in the cool of the night, pounding the green slime with their feet. Each night the chemicals eat away more skin and very quickly open ulcers erupt. Some young men in the Chapare now have feet that are so diseased that they are incapable of standing, much less walking. So, instead, they use their hands to mix the *pasta,* but their hands are eaten away even faster than their feet. Thousands and possibly tens of thousands of young Bolivian men now look like lepers with permanently disfigured hands and feet. It is unlikely that any could return to Pocona and make a decent farmer.

Because this work is painful, the *pisacocas* smoke addictive cigarettes coated with *pasta.* This alleviates their pain and allows them to continue walking the coca throughout the night. The *pasta* is contaminated with chemical residues, and smoking it warps their minds as quickly as the acids eat their hands and feet. Like Mariana's brother, the users become irrational, easily angered, and frequently violent.

Once the boys are no longer able to mix coca because of their mental or their physical condition, they usually become unemployed. If their wounds heal, they may be able to work as loaders or haulers, carrying the cocaine or transporting the controlled chemicals used to process it. By and large, however, women and very small children, called *hormigas* (ants), are better at this work. Some of the young men then return home to their villages; others wander to Cochabamba, where they might live on the streets or try to earn money buying and selling dollars on the black market.

The cocaine manufacturers not only supply their workers with food and drugs, they keep them sexually supplied with young girls who serve as prostitutes as well. Bolivian health officials estimate that nearly half of the people living in the Chapare today have venereal disease. As the boys and girls working there return to their villages, they take these diseases with them. Increasing numbers of children born to infected mothers now have bodies covered in syphilitic sores. In 1985, a worse disease hit with the first case of AIDS. Soon after the victim died, a second victim was diagnosed.

In an effort to control its own drug problem, the United States is putting pressure on Bolivia to eradicate coca production in the Andean countries. The army invaded the Chapare during January of 1986, but after nearly three weeks of being surrounded by the workers in the narcotics industry and cut off from their supply bases, the army surrendered. In a nation the size of Texas and California combined, but with a population approximately the size of the city of Chicago, it is difficult for the government to control its own territory. Neither the Incas nor the Spanish conquistadores were ever able to conquer and administer the jungles of Bolivia, where there are still nomadic bands of Indians who have retreated deep into the jungle to escape Western encroachment. The army of the poorest government in South America is no better able to control this country than its predecessors. The government runs the cities, but the countryside and the jungles operate under their own laws.

One of the most significant effects of the coca trade and of the campaigns to eradicate it has come on the most remote Indians of the jungle area. As the campaign against drugs has pushed production into more inaccessible places and as the world demand has promoted greater cultivation of coca, the coca growers are moving into previously unexplored areas. A coca plantation has been opened along the Chimore river less than an hour's walk from one of the few surviving bands of Yuqui Indians. The Yuquis, famous for their eight-foot-long bows and their six-foot arrows, are now hovering on the brink of extinction. In the past year, the three bands of a few hundred Yuquis have lost eleven members in skirmishes with outsiders. In turn, they killed several outsiders this year and even shot the missionary who is their main champion against outside invaders.

According to the reports of missionaries, other Indian bands have been enlisted as workers in cocaine production and trafficking, making virtual slaves out of them. A Bolivian medical doctor explained to me that the Indians are fed the cocaine in their food as a way of keeping them working and preventing their escape. Through cocaine, the drug traffickers may be able to conquer and control these last remnants of the great Indian nations of the Americas. If so, they will accomplish what many have failed to do in the five-hundred-year campaign of Europeans to conquer the free Indians.

The fate of the Indians driven out of their homelands is shown in the case of Juan, a thirteen-year-old Indian boy from the Chimore river where the Yuquis live. I found him one night in a soup kitchen for street children operated in the corner of a potato warehouse by the Maryknoll priests.

Juan wore a bright orange undershirt that proclaimed in bold letters Fairfax District Public Schools. I sat with him at the table coated in potato dust while he ate his soup with his fellow street children, some of whom were as young as four years old. He told me what he could remember of his life on the Chimore; he did not know to which tribe he was born or what language he had spoken with his mother. It was difficult for Juan to talk about his Indian past in a country where it is a grave insult to be called an Indian. Rather than talk about the Chimore or the Chapare, he wanted to ask me questions because I was the first American he had ever met. Was I stronger than everyone else, because he had heard that Americans were the strongest people in the world? Did we really have wolves and bears in North America, and was I afraid of them? Had I been to the Chapare? Did I use cocaine?

In between his questions, I found out that Juan had come to Cochabamba several years ago with his mother. The two had fled the Chapare, but he did not know why. Once in the city they lived on the streets for a few years until his mother died, and he had been living alone ever since. He had become a *polilla* (moth), as they call such street boys. To earn money he washed cars and sold cigarettes laced with *pasta*. When he tired of talking about himself and asking about the animals of North America, he and his two friends made plans to go out to one of the nearby *pasta* villages the next day.

Both the Chapare (which supplied the land for growing coca) and highland villages such as Pocona (which supplied the labor) were suffering from the cocaine boom. Where, then, is the profit? The only other sites in Bolivia are the newly developed manufacturing towns where cocaine is refined. Whereas in the past most of this refining took place in Colombia, both the manufacturers and the traffickers find it easier and cheaper to have the work done in Bolivia, closer to the source of coca leaves and closer to much cheaper sources of labor. The strength of the Colombian government and its closeness to the United States also make the drug trafficking more difficult there than in Bolivia, with its weak, unstable government in La Paz.

Toco is one of the villages that has turned into a processing point for cocaine. Located at about the same altitude as Pocona but only a half-day by truck from the Chapare, Toco cannot grow coca, but the village is close enough to the source to become a major producer of the *pasta*. Traffickers bring in large shipments of coca leaves and work them in backyard "kitchens." Not only does Toco still have its young men at home and still have food and electricity, but it has work for a few hundred young men from other villages.

Unlike Pocona, for which there are only a few trucks each week, trucks flow in and out of Toco every day. Emblazoned with names such as Rambo, El Padrino (The Godfather), and Charles Bronson rather than the traditional truck names of San José, Virgen de Copacabana, or Flor de Urkupina, these are the newest and finest trucks found in Bolivia. Going in with a Bolivian physician and another anthropologist from the United States, I easily got a ride, along with a dozen Indians, on a truck which was hauling old car batteries splattered with what appeared to be vomit.

A few kilometers outside of Toco we were stopped by a large crowd of Indian peasants. Several dozen women sat around on the ground and in the road spinning yarn and knitting. Most of the women had babies tied to their shoulders in the brightly colored *awayu* cloth, which the women use to carry everything from potatoes to lambs. Men stood around with farm tools, which they now used to block the roads. The men brandished their machetes and rakes at us, accusing us all of being smugglers and *pisacocas*. Like the Indians on the truck with us, the three of us stood silent and expressionless in the melee.

The hostile peasants were staging an ad hoc strike against the coca trade. They had just had their own fields of potatoes washed away in a flash flood. Now without food and without money to replant, they were demanding that someone help them or they would disrupt all traffic to and from Toco. Shouting at us, several of them climbed on board the truck. Moving among the nervous passengers, they checked for a shipment of coca leaves, kerosene, acid, or anything else that might be a part of the coca trade. Having found nothing, they reluctantly let us pass with stern warnings not to return with cocaine or *pasta*. A few weeks after our encounter with the strikers, their strike ended and most of the men went off to look for work in the Chapare and in Toco; without a crop, the cocaine traffic was their only hope of food for the year.

On our arrival in Toco we found out that the batteries loaded with us in the back of the truck had been hollowed out and filled with acid to be used in making *pasta*. *Chicha* vomit had been smeared around to discourage anyone from checking them. After removal of the acid, the same batteries were then filled with plastic bags of cocaine to be smuggled out of Toco and into the town of Cliza and on to Cochabamba and the outside world.

Toco is an expanding village with new cement-block buildings going up on the edge of town and a variety of large plumbing pipes, tanks, and drains being installed. It also has a large number of motorcycles and cars. By Bolivian standards it is a rich village, but it is still poorer than the average village in Mexico or Brazil. Soon after our arrival in Toco, we were followed by a handful of men wanting to sell us *pasta*, and within a few minutes the few had grown to nearly fifty young men anxious to assist us. Most of them were on foot, but some of them circled us in motorcycles, and many of them were armed with guns and machetes. They became suspicious and then openly hostile when we convinced them that we did not want to buy *pasta*. To escape them we took refuge in the home of an Indian family and waited for the mob to disperse.

When we tried to leave the village a few hours later, we were trapped by a truckload of young men who did not release us until they had checked with everyone we had met with in the village. They wondered why we were there if not to buy *pasta*. We were rescued by the doctor who accompanied us; she happened to be the niece of a popular Quechua writer. Evoking the memory of her uncle who had done so much for the Quechua people, she convinced the villagers of Toco that we were Bolivian doctors who worked with her in Cochabamba, and that we were not foreigners coming to buy *pasta* or to spy on them. An old veteran who claimed that he had served in the Chaco War with her uncle vouched for us, but in return for having saved us he then wanted us to buy *pasta* from him.

The wealth generated by the coca trade from Bolivia is easy to see. It is in the European cars cruising the streets of Cochabamba and Santa Cruz, and in the nice houses in the suburbs. It is in the motorcycles and jeeps in Toco, Cliza, and Trinidad. The poverty is difficult to see because it is in the remote villages like Pocona, among the impoverished miners in the village of Porco, and intertwined in the lives of peasants throughout the highland districts of Potosí and Oruro. But it is in communities such as Pocona that 70 percent of the population of Bolivia lives. For every modern home built with cocaine money in Cochabamba, a tin mine lies abandoned in Potosí that lost many of its miners when the world price for tin fell and they had to go to the Chapare for food. For every new car in Santa Cruz or every new motorcycle in Toco, a whole village is going hungry in the mountains.

The money for coca does not go to the Bolivians. It goes to the criminal organizations that smuggle the drugs out of the country and into the United States and Europe. A gram of pure cocaine on the streets of Cochabamba costs five dollars; the same gram on the streets of New York, Paris, or Berlin costs over a hundred dollars. The price increase occurs outside Bolivia.

The financial differential is evident in the case of the American housewife and mother sentenced to the Cochabamba prison after being caught with six and a half kilograms of cocaine at the airport. Like all the other women in the prison, she now earns money washing laundry by hand at a cold-water tap in the middle of the prison yard. She receives the equivalent of twenty cents for each pair of pants she washes, dries, and irons. In Bolivian prisons, the prisoner has to furnish his or her own food, clothes, medical attention, and even furniture.

She was paid five thousand dollars to smuggle the cocaine out of Bolivia to the Caribbean. Presumably someone else was then to be paid even more to smuggle it into the United States or Europe. The money that the American housewife received to smuggle the cocaine out of the country would pay the salary of eighty *pisacocas* for a month. It would also pay the monthly wages of two hundred fifty Bolivian schoolteachers, who earn the equivalent of twenty U.S. dollars per month in pay. Even though her price seemed high by Bolivian standards, it is a small part of the final money generated by the drugs. When cut and sold on the streets of the United States, her shipment of cocaine would probably bring in five to seven million dollars. Of that amount, however, only about five hundred dollars goes to the Bolivian farmer.

The peasant in the Chapare growing the coca earns three times as much for a field of coca as he would for a field of papayas. But he is only the first in a long line of people and transactions that brings the final product of cocaine to the streets of the West. At the end of the line, cocaine sells for four to five times its weight in gold.

The United States government made all aid programs and loans to Bolivia dependent on the country's efforts to destroy coca. This produces programs in which Bolivian troops go into the most accessible areas and uproot a few fields of aging or diseased coca plants. Visiting drug-enforcement agents from the United States together with American congressmen applaud, make their reports on the escalating war against drugs, and then retire to a city hotel where they drink hot cups of coca tea and cocktails.

These programs hurt primarily the poor farmer who tries to make a slightly better living by growing coca rather than papayas. The raids on the fields and cocaine factories usually lead to the imprisonment of ulcerated *pisacocas* and women and children *hormigas* from villages throughout Bolivia. Local authorities present the burned fields and full prisons to Washington visitors as proof that the Bolivian government has taken a hard stance against drug trafficking.

International crime figures with bank accounts in New York and Zurich get the money. Bolivia ends up with hunger in its villages, young men with their hands and feet permanently maimed, higher rates of venereal disease, chronic food shortages, less kerosene, higher school dropout rates, increased drug addiction, and a worthless peso.

REVIEW QUESTIONS

1. List and describe the major effects of the cocaine trade on rural Bolivian life.
2. Why have the production of coca and the manufacture of cocaine created a health hazard in Bolivia?
3. Why has the cocaine trade benefited the Bolivian economy so little?
4. How has the cocaine trade disrupted village social organization in Bolivia?

VI

KINSHIP AND FAMILY

Social life is essential to human existence. We remain in the company of other people from the day we are born to the time of our death. People teach us to speak. They show us how to relate to our surroundings. They give us the help and the support we need to achieve personal security and mental well-being. Alone, we are relatively frail, defenseless primates; in groups we are astonishingly adaptive and powerful. Yet despite these advantages, well-organized human societies are difficult to achieve. Some species manage to produce social organization genetically. But people are not like bees or ants. We lack the genetically coded directions for behavior that make these insects successful social animals. Although we seem to inherit a general need for social approval, we also harbor individual interests and ambitions that can block or destroy close social ties. To overcome these divisive tendencies, human groups organize around several principles designed to foster cooperation and group loyalty. Kinship is among the strongest of these.

We may define *kinship* as the complex system of culturally defined social relationships based on marriage (the principle of *affinity*) and birth (the principle of *consanguinity*). The study of kinship involves consideration of such principles as descent, kinship status and roles, family and other kinship groups, marriage, and residence. In fact, kinship has been such an important organizing factor in many of the societies studied by anthropologists that it is one of the most elaborate areas of the discipline. What are some of the important concepts?

First is descent. *Descent* is based on the notion of a common heritage. It is a cultural rule tying together people on the basis of reputed common ancestry. Descent functions to guide inheritance, group loyalty, and, above all, the formation of families and extended kinship groups.

There are three main rules of descent. One is *patrilineal descent*, which links relatives through males only. In patrilineal systems, females are part of their father's line, but their children descend from the husbands.

Matrilineal descent links relatives through females only. Males belong to their mother's line; the children of males descend from the wives. *Bilateral descent* links a person to kin through both males and females simultaneously. We Americans are said to have bilateral descent, whereas most of the people in India, Japan, and China are patrilineal. Such groups as the Apache and Trobriand Islanders are matrilineal.

Descent often defines groups called, not surprisingly, *descent groups*. One of these is the *lineage*, a localized group that is based on unilineal (patrilineal or matrilineal) descent and that usually has some corporate powers. In the Marshall Islands, for example, the matriline holds rights to land, which, in turn, it allots to its members. Lineages in India sometimes hold rights to land but are a more important arena for other kinds of decisions such as marriage. Lineage mates must be consulted about the advisability, timing, and arrangements for weddings.

Clans are composed of lineages. Clan members believe they are all descended from a common ancestor, but because clans are larger, members cannot trace their genealogical relationships to everyone in the group. In some societies, clans may be linked together in even larger groups called *phratries*. Because phratries are usually large, the feeling of common descent they offer is weaker.

Ramages, or cognatic kin groups, are based on bilateral descent. They often resemble lineages in size and function but provide more recruiting flexibility. An individual can choose membership from among several ramages where he or she has relatives.

Another important kinship group is the family. This unit is more difficult to define than we may think, because people have found so many different ways to organize "familylike" groups. Here we will follow anthropologist George P. Murdock's approach and define the *family* as a kin group consisting of at least one married couple sharing the same residence with their children and performing sexual, reproductive, economic, and educational functions. A *nuclear family* consists of a single married couple and their children. An *extended family* consists of two or more married couples and their children. Extended families have a quality all their own and are often found in societies where family performance and honor are paramount to the reputation of individual family members. Extended families are most commonly based on patrilineal descent. Women marry into such families and must establish themselves among the line members and other women who live there.

Marriage, the socially approved union of a man and a woman, is a second major principle of kinship. The regulation of marriage takes elaborate forms from one society to the next. Marriage may be *exogamous*, meaning marriage outside any particular named group, or *endogamous*, indicating the opposite. Bhil tribals of India, for example, are clan and village exogamous (they should marry outside these groups), but tribal endogamous (they should marry other Bhils).

Marriage may also be *monogamous,* where it is preferred that only one woman should be married to one man at a time, or *polygamous,* meaning that one person may be married to more than one person simultaneously. There are two kinds of polygamy, *polygyny,* the marriage of one man with more than one woman simultaneously, and *polyandry,* the marriage of one woman with more than one man.

Many anthropologists view marriage as a system of alliances between families and descent lines. Viewed in these terms, rules such as endogamy and exogamy can be explained as devices to link or internally strengthen various kinship groups. The *incest taboo,* a legal rule that prohibits sexual intercourse or marriage between particular classes of kin, is often explained as a way to extend alliances between kin groups.

Finally, the regulation of marriage falls to the parents and close relatives of eligible young people in many societies. These elders concern themselves with more than wedding preparations; they must also see to it that young people marry appropriately, which means they consider the reputation of prospective spouses and their families' economic strength and social rank.

The selections in Part VI illustrate several aspects of kinship systems. In the first article, Nancy Scheper-Hughes looks at the relationship that poor Brazilian mothers have with their infants. Because babies die so often, mothers must delay forming attachments until their children show they can survive. The second article, by Melvyn Goldstein, looks at a rare form of marriage—polyandry—and shows why, despite other choices, Tibetan brothers often choose to share a single wife among them. The role of the incest taboo in forging marriage alliances and its restricted application in modern society is the subject of the third article, by Yehudi Cohen. If its functions are met in other ways, he concludes, the taboo may disappear altogether. Finally, Margery Wolf looks at the structure of the Taiwanese extended family from the point of view of the women who constitute it. It is only by establishing her own uterine family that a woman can gain power within the patrilineal group.

KEY TERMS

kinship	family
affinity	extended family
consanguinity	nuclear family
descent	marriage
patrilineal descent	exogamy
matrilineal descent	endogamy
bilateral descent	monogamy
descent groups	polygamy

lineage   polygyny
clan   polyandry
phratry   incest taboo
ramage

READINGS IN THIS SECTION

17

Mother's Love:
Death Without Weeping

Nancy Scheper-Hughes

Kinship systems are based on marriage and birth. Both, anthropologists assume, create ties that can link kin into close, cooperative, enduring structures. What happens to such ties, however, in the face of severe hardship imposed by grinding poverty and urban migration? Can we continue to assume, for example, that there will be a close bond between mother and child? This is the question pursued by Nancy Scheper-Hughes in the following article about the mother-infant relationship among poor women in a Brazilian shantytown. The author became interested in the question following a "baby die-off" in the town of Bom Jesus in 1965. She noticed that mothers seemed to take these events casually. After 25 years of research in the Alto do Cruzeiro shantytown there, she has come to see such indifference as a cultural response to high rates of infant death due to poverty and malnutrition. Mothers, and surrounding social institutions such as the Catholic Church, expect babies to die easily. Mothers concentrate their support on babies who are "fighters" and let themselves grow attached to their children only when they are reasonably sure that

*the offspring will survive. The article also provides an excellent illus-
tration of what happens to kinship systems in the face of poverty and
social dislocation. Such conditions may easily result in the formation
of woman-headed families, and in a lack of the extended kinship networks so often found in more stable, rural societies.*

I have seen death without weeping
The destiny of the Northeast is death
Cattle they kill
To the people they do something worse

—ANONYMOUS BRAZILIAN SINGER (1965)

"Why do the church bells ring so often?" I asked Nailza de Ar-
ruda soon after I moved into a corner of her tiny mud-
walled hut near the top of the shantytown called the Alto do Cruzeiro
(Crucifix Hill). I was then a Peace Corps volunteer and a community de-
velopment/health worker. It was the dry and blazing hot summer of 1965,
the months following the military coup in Brazil, and save for the rusty,
clanging bells of N. S. das Dores Church, an eerie quiet had settled over the
market town that I call Bom Jesus da Mata. Beneath the quiet, however,
there was chaos and panic. "It's nothing," replied Nailza, "just another little angel gone to heaven."

Nailza had sent more than her share of little angels to heaven, and
sometimes at night I could hear her engaged in a muffled but passionate
discourse with one of them, two-year-old Joana. Joana's photograph, taken
as she lay propped up in her tiny cardboard coffin, her eyes open, hung on
a wall next to one of Nailza and Ze Antonio taken on the day they eloped.

Nailza could barely remember the other infants and babies who came
and went in close succession. Most had died unnamed and were hastily
baptized in their coffins. Few lived more than a month or two. Only Joana,
properly baptized in church at the close of her first year and placed under
the protection of a powerful saint, Joan of Arc, had been expected to live.
And Nailza had dangerously allowed herself to love the little girl.

In addressing the dead child, Nailza's voice would range from tearful
imploring to angry recrimination: "Why did you leave me? Was your patron saint so greedy that she could not allow me one child on this earth?"
Ze Antonio advised me to ignore Nailza's odd behavior, which he understood as a kind of madness that, like the birth and death of children, came
and went. Indeed, the premature birth of a stillborn son some months later
"cured" Nailza of her "inappropriate" grief, and the day came when she
removed Joana's photo and carefully packed it away.

More than fifteen years elapsed before I returned to the Alto do
Cruzeiro, and it was anthropology that provided the vehicle of my return.
Since 1982 I have returned several times in order to pursue a problem that
first attracted my attention in the 1960s. My involvement with the people

of the Alto do Cruzeiro now spans a quarter of a century and three generations of parenting in a community where mothers and daughters are
often simultaneously pregnant.

The Alto do Cruzeiro is one of three shantytowns surrounding the
large market town of Bom Jesus in the sugar plantation zone of Pernam-
buco in Northeast Brazil, one of the many zones of neglect that have
emerged in the shadow of the now tarnished economic miracle of Brazil.
For the women and children of the Alto do Cruzeiro the only miracle is
that some of them have managed to stay alive at all.

The Northeast is a region of vast proportions (approximately twice the
size of Texas) and of equally vast social and developmental problems. The
nine states that make up the region are the poorest in the country and are
representative of the Third World within a dynamic and rapidly industri-
alizing nation. Despite waves of migrations from the interior to the teem-
ing shantytowns of coastal cities, the majority still live in rural areas on
farms and ranches, sugar plantations and mills.

Life expectancy in the Northeast is only forty years, largely because of
the appallingly high rate of infant and child mortality. Approximately one
million children in Brazil under the age of five die each year. The children
of the Northeast, especially those born in shantytowns on the periphery of
urban life, are at a very high risk of death. In these areas, children are born
without the traditional protection of breast-feeding, subsistence gardens,
stable marriages, and multiple adult caretakers that exists in the interior.
In the hillside shantytowns that spring up around cities or, in this case, interior market towns, marriages are brittle, single parenting is the norm,
and women are frequently forced into the shadow economy of domestic
work in the homes of the rich or into unprotected and oftentimes "scab"
wage labor on the surrounding sugar plantations, where they clear land
for planting and weed for a pittance, sometimes less than a dollar a day.
The women of the Alto may not bring their babies with them into the
homes of the wealthy, where the often-sick infants are considered sources
of contamination, and they cannot carry the little ones to the riverbanks
where they wash clothes because the river is heavily infested with schis-
tosomes and other deadly parasites. Nor can they carry their young children to the plantations, which are often several miles away. At wages of a
dollar a day, the women of the Alto cannot hire baby sitters. Older children who are not in school will sometimes serve as somewhat indifferent
caretakers. But any child not in school is also expected to find wage work.
In most cases, babies are simply left at home alone, the door securely fas-
tened. And so many also die alone and unattended.

Bom Jesus da Mata, centrally located in the plantation zone of Per-
nambuco, is within commuting distance of several sugar plantations and
mills. Consequently, Bom Jesus has been a magnet for rural workers
forced off their small subsistence plots by large landowners wanting to use
every available piece of land for sugar cultivation. Initially, the rural mi-

grants to Bom Jesus were squatters who were given tacit approval by the mayor to put up temporary straw huts on each of the three hills overlooking the town. The Alto do Cruzeiro is the oldest, the largest, and the poorest of the shantytowns. Over the past three decades many of the original migrants have become permanent residents, and the primitive and temporary straw huts have been replaced by small homes (usually of two rooms) made of wattle and daub, sometimes covered with plaster. The more affluent residents use bricks and tiles. In most Alto homes, dangerous kerosene lamps have been replaced by light bulbs. The once tattered rural garb, often fashioned from used sugar sacking, has likewise been replaced by store-bought clothes, often castoffs from a wealthy *patrão* (boss). The trappings are modern, but the hunger, sickness, and death that they conceal are traditional, deeply rooted in a history of feudalism, exploitation, and institutionalized dependency.

My research agenda never wavered. The questions I addressed first crystallized during a veritable "die-off" of Alto babies during a severe drought in 1965. The food and water shortages and the political and economic chaos occasioned by the military coup were reflected in the handwritten entries of births and deaths in the dusty, yellowed pages of the ledger books kept at the public registry office in Bom Jesus. More than 350 babies died in the Alto during 1965 alone—this from a shantytown population of little more than 5,000. But that wasn't what surprised me. There were reasons enough for the deaths in the miserable conditions of shantytown life. What puzzled me was the seeming indifference of Alto women to the death of their infants, and their willingness to attribute to their own tiny offspring an aversion to life that made their death seem wholly natural, indeed all but anticipated.

Although I found that it was possible, and hardly difficult, to rescue infants and toddlers from death by diarrhea and dehydration with a simple sugar, salt, and water solution (even bottled Coca-Cola worked fine), it was more difficult to enlist a mother herself in the rescue of a child she perceived as ill-fated for life or better off dead, or to convince her to take back into her threatened and besieged home a baby she had already come to think of as an angel rather than as a son or daughter.

I learned that the high expectancy of death, and the ability to face child death with stoicism and equanimity, produced patterns of nurturing that differentiated between those infants thought of as thrivers and survivors and those thought of as born already "wanting to die." The survivors were nurtured, while stigmatized, doomed infants were left to die, as mothers say, *a mingua*, "of neglect." Mothers stepped back and allowed nature to take its course. This pattern, which I call mortal selective neglect, is called passive infanticide by anthropologist Marvin Harris. The Alto situation, although culturally specific in the form that it takes, is not unique to Third World shantytown communities and may have its correlates in our own impoverished urban communities in some cases of "failure to thrive" infants.

I use as an example the story of Zezinho, the thirteen-month-old tod-dler of one of my neighbors, Lourdes. I became involved with Zezinho when I was called in to help Lourdes in the delivery of another child, this one a fair and robust little tyke with a lusty cry. I noted that while Lourdes showed great interest in the newborn, she totally ignored Zezinho who, wasted and severely malnourished, was curled up in a fetal position on a piece of urine- and feces-soaked cardboard placed under his mother's hammock. Eyes open and vacant, mouth slack, the little boy seemed doomed.

When I carried Zezinho up to the community day-care center at the top of the hill, the Alto women who took turns caring for one another's children (in order to free themselves for part-time work in the cane fields or washing clothes) laughed at my efforts to save Ze, agreeing with Lour-des that here was a baby without a ghost of a chance. Leave him alone, they cautioned. It makes no sense to fight with death. But I did do battle with Ze, and after several weeks of force-feeding (malnourished babies lose their interest in food), Ze began to succumb to my ministrations. He acquired some flesh across his taut chest bones, learned to sit up, and even tried to smile. When he seemed well enough, I returned him to Lourdes in her miserable scrap-material lean-to, but not without guilt about what I had done. I wondered whether returning Ze was at all fair to Lourdes and to his little brother. But I was busy and washed my hands of the matter. And Lourdes did seem more interested in Ze now that he was looking more human.

When I returned in 1982, there was Lourdes among the women who formed my sample of Alto mothers—still struggling to put together some semblance of life for a now grown Ze and her five other surviving chil-dren. Much was made of my reunion with Ze in 1982, and everyone en-joyed retelling the story of Ze's rescue and of how his mother had given him up for dead. Ze would laugh the loudest when told how I had had to force-feed him like a fiesta turkey. There was no hint of guilt on the part of Lourdes and no resentment on the part of Ze. In fact, when questioned in private as to who was the best friend he ever had in life, Ze took a long drag on his cigarette and answered without a trace of irony, "Why my mother, of course!" "But of course," I replied.

Part of learning how to mother in the Alto do Cruzeiro is learning when to let go of a child who shows that it "wants" to die or that it has no "knack" or no "taste" for life. Another part is learning when it is safe to let oneself love a child. Frequent child death remains a powerful shaper of maternal thinking and practice. In the absence of firm expectation that a child will survive, mother love as we conceptualize it (whether in popular terms or in the psychobiological notion of maternal bonding) is attenuated and delayed with consequences for infant survival. In an environment al-ready precarious to young life, the emotional detachment of mothers to-ward some of their babies contributes even further to the spiral of high mortality—high fertility in a kind of macabre lock-step dance of death.

The average woman of the Alto experiences 9.5 pregnancies, 3.5 child deaths, and 1.5 stillbirths. Seventy percent of all child deaths in the Alto occur in the first six months of life, and 82 percent by the end of the first year. Of all deaths in the community each year, about 45 percent are of children under the age of five.

Women of the Alto distinguish between child deaths understood as natural (caused by diarrhea and communicable diseases) and those resulting from sorcery, the evil eye, or other magical or supernatural afflictions. They also recognize a large category of infant deaths seen as fated and inevitable. These hopeless cases are classified by mothers under the folk terminology "child sickness" or "child attack." Women say that there are at least fourteen different types of hopeless child sickness, but most can be subsumed under two categories—chronic and acute. The chronic cases refer to infants who are born small and wasted. They are deathly pale, mothers say, as well as weak and passive. They demonstrate no vital force, no liveliness. They do not suck vigorously; they hardly cry. Such babies can be this way at birth or they can be born sound but soon show no resistance, no "fight" against the common crises of infancy: diarrhea, respiratory infections, tropical fevers.

The acute cases are those doomed infants who die suddenly and violently. They are taken by stealth overnight, often following convulsions that bring on head banging, shaking, grimacing, and shrieking. Women say it is horrible to look at such a baby. If the infant begins to foam at the mouth or gnash its teeth or go rigid with its eyes turned back inside its head, there is absolutely no hope. The infant is "put aside"—left alone—often on the floor in a back room, and allowed to die. These symptoms (which accompany high fevers, dehydration, third-stage malnutrition, and encephalitis) are equated by Alto women with madness, epilepsy, and worst of all, rabies, which is greatly feared and highly stigmatized.

Most of the infants presented to me as suffering from chronic child sickness were tiny, wasted famine victims, while those labeled as victims of acute child attack seemed to be infants suffering from the deliriums of high fever or the convulsions that can accompany electrolyte imbalance in dehydrated babies.

Local midwives and traditional healers, praying women, as they are called, advise Alto women on when to allow a baby to die. One midwife explained: "If I can see that a baby was born unfortuitously, I tell the mother that she need not wash the infant or give it a cleansing tea. I tell her just to dust the infant with baby powder and wait for it to die." Allowing nature to take its course is not seen as sinful by these often very devout Catholic women. Rather, it is understood as cooperating with God's plan.

Often I have been asked how consciously women of the Alto behave in this regard. I would have to say that consciousness is always shifting between allowed and disallowed levels of awareness. For example, I was awakened early one morning in 1987 by two neighborhood children who had been sent to fetch me to a hastily organized wake for a two-month-old infant whose mother I had unsuccessfully urged to breast-feed. The infant was being sustained on sugar water, which the mother referred to as *soro* (serum), using a medical term for the infant's starvation regime in light of his chronic diarrhea. I had cautioned the mother that an infant could not live on *soro* forever.

The two girls urged me to console the young mother by telling her that it was "too bad" that her infant was so weak that Jesus had to take him. They were coaching me in proper Alto etiquette. I agreed, of course, but asked, "And what do *you* think?" Xoxa, the eleven-year-old, looked down at her dusty flip-flops and blurted out, "Oh, Dona Nanci, that baby never got enough to eat, but you must never say that!" And so the death of hungry babies remains one of the best kept secrets of life in Bom Jesus da Mata.

Most victims are waked quickly and with a minimum of ceremony. No tears are shed, and the neighborhood children form a tiny procession, carrying the baby to the town graveyard where it will join a multitude of others. Although a few fresh flowers may be scattered over the tiny grave, no stone or wooden cross will mark the place, and the same spot will be reused within a few months' time. The mother will never visit the grave, which soon becomes an anonymous one.

What, then, can be said of these women? What emotions, what sentiments motivate them? How are they able to do what, in fact, must be done? What does mother love mean in this inhospitable context? Are grief, mourning, and melancholia present, although deeply repressed? If so, where shall we look for them? And if not, how are we to understand the moral visions and moral sensibilities that guide their actions?

I have been criticized more than once for presenting an unflattering portrait of poor Brazilian women, women who are, after all, themselves the victims of severe social and institutional neglect. I have described these women as allowing some of their children to die, as if this were an unnatural and inhuman act rather than, as I would assert, the way any one of us might act, reasonably and rationally, under similarly desperate conditions. Perhaps I have not emphasized enough the real pathogens in this environment of high risk: poverty, deprivation, sexism, chronic hunger, and economic exploitation. If mother love is, as many psychologists and some feminists believe, a seemingly natural and universal maternal script, what does it mean to women for whom scarcity, loss, sickness, and deprivation have made that love frantic and robbed them of their grief, seeming to turn their hearts to stone?

Throughout much of human history—as in a great deal of the impoverished Third World today—women have had to give birth and to nurture children under ecological conditions and social arrangements hostile to child survival, as well as to their own well-being. Under circumstances of high childhood mortality, patterns of selective neglect and passive infanticide may be seen as active survival strategies.

They also seem to be fairly common practices historically and across cultures. In societies characterized by high childhood mortality and by a correspondingly high (replacement) fertility, cultural practices of infant and child care tend to be organized primarily around survival goals. But what this means is a pragmatic recognition that not all of one's children can be expected to live. The nervousness about child survival in areas of northeast Brazil, northern India, or Bangladesh, where a 30 percent or 40 percent mortality rate in the first years of life is common, can lead to forms of delayed attachment and a casual or benign neglect that serves to weed out the worst bets so as to enhance the life chances of healthier siblings, including those yet to be born. Practices similar to those that I am describing have been recorded for parts of Africa, India, and Central America.

Life in the Alto do Cruzeiro resembles nothing so much as a battlefield or an emergency room in an overcrowded inner-city public hospital. Consequently, morality is guided by a kind of "lifeboat ethics," the morality of triage. The seemingly studied indifference toward the suffering of some of their infants, conveyed in such sayings as "little critters have no feelings," is understandable in light of these women's obligation to carry on with their reproductive and nurturing lives.

In their slowness to anthropomorphize and personalize their infants, everything is mobilized so as to prevent maternal overattachment and, therefore, grief at death. The bereaved mother is told not to cry, that her tears will dampen the wings of her little angel so that she cannot fly up to her heavenly home. Grief at the death of an angel is not only inappropriate, it is a symptom of madness and of a profound lack of faith.

Infant death becomes routine in an environment in which death is anticipated and bets are hedged. While the routinization of death in the context of shantytown life is not hard to understand, and quite possible to empathize with, its routinization in the formal institutions of public life in Bom Jesus is not as easy to accept uncritically. Here the social production of indifference takes on a different, even a malevolent, cast.

In a society where triplicates of every form are required for the most banal events (registering a car, for example), the registration of infant and child death is informal, incomplete, and rapid. It requires no documentation, takes less than five minutes, and demands no witnesses other than office clerks. No questions are asked concerning the circumstances of the death, and the cause of death is left blank, unquestioned and unexamined. A neighbor, grandmother, older sibling, or common-law husband may register the death. Since most infants die at home, there is no question of a medical record.

From the registry office, the parent proceeds to the town hall, where the mayor will give him or her a voucher for a free baby coffin. The full-time municipal coffinmaker cannot tell you exactly how many baby coffins are dispatched each week. It varies, he says, with the seasons. There are more needed during the drought months and during the big festivals of Carnaval and Christmas and São Joao's Day because people are too busy, he supposes, to take their babies to the clinic. Record keeping is sloppy.

Similarly, there is a failure on the part of city-employed doctors working at two free clinics to recognize the malnutrition of babies who are weighed, measured, and immunized without comment and as if they were not, in fact, anemic, stunted, fussy, and irritated starvation babies. At best the mothers are told to pick up free vitamins or a health "tonic" at the municipal chambers. At worst, clinic personnel will give tranquilizers and sleeping pills to quiet the hungry cries of "sick-to-death" Alto babies.

The church, too, contributes to the routinization of, and indifference toward, child death. Traditionally, the local Catholic church taught patience and resignation to domestic tragedies that were said to reveal the imponderable workings of God's will. If an infant died suddenly, it was because a particular saint had claimed the child. The infant would be an angel in the service of his or her heavenly patron. It would be wrong, a sign of a lack of faith, to weep for a child with such good fortune. The infant funeral was, in the past, an event celebrated with joy. Today, however, under the new regime of "liberation theology," the bells of N. S. das Dores parish church no longer peal for the death of Alto babies, and no priest accompanies the procession of angels to the cemetery where their bodies are disposed of casually and without ceremony. Children bury children in Bom Jesus da Mata. In this most Catholic of communities, the coffin is handed to the disabled and irritable municipal gravedigger, who often chides the children for one reason or another. It may be that the coffin is larger than expected and the gravedigger can find no appropriate space. The children do not wait for the gravedigger to complete his task. No prayers are recited and no sign of the cross made as the tiny coffin goes into its shallow grave.

When I asked the local priest, Padre Marcos, about the lack of church ceremony surrounding infant and childhood death today in Bom Jesus, he replied: "In the old days, child death was richly celebrated. But those were the baroque customs of a conservative church that wallowed in death and misery. The new church is a church of hope and joy. We no longer celebrate the death of child angels. We try to tell mothers that Jesus doesn't want all the dead babies they send him." Similarly, the new church has changed its baptismal customs, now often refusing to baptize dying babies brought to the back door of a church or rectory. The mothers are scolded by the church attendants and told to go home and take care of their sick babies. Baptism, they are told, is for the living; it is not to be confused with the sacrament of extreme unction, which is the anointing of the dying. And so it appears to the women of the Alto that even the church has turned away from them, denying the traditional comfort of folk Catholicism.

The contemporary Catholic church is caught in the clutches of a double bind. The new theology of liberation imagines a kingdom of God on earth based on justice and equality, a world without hunger, sickness, or childhood mortality. At the same time, the church has not changed its official position on sexuality and reproduction, including its sanctions against birth control, abortion, and sterilization. The padre of Bom Jesus da Mata recognizes this contradiction intuitively, although he shies away from discussions on the topic, saying that he prefers to leave questions of family planning to the discretion and the "good consciences" of his impoverished parishioners. But this, of course, sidesteps the extent to which those good consciences have been shaped by traditional church teachings in Bom Jesus, especially by his recent predecessors. Hence, we can begin to see that the seeming indifference of Alto mothers toward the death of some of their infants is but a pale reflection of the official indifference of church and state to the plight of poor women and children.

Nonetheless, the women of Bom Jesus are survivors. One woman, Biu, told me her life history, returning again and again to the themes of child death, her first husband's suicide, abandonment by her father and later by her second husband, and all the other losses and disappointments she had suffered in her long forty-five years. She concluded with great force, reflecting on the days of Carnaval '88 that were fast approaching:

> No, Dona Nanci, I won't cry, and I won't waste my life thinking about it from morning to night. . . . Can I argue with God for the state that I'm in? No! And so I'll dance and I'll jump and I'll play Carnaval! And yes, I'll laugh and people will wonder at a *pobre* like me who can have such a good time.

And no one did blame Biu for dancing in the streets during the four days of Carnaval—not even on Ash Wednesday, the day following Carnaval '88 when we all assembled hurriedly to assist in the burial of Mercea, Biu's beloved *casula,* her last-born daughter who had died at home of pneumonia during the festivities. The rest of the family barely had time to change out of their costumes. Severino, the child's uncle and godfather, sprinkled holy water over the little angel while he prayed: "Mercea, I don't know whether you were called, taken, or thrown out of this world. But look down at us from your heavenly home with tenderness, with pity, and with mercy." So be it.

REVIEW QUESTIONS

1. What did Scheper-Hughes notice about mother's reactions during the baby die-off of 1965 in Bom Jesus, Brazil?
2. How do poor Brazilian mothers react to their infants' illnesses and death? How do other institutions, such as the church, clinic, and civil authorities respond? Give examples.
3. How does Scheper-Hughes explain the apparent indifference of mothers to the death of their infants?
4. What does the indifference of mothers to the deaths of their children say about basic human nature, especially the mother-child bond?

18

Polyandry: When Brothers Take a Wife

Melvyn C. Goldstein

Many of the world's societies permit polygamy, the marriage of an individual to more than one spouse. The most common form of polygamy is polygyny, an arrangement in which a man marries more than one wife. Polygyny may exist for many reasons, not the least of which is its relationship to the substantial economic contributions of women. But there is a second kind of polygamy called polyandry, organized around the marriage of a woman to more than one husband, and its causes may seem less clear. In this article, Melvyn Goldstein describes the fraternal polyandry practiced by Tibetans living in Northern Nepal and seeks to explain why, despite having a choice of marriage forms including monogamy and polygyny, men and women often choose this rare form of marriage. He argues that, by marrying a single wife, a group of brothers can more easily preserve their family resources, whereas monogamous or polygynous marriage usually costs a man his inheritance and requires him to make a fresh start.

Originally published as "When Brothers Take a Wife." With permission from *Natural History*, March 1987. Copyright © the American Museum of Natural History, 1987.

Eager to reach home. Dorje drives his yaks hard over the seventeen-thousand-foot mountain pass, stopping only once to rest. He and his two older brothers, Pema and Sonam, are jointly marrying a woman from the next village in a few weeks, and he has to help with the preparations.

Dorje, Pema, and Sonam are Tibetans living in Limi, a two-hundred-square-mile area in the northwest corner of Nepal, across the border from Tibet. The form of marriage they are about to enter—fraternal polyandry in anthropological parlance—is one of the world's rarest forms of marriage but is not uncommon in Tibetan society, where it has been practiced from time immemorial. For many Tibetan social strata, it traditionally represented the ideal form of marriage and family.

The mechanics of fraternal polyandry are simple. Two, three, four, or more brothers jointly take a wife, who leaves her home to come and live with them. Traditionally, marriage was arranged by parents, with children, particularly females, having little or no say. This is changing somewhat nowadays, but it is still unusual for children to marry without their parents' consent. Marriage ceremonies vary by income and region and range from all the brothers sitting together as grooms to only the eldest one formally doing so. The age of the brothers plays an important role in determining this: very young brothers almost never participate in actual marriage ceremonies, although they typically join the marriage when they reach their midteens.

The eldest brother is normally dominant in terms of authority, that is, in managing the household, but all the brothers share the work and participate as sexual partners. Tibetan males and females do not find the sexual aspect of sharing a spouse the least bit unusual, repulsive, or scandalous, and the norm is for the wife to treat all the brothers the same.

Offspring are treated similarly. There is no attempt to link children biologically to particular brothers, and a brother shows no favoritism toward his child even if he knows he is the real father because, for example, his other brothers were away at the time the wife became pregnant. The children, in turn, consider all of the brothers as their fathers and treat them equally, even if they also know who is their real father. In some regions children use the term "father" for the eldest brother and "father's brother" for the others, while in other areas they call all the brothers by one term, modifying this by the use of "elder" and "younger."

Unlike our own society, where monogamy is the only form of marriage permitted, Tibetan society allows a variety of marriage types, including monogamy, fraternal polyandry, and polygyny. Fraternal polyandry and monogamy are the most common forms of marriage, while polygyny typically occurs in cases where the first wife is barren. The widespread practice of fraternal polyandry, therefore, is not the outcome of a law requiring brothers to marry jointly. There is choice, and in fact, divorce traditionally was relatively simple in Tibetan society. If a brother in a polyandrous marriage became dissatisfied and wanted to separate, he simply left the main house and set up his own household. In such cases, all the children stayed in the main household with the remaining brother(s), even if the departing brother was known to be the real father of one or more of the children.

The Tibetans' own explanation for choosing fraternal polyandry is materialistic. For example, when I asked Dorje why he decided to marry with his two brothers rather than take his own wife, he thought for a moment, then said it prevented the division of his family's farm (and animals) and thus facilitated all of them achieving a higher standard of living. And when I later asked Dorje's bride whether it wasn't difficult for her to cope with three brothers as husbands, she laughed and echoed the rationale of avoiding fragmentation of the family and land, adding that she expected to be better off economically, since she would have three husbands working for her and her children.

Exotic as it may seem to Westerners, Tibetan fraternal polyandry is thus in many ways analogous to the way primogeniture functioned in nineteenth-century England. Primogeniture dictated that the eldest son inherited the family estate, while younger sons had to leave home and seek their own employment—for example, in the military or the clergy. Primogeniture maintained family estates intact over generations by permitting only one heir per generation. Fraternal polyandry also accomplishes this but does so by keeping all the brothers together with just one wife so that there is only one *set* of heirs per generation.

While Tibetans believe that in this way fraternal polyandry reduces the risk of family fission, monogamous marriages among brothers need not necessarily precipitate the division of the family estate: brothers could continue to live together, and the family land could continue to be worked jointly. When I asked Tibetans about this, however, they invariably responded that such joint families are unstable because each wife is primarily oriented to her own children and interested in their success and well-being over that of the children of the other wives. For example, if the youngest brother's wife had three sons while the eldest brother's wife had only one daughter, the wife of the youngest brother might begin to demand more resources for her children since, as males, they represent the future of the family. Thus, the children from different wives in the same generation are competing sets of heirs, and this makes such families inherently unstable. Tibetans perceive that conflict will spread from the wives to their husbands and consider this likely to cause family fission. Consequently, it is almost never done.

Although Tibetans see an economic advantage to fraternal polyandry, they do not value the sharing of a wife as an end in itself. On the contrary, they articulate a number of problems inherent in the practice. For example, because authority is customarily exercised by the eldest brother, his younger male siblings have to subordinate themselves with little hope of changing their status within the family. When these younger brothers are aggressive and individualistic, tensions and difficulties often occur despite there being only one set of heirs.

In addition, tension and conflict may arise in polyandrous families because of sexual favoritism. The bride normally sleeps with the eldest brother, and the two have the responsibility to see to it that the other males have opportunities for sexual access. Since the Tibetan subsistence economy requires males to travel a lot, the temporary absence of one or more brothers facilitates this, but there are also other rotation practices. The cultural ideal unambiguously calls for the wife to show equal affection and sexuality to each of the brothers (and vice versa), but deviations from this ideal occur, especially when there is a sizable difference in age between the partners in the marriage.

Dorje's family represents just such a potential situation. He is fifteen years old and his two older brothers are twenty-five and twenty-two years old. The new bride is twenty-three years old, eight years Dorje's senior. Sometimes such a bride finds the youngest husband immature and adolescent and does not treat him with equal affection; alternatively, she may find his youth attractive and lavish special attention on him. Apart from that consideration, when a younger male like Dorje grows up, he may consider his wife "ancient" and prefer the company of a woman his own age or younger. Consequently, although men and women do not find the idea of sharing a bride or a bridegroom repulsive, individual likes and dislikes can cause familial discord.

Two reasons have commonly been offered for the perpetuation of fraternal polyandry in Tibet: that Tibetans practice female infanticide and therefore have to marry polyandrously, owing to a shortage of females; and that Tibet, lying at extremely high altitudes, is so barren and bleak that Tibetans would starve without resort to this mechanism. A Jesuit who lived in Tibet during the eighteenth century articulated this second view: "One reason for this most odious custom is the sterility of the soil, and the small amount of land that can be cultivated owing to the lack of water. The crops may suffice if the brothers all live together, but if they form separate families they would be reduced to beggary."

Both explanations are wrong, however. Not only has there never been institutionalized female infanticide in Tibet, but Tibetan society gives females considerable rights, including inheriting the family estate in the absence of brothers. In such cases, the woman takes a bridegroom who comes to live in her family and adopts her family's name and identity. Moreover, there is no demographic evidence of a shortage of females. In Limi, for example, there were (in 1974) sixty females and fifty-three males in the fifteen- to thirty-five-year age category, and many adult females were unmarried.

The second reason is also incorrect. The climate in Tibet is extremely harsh, and ecological factors do play a major role in perpetuating polyandry, but polyandry is not a means of preventing starvation. It is characteristic, not of the poorest segments of the society, but rather of the peasant landowning families.

In the old society, the landless poor could not realistically aspire to prosperity, but they did not fear starvation. There was a persistent labor shortage throughout Tibet, and very poor families with little or no land and few animals could subsist through agricultural labor, tenant farming, craft occupations such as carpentry, or by working as servants. Although the per-person family income could increase somewhat if brothers married polyandrously and pooled their wages, in the absence of inheritable land, the advantage of fraternal polyandry was not generally sufficient to prevent them from setting up their own households. A more skilled or energetic younger brother could do as well or better alone, since he would completely control his income and would not have to share it with his siblings. Consequently, while there was and is some polyandry among the poor, it is much less frequent and more prone to result in divorce and family fission.

An alternative reason for the persistence of fraternal polyandry is that it reduces population growth (and thereby reduces the pressure on resources) by relegating some females to lifetime spinsterhood (see Figure I). Fraternal polyandrous marriages in Limi (in 1974) averaged 2.35 men per woman, and not surprisingly, 31 percent of the females of child-bearing age (twenty to forty-nine) were unmarried. These spinsters either continued to live at home, set up their own households, or worked as servants for other families. They could also become Buddhist nuns. Being unmarried is not synonymous with exclusion from the reproductive pool. Discreet extramarital relationships are tolerated, and actually half of the adult unmarried women in Limi had one or more children. They raised these children as single mothers, working for wages or weaving cloth and blankets for sale. As a group, however, the unmarried women had far fewer offspring than the married women, averaging only 0.7 children per woman, compared with 3.3 for married women, whether polyandrous, monogamous, or polygynous. When polyandry helps regulate population, this function of polyandry is not consciously perceived by Tibetans and is not the reason they consistently choose it.

If neither a shortage of females nor the fear of starvation perpetuates fraternal polyandry, what motivates brothers, particularly younger brothers, to opt for this system of marriage? From the perspective of the younger brother in a landholding family, the main incentive is the attainment or maintenance of the good life. With polyandry, he can expect a more secure and higher standard of living, with access not only to his family's land and animals but also to its inherited collection of clothes, jewelry, rugs, saddles, and horses. In addition, he will experience less work pressure and much greater security because all responsibility does not fall on one "father." For Tibetan brothers, the question is whether to trade off the greater personal freedom inherent in monogamy for the real or potential

Figure I

Family planning in Tibet

An economic rationale for fraternal polyandry is outlined in the diagram below, which emphasizes only the male offspring in each generation. If every wife is assumed to bear three sons, a family splitting up into monogamous households would rapidly multiply and fragment the family land. In this case, a rule of inheritance, such as primogeniture, could retain the family land intact, but only at the cost of creating many landless male offspring. In contrast, the family practicing fraternal polyandry maintains a steady ratio of persons to land.

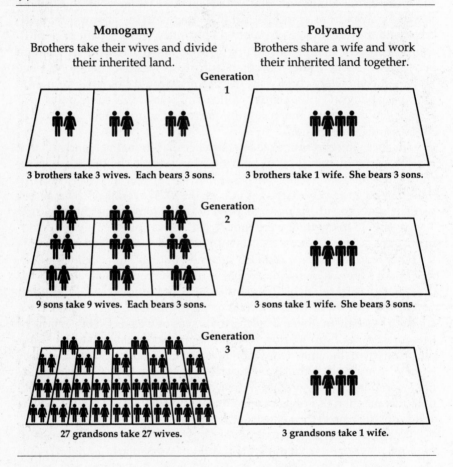

Monogamy
Brothers take their wives and divide their inherited land.

Polyandry
Brothers share a wife and work their inherited land together.

Generation 1

3 brothers take 3 wives. Each bears 3 sons.   3 brothers take 1 wife. She bears 3 sons.

Generation 2

9 sons take 9 wives. Each bears 3 sons.   3 sons take 1 wife. She bears 3 sons.

Generation 3

27 grandsons take 27 wives.   3 grandsons take 1 wife.

economic security, affluence, and social prestige associated with life in a larger, labor-rich polyandrous family.

A brother thinking of separating from his polyandrous marriage and taking his own wife would face various disadvantages. Although in the majority of Tibetan regions all brothers theoretically have rights to their family's estate, in reality Tibetans are reluctant to divide their land into small fragments. Generally, a younger brother who insists on leaving the family will receive only a small plot of land, if that. Because of its power and wealth, the rest of the family usually can block any attempt of the younger brother to increase his share of land through litigation. Moreover, a younger brother may not even get a house and cannot expect to receive much above the minimum in terms of movable possessions, such as furniture, pots, and pans. Thus, a brother contemplating going it on his own must plan on achieving economic security and the good life not through inheritance but through his own work.

The obvious solution for younger brothers—creating new fields from virgin land—is generally not a feasible option. Most Tibetan populations live at high altitudes (above 12,000 feet), where arable land is extremely scarce. For example, in Dorje's village, agriculture ranges only from about 12,900 feet, the lowest point in the area, to 13,300 feet. Above that altitude, early frost and snow destroy the staple barley crop. Furthermore, because of the low rainfall caused by the Himalayan rain shadow, many areas in Tibet and northern Nepal that are within the appropriate altitude range for agriculture have no reliable sources of irrigation. In the end, although there is plenty of unused land in such areas, most of it is either too high or too arid.

Even where unused land capable of being farmed exists, clearing the land and building the substantial terraces necessary for irrigation constitute a great undertaking. Each plot has to be completely dug out to a depth of two to two and a half feet so that the large rocks and boulders can be removed. At best, a man might be able to bring a few new fields under cultivation in the first years after separating from his brothers, but he could not expect to acquire substantial amounts of arable land this way.

In addition, because of the limited farmland, the Tibetan subsistence economy characteristically includes a strong emphasis on animal husbandry. Tibetan farmers regularly maintain cattle, yaks, goats, and sheep, grazing them in the areas too high for agriculture. These herds produce wool, milk, cheese, butter, meat, and skins. To obtain these resources, however, shepherds must accompany the animals on a daily basis. When first setting up a monogamous household, a younger brother like Dorje would find it difficult to both farm and manage animals.

In traditional Tibetan society, there was an even more critical factor that operated to perpetuate fraternal polyandry—a form of hereditary servitude somewhat analogous to serfdom in Europe. Peasants were tied to large estates held by aristocrats, monasteries, and the Lhasa government. They were allowed the use of some farmland to produce their own subsistence but were required to provide taxes in kind and corvée (free labor) to their lords. The corvée was a substantial hardship, since a peasant household was in many cases required to furnish the lord with one laborer daily for most of the year and more on specific occasions such as the harvest. This enforced labor, along with the lack of new land and the ecological pressure to pursue both agriculture and animal husbandry, made polyandrous families particularly beneficial. The polyandrous family allowed an internal division of adult labor, maximizing economic advantage. For example, while the wife worked the family fields, one brother could perform the lord's corvée, another could look after the animals, and a third could engage in trade.

Although social scientists often discount other people's explanations of why they do things, in the case of Tibetan fraternal polyandry, such explanations are very close to the truth. The custom, however, is very sensitive to changes in its political and economic milieu and, not surprisingly, is in decline in most Tibetan areas. Made less important by the elimination of the traditional serf-based economy, it is disparaged by the dominant non-Tibetan leaders of India, China, and Nepal. New opportunities for economic and social mobility in these countries, such as the tourist trade and government employment, are also eroding the rationale for polyandry, and so it may vanish within the next generation.

REVIEW QUESTIONS

1. What is fraternal polyandry and how does this form of marriage manage potential conflict over sex, children, and inheritance?
2. Why do many Tibetans choose polyandry over monogamous or polygynous marriage?
3. According to Tibetans, what are some of the disadvantages of polyandry?
4. What is wrong with the theory that Tibetan polyandry either is caused either by a shortage of women due to infanticide or is a way to prevent famine by limiting population and land pressure?
5. Why might Tibetan polyandry disappear under modern conditions?

19

Marriage, Alliance, and the Incest Taboo

Yehudi Cohen

The incest taboo, a legal proscription against mating and marriage among certain designated kin, is often considered a human universal. In this article, Yehudi Cohen argues that the taboo as a feature of law may disappear in some societies, because its original functions are being met in other ways. The incest taboo, he claims, originated out of a need for families in technologically and socially simple groups to forge trade alliances. As that need was filled by other institutions, the taboo came to apply to fewer and fewer individuals until, in industrial society, it was limited to primary relatives. For the industrial family, the taboo still prevents isolation and promotes social maturity. Cohen concludes, however, that this function may soon be met in other ways, leading to the demise of the taboo.

Several years ago a minor Swedish bureaucrat, apparently with nothing better to do, was leafing through birth and marriage records, matching people with their natural parents. To his amazement he found a full brother and sister who were married and had several children. The couple were arrested and brought to trial. It emerged that they had been brought up by separate sets of foster parents and never knew of each other's existence. By a coincidence reminiscent of a Greek tragedy, they met as adults, fell in love, and married, learning of their biological tie only after their arrest. The local court declared their marriage illegal and void.

The couple appealed the decision to Sweden's Supreme Court. After lengthy testimony on both sides of the issue, the court overturned the decision on the grounds that the pair had not been reared together. The marriage was declared legal and valid. In the wake of the decision, a committee appointed by Sweden's Minister of Justice to examine the question has proposed that criminal sanctions against incest be repealed. The committee's members were apparently swayed by Carl-Henry Alstrom, a professor of psychiatry. Alstrom argued that psychological deterrents to incest are stronger than legal prohibitions. . . .

Aside from illustrating the idea that the most momentous changes in human societies often occur as a result of unforeseen events, this landmark case raises questions that go far beyond Sweden's (or any other society's) borders. Some people may be tempted to dismiss the Swedish decision as an anomaly, as nothing more than a part of Sweden's unusual experiments in public welfare and sexual freedom.

But the probable Swedish decision to repeal criminal laws against incest cannot be regarded so lightly; this simple step reflects a trend in human society that has been developing for several thousand years. When we arrange human societies along a continuum from the least to the most complex, from those with the smallest number of interacting social groups to those with the highest number of groups, from those with the simplest technology to those with the most advanced technology, we observe that the incest taboo applies to fewer and fewer relatives beyond the immediate family.

Though there are exceptions, the widest extension of incest taboos beyond the nuclear family is found in the least complex societies. In a few societies, such as the Cheyenne of North America and the Kwoma of New Guinea, incest taboos extend to many remote relatives, including in-laws and the in-laws of in-laws. In modern industrial societies, incest taboos are usually confined to members of the immediate household. This contraction in the range of incest taboos is reaching the point at which they may disappear entirely.

The source of these changes in incest taboos lies in changing patterns of external trade. Trade is a society's jugular. Because every group lives in a milieu lacking some necessities that are available in other habitats, the flow of goods and resources is a society's lifeblood. But it is never sufficient merely to encourage people to form trade alliances with others in different areas. Incest taboos force people to marry outside their own group, to form alliances and to maintain trade networks. As other institutions—governments, business organizations—begin to organize trade, incest taboos become less necessary for assuring the flow of the society's lifeblood; they start to contract.

Other explanations of the incest taboo do not, under close examination, hold up. The most common assumption is that close inbreeding is biologically deleterious and will lead to the extinction of those who practice it. But there is strong evidence that inbreeding does not materially increase the rate of maladies such as albinism, total color blindness, or various forms of idiocy, which generally result when each parent carries the same recessive gene. In most cases these diseases result from chance combinations of recessive genes or from mutation.

According to Theodosius Dobzhansky, a geneticist, "The increase of the incidence of hereditary diseases in the offspring of marriages between relatives (cousins, uncle and niece or aunt and nephew, second cousins, etc.) over that in marriages between persons not known to be related is slight—so slight that geneticists hesitate to declare such marriages disgenic." Inbreeding does carry a slight risk. The progeny of relatives include more stillbirths and infant and early childhood deaths than the progeny of unrelated people. But most of these deaths are due to environmental rather than genetic factors. Genetic disadvantages are not frequent enough to justify a prohibition. Moreover, it is difficult to justify the biological explanation for incest taboos when many societies prescribe marriage to one cousin and prohibit marriage to another. Among the Lesu of Melanesia a man must avoid sexual contact with his parallel cousins, his mother's sisters' daughters and his father's brothers' daughters, but is supposed to marry his cross cousins, his mother's brothers' daughters and his father's sisters' daughters. Even though both types of cousins have the same genetic relationship to the man, only one kind is included in the incest taboo. The taboo is apparently a cultural phenomenon based on the cultural classification of people and can not be explained biologically.

Genetic inbreeding may even have some advantages in terms of natural selection. Each time a person dies of a hereditary disadvantage, his detrimental genes are lost to the population. By such a process of genetic cleansing, inbreeding may lead to the elimination, or at least to reduced frequencies, of recessive genes. The infant mortality rate may increase slightly at first, but after the sheltered recessive genes are eliminated, the population may stabilize. Inbreeding may also increase the frequency of beneficial recessive genes, contributing to the population's genetic fitness. In the end, inbreeding seems to have only a slight effect on the offspring and a mixed effect, some good and some bad, on the gene pool itself. This mild consequence hardly justifies the universal taboo on incest.

Another explanation of the incest taboo is the theory of natural aversion, first propounded by Edward Westermarck in his 1891 book, *The History of Human Marriage.* According to Westermarck, children reared in the same household are naturally averse to having sexual relations with one another in adulthood. But this theory has major difficulties. First, it has a basic logical flaw: If there were a natural aversion to incest, the taboo would be unnecessary. As James Frazer pointed out in 1910, "It is not easy to see why any deep human instinct should need to be reinforced by law. There is no law commanding men to eat and drink or forbidding them to put their hands in the fire. . . . The law only forbids men to do what their instincts incline them to do; what nature itself prohibits and punishes, it would be superfluous for the law to prohibit and punish. . . . Instead of assuming, therefore, from the legal prohibition of incest that there is a natural aversion to incest, we ought rather to assume that there is a natural instinct in favour of it."

Second, the facts play havoc with the notion of natural aversion. In many societies, such as the Arapesh of New Guinea studied by Margaret Mead, and the Eskimo, young children are betrothed and raised together, usually by the boy's parents, before the marriage is consummated. Arthur Wolf, an anthropologist who studied a village in northern Taiwan, describes just such a custom: "Dressed in the traditional red wedding costume, the bride enters her future husband's home as a child. She is seldom more than three years of age and often less than a year. . . . [The] last phase in the marriage process does not take place until she is old enough to fulfill the role of wife. In the meantime, she and her parents are affinally related to the groom's parents, but she is not in fact married to the groom."

One of the examples commonly drawn up to support Westermarck's theory of aversion is the Israeli *kibbutz*, where children who have been raised together tend to avoid marrying. But this avoidance has been greatly exaggerated. There is some tendency among those who have been brought up in the same age group in a communal "children's house" to avoid marrying one another, but this arises from two regulations that separate young adults from their *kibbutz* at about the age when they might marry. The first is a regulation of the Israel Defense Forces that no married woman may serve in the armed forces. Conscription for men and women is at 18, usually coinciding with their completion of secondary school, and military service is a deeply felt responsibility for most *kibbutz*-reared Israelis. Were women to marry prior to 18, they would be denied one of their principal goals. By the time they complete their military service, many choose urban spouses whom they have met in the army. Thus the probability of marrying a person one has grown up with is greatly reduced.

The second regulation that limits intermarriage on a *kibbutz* is a policy of the federations to which almost all *kibbutzim* belong. Each of the four major federations reserves the right to transfer any member to any other settlement, especially when a new one is being established. These "seeds," as the transferred members are called, are recruited individually from different settlements and most transfers are made during a soldier's third or fourth year of military service. When these soldiers leave the army to live on a *kibbutz*, they may be separated from those they were reared with. The frequency of marriage among people from working-class backgrounds who began and completed school together in an American city or town is probably higher than for an Israeli *kibbutz;* the proclivity among American college graduates to marry outside their neighborhoods or towns is no more an example of exogamy or incest avoidance than is the tendency in Israeli *kibbutzim* to marry out.

Just as marriage within a neighborhood is accepted in the United States, so is marriage within a *kibbutz* accepted in Israel. During research I conducted in Israel between 1967 and 1969, I attended the wedding of two people in a *kibbutz* who supposedly were covered by this taboo or rule of avoidance. As my tape recordings and photographs show, it would be difficult to imagine a more joyous occasion. When I questioned members of the *kibbutz* about this, they told me with condescending smiles that they had "heard of these things the professors say."

A third, "demographic," explanation of the incest taboo was originally set forth in 1950 by Wilson Wallis and elaborated in 1959 by Mariam Slater. According to this theory, mating within the household, especially between parents and children, was unlikely in early human societies because the life span in these early groups was so short that by the time offspring were old enough to mate, their parents would probably have died. Mating between siblings would also have been unlikely because of the average of eight years between children that resulted from breastfeeding and high rates of infant mortality. But even assuming this to have been true for the first human societies, there is nothing to prevent mating among the members of a nuclear family when the life span is lengthened.

A fourth theory that is widely subscribed to focuses on the length of the human child's parental dependency, which is the longest in the animal kingdom. Given the long period required for socializing children, there must be regulation of sexual activity so that children may learn their proper roles. If the nuclear family's members are permitted to have unrestricted sexual access to one another, the members of the unit would be confused about their roles. Parental authority would be undermined, and it would be impossible to socialize children. This interpretation has much to recommend it as far as relationships between parents and children are concerned, but it does not help explain brother-sister incest taboos or the extension of incest taboos to include remote relatives.

The explanation closest to my interpretation of the changes in the taboo is the theory of alliance advocated by the French anthropologist Claude Levi-Strauss, which suggests that people are compelled to marry outside their groups in order to form unions with other groups and promote harmony among them. A key element in the theory is that men exchange their sisters and daughters in marriage with men of other groups. As originally propounded, the theory of alliance was based on the assumption that men stay put while the women change groups by marrying out, moved about by men like pieces on a chessboard. But there are many instances in which the women stay put while the men change groups by marrying out. In either case, the result is the same. Marriage forges alliances.

These alliances freed early human societies from exclusive reliance on their own limited materials and products. No society is self-sustaining or self-perpetuating; no culture is a world unto itself. Each society is compelled to trade with others and this was as true for tribal societies as it is for modern industrial nations. North America, for instance, was criss-crossed with elaborate trade networks before the Europeans arrived. Similar trade networks covered aboriginal New Guinea and Australia. In these trade networks, coastal or riverine groups gave shells and fish to hinterland people in exchange for cultivated foods, wood, and manufactured items.

American Indian standards of living were quite high before the Europeans destroyed the native trade networks, and the same seems to have been true in almost all other parts of the world. It will come as no surprise to economists that the material quality of people's lives improves to the extent that they engage in external trade.

But barter and exchange do not automatically take place when people meet. Exchange involves trust, and devices are needed to establish trust, to distinguish friend from foe, and to assure a smooth, predictable flow of trade goods. Marriage in the tribal world established permanent obligations and reciprocal rights and privileges among families living in different habitats.

For instance, when a young Cheyenne Indian man decided on a girl to marry, he told his family of his choice. If they agreed that his selection was good, they gathered a store of prized possessions—clothing, blankets, guns, bows and arrows—and carefully loaded them on a fine horse. A friend of the family, usually a respected old woman, led the horse to the tepee of the girl's elder brother. There the go-between spread the gifts for everyone to see while she pressed the suitor's case. The next step was for the girl's brother to assemble all his cousins for a conference to weigh the proposal. If they agreed to it, the cousins distributed the gifts among themselves, the brother taking the horse. Then the men returned to their tepees to find suitable gifts to give in return. Within a day or two, each returned with something roughly equal in value to what he had received. While this was happening, the bride was made beautiful. When all arrangements were completed, she mounted one horse while the return gifts were loaded on another. The old woman led both horses to the groom's camp. After the bride was received, her accompanying gifts were distributed among the groom's relatives in accordance with what each had given. The exchanges between the two families did not end with the marriage ceremony, however; they continued as a permanent part of the marriage ties. This continual exchange, which took place periodically, is why the young man's bridal choice was so important for his entire family.

Marriage was not the only integral part of external trade relationships. Another was ritualized friendship, "blood brotherhood," for example. Such bonds were generally established between members of different groups and were invariably trade partnerships. Significantly, these ritualized friendships often included taboos against marriage with the friend's sisters; sometimes the taboo applied to all their close relatives. This extension of a taboo provides an important key for understanding all incest taboos. Sexual prohibitions do not necessarily grow out of biological ties. Both marriage and ritualized friendships in primitive societies promote economic alliances and both are associated with incest taboos.

Incest taboos force people into alliances with others in as many groups as possible. They promote the greatest flow of manufactured goods and raw materials from the widest variety of groups and ecological niches and force people to spread their social nets. Looked at another way, incest taboos prevent localism and economic provincialism; they block social and economic inbreeding.

Incest taboos have their widest extensions outside the nuclear family in those societies in which technology is least well developed and in which people have to carry their own trade goods for barter or exchange with members of other groups. Often in these small societies, everyone in a community is sexually taboo to the rest of the group. When the technology surrounding trade improves and shipments of goods and materials can be concentrated (as when people learn to build and navigate ocean-going canoes or harness pack animals), fewer and fewer people have to be involved in trade. As this happens, incest taboos begin to contract, affecting fewer and fewer people outside the nuclear family.

This process has been going on for centuries. Today, in most industrial societies, the only incest taboos are those that pertain to members of the nuclear family. This contraction of the range of the taboo is inseparable from the fact that we no longer engage in personal alliances and trade agreements to get the food we eat, the clothes we wear, the tools and materials we use, the fuels on which we depend. Goods are brought to distribution points near our homes by a relatively tiny handful of truckers, shippers, merchants, entrepreneurs, and others. Most of us are only vaguely aware of the alliances, negotiations, and relationships that make this massive movement of goods possible. When we compare tribal and contemporary industrialized societies, the correspondence between the range of incest taboos and the material conditions of life cannot be dismissed as mere coincidence.

Industrialization does not operate alone in affecting the degree to which incest taboos extend beyond the nuclear family. In the history of societies, political institutions developed as technology advanced. Improvements in packaging and transportation have led not only to reductions in the number of people involved in external trade, but also to greater and greater concentrations of decision making in the hands of fewer and fewer people. Trade is no longer the responsibility of all members of a society, and the maintenance of relationships between societies has become the responsibility of a few people—a king and his bureaucracy, impersonal governmental agencies, national and multinational corporations.

To the extent that trade is conducted and negotiated by a handful of people, it becomes unnecessary to use incest taboos to force the majority of people into alliances with other groups. Treaties, political alliances, and negotiations by the managers of a few impersonal agencies have replaced marital and other personal alliances. The history of human societies suggests that incest taboos may have outlived their original purpose.

But incest taboos still serve other purposes. For social and emotional reasons rather than economic ones, people in modern industrial societies still need to prevent localism. Psychological well-being in a diversified society depends largely on the ability to tap different ideas, points of view, life styles, and social relationships. The jugulars that must now be kept open by the majority of people may no longer be for goods and resources, but for variety and stimulation. This need for variety is what, in part, seems to underlie the preference of Israelis to marry outside the communities in which they were born and brought up. The taboo against sex within the nuclear family leads young people to explore, to seek new experiences. In a survey of a thousand cases of incest, Christopher Bagley found that incestuous families are cut off from their society's social and cultural mainstream. Whether rural or urban, he writes, "the family seems to withdraw from the general community, and initiates its own 'deviant' norms of sexual behavior, which are contained within the family circle." "Such a family," he continues, "is an isolated cultural unit, relatively untouched by external social norms." This social and cultural inbreeding is the cause of the profound malaise represented by incest.

To illustrate the correspondence between incest and social isolation, let me describe an incestuous family reported by Peter Wilson, an anthropologist. Wilson sketched a sequence of events in which a South American family became almost totally isolated from the community in which it lived, and began to practice almost every variety of incest. The decline into incest began many years before Wilson appeared on the scene to do anthropological research, when the father of five daughters and four sons made the girls (who ranged in age from 18 to 33) sexually available to some sailors for a small sum of money. As a result, the entire household was ostracized by the rest of the village. "But most important," Wilson writes, "the Brown family was immediately cut off from sexual partners. No woman would have anything to do with a Brown man; no man would touch a Brown woman."

The Browns' isolation and incest continued for several years, until the women in the family rebelled—apparently because a new road connecting their hamlet to others provided the opportunity for social contact with people outside the hamlet. At the same time the Brown men began working in new light industry in the area and spending their money in local stores. The family slowly regained some social acceptance in Green Fields, the larger village to which their hamlet belonged. Little by little they were reintegrated into the hamlet and there seems to have been no recurrence of incest among them.

A second example is an upper-middle class, Jewish, urban American family that was described to me by a colleague. The Erva family (a pseudonym) consists of six people—the parents, two daughters aged 19 and 22, and two sons, aged 14 and 20. Mr. Erva is a computer analyst and his wife a dentist. Twenty-five years ago, the Ervas seemed relatively normal, but shortly after their first child was born, Mr. and Mrs. Erva took to wandering naked about their apartment, even when others were present. They also began dropping in on friends for as long as a week; their notion of reciprocity was to refuse to accept food, to eat very little of what was offered them, or to order one member of their family not to accept any food at all during a meal. Their rationale seemed to be that accepting food was receiving a favor, but occupying a bed was not. This pattern was accompanied by intense family bickering and inadvertent insults to their hosts. Not surprisingly, most of their friends wearied of their visits and the family was left almost friendless.

Reflecting Bagley's general description of incestuous families, the Ervas had withdrawn from the norms of the general community after the birth of their first child and had instituted their own "deviant" patterns of behavior. They thereby set the stage for incest.

Mr. Erva began to have intercourse with his daughters when they were 14 and 16 years old. Neither of them was self-conscious about the relationship and it was common for the father to take both girls into bed with him at the same time when they were visiting overnight. Mrs. Erva apparently did not have intercourse with her sons. The incest became a matter of gossip and added to the family's isolation.

The Erva family then moved to the Southwest to start over again. They built a home on a parcel of land that had no access to water. Claiming they could not afford a well of their own, the family began to use the bathrooms and washing facilities of their neighbors. In the end these neighbors, too, wanted nothing to do with them.

Mr. and Mrs. Erva eventually separated, he taking the daughters and she the sons. Later the younger daughter left her father to live alone, but the older daughter still shares a one-bedroom apartment with her father.

Social isolation and incest appear to be related, and social maturity and a taboo on incest are also related. Within the modern nuclear family, social and emotional relationships are intense, and sexuality is the source of some of the strongest emotions in human life. When combined with the intensity of family life, sexually stimulated emotions can be overwhelming for children. Incest taboos are a way of limiting family relationships. They are assurances of a degree of emotional insularity, of detachment on which emotional maturity depends.

On balance, then, we can say that legal penalties for incest were first instituted because of the adverse economic effects of incestuous unions on society, but that today the negative consequences of incest affect only individuals. Some will say that criminal penalties should be retained if only to protect children. But legal restraints alone are unlikely to serve as deterrents. Father-daughter incest is regarded by many social workers, judges, and psychiatrists as a form of child abuse, but criminal penalties have not deterred other forms of child abuse. Moreover, incest between brothers and sisters cannot be considered child abuse. Some have even suggested that the concept of abuse may be inappropriate when applied to incest. "Many psychotherapists," claims psychologist James McCary in *Human Sexuality*, "believe that a child is less affected by actual incest than by seductive behavior on the part of a parent that never culminates in any manifest sexual activity."

Human history suggests that the incest taboo may indeed be obsolete. As in connection with changing attitudes toward homosexuality, it may be maintained that incestuous relations between consenting mature adults and their concern alone and no one else's. At the same time, however, children must be protected. But questions still remain about how they should be protected and until what age.

If a debate over the repeal of criminal laws against incest is to begin in earnest . . . one other important fact about the social history of sexual behavior must be remembered. Until about a century ago, many societies punished adultery and violations of celibacy with death. When it came time to repeal those laws, not a few people favored their retention on the grounds that extramarital sexual relationships would adversely affect the entire society. Someday people may regard incest in the same way they now regard adultery and violations of celibacy. Where the threat of punishment once seemed necessary, social and emotional dissuasion may now suffice.

REVIEW QUESTIONS

1. What is the incest taboo, and why does Cohen believe it might disappear?
2. What explanations of the incest taboo have been suggested by anthropologists? What are the criticisms of each?
3. What is Cohen's explanation for the taboo, and what supporting evidence does he cite?
4. What is the function of the incest taboo in industrial societies? What is the evidence of this function?
5. What social forces (not legal ones) work to prevent incest from occurring in industrial society families?

20

Uterine Families and the Women's Community

Margery Wolf

The size and organization of extended families vary from one society to the next, but extended families often share some important attributes. They are most often based on a rule of patrilineal descent. For men, the patrilineal family extends in an unbroken line of ancestors and descendants. Membership is permanent; loyalty assured. For women, the patrilineal family is temporary. Born into one family and married into another, women discover that their happiness and interests depend on bearing children to create their own uterine family. This and the importance of a local women's group are the subjects of this article by Margery Wolf in her discussion of Taiwanese family life.

F ew women in China experience the continuity that is typical of the lives of the menfolk. A woman can and, if she is ever to have any economic security, must provide the links in the male chain of descent, but she will never appear in anyone's genealogy as that all-important name

Reprinted from *Women and the Family in Rural Taiwan* by Margery Wolf with the permission of the publishers, Stanford University Press. © 1972 by the Board of Trustees of the Leland Stanford Junior University.

connecting the past to the future. If she dies before she is married, her tablet will not appear on her father's altar; although she was a temporary member of his household, she was not a member of his family. A man is born into his family and remains a member of it throughout his life and even after his death. He is identified with the family from birth, and every action concerning him, up to and including his death, is in the context of that group. Whatever other uncertainties may trouble his life, his place in the line of ancestors provides a permanent setting. There is no such secure setting for a woman. She will abruptly leave the household into which she is born, either as an infant or as an adult bride, and enter another whose members treat her with suspicion or even hostility.

A man defines his family as a large group that includes the dead, and not-yet-born, and the living members of his household. But how does a woman define her family? This is not a question that China specialists often consider, but from their treatment of the family in general, it would seem that a woman's family is identical with that of the senior male in the household in which she lives. Although I have never asked, I imagine a Taiwanese man would define a woman's family in very much those same terms. Women, I think, would give quite a different answer. They do not have an unchanging place, assigned at birth, in any group, and their view of the family reflects this.

When she is a child, a woman's family is defined for her by her mother and to some extent by her grandmother. No matter how fond of his daughter the father may be, she is only a temporary member of his household and useless to his family—he cannot even marry her to one of his sons as he could an adopted daughter. Her irrelevance to her father's family in turn affects the daughter's attitude toward it. It is of no particular interest to her, and the need to maintain its continuity has little meaning for her beyond the fact that this continuity matters a great deal to some of the people she loves. As a child she probably accepts to some degree her grandmother's orientation toward the family: the household, that is, those people who live together and eat together, including perhaps one or more of her father's married brothers and their children. But the group that has the most meaning for her and with which she will have the most lasting ties is the smaller, more cohesive unit centering on her mother, that is, the uterine family—her mother and her mother's children. Father is important to the group, just as grandmother is important to some of the children, but he is not quite a member of it, and for some uterine families he may even be "the enemy." As the girl grows up and her grandmother dies and a brother or two marries, she discovers that her mother's definition of the family is becoming less exclusive and may even include such outsiders as her brother's new wife. Without knowing precisely when it happened, she finds that her brother's interests and goals have shifted in a direction she cannot follow. Her mother does not push her aside, but when the mother speaks of the future, she speaks in terms of her son's future. Although the mother sees her uterine family as adding new members and another generation, her daughter sees it as dissolving, leaving her with strong particular relationships, but with no group to which she has permanent loyalties and obligations.

When a young woman marries, her formal ties with the household of her father are severed. In one of the rituals of the wedding ceremony the bride's father or brothers symbolically inform her by means of split water that she, like the water, may never return, and when her wedding sedan chair passes over the threshold of her father's house, the doors are slammed shut behind her. If she is ill-treated by her husband's family, her father's family may intervene, but unless her parents are willing to bring her home and support her for the rest of her life (and most parents are not), there is little they can do beyond shaming the other family. This is usually enough.

As long as her mother is alive, the daughter will continue her contacts with her father's household by as many visits as her new situation allows. If she lives nearby she may visit every few days, and no matter where she lives she must at least be allowed to return at New Year. After her mother dies her visits may become perfunctory, but her relations with at least one member of her uterine family, the group that centered on her mother, remain strong. Her brother plays an important ritual role throughout her life. She may gradually lose contact with her sisters as she and they become more involved with their own children, but her relations with her brother continue. When her sons marry, he is the guest of honor at the wedding feasts, and when her daughters marry he must give a small banquet in their honor. If her sons wish to divide their father's estate, it is their mother's brother who is called on to supervise. And when she dies, the coffin cannot be closed until her brother determines to his own satisfaction that she died a natural death and that her husband's family did everything possible to prevent it.

With the ritual slam of her father's door on her wedding day, a young woman finds herself quite literally without a family. She enters the household of her husband—a man who in an earlier time, say fifty years ago, she would never have met and who even today, in modern rural Taiwan, she is unlikely to know very well. She is an outsider, and for Chinese an outsider is always an object of deep suspicion. Her husband and her father-in-law do not see her as a member of their family. But they do see her as essential to it; they have gone to great expense to bring her into their household for the purpose of bearing a new generation for their family. Her mother-in-law, who was mainly responsible for negotiating the terms of her entry, may harbor some resentment over the hard bargaining, but she is nonetheless eager to see another generation added to *her* uterine family. A mother-in-law often has the same kind of ambivalence toward her daughter-in-law as she has toward her husband—the younger woman seems a member of her family at times and merely a member of the household at others. The new bride may find that her husband's sister is hostile or at best condescending, both attitudes reflecting the daughter's distress at an outsider who seems to be making her way right into the heart of the family.

Chinese children are taught by proverb, by example, and by experience that the family is the source of their security, and relatives the only people who can be depended on. Ostracism from the family is one of the harshest sanctions that can be imposed on erring youth. One of the reasons mainlanders as individuals are considered so untrustworthy on Taiwan is the fact that they are not subject to the controls of (and therefore have no fear of ostracism from) their families. If a timid new bride is considered an object of suspicion and potentially dangerous because she is a stranger, think how uneasy her own first few months must be surrounded by strangers. Her irrelevance to her father's family may result in her having little reverence for descent lines, but she has warm memories of the security of the family her mother created. If she is ever to return to this certainty and sense of belonging, a woman must create her own uterine family by bearing children, a goal that happily corresponds to the goals of the family into which she has married. She may gradually create a tolerable niche for herself in the household of her mother-in-law, but her family will not be formed until she herself forms it of her own children and grandchildren. In most cases, by the time she adds grandchildren, the uterine family and the household will almost completely overlap, and there will be another daughter-in-law struggling with loneliness and beginning a new uterine family.

The ambiguity of a man's position in relation to the uterine families accounts for much of the hostility between mother-in-law and daughter-in-law. There is no question in the mind of the older woman but that her son *is* her family. The daughter-in-law might be content with this situation once her sons are old enough to represent her interests in the household and in areas strictly under men's control, but until then, she is dependent on her husband. If she were to be completely absorbed into her mother-in-law's family—a rare occurrence unless she is a *simpua*—there would be little or no conflict; but under most circumstances she must rely on her husband, her mother-in-law's son, as her spokesman, and here is where the trouble begins. Since it is usually events within the household that she wishes to affect, and the household more or less overlaps with her mother-in-law's uterine family, even a minor foray by the younger woman suggests to the older one an all-out attack on everything she has worked so hard to build in the years of her own loneliness and insecurity. The birth of grandchildren further complicates their relations, for the one sees them as new members for her family and the other as desperately needed recruits to her own small circle of security.

In summary, my thesis contends . . . that because we have heretofore focused on men when examining the Chinese family—a reasonable approach to a patrilineal system—we have missed not only some of the system's subtleties but also its near-fatal weaknesses. With a male focus we see the Chinese family as a line of descent, bulging to encompass all the members of a man's household and spreading out through his descendants. With a female focus, however, we see the Chinese family not as a continuous line stretching between the vague horizons of past and future, but as a contemporary group that comes into existence out of one woman's need and is held together insofar as she has the strength to do so, or, for that matter, the need to do so. After her death the uterine family survives only in the mind of her son and is symbolized by the special attention he gives her earthly remains and her ancestral tablet. The rites themselves are demanded by the ideology of the patriliny, but the meaning they hold for most sons is formed in the uterine family. The uterine family has no ideology, no formal structure, and no public existence. It is built out of sentiments and loyalties that die with its members, but it is no less real for all that. The descent lines of men are born and nourished in the uterine families of women, and it is here that a male ideology that excludes women makes its accommodations with reality.

Women in rural Taiwan do not live their lives in the walled courtyards of their husband's households. If they did, they might be as powerless as their stereotype. It is in their relations in the outside world (and for women in rural Taiwan that world consists almost entirely of the village) that women develop sufficient backing to maintain some independence under their powerful mothers-in-law and even occasionally to bring the men's world to terms. A successful venture into the men's world is no small feat when one recalls that the men of a village were born there and are often related to one another, whereas the women are unlikely to have either the ties of childhood or the ties of kinship to unite them. All the same, the needs, shared interests, and common problems of women are reflected in every village in a loosely knit society that can when needed be called on to exercise considerable influence.

Women carry on as many of their activities as possible outside the house. They wash clothes on the riverbank, clean and pare vegetables at a communal pump, mend under a tree that is a known meetingplace, and stop to rest on a bench or group of stones with other women. There is a continual moving back and forth between kitchens, and conversations are carried on from open doorways through the long, hot afternoons of summer. The shy young girl who enters the village as a bride is examined as frankly and suspiciously by the women as an animal that is up for sale. If she is deferential to her elders, does not criticize or compare her new world unfavorably with the one she has left, the older residents will gradually accept her presence on the edge of their conversations and stop changing the topic to general subjects when she brings the family laundry to scrub on the rocks near them. As the young bride meets other girls in her position, she makes allies for the future, but she must also develop relationships with the older women. She learns to use considerable discretion in making and receiving confidences, for a girl who gossips freely about the affairs of her husband's household may find herself labeled a troublemaker. On the other hand, a girl who is too reticent may find herself always on the outside of the group, or worse yet, accused of snobbery. I described in *The House of Lim* the plight of Lim Chui-ieng, who had little village backing in her troubles with her husband and his family as the result of her arrogance toward the women's community. In Peihotien the young wife of the storekeeper's son suffered a similar lack of support. Warned by her husband's parents not to be too "easy" with the other villagers lest they try to buy things on credit, she obeyed to the point of being considered unfriendly by the women of the village. When she began to have serious troubles with her husband and eventually his family, there was no one in the village she could turn to for solace, advice, and, most important, peacemaking.

Once a young bride has established herself as a member of the women's community, she has also established for herself a certain amount of protection. If the members of her husband's family step beyond the limits of propriety in their treatment of her—such as refusing to allow her to return to her natal home for her brother's wedding or beating her without serious justification—she can complain to a woman friend, preferably older, while they are washing vegetables at the communal pump. The story will quickly spread to the other women, and one of them will take it on herself to check the facts with another member of the girl's household. For a few days the matter will be thoroughly discussed whenever a few women gather. In a young wife's first few years in the community, she can expect to have her mother-in-law's side of any disagreement given fuller weight than her own—her mother-in-law has, after all, been a part of the community a lot longer. However, the discussion itself will serve to curb many offenses. Even if the older woman knows that public opinion is falling to her side, she will still be somewhat more judicious about refusing her daughter-in-law's next request. Still, the daughter-in-law who hopes to make use of the village forum to depose her mother-in-law or at least gain herself special privilege will discover just how important the prerogatives of age and length of residence are. Although the women can serve as a powerful protective force for their defenseless younger members, they are also a very conservative force in the village.

Taiwanese women can and do make use of their collective power to lose face for their menfolk in order to influence decisions that are ostensibly not theirs to make. Although young women may have little or no influence over their husbands and would not dare express an unsolicited opinion (and perhaps not even a solicited one) to their fathers-in-law, older women who have raised their sons properly retain considerable influence over their sons' actions, even in activities exclusive to men. Further, older women who have displayed years of good judgment are regularly consulted by their husbands about major as well as minor economic and social projects. But even men who think themselves free to ignore the opinions of their women are never free of their own concept, face. It is much easier to lose face than to have face. We once asked a male friend in Peihotien just what "having face" amounted to. He replied, "When no one is talking about a family, you can say it has face." This is precisely where women wield their power. When a man behaves in a way that they consider wrong, they talk about him—not only among themselves, but to their sons and husbands. No one "tells him how to mind his own business," but it becomes abundantly clear that he is losing face and by continuing in this manner may bring shame to the family of his ancestors and descendants. Few men will risk that.

The rules that a Taiwanese man must learn and obey to be a success-ful member of his society are well developed, clear, and relatively easy to stay within. A Taiwanese woman must also learn the rules, but if she is to be a successful woman, she must learn not to stay within them, but to *ap-pear* to stay within them; to manipulate them, but not to appear to be ma-nipulating them; to teach them to her children, but not to depend on her children for her protection. A truly successful Taiwanese woman is a rugged individualist who has learned to depend largely on herself while appearing to lean on her father, her husband, and her son. The contrast be-tween the terrified young bride and the loud, confident, often lewd old woman who has outlived her mother-in-law and her husband reflects the tests met and passed by not strictly following the rules and by making pur-poseful use of those who must. The Chinese male's conception of women as "narrow-hearted" and socially inept may well be his vague recognition of this facet of women's power and technique.

The women's subculture in rural Taiwan is, I believe, below the level of consciousness. Mothers do not tell their about-to-be-married daughters how to establish themselves in village society so that they may have some protection from an oppressive family situation, nor do they warn them to gather their children into an exclusive circle under their own control. But girls grow up in village society and see their mothers and sisters-in-law settling their differences to keep them from a public airing or presenting them for the women's community to judge. Their mothers have created around them the meaningful unit in their father's households, and when they are desperately lonely and unhappy in the households of their hus-bands, what they long for is what they have lost. . . . [Some] areas in the subculture of women . . . mesh perfectly into the main culture of the soci-ety. The two cultures are not symbiotic because they are not sufficiently in-dependent of one another, but neither do they share identical goals or nec-essarily use the same means to reach the goals they do share. Outside the village the women's subculture seems not to exist. The uterine family also has no public existence, and appears almost as a response to the traditional family organized in terms of a male ideology.

REVIEW QUESTIONS

1. According to Wolf, what is a uterine family, and what relatives are likely to be members?
2. Why is the uterine family important to Chinese women who live in their husband's patrilineal extended families?
3. What is the relationship between a woman's uterine family and her power within her husband's family?
4. Why might the existence of the uterine family contribute to the division of extended families into smaller constituent parts?
5. How do you think a Chinese woman's desire to have a uterine family affects attempts to limit the Chinese population?

VII

ROLES AND INEQUALITY

F or most of us, social interaction is unconscious and automatic. We associate with other people from the time we are born. Of course we experience moments when we feel socially awkward and out of place, but generally we learn to act toward others with confidence. Yet our unconscious ease masks an enormously complex process. When we enter a social situation, how do we know what to do? What should we say? How are we supposed to act? Are we dressed appropriately? Are we talking to the right person? Without knowing it, we have learned a complex set of cultural categories for social interaction that enables us to estimate the social situation, identify the people in it, act appropriately, and recognize larger groups of people.

Status and role are basic to social intercourse. *Status* refers to the categories of different kinds of people who interact. The old saying, "You can't tell the players without a program," goes for our daily associations as well. Instead of a program, however, we identify the actors by a range of signs, from the way they dress to the claims they make about themselves. Most statuses are named, so we may be heard to say things like, "That's President Gavin," or "She's a lawyer," when we explain social situations to others. This identification of actors is a prerequisite for appropriate social interaction.

Roles are the rules for action associated with particular statuses. We use them to interpret and generate social behavior. For example, a professor plays a role in the classroom. Although often not conscious of this role, the professor will stand, use the blackboard, look at notes, and speak with a slightly more formal air than usual. The professor does not wear blue jeans and a T-shirt, chew gum, sit cross-legged on the podium, or sing. These actions might be appropriate for this person when assuming the identity of "friend" at a party, but they are out of place in the classroom.

People also always relate to each other in *social situations*, the settings in which social interaction takes place. Social situations consist of a combination of times, places, objects, and events. For example, if we see a stranger carrying a television set across campus at four o'clock in the afternoon, we will probably ignore the activity. Most likely someone is simply moving. But if we see the same person carrying the set at four in the morning, we may suspect a theft. Only the time has changed, but it is a significant marker of the social situation. Similarly, we expect classrooms to be associated with lectures, and stethoscopes to be part of medical exams. Such places and objects mark the social situations of which they are part.

Some degree of *inequality* is part of most human interaction. One spouse may dominate another; a child may receive more attention than his or her siblings; the boss's friends may be promoted faster than other employees. But inequality becomes most noticeable when it systematically affects whole classes of people. In its most obvious form, inequality emerges as *social stratification*, which is characterized by regularly experienced unequal access to valued economic resources and prestige.

Anthropologists recognize at least two kinds of social stratification: class and caste. *Class* stratification restricts individuals' access to valued resources and prestige within a partially flexible system. Although it is often a difficult process, individuals may change rank in a class system if they manage to acquire the necessary prerequisites.

Many sociologists and anthropologists believe that there is an American class system and use terms such as *lower class, working class, middle class,* and *upper class* to designate the unequal positions within it. Americans born into poverty lack access to goods and prestige in this system but can change class standing if they acquire wealth and symbols of higher standing on a continuing basis. Upward mobility is difficult to achieve, however, and few people at the bottom of the system manage to change rank significantly. Indeed, many social scientists feel there is now a permanent underclass in the United States.

Caste defines a second kind of social stratification, one based on permanent membership. People are born into castes and cannot change membership, no matter what they do. In India, for example, caste is a pervasive feature of social organization. South Asians are born into castes and remain members for life; intercaste marriage is forbidden. In the past, castes formed the building blocks of rural Indian society. They were governed by strict rules of deference and served to allocate access to jobs, land, wealth, and power. Cash labor and new industrial jobs have eroded the economic aspect of the system today, but caste persists as a form of rank throughout most of the Indian subcontinent.

Several anthropologists and sociologists have argued that American racial groups are the equivalent of Indian castes. Black and white Americans keep their racial identity for life; nothing can change one's race. Racial identity clearly affects chances for the acquisition of prestige and economic success.

Caste identity, whether Indian or American, tends to preserve and create cultural difference. There is noticeable cultural variation among members of castes in most Indian villages, just as cultural variation occurs among black and white people in the United States.

Using the idea of social stratification, anthropologists have constructed a rough classification of societies into three types: egalitarian, rank, and stratified. *Egalitarian societies* lack formal social stratification. They may display inequality in personal relations based on age, gender, or personal ability, but no category of persons within the same sex or age group has special privilege. Hunter-gatherer societies are most likely to be egalitarian.

Rank societies contain unequal access to prestige, but not to valued economic resources. In such societies there may be chiefs or other persons with authority and prestige, and they may gain access to rank by birth, but their positions give them no substantial economic advantage. Horticultural societies, including some chiefdomships, fit this category.

Stratified societies organize around formal modes of social stratification, as their name suggests. Members of stratified societies are likely to form classes or castes, and inequality affects access to both prestige and economic resources. Most complex societies, including agrarian and industrialized states, fit into this type.

Inequality may also be based on other human attributes, such as age and gender. In many societies, including our own, age and gender affect access to prestige, power, and resources. It is common for men to publicly outrank women along these dimensions, particularly in societies threatened by war or other adversity that requires male intervention.

The articles in this section explore the nature of status, role, and inequality especially as these relate to gender. The first, by linguist Deborah Tannen, looks at the differences in the way little boys and little girls learn to communicate and explores the consequences of this interaction for adult men and women. The second selection, by David Gilmore, suggests that there is a strong similarity among the world's societies in the way manhood is defined. It goes on to describe the definition and explain why so many societies require boys to endure tests of their manhood. The third article, by Ernestine Friedl, explores the reasons behind difference in power experienced by women in hunting and gathering societies. Friedl concludes that women's power is governed by access to public resources. The final selection, by Elizabeth and Robert Fernea, describes the importance of the veil as a symbol defining the role and rank of women in the Middle East.

KEY TERMS

role	caste
status	racial inequality
social situation	egalitarian societies
inequality	rank societies

social stratification   stratified societies
class   sexual inequality

READINGS IN THIS SECTION

21

Children's Talk: Learning Gender

Deborah Tannen

Girls and boys in every society must learn the cultural rules that shape their roles as adult women and men. But, at least in the United States, many people ignore distinctive gender-related behavior in daily interaction. This is the subject of this selection, a small part of a much larger work on the way American women and men communicate, by Deborah Tannen. Focusing on second-graders, she contrasts the body language, conversational content, level of physical activity, seriousness, and level of apparent mutual concern displayed by boys and girls. She concludes that the gender differences begun in childhood largely continue throughout life and often go undetected by adults.

One source of inspiration for this book was a research project I participated in, dealing with how friends talk to each other at grade levels ranging from second grade to university. Although I had not intended to examine gender differences, when I watched the set of video-

From "'Look at Me When I'm Talking to You!': Cross Talk Across the Ages," Chapter 9 in *You Just Don't Understand: Women and Men in Conversation*, William Morrow & Company, 1990; paperback edition, Ballintine, 1991. Copyright © 1990 by Deborah Tannen. Reprinted by permission of the author.

tapes recorded by Bruce Dorval, I was overwhelmed by the differences that separated the females and males at each age, and the striking similarities that linked the females, on one hand, and the males, on the other, across the vast expanse of age. In many ways, the second-grade girls were more like the twenty-five-year-old women than like the second-grade boys.

The two categories of differences between the male and female speakers in the videotapes that were most striking to me were what the friends talked about and their body language—how they oriented themselves to each other with their bodies and eyes.

Differences in physical alignment, or body language, leap out at anyone who looks at segments of the videotapes one after another. At every age, the girls and women sit closer to each other and look at each other directly. At every age, the boys and men sit at angles to each other—in one case, almost parallel—and never look directly into each other's faces. I developed the term *anchoring gaze* to describe this visual home base. The girls and women anchor their gaze on each other's faces, occasionally glancing away, while the boys and men anchor their gaze elsewhere in the room, occasionally glancing at each other.

The boys' and men's avoidance of looking directly at each other is especially important because researchers, and conventional wisdom, have emphasized that girls and women tend to be more indirect than boys and men in their speech. Actually, women and men tend to be indirect about different things. In physical alignment, and in verbally expressing personal problems, the men tend to be more indirect.

TEASING AND TELLING STORIES AT SECOND GRADE

The two pairs of second-graders provide the most obvious contrast in physical alignment and in what they talk about. The second-grade boys, Kevin and Jimmy, move so incessantly that it seems the chairs they are sitting on can't contain them. They never look directly at each other. They look around the room, at the ceiling, and at the video camera set up in the room. They squirm, jump out of their chairs, rhythmically kick their feet, make faces at each other and the camera, and point to objects in the room. One boy continually pummels the arms of his chair. They sing, make motor sounds by trilling their lips, and utter nonsense syllables.

And what are the boys talking about amid all this hubbub? They make a show of misbehaving by mugging for the camera, saying dirty words, laughing, and then clamping their hands over their giggles and shushing each other up. They tease: Jimmy tells Kevin over and over, "Your hair is standing up! Your hair always sticks up!" and Jimmy tries to smooth his hair, since he has no mirror to see that it looks just fine. They jump from topic to topic, as they try to find "something to do."

"WHAT GAMES DOES HE HAVE?"

For the second-grade boys, "something to do" is "games to play." For example, they look around the room in which they have been placed (Professor Dorval's university office), in search of games:

JIMMY: Look. You know what the game—what the game is over there? We play—we had that in first grade. What games do we—does he have?
KEVIN: I don't know.
JIMMY: Probably only that. That's a dumb game, isn't it?
KEVIN: Looks pretty good though.
JIMMY: I can't wait until we play games.

Since they can't find any games to play (or don't feel they can help themselves to games they see in the room), they try to think of other things they can do:

JIMMY: Well, if you have something to do, do it.
KEVIN: Here he comes back in. What would you like to do?
JIMMY: Play football.

Though he obviously can't do it right now, Jimmy has no trouble thinking of what he would like to do: play football. He'd like to be outside, running around with a group of boys, not sitting in a chair talking to one friend. Since they can't be physically active now, they talk about being so in the future; Kevin says, "You want to come over to my house one day? Ride my bike?"

The boys do find "something to do," though it is not their first choice. In a tone that shows mock impatience, Jimmy demands that Kevin find something to do and Kevin obliges, making a suggestion that the boys take up:

JIMMY: Would *you* find something to *do?*
KEVIN: Patty cake.
JIMMY: [Laugh] Look. Patty cake. Come on, let's do patty cake. Come on.

All these excerpts give the impression of young children with a lot of energy—much like any young children, I might have thought, until I viewed the videotape of two girls of the same age. The picture the second-grade girls present seems truly to be of another world. Jane and Ellen sit very still, practically nose to nose for much of the time. One or the other or both sit at the edge of their chairs, and they look directly into each other's faces. They calmly look elsewhere in the room only when they are thinking of what to say next. They do not cast about for something to do; they seem satisfied that they are already doing something: talking to each other.

Looking at the two transcripts side by side shows how different these conversations are: Whereas the second-grade boys' transcript is a mass of short spurts of speech, each boy's turn rarely taking more than a line, the transcript of the second-grade girls' conversation shows big blocks of talk, so that a single page of transcript might have one or two turns. This is because the girls are telling each other stories about things that have happened to them and other people. But these are not just any stories. They are about accidents and mishaps, illnesses and hospital visits.

"THAT'S SERIOUS!"

Telling stories about misfortunes seemed to me a rather strange thing to do, until I realized that the girls were strictly following the orders they had been given. Dorval had instructed them, as he did the boys and all the other pairs of friends in his study, to consult with each other and find something serious to talk about. So when he left the room, the girls huddled and whispered and then separated, faced each other, and began to exchange stories about things they considered serious. The stories in the following excerpt are rather short, but otherwise they are typical of the second-grade girls' conversation.

ELLEN: Remember? What—when I told you about my uncle? He went up the ladder after my grandpa? And he fell and, um, cracked his head open? He's—and you know what? It still hasn't healed.

JANE: One time, my uncle, he was, uh, he has like this bull ranch? In Millworth? And the bull's horns went right through his head.

ELLEN: That's serious.

The way Ellen shows approval of Jane's story, "That's serious," shows that telling stories about disasters was meant to comply with the instructions they had been given.

Comparing the boys and girls of the same age, I had the feeling I was looking at two different species. The request to talk to each other about something serious seemed to make sense to the girls; they were asked to do something they often do by choice: sit together and talk. But the same request was a different one for boys, who are far less likely just to sit together and talk to each other in the course of their play. They are more used to *doing* things together—running around outside or playing games inside.

Looking at the tapes from the perspective of status and connection, or of oppositional versus supportive frameworks, I could see the patterns clearly. The boys, who have identified each other as best friends, show their affection for each other in an oppositional framework. Jimmy's repeated teasing, making Kevin think his hair is standing up when it's not, is one example. Jimmy also pretends to shoot Kevin, saying, "You're under arrest." And he says something intentionally mean: "I know William doesn't like you at all." Both boys play-fight, taking harmless swipes at each other.

FLOUTING AUTHORITY

The boys continually show their awareness of the authority figure who has placed them in this situation, as in the brief example above, where Kevin says, "Here he comes back in." They seek to undercut the experimenter's authority by resisting doing what they have been told (to talk about something serious) and by playful defiance. For example, they jump up and make faces at the camera, then giggle and shush each other, pretending momentarily to look like good little boys. They invoke the experimenter to flout his authority when he is nowhere in sight, as when Jimmy says, ". . . and then made a fart—here he comes!" Here, as elsewhere, their "misbehavior" seems aimed at the adult who has told them what to do.

Since they were instructed to talk about something serious, what better way to avoid compliance than to tell jokes? This the boys do:

KEVIN: Knock knock.
JIMMY: Who's there?
KEVIN: Fruit.
JIMMY: Fruit who?
KEVIN: Fruit bar.
JIMMY: What do you call a sleeping bull?
KEVIN: Bull chase. What?
JIMMY: Well? Well?
KEVIN: I don't know.
JIMMY: Bulldozer. You get it? Bulldozer.

Sometimes the jokes are scatological, and it is clear that they are breaking the rules of decorum with the adult authority in mind:

KEVIN: Knock knock.
JIMMY: Who's there?
KEVIN: [Jumping in his seat] Knock knock knock knock.
JIMMY: Who's there? [Pause] Tu tu. Tu tu who? You got tu tu in your panties.
KEVIN: I don't either.
JIMMY: I wonder if he hears us—he can—just move your mouth. [Both boys proceed to do so.]

This brief example has it all: Jimmy tells a joke; he teasingly puts Kevin down; he refers to a taboo subject; he shows his preoccupation with the authority figure who might object to their breaking these rules; and he defies and mocks the situation by pretending (and getting Kevin to pretend) to talk without producing sound. If telling a joke is a kind of performance that sets the teller at center stage, Jimmy is so exuberant in telling his tu-tu joke that he hogs the stage for the audience participation part as well, speaking all four lines of the knock-knock dialogue. On the other hand, he may simply be filling in for Kevin, who started the routine with "Knock knock," but didn't seem to have a joke in mind to follow through.

PLAYING "INTERVIEW"

Finding themselves sitting together and talking seems to suggest to these boys the hierarchical situation of being questioned by an adult. Playacting and mocking this framework, Jimmy takes the role of interviewer:

JIMMY: I've got four things to say.
KEVIN: Yeah?
JIMMY: I've got four things to say.
KEVIN: Tell me.
JIMMY: You doing good in your schoolwork, huh?
KEVIN: Yeah.
JIMMY: Um, play soccer good?
KEVIN: Uh huh.
JIMMY: You're nice. What was the last one? How are you?
KEVIN: Fine.
JIMMY: It's your turn.

Kevin's and Jimmy's turns are all very short—just a few words—with only two exceptions: one in which Jimmy explains a video game, and another in which he explains how to play patty cake (even though it was Kevin who proposed playing it). In both, he is taking the role of teacher.

A WORLD OF DIFFERENCE

These are just a few examples of what is pervasive in the twenty-minute videotape: The boys are physically restless; their idea of what to do involves physical activities; they are continually aware of the hierarchical framework they are in, and they do what they can to mock and resist it; and they show their affection for each other in an oppositional format. They directly disagree with each other, but then disagreement is a natural response to the putdowns and mock assaults that are initiated. For example, Kevin protests, "I don't either" when Jimmy tells him he has "tu tu" in his panties, and "No, I'm not" when Jimmy tells him he is under arrest.

The second-grade girls' conversation in the same situation includes nothing that resembles any of the ways of talking just described for the boys. The girls too are aware of the authoritarian framework they are in, but they are complying with it rather than defying or mocking it. And, far from playfully attacking each other, they support each other by agreeing with and adding to what the other says. Rather than colluding to defy authority, they reassure each other that they are successfully complying, as when Ellen tells Jane, "That's serious." In contrast to the teasing by which each boy implies that the other is doing things wrong, the girls offer reassurance that they are doing things right.

The brief stories the girls tell in the excerpt above are also typical of the ways the stories are linked to each other and to the girls' shared experience. By starting out with "Remember?" Ellen reminds Jane that Jane was there or has heard the story before. Already, in second grade, these little girls tell stories with the characteristic rising intonation that makes every phrase sound like a question. Like so many ways of talking that are characteristic of girls and women, when looked at from the perspective of status, this rising intonation could be interpreted as a request for approval and therefore evidence of insecurity. But it could also be seen—and, I think, is more accurately seen—as a way of inviting the listener to participate by saying something like "uh huh," or nodding. Jane also begins many of her stories by saying her friend's name—another mark of involvement.

The short example above is also typical of the longer conversation in that Jane follows Ellen's story with a similar story. Jane's story matches Ellen's not only in being about an accident, but also in being about an uncle and a head wound.

The second-grade girls, like the boys, talk about future activities, but what they propose is different from what the boys propose. Whereas Kevin invites Jimmy to come over and ride his bike, Jane tells Ellen that she has just read a Bible story that she liked a lot. She says Ellen can come over to her house so that Jane can read it to her—or she can read it herself. Not only does Ellen propose a talking activity, in contrast to Kevin's suggestion of a physical activity, but Jane also avoids framing Ellen as lower in status by assuring her that she can read the story herself rather than being read to, if she prefers.

Before the investigator entered the room and reminded them to talk about something serious, the girls were exchanging different kinds of stories. Like women who tell troubles as a kind of rapport-talk, these second-grade girls were exchanging matching complaints. For example, Jane complained that her little brother kept asking her to read stories to him but wouldn't let her finish any of them; he kept bringing out new books for her to start reading. Ellen responded with a matching story about reading to *her* brother, only her problem was that he had chosen a long book, and each time she finished a chapter and thought she was done reading to him, he'd insist on hearing one more. Here they were, in second grade, establishing rapport by complaining about others who were close to them and by matching and supporting each other's stories.

Men and women to whom I showed these videotapes had very different reactions to these second-graders. My reaction was typical of women's: I thought Jane and Ellen were sweet little girls, and I smiled to see them. I was touched by their eagerness to fulfill the experimenter's request. My heart went out to them. But the little boys made me nervous. I wished they'd *sit still!* I thought their joking silly, and I didn't like their teasing and mock attacks. I felt sorry for poor Kevin, who kept trying to smooth down his hair and was told that another little boy didn't like him.

But men I showed the tapes to reacted very differently. They thought the boys cute, and they found their energy and glee touching. They were sympathetic to the boys' impulse to poke fun at the situation and defy the experimenter's authority. The girls seemed to them like a pair of Goody Two Shoes. Some men commented that they didn't trust the girls' behavior; they felt that little children couldn't really enjoy sitting so still—they must be on their best behavior to kiss up to the experimenter.

So there it is: Boys and girls grow up in different worlds, but we think we're in the same one, so we judge each other's behavior by the standards of our own.

REVIEW QUESTIONS

1. What are the most distinctive attributes of the way second-grade boys interact with one another, according to Tannen?
2. What are the most important features of communication between second-grade girls?
3. How do men and women viewing tapes of the children's interaction react to what they see? Why?
4. What do you think these data imply about interaction between adult men and women?

22

Manhood

David D. Gilmore

Among the people of an Andalusian village in Spain, men should work hard, protect dependents, produce babies, and act with energy and bravery. Violence against women is a weakness. Based on these observations from his fieldwork, David Gilmore looks at the definition of manhood worldwide. He discovers that, although definitions vary from one culture to the next, most see real men as protectors, providers, and impregnators. To instill a value of manliness and to prevent boys from experiencing psychic regression, Gilmore argues, most societies require their boys to undergo public tests of their manliness.

Masculinity is not something given to you, something you're born with, but something you gain. . . . And you gain it by winning small battles with honor.
—NORMAN MAILER, "CANNIBALS AND CHRISTIANS"

We Westerners have always been concerned with manhood as a matter of personal identity or reputation, but this concern is not confined to the West. On Truk Island, a little atoll in the South Pacific, for example, men are also obsessed with being masculine. Echoing Lady

Macbeth, a common challenge there is: "Are you a man? Come, I will take your life now." In East Africa, young boys from cattleherding tribes, including the Masai, Rendille, Jie, and Samburu, are taken away from their mothers and subjected to painful circumcision rites by which they become men. If the Samburu boy cries out while his flesh is being cut, if he so much as blinks an eye, he is shamed for life as unworthy of manhood. The Amhara, an Ethiopian tribe, have a passionate belief in masculinity called wand-nat. To show their wand-nat, Amhara youths are forced to engage in bloody whipping contests known as buhe. Far away, in the high mountains of Melanesia, young boys undergo similar trials before being admitted into the select club of manhood. They are torn from their mothers and forced to undergo a series of brutal rituals. These include whipping, bloodletting, and beating, all of which the boys must endure stoically. The Tewa people of New Mexico also believe that boys must be "made" into men. Tewa boys are taken away from their homes, purified by ritual means, and then whipped mercilessly by the kachina spirits (their fathers in disguise). Each boy is lashed on the back with a crude yucca whip that draws blood and leaves permanent scars. "You are made a man," the elders tell them afterward.

Why must manhood be vindicated in so many cultures through tests and challenges? And how widespread are such rites of masculinity? My own interest in this subject arose through experiences in the field—in my case, a rural *pueblo* (town or village) in Andalusia, a region of southern Spain. There I noticed a heavy emphasis on being manly, or *macho* as Andalusians say, using the Spanish word for "male" (a word that, significantly, has worked its way into many languages as *machismo*). Hardly a day passed by when this subject went unmentioned. I found that it was hard to measure up in this regard. Indeed, it became a minor personal crisis when some male friends requested my company—rather insistently—on a nocturnal visit to a whorehouse so that I could prove that I was a "man."

Trained to see each culture as unique, cultural anthropologists emphasize human differences, but sometimes common themes draw them ineluctably to the contemplation of human similarities. As I pondered my friends' invitation, I experienced a curious sense of familiarity. I sensed affinity not only with the cultures described above but also with my own. I had grown up absorbing the manly fiction of Ernest Hemingway, Jack London, Norman Mailer, Tom McGuane, and James Dickey. Like many of my friends I, too, had gone to Pamplona to run with the bulls in imitation of Jake Barnes in *The Sun Also Rises,* a typical, if ersatz, rite of passage for college-age Americans. Later, when I returned home, I found the topic of manliness cropping up in discussions with colleagues. Almost every society, I found, has some specific notion about "true" manhood.

Sometimes, as in Andalusia, virility or potency is paramount; elsewhere, as among the Trukese and Amhara, physical toughness is more important. Sometimes economic "go-getting," athletic ability, or heavy drinking is the measure of a man. The ingredients vary, but in all these places a man has to pass some sort of test, measure up, accomplish something. Why is manhood a test in so many cultures? My quests for answers started in Spain.

There was a young man in the *pueblo* named Lorenzo. He was a perennial student and bachelor. A gentle character of outstanding native intelligence, Lorenzo was the only person from the *pueblo* ever to have gone to graduate school to pursue a doctorate, in this case in literature. But he was unable for various reasons ever to complete his dissertation, so he remained in a kind of occupational limbo, indecisive and feckless. Because of his erudition, Lorenzo was generally acknowledged as a sort of locally grown genius. Many people had high hopes for him. But the more traditionally minded were not among his admirers. In the very important matter of gender appropriateness, Lorenzo was eccentric, even deviant. "A grave case," as one man put it.

First, there were his living arrangements. Oddly, Lorenzo stayed indoors with his widowed mother, studying, reading books, rarely leaving his scholar's cloister. He had no discernible job. He lived off his uncomplaining old mother, hardworking but poor. Withdrawn and secretive, Lorenzo made no visible efforts to change this state of affairs; nor did he often, as men are supposed to do, enter the masculine world of the bars to drink or engage in the usual convivial banter. Rarely did he enter into the aggressive card games or the drunken bluster that men in his *pueblo* enjoy and expect.

Perhaps most bizarre, Lorenzo avoided women. He was actually intensely shy with girls. This is a very unusual dereliction indeed, one that is always greeted with real dismay by both men and women in Spain. Sexual shyness is more than a casual flaw; it is a serious, even tragic inadequacy. The entire village bemoans shyness as a personal calamity and collective disgrace. People said that Lorenzo was "afraid" of girls, afraid to try his luck. They believe that a real man must break down the wall of female resistance that separates the sexes. Otherwise there will be no children—God's gift to family, community, and nation. Being a sensitive soul, Lorenzo keenly felt the pressure to go out and run after women. He knew he was supposed to target a likely wife, get a paying job, and start a family. A cultural rebel by default, he felt himself to be a man of modern, "European" sensibilities, and he resisted.

One evening, after we had spent a pleasant hour talking about Cervantes, Lorenzo looked up at me with his great, melancholy eyes and confessed his cultural transgressions. He began by confiding his anxieties about the aggressive courting that is a man's presumed function. "I know you have to throw yourself violently at women," he said glumly, "but I prefer not to." Taking up a book, he shook his head with a shrug, awaiting a comforting word. It was obvious he was pathologically afraid of rejection.

Because he was a decent and honest man, Lorenzo had a small circle of friends in the town, all educated people, and he was the subject of much concern among them. They feared he would never marry, bachelorhood being accounted the most lamentable fate outside of blatant homosexuality. With the best intentions in mind, these people often asked me if I did not think it was sad that Lorenzo was so withdrawn and what should be done about him? Finally, one perceptive friend, discussing Lorenzo's case at length as we often did, summed up the problem in an unforgettable phrase. He noted his friend's debilitating unhappiness and social estrangement, and he told me in all seriousness that Lorenzo's problem was his failure "to be a man." When I asked him what he meant, he explained that in pursuing arcane knowledge, Lorenzo had "forgotten" how to be a man. Shaking his head sadly, he uttered a lapidary diagnosis: *como hombre, no sirve* (literally, as a man he just doesn't "serve," or work).

Spoken by a concerned friend in a tone of commiseration rather than reproach, the phrase *no sirve* has much meaning. Loosely translated, it means that as a man Lorenzo fails muster in some practical way, the Spanish verb *servir* meaning getting things done, "working" in the sense of proficiency: serviceability. This emphasis on serviceability, on efficiency and competence, provides a common thread in manly imagery and a clue to its deeper meanings. How does Lorenzo fail the test of manhood?

I had the good fortune, also, to encounter the model man. The opposite of Lorenzo was Juan, known to everyone by his nickname, Robustiano, "the robust one." He was tall and energetic, a worker who toiled hard in the fields from dawn till dusk, "sacrificed," as they say, to support his huge family. He was a fearless labor organizer, too, and during the dark days of the Franco dictatorship he had kept the faith alive among the town's workers and peasants by openly defying the police. He went to jail often and suffered many beatings, but even the tough Civil Guards could not break his spirit. They said that he resembled a mule in stubbornness, but that he had more *cojones* (balls) than a mountain of ministers—a begrudging way of complimenting a political opponent. *Muy hombre,* they admitted as they beat him, "a lot of man." In addition, Robustiano had fathered many children, with five sons among his brood. Only in his forties, Robustiano was a kind of culture hero.

These negative and positive examples sum up the qualities of manliness in Andalusia. A real man is one who provides for his family, protects dependents, and produces babies. He is not a bully, never a wife beater. On the contrary, he is a supporting prop of his community; above all, he is competent, a doer. He is willing to absorb punishment in pursuit of approved civic goals. He is fearless. On a more abstract level, one might summarize by saying he reproduces and augments the highest values of his culture by force of will. He creates something from nothing. In this way, he serves. Lorenzo's main failure, by contrast, is his fickle recessiveness, his timidity.

How can we conceptualize this composite image of manhood in Spain? It seems a threefold threshold: "man the protector" is also "man the provider" and, of course, "man the impregnator." This trinity of competencies is a recurrent image of communal hope. The emphasis on productivity and on omnicompetence is a common denominator that unites men and women in the re-creation of core values. It is this deeper function of creating and buttressing, not the specifics of form, that opens the door to cross-cultural comparison. Let us take a few brief examples from other cultures, far from Spain.

Among the aboriginal Mehinaku, a Stone Age tribe of farmers and fishermen living in the Amazon Basin in Brazil, there are "real men" and there are effeminate "trash yard men." A real man is one who displays efficiency in all walks of life. He gets up early to go on long, arduous fishing expeditions over dangerous terrain, ignoring hostile tribes that wait in ambush. When he returns, sometimes days later, he marches ostentatiously to the middle of the village where he throws down his catch for everyone to share. He is a fierce competitor in games and sports, especially wrestling—a favorite tribal pastime. He fathers many children, has many lovers, and satisfies his wife sexually. An incompetent man, one who is stingy, weak, or impotent, is scorned as effeminate.

Among the nonviolent Bushmen of the Kalahari Desert in southwest Africa, boys are not granted their manhood until they stalk and kill a large antelope singlehandedly. In this way they show that they are capable of providing meat for the entire band. Among the Sambia people of highland New Guinea, a boy cannot be a man until he has learned to disdain the sight of his own blood—basic training for the warrior's life that awaits him and upon which the security of the tribe depends. To be really a man, the Sambia tribesman must also father at least two children. Among the Masai of Kenya, a boy is not a man until he has stood up to a charging lion, established an independent household, and fathered more than one child. Among the Mende of West Africa, a boy is only a man when he shows he can survive unaided in the bush. In all these cases, the tests and accomplishments involved are those that will prepare boys and youths specifically for the skills needed in adult life to support, protect, and expand the living community. And it is only when these skills are mastered and displayed communally, in public, that manhood is conferred consensually upon the youth.

But still, we ask: why the stress and drama of manhood? Why is all this indoctrination needed, why the trials and tribulations? Why must males be literally pushed into such displays of performance? Here, as in most cases of human behavior where strong emotions are involved, we need a little guidance from psychological theory, and here, too, is where there is agreement with what feminists have said about the plasticity of gender roles. The key, I think, lies in the inherent weaknesses of human nature, in the inborn tendency of all human beings, male and female, to run from danger, to retreat from challenges, to return to the safety of the hearth and home. In psychoanalytic thinking, this tendency, exemplified perhaps by Lorenzo, is called psychic regression. It is defined as the tidal pull back toward the world of childhood, the pull back to the mother, the wish to return to the blissful, traumaless idyll of infancy.

Seen from this psychological perspective, we can interpret manhood as a moral instigation for performance—the moral force that culture erects against the eternal child in men, that makes retreat impossible by creating a cultural sanction literally worse than death: the theft of one's sexual identity.

Interestingly, manhood is not just a call to aggression. The brutal *machismo* of violent men is not real manhood in these cultures, but a mere-tricious counterfeit—the sign of weakness. A curious commonality is that true manhood is a call to nurturing. "Real" men are those who give more than they take, who, like "the robust one," serve others by being brave and protective. This "manly" nurturing is different from the female. It is less direct, more obscure; the "other" involved may be society in general rather than specific persons. Yet real men do nurture. They do this by shedding their blood, their sweat, their semen; by bringing home food, producing children, or dying if necessary in far away places to provide security for their families. But this masculine nurturing is paradoxical. To be support-ive, a man must first be tough in order to ward off enemies; to be gener-ous, he must first be selfish in order to amass goods; to be tender, he must be aggressive enough to court, seduce, "win" a wife.

Finally, with all this said, why should the challenges (and rewards) of these manhood codes be confined to males? We have seen that true man-hood often means serving society: accepting challenges, taking risks, be-ing expendable in the service of society. So why can't women be "real men" too? Why can't women also earn the glory of a risk successfully taken? But here we have to stop, for this is a question for the philosopher, not the cultural anthropologist.

REVIEW QUESTIONS

1. What evidence does Gilmore cite to support his contention that tests of manhood are important in many parts of the world?
2. What are the important elements of the male role found in the Andalu-sian village discussed by Gilmore?
3. How is the male role defined in other parts of the world?
4. What does Gilmore think accounts for why so many societies ask their boys to endure tests of manhood?

23

Society and Sex Roles

Ernestine Friedl

*Many anthropologists claim that males hold formal authority over
females in every society. Although the degree of masculine authority
may vary from one group to the next, males always have more
power. For some researchers, this unequal male-female relationship is the result of biological inheritance. As with other primates,
they argue, male humans are naturally more aggressive, females
more docile. Ernestine Friedl challenges this explanation in this selection. Comparing a variety of hunting and gathering groups, she
concludes that relations between men and women are shaped by a
culturally defined division of labor based on sex, not by inherited
predisposition. Given access to resources that circulate publicly,
women can attain equal or dominant status in any society, including our own.*

"**W**omen must respond quickly to the demands of their husbands," says anthropolgist Napoleon Chagnon, describing
the horticultural Yanomamö Indians of Venezuela. When a man returns
from a hunting trip, "the woman, no matter what she is doing, hurries

home and quietly but rapidly prepares a meal for her husband. Should the wife be slow in doing this, the husband is within his rights to beat her. Most reprimands . . . take the form of blows with the hand or with a piece of firewood. . . . Some of them chop their wives with the sharp edge of a machete or axe, or shoot them with a barbed arrow in some nonvital area, such as the buttocks or leg."

Among the Semai agriculturalists of central Malaya, when one person refuses the request of another, the offended party suffers *punan,* a mixture of emotional pain and frustration. "Enduring *punan* is commonest when a girl has refused the victim her sexual favors," reports Robert Dentan. "The jilted man's 'heart becomes sad.' He loses his energy and his appetite. Much of the time he sleeps, dreaming of his lost love. In this state he is in fact very likely to injure himself 'accidentally.'" The Semai are afraid of violence; a man would never strike a woman.

The social relationship between men and women has emerged as one of the principal disputes occupying the attention of scholars and the public in recent years. Although the discord is sharpest in the United States, the controversy has spread throughout the world. Numerous national and international conferences, including one in Mexico sponsored by the United Nations, have drawn together delegates from all walks of life to discuss such questions as the social and political rights of each sex and even the basic nature of males and females.

Whatever their position, partisans often invoke examples from other cultures to support their ideas about the proper role of each sex. Because women are clearly subservient to men in many societies, like the Yanomamö, some experts conclude that the natural pattern is for men to dominate. But among the Semai no one has the right to command others, and in West Africa women are often chiefs. The place of women in these societies supports the argument of those who believe that sex roles are not fixed, that if there is a natural order, it allows for many different arrangements.

The argument will never be settled as long as the opposing sides toss examples from the world's cultures at each other like intellectual stones. But the effect of biological differences on male and female behavior can be clarified by looking at known examples of the earliest forms of human society and examining the relationship between technology, social organization, environment, and sex roles. The problem is to determine the conditions in which different degrees of male dominance are found, to try to discover the social and cultural arrangements that give rise to equality or inequality between the sexes, and to attempt to apply this knowledge to our understanding of the changes taking place in modern industrial society.

As Western history and the anthropological record have told us, equality between the sexes is rare; in most known societies females are subordinate. Male dominance is so widespread that it is virtually a human universal; societies in which women are consistently dominant do not exist and have never existed.

Evidence of a society in which women control all strategic resources like food and water, and in which women's activities are the most prestigious, has never been found. The Iroquois of North America and the Lovedu of Africa came closest. Among the Iroquois, women raised food, controlled its distribution, and helped to choose male political leaders. Lovedu women ruled as queens, exchanged valuable cattle, led ceremonies, and controlled their own sex lives. But among both the Iroquois and Lovedu, men owned the land and held other positions of power and prestige. Women were equal to men; they did not have ultimate authority over them. Neither culture was a true matriarchy.

Patriarchies are prevalent, and they appear to be strongest in societies in which men control significant goods that are exchanged with people outside the family. Regardless of who produces food, the person who gives it to others creates the obligations and alliances that are at the center of all political relations. The greater the male monopoly on the distribution of scarce items, the stronger their control of women seems to be. This is most obvious in relatively simple hunter-gatherer societies.

Hunter-gatherers, or foragers, subsist on wild plants, small land animals, and small river or sea creatures gathered by hand; large land animals and sea mammals hunted with spears, bows and arrows, and blow guns; and fish caught with hooks and nets. The three hundred thousand hunter-gatherers alive in the world today include the Eskimos, the Australian aborigines, and the Pygmies of Central Africa.

Foraging has endured for two million years and was replaced by farming and animal husbandry only ten thousand years ago; it covers more than 99 percent of human history. Our foraging ancestry is not far behind us and provides a clue to our understanding of the human condition.

Hunter-gatherers are people whose ways of life are technologically simple and socially and politically egalitarian. They live in small groups of 50 to 200 and have neither kings, nor priests, nor social classes. These conditions permit anthropologists to observe the essential bases for inequalities between the sexes without the distortions induced by the complexities of contemporary industrial society.

The source of male power among hunter-gatherers lies in their control of a scarce, hard to acquire, but necessary nutrient—animal protein. When men in a hunter-gatherer society return to camp with game, they divide the meat in some customary way. Among the !Kung San of Africa, certain parts of the animal are given to the owner of the arrow that killed the beast, to the first hunter to sight the game, to the one who threw the first spear, and to all men in the hunting party. After the meat has been divided, each hunter distributes his share to his blood relatives and his in-laws, who in turn share it with others. If an animal is large enough, every member of the band will receive some meat.

Vegetable foods, in contrast, are not distributed beyond the immediate household. Women give food to their children, to their husbands, to other members of the household, and rarely, to the occasional visitor. No one outside the family regularly eats any of the wild fruits and vegetables that are gathered by the women.

The meat distributed by the men is a public gift. Its source is widely known, and the donor expects a reciprocal gift when other men return from a successful hunt. He gains honor as a supplier of a scarce item and simultaneously obligates others to him.

These obligations constitute a form of power or control over others, both men and women. The opinions of hunters play an important part in decisions to move the village; good hunters attract the most desirable women; people in other groups join camps with good hunters; and hunters, because they already participate in an internal system of exchange, control exchange with other groups for flint, salt, and steel axes. The male monopoly on hunting unites men in a system of exchange and gives them power; gathering vegetable food does not give women equal power even among foragers who live in the tropics, where the food collected by women provides more than half the hunter-gatherer diet.

If dominance arises from a monopoly on big-game hunting, why has the male monopoly remained unchallenged? Some women are strong enough to participate in the hunt and their endurance is certainly equal to that of men. Dobe San women of the Kalahari Desert in Africa walk an average of 10 miles a day carrying from 15 to 33 pounds of food plus a baby.

Women do not hunt, I believe, because of four interrelated factors: variability in the supply of game; the different skills required for hunting and gathering; the incompatability between carrying burdens and hunting; and the small size of seminomadic foraging populations.

Because the meat supply is unstable, foragers must make frequent expeditions to provide the band with gathered food. Environmental factors such as seasonal and annual variation in rainfall often affect the size of the wildlife population. Hunters cannot always find game, and when they do encounter animals, they are not always successful in killing their prey. In northern latitudes, where meat is the primary food, periods of starvation are known in every generation. The irregularity of the game supply leads hunter-gatherers in areas where plant foods are available to depend on these predictable foods a good part of the time. Someone must gather the fruits, nuts, and roots and carry them back to camp to feed unsuccessful hunters, children, the elderly, and anyone who might not have gone foraging that day.

Foraging falls to the women because hunting and gathering cannot be combined on the same expedition. Although gatherers sometimes notice signs of game as they work, the skills required to track game are not the same as those required to find edible roots or plants. Hunters scan the horizon and the land for traces of large game; gatherers keep their eyes to the ground, studying the distribution of plants and the texture of the soil for hidden roots and animal holes. Even if a woman who was collecting plants came across the track of an antelope, she could not follow it; it is impossible to carry a load and hunt at the same time. Running with a heavy load is difficult, and should the animal be sighted, the hunter would be off balance and could neither shoot an arrow nor throw a spear accurately.

Pregnancy and child care would also present difficulties for a hunter. An unborn child affects a woman's body balance, as does a child in her arms, on her back, or slung at her side. Until they are two years old, many hunter-gatherer children are carried at all times, and until they are four, they are carried some of the time.

An observer might wonder why young women do not hunt until they become pregnant, or why mature women and men do not hunt and gather on alternate days, with some women staying in camp to act as wet nurses for the young. Apart from the effects hunting might have on a mother's milk production, there are two reasons. First, young girls begin to bear children as soon as they are physically mature and strong enough to hunt, and second, hunter-gatherer bands are so small that there are unlikely to be enough lactating women to serve as wet nurses. No hunter-gatherer group could afford to maintain a specialized female hunting force.

Because game is not always available, because hunting and gathering are specialized skills, because women carrying heavy loads cannot hunt, and because women in hunter-gatherer societies are usually either pregnant or caring for young children, for most of the last two million years of human history men have hunted and women have gathered.

If male dominance depends on controlling the supply of meat, then the degree of male dominance in a society should vary with the amount of meat available and the amount supplied by the men. Some regions, like the East African grasslands and the North American woodlands, abounded with species of large mammals; other zones, like tropical forests and semideserts, are thinly populated with prey. Many elements affect the supply of game, but theoretically, the less meat provided exclusively by the men, the more egalitarian the society.

All known hunter-gatherer societies fit into four basic types: those in which men and women work together in communal hunts and as teams gathering edible plants, as did the Washo Indians of North America; those in which men and women each collect their own plant foods although the men supply some meat to the group, as do the Hadza of Tanzania; those in which male hunters and female gatherers work apart but return to camp each evening to share their acquisitions, as do the Tiwi of North Australia; and those in which the men provide all the food by hunting large game, as do the Eskimo. In each case the extent of male dominance increases directly with the proportion of meat supplied by individual men and small hunting parties.

Among the most egalitarian of hunter-gatherer societies are the Washo Indians, who inhabited the valleys of the Sierra Nevada in what is now southern California and Nevada. In the spring they moved north to Lake Tahoe for the large fish runs of sucker and native trout. Everyone—men, women, and children—participated in the fishing. Women spent the summer gathering edible berries and seeds while the men continued to fish. In the fall some men hunted deer, but the most important source of animal protein was the jackrabbit, which was captured in communal hunts. Men and women together drove the rabbits into nets tied end to end. To provide food for the winter, husbands and wives worked as teams in the late fall to collect pine nuts.

Since everyone participated in most food-gathering activities, there were no individual distributors of food and relatively little difference in male and female rights. Men and women were not segregated from each other in daily activities; both were free to take lovers after marriage; both had the right to separate whenever they chose; menstruating women were not isolated from the rest of the group; and one of the two major Washo rituals celebrated hunting while the other celebrated gathering. Men were accorded more prestige if they had killed a deer, and men directed decisions about the seasonal movement of the group. But if no male leader stepped forward, women were permitted to lead. The distinctive feature of groups such as the Washo is the relative equality of the sexes.

The sexes are also relatively equal among the Hadza of Tanzania, but this near-equality arises because men and women tend to work alone to feed themselves. They exchange little food. The Hadza lead a leisurely life in the seemingly barren environment of the East African Rift Gorge, which is, in fact, rich in edible berries, roots, and small game. As a result of this abundance, from the time they are ten years old, Hadza men and women gather much of their own food. Women take their young children with them into the bush, eating as they forage, and collect only enough food for a light family meal in the evening. The men eat berries and roots as they hunt for small game, and should they bring down a rabbit or a hyrax, they eat the meat on the spot. Meat is carried back to the camp and shared with the rest of the group only on those rare occasions when a poisoned arrow brings down a large animal—an impala, a zebra, an eland, or a giraffe.

Because Hadza men distribute little meat, their status is only slightly higher than that of the women. People flock to the camp of a good hunter and the camp might take on his name because of his popularity, but he is in no sense a leader of the group. A Hadza man and a woman have an equal right to divorce, and each can repudiate a marriage simply by living apart for a few weeks. Couples tend to live in the same camp as the wife's mother, but they sometimes make long visits to the camp of the husband's mother. Although a man may take more than one wife, most Hadza males cannot afford to indulge in this luxury. In order to maintain a marriage, a man must supply both his wife and his mother-in-law with some meat and trade goods, such as beads and cloth, and the Hadza economy gives few men the wealth to provide for more than one wife and mother-in-law. Washo equality is based on cooperation; Hadza equality is based on independence.

In contrast to both these groups, among the Tiwi of Melville and Bathurst Islands off the northern coast of Australia, male hunters dominate female gatherers. The Tiwi are representative of the most common form of foraging society, in which the men supply large quantities of meat, although less than half the food consumed by the group. Each morning Tiwi women, most with babies on their backs, scatter in different directions in search of vegetables, grubs, worms, and small game such as bandicoots, lizards, and opossums. To track the game, they use hunting dogs. On most days women return to camp with some meat and with baskets full of *korka,* the nut of a native palm, which is soaked and mashed to make a porridge-like dish. The Tiwi men do not hunt small game and do not hunt every day, but when they do they often return with kangaroo, large lizards, fish, and game birds.

The porridge is cooked separately by each household and rarely shared outside the family, but the meat is prepared by a volunteer cook, who can be male or female. After the cook takes one of the parts of the animal traditionally reserved for him or her, the animal's "boss," the one who caught it, distributes the rest to all near kin and then to all others residing with the band. Although the small game supplied by the women is distributed in the same way as the big game supplied by the men, Tiwi men are dominant because the game they kill provides most of the meat.

The power of Tiwi men is clearest in their betrothal practices. Among the Tiwi, a woman must always be married. To ensure this, female infants are betrothed at birth and widows are remarried at the gravesides of their late husbands. Men form alliances by exchanging daughters, sisters, and mothers in marriage, and some collect as many as twenty-five wives. Tiwi men value the quantity and quality of the food many wives can collect and the many children they can produce.

The dominance of the men is offset somewhat by the influence of adult women in selecting their next husbands. Many women are active strategists in the political careers of their male relatives, but to the exasperation of some sons attempting to promote their own futures, widowed mothers sometimes insist on selecting their own partners. Women also influence the marriages of their daughters and granddaughters, especially when the selected husband dies before the bestowed child moves to his camp.

Among the Eskimo, representative of the rarest type of forager society, inequality between the sexes is matched by inequality in supplying the group with food. Inland Eskimo men hunt caribou throughout the year to provision the entire society, and maritime Eskimo men depend on whaling, fishing, and some hunting to feed their extended families. The women process the carcasses, cut and sew skins to make clothing, cook, and care for the young; but they collect no food of their own and depend on the men to supply all the raw materials for their work. Since men provide all the meat, they also control the trade in hides, whale oil, seal oil, and other items that move between the maritime and inland Eskimos.

Eskimo women are treated almost exclusively as objects to be used, abused, and traded by men. After puberty all Eskimo girls are fair game for any interested male. A man shows his intentions by grabbing the belt of a woman, and if she protests, he cuts off her trousers and forces himself upon her. These encounters are considered unimportant by the rest of the group. Men offer their wives' sexual services to establish alliances with trading partners and members of hunting and whaling parties.

Despite the consistent pattern of some degree of male dominance among foragers, most of these societies are egalitarian compared with agricultural and industrial societies. No forager has any significant opportunity for political leadership. Foragers, as a rule, do not like to give or take orders, and assume leadership only with reluctance. Shamans (those who are thought to be possessed by spirits) may be either male or female. Public rituals conducted by women in order to celebrate the first menstruation of girls are common, and the symbolism in these rituals is similar to that in the ceremonies that follow a boy's first kill.

In any society, status goes to those who control the distribution of valued goods and services outside the family. Equality arises when both sexes work side by side in food production, as do the Washo, and the products are simply distributed among the workers. In such circumstances, no person or sex has greater access to valued items than do others. But when women make no contribution to the food supply, as in the case of the Eskimo, they are completely subordinate.

When we attempt to apply these generalizations to contemporary industrial society, we can predict that as long as women spend their discretionary income from jobs on domestic needs, they will gain little social recognition and power. To be an effective source of power, money must be exchanged in ways that require returns and create obligations. In other words, it must be invested.

Jobs that do not give women control over valued resources will do little to advance their general status. Only as managers, executives, and professionals are women in a position to trade goods and services, to do others favors, and therefore to obligate others to them. Only as controllers of valued resources can women achieve prestige, power, and equality.

Within the household, women who bring in income from jobs are able to function on a more nearly equal basis with their husbands. Women who contribute services to their husbands and children without pay, as do some middle-class Western housewives, are especially vulnerable to dominance. Like Eskimo women, as long as their services are limited to domestic distribution they have little power relative to their husbands and none with respect to the outside world.

As for the limits imposed on women by their procreative functions in hunter-gatherer societies, childbearing and child care are organized around work as much as work is organized around reproduction. Some foraging groups space their children three to four years apart and have an average of only four to six children, far fewer than many women in other cultures. Hunter-gatherers nurse their infants for extended periods, sometimes for as long as four years. This custom suppresses ovulation and limits the size of their families. Sometimes, although rarely, they practice infanticide. By limiting reproduction, a woman who is gathering food has only one child to carry.

Different societies can and do adjust the frequency of birth and the care of children to accommodate whatever productive activities women customarily engage in. In horticultural societies, where women work long hours in gardens that may be far from home, infants get food to supplement their mothers' milk, older children take care of younger children, and pregnancies are widely spaced. Throughout the world, if a society requires a woman's labor, it finds ways to care for her children.

In the United States, as in some other industrial societies, the accelerated entry of women with preschool children into the labor force has resulted in the development of a variety of child-care arrangements. Individual women have called on friends, relatives, and neighbors. Public and private child-care centers are growing. We should realize that the declining birth rate, the increasing acceptance of childless or single-child families, and de-emphasis on motherhood are adaptations to a sexual division of labor reminiscent of the system of production found in hunter-gatherer societies.

In many countries where women no longer devote most of their productive years to childbearing, they are beginning to demand a change in the social relationship of the sexes. As women gain access to positions that control the exchange of resources, male dominance may become archaic, and industrial societies may one day become as egalitarian as the Washo.

REVIEW QUESTIONS

1. According to Friedl, what factor accounts for the different degrees of dominance and power between males and females found in hunter-gatherer societies?

2. What are the four types of hunter-gatherer societies considered by Friedl in this article, and what is it about the structure of each that relates to the distribution of power and dominance between males and females?
3. Some anthropologists believe that male dominance is inherited. Comment on this assertion in light of Friedl's article.
4. Why does Friedl believe that women will gain equality with men in industrial society?

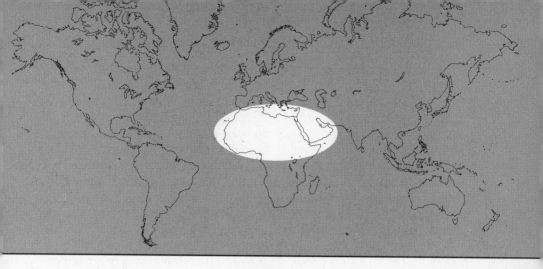

24

Symbolizing Roles: Behind the Veil

Elizabeth W. Fernea and Robert A. Fernea

*Most societies have some things that serve as key symbols. The flag
of the United States, for example, stands not only for the nation, but
for a variety of important values that guide American behavior and
perception. In this article, Elizabeth and Robert Fernea trace the
meaning of another key symbol: the veil worn by women in the
Middle East. Instead of reference to a national group, the veil codes
many of the values surrounding the role of women. Often viewed
by Westerners as a symbol of female restriction and inequality, for
the women who wear it the veil signals honor, personal protection,
the sanctity and privacy of the family, wealth and high status, and
city life.*

Blue jeans have come to mean America all over the world; three-piece
wool suits signal businessmen; and in the 1980s pink or green hair
said "punk." What do we notice, however, in societies other than our
own? Ishi, the last of a "lost" tribe of North American Indians who stum-
bled into twentieth-century California in 1911, is reported to have said that

the truly interesting objects in the white culture were pockets and matches. Rifa'ah Tahtawi, one of the first young Egyptians to be sent to Europe to study in 1826, wrote an account of French society in which he noted that Parisians used many unusual objects of dress, among them something called a belt. Women wore belts, he said, apparently to keep their bosoms erect, and to show off the slimness of their waists and the fullness of their hips. Europeans are still fascinated by the Stetson hats worn by American cowboys; an elderly Dutch woman of our acquaintance recently carried six enormous Stetsons back to the Hague as presents for the male members of her family.

Like languages (Inca, French) or food (tacos, hamburgers), clothing has special meaning for people who wear it that strangers may not understand. But some objects become charged with meaning to other cultures. The veil is one article of clothing used in Middle Eastern societies that stirs strong emotions in the West. "The feminine veil has become a symbol: that of the slavery of one portion of humanity," wrote French ethnologist Germaine Tillion in 1966. A hundred years earlier, Sir Richard Burton, British traveler, explorer, and translator of the *Arabian Nights*, recorded a different view. "Europeans inveigh against this article [the face veil] . . . for its hideousness and jealous concealment of charms made to be admired," he wrote in 1855. "It is, on the contrary, the most coquettish article of women's attire . . . it conceals coarse skins, fleshy noses, wide mouths and vanishing chins, whilst it sets off to best advantage what in these lands is most lustrous and liquid—the eye. Who has not remarked this at a masquerade ball?"

In the present generation, the veil has become a focus of attention for Western writers, both popular and academic, who take a measure of Burton's irony and Tillion's anger to equate modernization of the Middle East with the discarding of the veil and to look at its return in Iran and in a number of Arab countries as a sure sign of retrogression. "Iran's 16 million women have come a long way since their floor-length cotton veil officially was abolished in 1935," an article noted in the 1970s, just before the Shah was toppled. Today [1986], with Ayatollah Khomeini in power, those 16 million Iranian women have put their veils back on again, as if to say that the long way they have come is not in the direction of the West.

The thousands of words written about the appearance and disappearance of the veil and of *purdah* (the seclusion of women) do little to help us understand the Middle East or the cultures that grew out of the same Judeo-Christian roots as our own. The veil and the all-enveloping garments that inevitably accompany it (the *milayah* in Egypt, the *abbayah* in Iraq, the *chadoor* in Iran, the *yashmak* in Turkey, the *burga'* in Afghanistan, and the *djellabah* and the *haik* in North Africa) are only the outward manifestations of cultural practices and meanings that are rooted deep in the history of Mediterranean and Southwest Asian society and are now finding expression once again. Today, with the resurgence of Islam, the veil has become a statement of difference between the Middle East and the Western world, a boundary no easier to cross now than it was during the Crusades or during the nineteenth century, when Western colonial powers ruled the area.

In English, the world *veil* has many definitions, and some of them are religious, just as in the Middle East. In addition to a face cover, the term also means "a piece of material worn over the head and shoulders, a part of a nun's head dress." The Arabic word for veiling and secluding comes from the root word *hajaba*, meaning "barrier." A *hijab* is an amulet worn to keep away the evil eye; it also means a diaphragm used to prevent conception. The gatekeeper or doorkeeper who guards the entrance to a government minister's office is a *hijab*, and in a casual conversation a person might say, "I want to be more informal with my friend so-and-so, but she always puts a *hijab* [barrier] between us."

In Islam, the Koranic verse that sanctions a barrier between men and women is called the Sura of the *hijab* (curtain): "Prophet, enjoin your wives, your daughters and the wives of true believers to draw their garments close round them. That is more proper, so that they may be recognized and not molested. Allah is forgiving and merciful." Notice, however, that veils of the first true believers did not conceal but rather announced the religious status of the women who wore them, drawing attention to the fact that they were Muslims and therefore to be treated with respect. The special Islamic dress worn by increasing numbers of modern Muslim women has much the same effect; it also says, "Treat me with respect."

Certainly some form of seclusion and of veiling was practiced before the time of Muhammad, at least among the urban elites and ruling families, but it was his followers, the first converts to Islam, who used veiling to signal religious faith. According to historic traditions, the *hijab* was established after the wives of the Prophet Muhammad were insulted by people coming to the mosque in search of the Prophet. Muhammad's wives, they said, had been mistaken for slaves. The custom of the *hijab* was thus established, and in the words of historian Nabia Abbott, "Muhammad's women found themselves, on the one hand, deprived of personal liberty, and on the other hand, raised to a position of honor and dignity." It is true, nonetheless, that the forms and uses of veiling and seclusion have varied greatly in practice over the last thousand years since the time of the Prophet, and millions of Muslim women have never been veiled at all. It is a luxury poorer families cannot afford, since any form of arduous activity, such as working in the fields, makes its use impossible. Thus it is likely that the use of the veil was envied by those who could not afford it, for it signaled a style of life that was generally admired. Burton, commenting on the Muslims portrayed in the *Arabian Nights*, says, "The women, who delight in restrictions which tend to their honour, accepted it willingly and still affect it, they do not desire a liberty or rather a license which they have learned to regard as inconsistent with their time-honored notions of feminine decorum and delicacy. They would think very meanly of a husband who permitted them to be exposed, like hetairae, to the public gaze."

The veil bears many messages about its wearers and their society, and many men and women in Middle Eastern communities today would quickly denounce nineteenth-century Orientalists like Sir Richard Burton and deny its importance. Nouha al Hejelan, wife of the Saudi Arabian ambassador to London, told Sally Quinn of *The Washington Post,* "If I wanted to take it all off [the *abbayah* and veil], I would have long ago. It wouldn't mean as much to me as it does to you." Basima Bezirgan, a contemporary Iraqi feminist, says, "Compared to the real issues that are involved between men and women in the Middle East today, the veil itself is unimportant." A Moroccan linguist, who buys her clothes in Paris, laughs when asked about the veil. "My mother wears a *djellabah* and a veil. I have never worn them. But so what? I still cannot get divorced as easily as a man, and I am still a member of my family group and responsible to them for everything I do. What is the veil? A piece of cloth." However, early Middle Eastern feminists felt differently. Huda Sharawi, an early Egyptian activist who formed the first Women's Union, removed her veil in public in 1923, a dramatic gesture to demonstrate her dislike of society's attitude toward women and her defiance of the system.

"The seclusion of women has many purposes," states Egyptian anthropologist Nadia Abu Zahra. "It expresses men's status, power, wealth, and manliness. It also helps preserve men's image of virility and masculinity, but men do not admit this; on the contrary they claim that one of the purposes of the veil is to guard women's honor." The veil and *purdah* are symbols of restriction, in men's behavior as well as women's. A respectable woman wearing conservative Islamic dress today on a public street is signaling, "Hands off! Don't touch me or you'll be sorry." Cowboy Jim Sayre of Deadwood, South Dakota, says, "If you deform a cowboy's hat, he'll likely deform you." A man who approaches a veiled woman is asking for similar trouble; not only the woman but also her family is shamed, and serious problems may result. "It is clear," says Egyptian anthropologist Ahmed Abou Zeid, "that honor and shame which are usually attributed to a certain individual or a certain kinship group have in fact a bearing on the total social structure, since most acts involving honor or shame are likely to affect the existing social equilibrium."

Veiling and seclusion almost always can be related to the maintenance of social status. The extreme example of the way the rich could use this practice was found among the wealthy sultans of pre-revolutionary Turkey. Stories of their women, kept in harems and guarded by eunuchs, formed the basis for much of the Western folklore concerning the nature of male-female relationships in Middle Eastern society. The forbidden nature of seclusion inflamed the Western imagination, but the Westerners who created erotic fantasies in films and novels would not have been able to enter the sultans' palaces any more than they could have penetrated their harems! It was eroticism plus opulence and luxury, the signs of wealth, that captured the imagination of the Westerners—and still does, as witnessed by the popularity of "Dallas" and "Dynasty."

The meaning associated with veiling or a lack of veiling changes according to locality. Most village women in the Egyptian delta have not veiled, nor have the Berber women of North Africa, but no one criticizes them for this. "In the village, no one veils, because everyone is considered a member of the same large family," explained Aisha Bint Muhammad, a working-class wife of Marrakesh. "But in the city, veiling is *sunnah*, required by our religion." Veiling has generally been found in towns and cities, among all classes, where families feel that it is necessary to distinguish themselves from strangers. Some women who must work without the veil in factories and hotels may put such garments on when they go out on holidays or even walk on the streets after work.

Veiling and *purdah* not only indicate status and wealth; they also have some religious sanction and protect women from the world outside the home. *Purdah* delineates private space and distinguishes between the public and private sectors of society, as does the traditional architecture of the area. Older Middle Eastern houses do not have picture windows facing on the street, nor do they have walks leading invitingly to front doors. Family life is hidden away from strangers; behind blank walls may lie courtyards and gardens, refuges from the heat, cold, and bustle of the outside world, the world of nonkin that is not to be trusted. Outsiders are pointedly excluded.

Even within the household, among her close relatives, a traditional Muslim woman may veil before those kinsmen whom she could legally marry. If her maternal or paternal cousins, her brothers-in-law, or her sons-in-law come to call, she covers her head, or perhaps her whole face. To do otherwise, to neglect such acts of respect and modesty, would be considered shameless.

The veil does more than protect its wearers from known and unknown intruders; it can also conceal identity. Behind the anonymity of the veil, women can go about a city unrecognized and uncriticized. Nadia Abu Zahra reports anecdotes of men donning women's veils in order to visit their lovers undetected; women may do the same. The veil is such an effective disguise that Nouri Al-Sa'id, the late prime minister of Iraq, attempted to escape death from revolutionary forces in 1958 by wearing the *abbayah* and veil of a woman; only his shoes gave him away. When houses of prostitution were closed in Baghdad in the early 1950s, the prostitutes donned the same clothing to cruise the streets. Flashing open their outer garments was an advertisement to potential customers.

Political dissidents in many countries have used the veil for their own ends. The women who marched, veiled, through Cairo during the Nationalist demonstrations against the British after World War I were counting on the strength of Western respect for the veil to protect them against British gunfire. At first they were right. Algerian women also used the protection of the veil to carry bombs through French army checkpoints during the Algerian revolution. But when the French discovered the ruse, Algerian women discarded the veil and dressed like Europeans to move about freely.

The multiple meanings and uses of *purdah* and the veil do not fully explain how such practices came to be so deeply embedded in Mediterranean society. However, their origins lie in the asymmetrical relationship between men and women and the resulting attitudes about men's and women's roles. Women, according to Fatma Mernissi, a Moroccan sociologist, are seen by men in Islamic societies as in need of protection because they are unable to control their sexuality and hence are a danger to the social order. In other words, they need to be restrained and controlled so that men do not give way to the impassioned desire they inspire, and society can thus function in an orderly way.

The notion that women present a danger to the social order is scarcely limited to Muslim society. Anthropologist Julian Pitt-Rivers has pointed out that the supervision and seclusion of women was also found in Christian Europe, even though veiling was not usually practiced there. "The idea that women not subjected to male authority are a danger is a fundamental one in the writings of the moralists from the Archpriest of Talavera to Padre Haro, and it is echoed in the modern Andalusian *pueblo*. It is bound up with the fear of ungoverned female sexuality which had been an integral element of European folklore ever since prudent Odysseus lashed himself to the mast to escape the sirens."

Pitt-Rivers is writing about northern Mediterranean communities, which, like those of the Middle Eastern societies, have been greatly concerned with family honor and shame rather than with individual guilt. The honor of the Middle Eastern extended family, its ancestors and its descendants, is the highest social value. The misdeeds of the grandparents are indeed visited on their grandchildren, but so also grandparents may be disgraced by grandchildren. Men and women always remain members of their natal families. Marriage is a legal contract, but a fragile one that is often broken; the ties between brother and sister, mother and child, father and child are lifelong and enduring. The larger natal family is the group to which the individual man or woman belongs and to which the individual owes responsibility in exchange for the social and economic security that the family group provides. It is the group that is socially honored—or dishonored—by the behavior of the individual.

Both male honor and female honor are involved in the honor of the family, but each is expressed differently. The honor of a man, *sharaf*, is a public matter, involving bravery, hospitality, and piety. It may be lost, but it may also be regained. The honor of a woman, *'ard*, is a private matter involving only one thing, her sexual chastity. Once believed to be lost, it cannot be regained. If the loss of female honor remains only privately known, a rebuke may be all that takes place. But if the loss of female honor becomes public knowledge, the other members of the family may feel bound to cleanse the family name. In extreme cases, the cleansing may require the death of the offending female member. Although such killings are now criminal offenses in the Middle East, suspended sentences are often given, and the newspapers in Cairo and Baghdad frequently carry sad stories of runaway sisters "gone bad" in the city, and the revenge taken upon them in the name of family honor by their brothers or cousins.

This emphasis on female chastity, many say, originated in the patrilineal society's concern with the paternity of the child and the inheritance that follows the male line. How could the husband know that the child in his wife's womb was his son? He could not know unless his wife was a virgin at marriage. Marriages were arranged by parents, and keeping daughters secluded from men was the best way of seeing that a girl remained a virgin until her wedding night.

Middle Eastern women also look upon seclusion as practical protection. In the Iraqi village where we lived from 1956 to 1958, one of us (Elizabeth) wore the *abbayah* and found that it provided a great deal of protection from prying eyes, dust, heat, and flies. Parisian women visiting Istanbul in the sixteenth century were so impressed by the ability of the all-enveloping garment to keep dresses clean of mud and manure and to keep women from being attacked by importuning men that they tried to introduce it into French fashion. Many women have told us that they felt self-conscious, vulnerable, and even naked when they first walked on a public street without the veil and *abbayah*—as if they were making a display of themselves.

The veil, as it has returned in the last decade in a movement away from wearing Western dress, has been called a form of "portable seclusion," allowing women to maintain a modest appearance that indicates respectability and religious piety in the midst of modern Middle Eastern urban life. This new style of dress always includes long skirts, long sleeves, and a head covering (scarf or turban). Some outfits are belted, some are loose, and some include face veils and shapeless robes, as well as gloves so that no skin whatsoever is exposed to the public eye. However, these clothes are seldom black, like the older garments. The women wearing such clothes in Egypt may work in shops or offices or go to college; they are members of the growing middle class.

This new fashion has been described by some scholars as an attempt by men to reassert their Muslim identity and to reestablish their position as heads of families, even though both spouses often must work outside the home. According to this analysis, the presence of the veil is a sign that the males of the household are in control of their women and are more able to assume the responsibilities disturbed or usurped by foreign colonial powers, responsibilities which continue to be threatened by Western politics and materialism. Other scholars argue that it is not men who are choosing the garb today but women themselves, using modest dress as a way of communicating to the rest of the world that though they may work outside their homes, they are nonetheless pious Muslims and respectable women.

The veil is the outward sign of a complex reality. Observers are often deceived by the absence of that sign and fail to see that in Middle Eastern societies (and in many parts of Europe) where the garb no longer exists, basic attitudes are unchanged. Women who have taken off the veil continue to play the old roles within the family, and their chastity remains crucial. A woman's behavior is still the key to the honor and the reputation of her family, no matter what she wears.

In Middle Eastern societies, feminine and masculine continue to be strong poles of identification. This is in marked contrast to Western society, where for more than a generation greater equality between men and women has been reflected in the blurring of distinctions between male and female clothing. Western feminists continue to state that biology is not the basis of behavior and therefore should not be the basis for understanding men's and women's roles. But almost all Middle Eastern reformers, whether upper or middle class, intellectuals or clerics, argue from the assumption of a fundamental, God-given difference, social and psychological as well as physical, between men and women. There are important disagreements among these reformers today about what should be done, however.

Those Muslim reformers still strongly influenced by Western models call for equal access to divorce, child custody, and inheritance; equal opportunities for education and employment; abolition of female circumcision and "crimes of honor"; an end to polygamy; and a law regulating the age of marriage. But of growing importance are reformers of social practice who call for a return to the example set by the Prophet Muhammad and his early followers; they wish to begin by eliminating what they feel to be the licentious practices introduced by Western influence, such as sexual laxity and the consumption of alcohol. To them, change in the laws affecting women should be in strict accord with their view of Islamic law, and women should begin by expressing their modesty and piety by wearing the new forms of veiling in public life. Seclusion may be impossible in modern urban societies, but conservative dress, the new form of veiling, is an option for women that sets the faithful Muslim apart from the corrupt world of the nonbeliever as it was believed to do in the time of the Prophet.

A female English film director, after several months in Morocco, said in an interview, "This business about the veil is nonsense. We all have our veils, between ourselves and other people. The question is what the veils are used for, and by whom." Today the use of the veil continues to trigger

Western reaction, for as Islamic dress, it is not only a statement about the honor of the family or the boundary between family and stranger. Just as the changes in the nun's dress in the United States tell us something about the woman who wears it and the society of which she is a part, the various forms of veiling today communicate attitudes and beliefs about politics and religious morality as well as the roles of men and women in the Middle East.

REVIEW QUESTIONS

1. What is the meaning to Westerners of the veil worn by Middle Eastern women? How does this view reflect Western values?
2. List the symbolic meanings of the veil to Middle Eastern women. How do these meanings relate to the Muslim concept of *purdah* and to other important Middle Eastern values?
3. There has been a resurgence of the veil in several Middle Eastern societies over the past few years. How can you explain this change?
4. Using this article as a model, analyze the meaning of some American articles of clothing. How do these relate to core values in the country?

VIII

LAW AND POLITICS

I deally, culture provides the blueprint for a smoothly oiled social machine whose parts work together under all circumstances. But human society is not like a rigidly constructed machine. It is made of individuals who have their own special needs and desires. Personal interest, competition for scarce resources, and simple accident can cause nonconformity and disputes, resulting in serious disorganization.

One way we manage social disruption is through the socialization of children. As we acquire our culture, we learn the appropriate ways to look at experience, to define our existence, and to feel about life. Each system of cultural knowledge contains implicit values of what is desirable, and we come to share these values with other people. Slowly, with the acquisition of culture, most people find they *want* to do what they *must* do; the requirements of an orderly social life become personal goals.

Enculturation, however, is rarely enough. Disputes among individuals regularly occur in all societies, and how such disagreements are handled defines what anthropologists mean by the legal system. Some disputes are *infralegal*; they never reach a point where they are settled by individuals with special authority. Neighbors, for example, would engage in an infralegal dispute if they argued over who should pay for the damage caused by water that runs off one's land into the other's basement. So long as they don't take the matter to court or resort to violence, the dispute will remain infralegal. This dispute may become *extralegal*, however, if it occurs outside the law and escalates into violence. Had the neighbors come to blows over the waterlogged basement, the dispute would have become extralegal. Feuds and wars are the best examples of this kind of dispute.

Legal disputes, on the other hand, involve socially approved mechanisms for their settlement. *Law* is the cultural knowledge that people use to settle disputes by means of agents who have the recognized authority to do so. Thus, if the argument between neighbors cited above ended up in court before a judge or referee, it would have become legal.

Although we Americans often think of courts as synonymous with the legal system, societies have evolved a variety of structures for settling disputes. For example, some disputes may be settled by *self-redress,* meaning that wronged individuals are given the right to settle matters themselves. *Contests* requiring physical or mental combat between disputants may also be used to settle disputes. A trusted third party, or *go-between,* may be asked to negotiate with each side until a settlement is achieved. In some societies, supernatural power or beings may be used. In parts of India, for example, disputants are asked to take an oath in the name of a powerful deity or (at least in the past) to submit to a supernaturally controlled, painful, or physically dangerous test, called an *ordeal.* Disputes may also be taken to a *moot,* an informal community meeting where conflict may be aired. At the moot, talk continues until a settlement is reached. Finally, as we saw above, disputes are often taken to *courts,* which are formally organized and include officials with authority to make and enforce decisions.

Political systems are closely related to legal ones and often involve some of the same offices and actors. The *political system* contains the process for making and carrying out public policy according to cultural categories and rules; *policy* refers to guidelines for action. The *public* are the people affected by the policy. Every society must make decisions that affect all or most of its members. The Mbuti Pygmies of the Ituri Forest described by anthropologist Colin Turnbull, for example, occasionally decide to conduct a communal hunt. Hunters set their nets together and wait for the appearance of forest game. Men, women, and children must work together as beaters to drive the animals toward the nets. When the Mbuti decide to hold a hunt, they make a political decision.

The political process requires that people make and abide by a particular policy, often in the face of competing plans. To do so a policy must have *support,* which is anything that contributes to its adoption and enforcement. Anthropologists recognize two main kinds of support: legitimacy and coercion. *Legitimacy* refers to people's positive evaluation of public officials and public policy. A college faculty, for example, may decide to institute the quarter system because a majority feel that quarters rather than semesters represent the "right length" for courses. Theirs is a positive evaluation of the policy. Some faculty members will oppose the change but will abide by the decision because they value the authority of faculty governance. For them the decision, although unfortunate, is legitimate.

Coercion, on the other hand, is support derived from the threat or use of force or the promise of short-term gain. Had the faculty members adopted the quarter system because they had been threatened with termination by the administration, they would have acted under coercion.

There are also other important aspects of the political process. Some members of a society may be given *authority,* the right to make and enforce public policy. In our country, elected officials are given authority to make certain decisions and exercise particular powers. However, formal political offices with authority do not occur in every society. Most hunting and gathering societies lack such positions, as do many horticulturalists. *Leadership*, which is the ability to influence others to act, must be exercised informally in these societies.

The selections in this section illustrate several aspects of legal and political systems. In the first article, Napoleon Chagnon describes how the Yanomamö of Venezuela and Brazil organize violence into a series of increasingly deadly bouts, ending in lethal raids and the dreaded "trick." The second selection, by Mindie Lazarus-Black, looks at how poor women living on the Caribbean Island of Barbados use the state-sponsored legal system and child support laws to reinforce informal kinship rules and to control men. The third article, by Elizabeth Eames, looks at the political institution of bureaucracy. Drawing from the theory of Max Weber, she notes that bureaucracy, which is designed to be impersonal and even-handed in Europe and America, is a personal institution in Nigeria. The final selection, by Jack Weatherford, demonstrates the importance of kinship in the American Congress. Despite regular elections and open access to the electoral process, many Senators and Representatives belong to family dynasties that may even cross party lines and extend to power circles outside government.

KEY TERMS

infralegal	political system
extralegal	policy
law	public
self-redress	support
contest	legitimacy
go-between	coercion
ordeal	authority
moot	leadership
court	

READINGS IN THIS SECTION

25

Yanomamö: The Fierce People

Napoleon A. Chagnon

Every society provides a basis for authority and ways to gain sup-
port for such authority. In this article, Napoleon Chagnon describes
the Yanomamö, a group that bases its authority structure on a con-
tinuum of violence and on claims to fierceness or willingness to do
violence.

The Yanomamö Indians are a tribe in Venezuela and Brazil who practice a slash-and-burn way of horticultural life. Traditionally, they
have been an inland "foot" tribe, avoiding larger rivers and settling deep
in the tropical jungle. Until about 1950 they had no sustained contact with
other peoples except, to a minor extent, with another tribe, the Carib-
speaking Makiritaris to the northeast.

I recently lived with the Yanomamö for more than a year, doing research sponsored by the U.S. Public Health Service, with the cooperation
of the Venezuela Institute for Scientific Research. My purpose was to
study Yanomamö social organization, language, sex practices, and forms
of violence, ranging from treacherous raids to chest-pounding duels.

With permission from *Natural History*, January 1967. Copyright © the American Museum of Natural History, 1966.

Those Yanomamö who have been encouraged to live on the larger rivers (Orinoco, Mavaca, Ocamo, and Padamo) are slowly beginning to realize that they are not the only people in the world; there is also a place called Caraca-tedi (Caracas), from whence come foreigners of an entirely new order. These foreigners speak in incomprehensible language, probably a degenerate form of Yanomamö. They bring malaria pills, machetes, axes, cooking pots, and *copetas* (guns), have curious ideas about indecency, and speak of a new "spirit."

However, the Yanomamö remain a people relatively unadulterated by outside contacts. They are also fairly numerous. Their population is roughly ten thousand, the larger portion of them distributed throughout southern Venezuela. Here, in basins of the upper Orinoco and all its tributaries, they dwell in some seventy-five scattered villages, each of which contains from forty to three hundred individuals.

The largest, most all-embracing human reality to these people is humanity itself; *Yanomamö* means true human beings. Their conception of themselves as the only true "domestic" beings (those that dwell in houses) is demonstrated by the contempt with which they treat non-Yanomamö, who, in their language, are "wild." For instance, when referring to themselves, they use an honorific pronoun otherwise reserved for important spirits and headmen; when discussing *nabäs* ("non-Yanomamö"), an ordinary pronoun is enough. Again, in one of the myths about their origin, the first people to be created were the Yanomamö. All others developed by a process of degeneration and are, therefore, not quite on a par with the Yanomamö.

In addition to meaning "people," Yanomamö also refers to the language. Their tribal name does not designate a politically organized entity but is more or less equivalent to our concept of humanity. (This, of course, makes their most outstanding characteristic—chronic warfare, of which I shall speak in detail—seem rather an anomaly.) Sub-Yanomamö groupings are based on language differences, historical separation, and geographical location.

For instance, two distinguishable groups, Waika (from *waikaö*—"to kill off") and Shamatari, speak nearly identical dialects; they are differentiated mostly on the basis of a specific event that led to their separation. The Shamatari, the group I know best, occupy the area south of the Orinoco to, and including portions of, northern Brazil. Their differentiation from the Waika probably occurred in the past seventy-five years.

According to the Indians, there was a large village on a northern tributary of the upper Orinoco River, close to its headwaters. The village had several factions, one of which was led by a man called Kayabawä (big tree). A notably corpulent man, he also had the name Shamatari, derived from *shama*, the tapir, a robust ungulate found throughout tropical South America. As the story goes, Shamatari's faction got into a fight with the rest of the village over the possession of a woman, and the community split into two warring halves. Gradually the fighting involved more villages, and Shamatari led his faction south, crossed the Orinoco, and settled there. He was followed by members of other villages that had taken his part in the fight.

Those who moved to the south side of the Orinoco came to be called Shamataris by those living on the north side, and the term is now applied to any village in this area, whether or not it can trace its origin to the first supporters of Shamatari.

For the Yanomamö, the village is the maximum political unit and the maximum sovereign body, and it is linked to other villages by ephemeral alliances, visiting and trade relationships, and intermarriages. In essence, the village is a building—a continuous, open-roofed lean-to built on a circular plan and surrounded by a protective palisade of split palm logs. The roof starts at or near ground level, ascends at an angle of about 45 degrees, and reaches a height of some 20 to 25 feet. Individual segments under the continuous roof are not partitioned; from a hammock hung anywhere beneath it one can see (and hear, thanks to the band-shell nature of the structure) all that goes on within the village.

The palisade, about three to six feet behind the base of the roof, is some ten feet high and is usually in various stages of disrepair, depending on the current warfare situation. The limited number of entrances are covered with dry palm leaves in the evening; if these are moved even slightly, the sound precipitates the barking of a horde of ill-tempered, underfed dogs, whose bad manners preadapt the stranger to what lies beyond the entrance.

A typical "house" (a segment under the continuous roof) shelters a man, his wife or wives, their children, perhaps one or both of the man's parents, and, farther down, the man's brothers and their families. The roof is alive with cockroaches, scorpions, and spiders, and the ground is littered with the debris of numerous repasts—bird, fish, and animal bones; bits of fur; skulls of monkeys and other animals; banana and plantain peelings; feathers; and the seeds of palm fruits. Bows and arrows stand against housepoles all over the village, baskets hang from roof rafters, and firewood is stacked under the lower part of the roof where it slopes to the ground. Some men will be whittling arrow points with agouti-tooth knives or tying feathers to arrow shafts. Some women will be spinning cotton, weaving baskets, or making hammocks or cotton waistbands. The children, gathered in the center of the village clearing, frequently tie a string to a lizard and entertain themselves by shooting the animal full of tiny arrows. And, of course, many people will be outside the compound, working in their gardens, fishing, or collecting palm fruits in the jungle.

If it is a typical late afternoon, most of the older men are gathered in one part of the village, blowing one of their hallucinatory drugs (*ebene*) up each other's nostrils by means of a hollow tube and chanting to the forest demons (*hekuras*) as the drug takes effect. Other men may be curing a sick person by sucking, massaging, and exhorting the evil spirit from him. Everybody in the village is swatting vigorously at the voracious biting gnats, and here and there groups of people delouse each other's heads and eat the vermin.

In composition, the village consists of one or more groups of patrilineally related kin (*mashis*), but it also contains other categories, including people who have come from other villages seeking spouses. All villages try to increase their size and consider it desirable for both the young men and young women to remain at home after marriage. Since one must marry out of his *mashi*, villages with only one patrilineage frequently lose their young men to other villages; they must go to another village to *sio-hamou* (to "son-in-law") if they want wives. The parents of the bride-to-be, of course, want the young man to remain in their village to help support them in their old age, particularly if they have few or no sons. They will frequently promise a young man one or more of the sisters of his wife in order to make his stay more attractive.

He, on the other hand, would rather return to his home village to be with his own kin, and the tendency is for postmarital residence to be patrilocal (with the father of the groom). If a village is rich in axes and machetes, it can and does coerce its poorer trading partners into permitting their young women to live permanently with the richer village. The latter thus obtains more women, while the poorer village gains some security in the trading network. The poor village then coerces other villages even poorer, or they raid them and steal their women.

The patrilineages that maintain the composition of the villages, rich or poor, include a man and his brothers and sisters, his children and his brothers' children, and the children of his sons and brothers' sons. The ideal marriage pattern is for a group of brothers to exchange sisters with another group of brothers. Furthermore, it is both permissible and desirable for a man to marry his mother's brother's daughter (his matrilateral cross-cousin) and/or his father's sister's daughter (his patrilateral cross-cousin) and, as we have seen earlier, to remain in his parents' village. Hence, the "ideal" village would have at least two patrilineages that exchanged marriageable people.

There is a considerable amount of adherence to these rules, and both brother-sister exchange and cross-cousin marriage are common. However, there are also a substantial number of people in each village who are not related in these ways. For the most part they are women and their children who have been stolen from other villages, segments of lineages that have fled from their own village because of fights, and individuals— mostly young men—who have moved in and attached themselves to the household of one of the lineage (*mashi*) leaders.

Even if the sex ratio is balanced, there is a chronic shortage of women. A pregnant woman or one who is still nursing her children must not have sexual relationships. This means that for as many as three years, even allowing for violations of the taboos, a woman is asexual as far as the men are concerned. Hence, men with pregnant wives, and bachelors too, are potentially disruptive in every village because they constantly seek liaisons with the wives of other men. Eventually such relationships are discovered and violence ensues.

The woman, even if merely suspected of having affairs with other men, is beaten with a club; burned with a glowing brand; shot with a barbed arrow in a nonvital area, such as the buttocks, so that removal of the barb is both difficult and painful; or chopped on the arms or legs with a machete or axe. Most women over thirty carry numerous scars inflicted on them by their enraged husbands. My study of genealogies also indicates that not a few women have been killed outright by their husbands. The women's punishment for infidelity depends on the number of brothers she has in the village, for if her husband is too brutal, her brothers may club him or take her away and give her to someone else.

The guilty man, on the other hand, is challenged to a fight with clubs. This duel is rarely confined to the two parties involved, for their brothers and supporters join the battle. If nobody is seriously injured, the matter may be forgotten. But if the incidents are frequent, the two patrilineages may decide to split while they are still on relatively "peaceable" terms with each other and form two independent villages. They will still be able to reunite when threatened by a raid from a larger village.

This is only one aspect of the chronic warfare of the Yanomamö—warfare that has a basic effect on settlement pattern and demography, intervillage political relationships, leadership, and social organization. The collective aggressive behavior is caused by the desire to accent "sovereignty"—the capacity to initiate fighting and to demonstrate this capacity to others.

Although the Yanomamö are habitually armed with lethal bows and arrows, they have a graded system of violence within which they can express their *waiteri,* or "fierceness." The form of violence is determined by the nature of the affront or wrong to be challenged. The most benign form is a duel between two groups, in which an individual from each group stands (or kneels) with his chest stuck out, head up in the air, and arms held back, and receives a hard blow to the chest. His opponent literally winds up and delivers a close-fist blow from the ground, striking the man on the left pectoral muscle just above the heart. The impact frequently drops the man to his knees, and participants may cough up blood for several days after such a contest. After receiving several such blows, the man then has his turn to strike his opponent, while the respective supporters of each antagonist gather around and frenziedly urge their champion on.

All men in the two villages are obliged to participate as village representatives, and on one occasion I saw some individuals take as many as three or four turns of four blows each. Duels of this type usually result from minor wrongs, such as a village being guilty of spreading bad rumors about another village, questioning its generosity or fierceness, or accusing it of gluttony at a feast. A variant of this form of duel is side slapping, in which an open-handed blow is delivered across the flank just above the pelvis.

More serious are the club fights. Although these almost invariably result from cases in which a wife has been caught in an affair with another man, some fights follow the theft of food within the village. The usual procedure calls for a representative from each belligerent group. One man holds a ten-foot club upright, braces himself by leaning on the club and spreading his feet, then holds his head out for his opponent to strike. Following this comes his turn to do likewise to his adversary. These duels, more often than not, end in a free-for-all in which everybody clubs everybody else on whatever spot he can hit. Such brawls occasionally result in fatalities. However, since headmen of the respective groups stand by with bows drawn, no one dares deliver an intentionally killing blow, for if he does, he will be shot. The scalps of the older men are almost incredible to behold, covered as they are by as many as a dozen ugly welts. Yet, most of them proudly shave the top of their heads to display their scars.

Also precipitated by feuds over women are spear fights, which are even more serious than club fights. Members of a village will warn those of the offending village that they are coming to fight with spears. They specify that they are not planning to shoot arrows unless the others shoot first. On the day of the fight, the attackers enter the other village, armed with five or six sharpened clubs or slender shafts some eight feet long, and attempt to drive the defenders out. If successful, the invaders steal all the valuable possessions—hammocks, cooking pots, and machetes—and retreat. In the spear fight that occurred while I was studying the tribe, the attackers were successful, but they wounded several individuals so badly that one of them died. The fighting then escalated to a raid, the penultimate form of violence.

Such raids may be precipitated by woman-stealing or the killing of a visitor (visitors are sometimes slain because they are suspected of having practiced harmful magic that has led to a death in the host's village). Raids also occur if a man kills his wife in a fit of anger; her natal village is then obliged to avenge the death. Most raids, however, are in revenge for deaths that occurred in previous raids, and once the vendetta gets started, it is not likely to end for a long time. Something else may trigger a raid. Occasionally an ambitious headman wearies of peaceful times—a rarity, certainly—and deliberately creates a situation that will demonstrate his leadership.

A revenge raid is preceded by a feast in which the ground bones of the person to be avenged are mixed in a soup of boiled, ripe plantains (the mainstay of Yanomamö diet) and swallowed. Yanomamö are endocannibals, which means they consume the remains of members of their own group. This ceremony puts the raiders in the appropriate state of frenzy for the business of warfare. A mock raid—rather like a dress rehearsal—is conducted in their own village on the afternoon before the day of the raid, and a life-sized effigy of an enemy, constructed of leaves or a log, is slain. That evening all the participants march, one at a time, to the center of the village clearing, while clacking their bows and arrows and screaming their versions of the calls of carnivorous birds, mammals, and even insects.

When all have lined up facing the direction of the enemy village, they sing their war song, "I am a meat-hungry buzzard," and shout several times in unison until they hear the echo return from the jungle. They then disperse to their individual sections of the village to vomit the symbolic rotten flesh of the enemy that they, as symbolic carnivorous vultures and wasps, partook of in the lineup. The same thing, with the exception of the song, is repeated at dawn the following morning. Then the raiders, covered with black paint made of chewed charcoal, march out of the village in single file and collect the hammocks and plantains that their women have previously set outside the village for them. On each night they spend en route to the enemy they fire arrows at a dummy in a mock raid. They approach the enemy village itself under cover of darkness, ambush the first person they catch, and retreat as rapidly as possible. If they catch a man and his family, they will shoot the man and steal the woman and her children. At a safe distance from her village, each of the raiders rapes the woman, and when they reach their own village, every man in the village may, if he wishes, do likewise before she is given to one of the men as a wife. Ordinarily she attempts to escape, but if caught, she may be killed. So constant is the threat of raids that every woman leaves her village in the knowledge that she may be stolen.

The supreme form of violence is the *nomohoni*—the "trick." During the dry season, the Yanomamö do a great deal of visiting. An entire village will go to another village for a ceremony that involves feasting, dancing, chanting, curing, trading, and just plain gossiping. Shortly after arrival, the visitors are invited to recline in the hammocks of the hosts. By custom they lie motionless to display their fine decorations while the hosts prepare food for them. But now suppose that a village has a grudge to settle with another, such as deaths to avenge. It enlists the support of a third village to act as accomplice. This third village, which must be on friendly terms with the intended victims, will invite them to a feast. While the guests recline defenseless in the hammocks, the hosts descend on them with axes and sharpened poles, treacherously killing as many as they can. Those that manage to escape the slaughter inside the village are shot outside the palisade by the village that instigated the *nomohoni*. The women and children will be shared between the two accomplices.

Throughout all this ferocity there are two organizational aspects of violence. One concerns leadership: A man must be able to demonstrate his fierceness if he is to be a true leader. It is equally important, however, that

he have a large natural following—that is, he must have many male kinsmen to support his position and a quantity of daughters and sisters to distribute to other men. Lineage leaders cannot accurately be described as
unilateral initiators of activities; rather, they are the vehicles through
which the group's will is expressed. For example, when a certain palm
fruit is ripe and is particularly abundant in an area some distance from the
village, everybody knows that the whole village will pack its belongings
and erect a temporary camp at that spot to collect the fruit. The headman
does little more than set the date. When his kinsmen see him packing, they
know that the time has come to leave for the collecting trip. True, the headman does have some initiative in raiding, but not even this is completely
independent of the attitudes of his followers, which dictate that a death
must be avenged. However, when the purpose of a raid is to steal women,
the headman does have some freedom to act on his own initiative.

As a general rule, the smaller his natural following, the more he is
obliged to demonstrate his personal qualities of fierceness and leadership.
Padudiwä, the headman of one of the lineages in Bisaasi-tedi, took pains
to demonstrate his personal qualities whenever he could; he had only two
living brothers and four living sisters in his group. Most of his demonstrations of ferocity were cruel beatings he administered to his four wives,
none of whom had brothers in the village to take their part. Several young
men who attached themselves to his household admired him for this.

Padudiwä was also responsible for organizing several raids while I lived
with the villagers of Bisaasi-tedi. Every one of them was against
Patanowä-tedi, a village that was being raided regularly by some seven or
eight other villages, so that the danger of being raided in return was correspondingly reduced. On one occasion, when three young men from
Patanowä-tedi arrived as emissaries of peace, Padudiwä wanted to kill
them, although he had lived with them at one time and they were fairly
close relatives. The murder was prevented by the headman of the other—
and larger—lineage in the village, who warned that if an attempt were
made on the lives of the visitors he himself would kill Padudiwä.

Obviously, then, Padudiwä's reputation was built largely on calculated acts of fierceness, which carefully reduced the possibility of personal
danger to himself and his followers, and on cunning and cruelty. To some
extent he was obliged by the smallness of his gathering to behave in such
a way, but he was certainly a man to treat with caution.

Despite their extreme aggressiveness, the Yanomamö have at least
two qualities I admired. They are kind and indulgent with children and
can quickly forget personal angers. (A few even treated me almost as an
equal—in their culture this was a considerable concession.) But to portray
them as "noble savages" would be misleading. Many of them are delightful and charming people when confronted alone and on a personal basis,
but the greater number of them are much like Padudiwä—or strive to be

that way. As they frequently told me, *"Yanomamö täbä waiteri!"*—
"Yanomamö are fierce!"

REVIEW QUESTIONS

1. What is the most important value for men among the Yanomamö, and how is it acted out in the world of conflict and social control?
2. Describe the Yanomamö social and political organization. What accounts for the proliferation of Yanomamö villages over the past seventy-five years?
3. What are the different kinds of Yanomamö combat? Rank them according to their severity.
4. What are the major causes of disputes that set off physical combat among the Yanomamö?
5. How do men attain positions of leadership among the Yanomamö?

26

Why Women Take Men to Magistrate's Court

Mindie Lazarus-Black

Part of every legal system is substantive law, *the legal statutes that define right and wrong. Such statutes may be written down or may simply be agreed-upon principles. When statutes are violated, the law comes into play. But people often use the legal system in ways that transcend the literal meaning of substantive law, as Mindie Lazarus-Black demonstrates in this article about how lower-class Antiguan women use the magistrate's court. Antiguan substantive law requires men to pay support for their children when the latter are born outside of formal marriage. Women, however, rarely take the fathers of their children to court for this reason. Instead, they use this statute against men who fail to meet a variety of other, less formally defined, kinship obligations or who refuse to treat the mothers of their children with proper respect. "Big men," who are most easily shamed by court proceedings, are the most likely targets. In this way, women use the court to control men's behavior and enforce important kinship values.*

E very Thursday afternoon a list of "Order in Bastardy, Maintenance, and Arrears" is posted on the wall of the St. John's magistrate's court in Antigua, West Indies. In a typical week, six to eight new cases are scheduled for hearing, while twenty or thirty others are brought by the collecting officer of the state against men who have neglected to pay child support. There were 1,493 cases of maintenance and arrears in 1984, 1,287 cases in 1985. Given a population of approximately 65,000 in Antigua and Barbuda, such case loads indicate that the court is frequently utilized.

Academic, legal, and popular wisdom holds that these West Indian women are going to magistrate's court for money because the babies' fathers fail to support them or to pay regularly enough. They go to court because they are unemployed or underemployed with too many illegitimate children to raise and too few dollars with which to do so. But when I asked one woman if she went to court for money, her answer surprised me. She looked at me indignantly and said, "I carry my case up there for justice. I complain him for justice."

This article explores ideas about justice which are integral to kinship relations in Antigua and Barbuda. "Carrying a case" to the magistrate's court exemplifies the interaction between state forms and community norms and demonstrates that certain rules and judicial processes of the Antiguan state are now constituent of local family ideology and practice. That is, Antiguan women regularly take cases to court to demand justice in their kinship relations, to assert their autonomy and rights, and to resist the pervasive hierarchical structures of gender and class.

THE LEGACY OF COLONIALISM

British and European colonists brought to the West Indies cultural traditions in which families were legally constituted and then duly went about relegislating kinship. In the case of Antigua, as early as 1672 and at regular intervals over the next three centuries, legal codes were absolutely critical to creating and maintaining different social ranks in the colony and to regulating families, gender and race. Local legislators wrestled with questions about who might marry whom, which persons constituted "family," and what rights and duties such connections bestowed. The kinship order these lawmakers instituted for Antiguans departed dramatically from the rules that guided kinship in Great Britain. The legacy of colonialism included both detailed kinship laws and an elaborate hierarchy of courts.

Antigua was first colonized in 1632, mainly by English and Irish adventurers, soldiers, farmers, and laborers. Early lawmakers and judges consisted of a very small group of men of property, most of them planters. The switch from tobacco and cotton to sugar began in the 1650s. At that time, the colony was comprised of small farmers and a good number of European indentured servants. A century later, 93.5 percent of the population were slaves and most worked on large sugar plantations. . . .

The kinship laws Antiguan planters wrote were directed at controlling marriage and human reproduction, and also at reproducing the hierarchical social and economic structure of capitalism. Codes made it illegal for slaves to marry free persons, prevented indentured servants from marrying without their masters' permission, granted the right to perform marriage ceremonies only to Anglican ministers, and made white men responsible for their white bastard children.

The *Leeward Islands Amelioration Act,* passed in Antigua in 1798, also set up a separate system of marriage for slaves. According to this act, a slave marriage was monogamous but not contractual, since the nuptials bestowed none of the rights and duties implied in marriages of free persons. Nor did a slave marriage convey upon children the status or title of the husband/father. The law did include provision for public declaration of a couple's intention to live together and for monetary awards from their masters.

The colonists also established a hierarchy of courts. By the end of the eighteenth century, there was a Court of Chancery, a Court of Error and Appeal, a Court of King's Bench and Grand Sessions, a Court of Common Pleas, a Court Ordinary, a Court Merchant, and a Court of Admiralty. In addition, complaints between indentured servants and masters, and masters and slaves, were heard by itinerant justices of the peace.

Slavery was abolished in Antigua in 1834. In reality, abolition brought few dramatic changes to the lives of the ex-slaves. Limited availability of free land and the infamous Contract Act, which set new terms between workers and planters, combined to make it difficult to leave the estates. The Contract Act not only made it arduous to find a new employer, it also directed who might legally reside with whom in the estate huts, and commanded labor from each member of a man's family. Other social welfare legislation of this period made the destitute, the infirm, and the elderly the economic responsibility of their kin, not of the government.

Lawmakers passed in 1875 *An Act for the Better Support of Natural Children, and to afford Facilities for obliging the Putative Father to assist in the Maintenance of such Children.* The statute set procedures for obtaining affiliation orders, bestowed power upon magistrates to establish relationships between illegitimate children and their fathers, and designated stipends for men to provide for their offspring. Any woman who delivered a bastard child could apply for a support order. The request had to be made within a year after the baby's birth unless she could prove that previously the man had cared for the child. At the hearing parties could bring witnesses and had the right to counsel.

Weekly support payments were limited to five shillings for the first six weeks and to two shillings and six pence thereafter until the child attained the age of twelve or until the mother married. Stipends were payable directly to the mother and she had to apply for arrears within thirteen weeks or they were forfeited. The magistrate also had discretionary power to order the father to pay the costs of the case, a payment to the midwife, and funeral expenses if necessary. He could appoint a guardian for a child if the mother died, was of unsound mind, or went to prison. A putative father could appeal his case to the High Court, but the magistrate had power to send him to jail and to sell his property for failure to comply with the bastardy order.

With only slight modifications, the bastardy law still functions today. The act exemplifies both the continuous intervention of the state in matters of kinship and the hegemonic character of legalities in local communities. The bastardy law is regularly invoked by contemporary Antiguan women, although not always for reasons envisioned by nineteenth-century and later lawmakers.

THE ECONOMIC AND POLITICAL CONTEXT

Antigua's present population is almost entirely African-Caribbean. A few people have British and other European forefathers, others are descendants of Syrian and Lebanese traders who arrived early in the twentieth century, and there are some expatriate Americans and Canadians. English is the standard language, although there is a creole dialect. Most islanders are literate and most consider themselves Christian.

Historic dependence upon sugar exports prevented Antigua from achieving economic self-sufficiency. Agriculture remains in general decline today, despite a variety of efforts to revive it. Manufacturing and industry are developing slowly, but in the last two decades tourism has emerged as the most important economic sector. . . . Its direct value now accounts for approximately 21 percent of the gross domestic product, and at least 12 percent of the labor force works in tourism. . . . Government employs about 30 percent of all working persons. Unemployment remained at around 20 percent through the first half of the 1980s. . . .

Antiguan planters controlled local politics until labor unrest heralded a movement for social and economic reform early in this century. Unions were legalized in 1940 and adult suffrage was granted in 1951. Shortly thereafter, election rules were changed to allow greater representation of the working people. In 1979, the islands became an Associated State, gaining control over local affairs but still under British authority with respect to external relations and defense. Independence came in 1981. Antigua and Barbuda is now a parliamentary democracy with a Prime Minister, Senate, and House of Representative. The government proclaimed a non-aligned foreign policy at independence, but maintains strongest political and economic ties with Britain, Canada, and the United States.

Antigua's two social classes, middle and lower, can be differentiated into smaller strata based upon members' socioeconomic status and ability to wield formal political power. At the top of the present hierarchy is a small local elite which holds elected political authority. In contrast to the days when sugar dominated, this elite is Antiguan-born, black, and increasingly educated in the Caribbean. Within this same stratum are foreign businessmen and expatriates who play important roles in the economy but who are noticeably absent from the official political process. The lifestyle and domestic organization of the elite, however, are virtually indistinguishable from Antigua's middle class. Such similarities help explain why middle-class persons almost always say that Antigua has only two classes. Middle-class women rarely use the magistrate's court to order their kinship relations. Moreover, the ideology of class protects middle-class men from being named publicly as the fathers of illegitimate children.

Quite the opposite is true of the lower class, which uses the courts regularly. In some respects, the lower class is also more heterogeneous than the middle class. Its upper stratum consists of a petite bourgeoisie, "who own small amounts of productive resources and have control over their working conditions in ways that proletarians do not." . . .[1] Petite bourgeoisie men are often jacks-of-all-trades. They may own some land, raise a few cattle or goats, and work a job or two for weekly cash. Petite bourgeoisie women run their own small shops or work from their homes as seamstresses or hairdressers. In contrast, members of the working class have little or no property and only their own labor to sell. They include agricultural workers, fishermen, sales persons, domestics, hotel workers, and laborers. They are low-income, hard-working people for whom multiple jobs and job-sharing are common.

In contrast to Antigua, class is not relevant in Barbuda. Antigua's sister island was leased to the Codrington family in 1685 and 1705. The Codringtons used Barbuda as a supply depot and manufacturing center for their estates in Antigua. Until 1898 when the Antiguan legislature assumed financial responsibility for its government, Barbuda was virtually without political representation, welfare or educational services, or legal institutions.

The island has remained sparsely populated. Codrington, the only village, is home to approximately 1,200 people—almost all descendants of Codrington's slaves. Today many Barbudan men fish for their living. Others raise cattle. Both men and women work subsistence gardens and continue to insist upon communal ownership of land outside the village despite opposition from the government in Antigua. . . . Barbuda has a few shops, a couple of hotels where people find seasonal work, an elementary school, a health clinic, several churches, and a few government buildings. During my field work, a room in the police station served as a temporary courtroom upon the arrival of the magistrate.

---

[1] R. Rapp, "Family and Class in Contemporary America: Notes Toward an Understanding of Ideology," in *Rethinking the Family: Some Feminist Questions*, edited by B. Thorne (New York: Longman 1982), 180.

THE COURTS, THE CODES, AND THE LITIGANTS

The organization of the courts and the legal codes partially determine who comes to the magistrate's court, the types of complaints that are filed, and how any particular case will fare. A four-tiered court system presently serves the islands. The first tier consists of the magistrate's courts. Affiliation and maintenance cases, arrears, disputes between persons over small property claims, personal grievances, traffic matters, and minor assaults are brought to these courts. In addition to the magistrate's court serving the capitol city of St. John's, three "country courts" meet weekly in the villages of Bolans, All Saints, and Parham. By law, the magistrate holds court in Barbuda four times a year for two or three days, depending upon the case load. The Barbuda court draws quite a crowd. Interested bystanders make humorous comments about the litigants and their cases, sometimes to the chagrin of the magistrate.

The second tier in the legal system is the High Court. The High Court also settles major property and criminal cases, and family matters such as divorce, adoption, and contested wills. The third tier, the Appellate Division of the Supreme Court of the Eastern Caribbean, meets intermittently in the different Leeward Islands. Finally, since Antigua and Barbuda is a member of the Commonwealth, cases decided by the Supreme Court may be appealed, as a last resort, to the Privy Council in England.

Kinship statutes instruct who shall use which of these courts to resolve family disputes. When I conducted field work, statutes distinguished persons on the basis of their marital status (single or married) and their birth status (legitimate or illegitimate). Married persons have the option of applying either to the High Court or the magistrate's court for legal remedy with respect to certain kinship disputes. For example, a married woman may apply to the magistrate for relief if a spouse has committed adultery or aggravated assault upon the applicant, or is guilty of persistent cruelty or desertion, or is a habitual drunkard. The magistrate has authority to order that the complainant no longer be bound to cohabit with the defendant, award legal custody of children to the applicant, and direct the defendant to pay weekly support for the plaintiff and any "children of the family" for whom the man is legally responsible. Only a woman in a legal union can ask for support for herself. . . . All conflicts between unmarried couples over child care and maintenance must be adjudicated in the magistrate's court.

The persistence of these two alternative legal channels preserves the hierarchical social structure. The system, in place since the nineteenth century, funnels women with illegitimate children through one set of processes and married women through another. The law also differentiates in practice between persons of different social classes, since the two courts are widely acknowledged to have quite different consequences for individuals' family ties and the economy of their households. When I asked whether the magistrate's court might be characterized as a "poor peoples' court," eighteen of twenty-one attorneys concurred.

There are structural, economic, and ideological reasons beyond the factor of legal jurisdiction as to why that characterization holds. First, the magistrate's court is more readily accessible to the lower class. It is cheap to take a case there: the cost of a three-dollar stamp. One need not hire an attorney and, indeed, the majority of litigants with maintenance cases are not represented. Second, in 1987 a magistrate could award a maximum of fifteen Eastern Caribbean dollars per week for child support ($5.67 U.S.) and up to twenty-five E.C. dollars per week ($9.36 U.S.) for support for a married woman. Such small sums are unlikely to draw middle-class women to the court. Moreover, since they are usually married, middle-class women prefer to divide their property and arrange for the welfare of their children at the High Court where judges have much greater discretion in awarding support. In contrast to magistrates, High Court judges investigate the income and property of both parties and the ages and educational needs of the children. Finally, there are ideological reasons why the middle class avoids the magistrate's court. Members of this class, and some lower-class persons as well, consider kinship cases analogous to "hanging one's dirty laundry in public." The court's long association with persons of low status—with rogues and criminals—also dissuades Antiguans concerned about reputation from bringing a case there.

For all of these reasons, the magistrates primarily hear kinship disputes of working-class persons. The large number of family cases is partly due to the frequency with which men who have been adjudged as legal fathers and ordered to pay weekly support fail to make those payments. When a man does not pay for five or six consecutive weeks, the collecting officer requests the magistrate to order the man to give reason why he has neglected to pay. At present, if he chooses not to pay he does not pay until the police track him down. Meanwhile, the number of cases against him continues to multiply on the books.

After cases of unpaid arrears, the most frequently heard family disputes are those in which a woman requests that the man be judged the putative father of her child and an order be made for the child's support. These petitions constituted about 70 percent of all new kinship cases brought before the magistrates each year between 1980 and 1986.

Excluding cases of arrears, almost all of the kinship cases heard by the court are brought by women. Women rely on the courts to establish affiliation and maintenance, to increase support orders, to deny husbands the right to cohabitation, to request maintenance for themselves and their children, to protect the financial interests of a child if a father is about leave the country, and to remove a youth from the home of a negligent parent. Men, on the other hand, file most of the requests for a discharge of a magistrate's order. They have that option as soon as a minor reaches the age of sixteen, if the child comes to reside with them, or if the mother takes the child out of the state.

The plaintiff with a kinship case in the magistrate's court is almost always a lower-class woman, finding herself at odds with a man and her children neglected. The woman may or may not have other children at home to support. In a great many instances, she juggles child care and some form of part-time employment to pay for shelter and food. Usually the union between the man and woman has not been a casual one; most frequently the couple have been seeing each other for over a year and up to several years. Of twenty-two such trials I observed in St. John's, seven involved one child, nine involved two children, four involved three children, and two involved four children. The parties tend to be young, commonly eighteen to thirty-five years of age, but the vast majority were not pregnant teens. Most plaintiffs had never been to court before and most were uncertain about what was expected of them.

The litigants usually did know, however, that a magistrate could award only up to $15 E.C. per week for child support. Indeed, the amount is so low that it can make a difference only to the most indigent. Moreover, if financial considerations were the primary cause for women going to court, we would expect to see a steady rise in the number of cases filed after 1982 when the stipend was raised from $7 to $15 E.C. That was not the case. There was an immediate but temporary rise in the number of requests for affiliation and maintenance in St. John's right after the stipend increased, probably due to the publicity surrounding the change in the law. This may have encouraged some women with easy access to this court to apply for aid for the first time and others to request an increase in the support they already received. Within two years of the passage of the bill, however, the number of new requests had dropped to earlier levels. The court records also show that over the relevant five-year period there were no significant changes in the number of new cases filed in any of the country courts or in Barbuda. Apparently neither urban nor village women were motivated to go to court for purely financial reasons.

WHY WOMEN USE THE MAGISTRATE'S COURT

Case histories, interviews with litigants and lawyers, and observations of trials at the magistrate's courts show that Antiguan women take men to court when those men violate local norms about respect, support, and appropriate relations between the sexes. Women invoke the state in the name of justice, using law and forensic processes to ritually enact the meaning, rights, and responsibilities of kin. Two case histories illustrate this phenomenon.

In 1985, Cicely was 38, unmarried, with four children, each of whom had a different father. Cicely supported herself and the children by cleaning offices two days a week, working in a private home one afternoon, and sometimes selling candy, cigarettes, drinks, and other small items on a street-corner from a tray perched upon a styrofoam cooler. Her regular salary was only $95 E.C. per week (about $35 U.S.) and she frequently needed help from her mother, who worked as a kitchen aid, or from her younger sister, a primary school teacher.

Her situation had improved somewhat a year later. She had a full-time cleaning job for which she earned $108 E.C. per week. She had also obtained some funds from an American organization which assisted poor children. The composition of her household had changed as well. Her oldest daughter had returned to live with her, but a little girl she had been "minding" in 1985 had gone to live with her father's sister. One thing was unchanged; Cicely had virtually no support for her children from their fathers. Yet Cicely took only two of those men to court. The first man was a bartender, the second was a police officer. The other fathers were laborers.

Josephine's story reveals some interesting parallels to Cicely's case. Her father, Tyronne, was a carpenter and electrician. Tyronne had no formal training, but he was a master at fixing and inventing things, and could connect a house to the government electricity without its knowledge. Tyronne ran a small shop and drove a big car. When he died in 1981, Josephine met siblings at his funeral that she had never known.

Josephine's mother, Evelyn, worked as a domestic servant. Evelyn and Tyronne had not stayed together long. When Evelyn married for the second time at the age of 44, she had had eight children by six different men. Only her first husband had consistently supported his two children. The other men, laborers and fishermen, went their separate ways. Only Tyronne, however, was taken to court. By coincidence, two other women also summoned Tyronne to court for maintenance on the same day and all three were awarded the maximum that the law allowed.

The timing of Tyronne's cases may have been coincidental; the fact that he and two of the fathers of Cicely's children were brought to court, was not. The case studies show that women use the courts selectively. The profiles of these men are keys to identifying ideas about family, gender, and status that explain why Antiguan women go to court and why these particular men received summons. Moreover, these notions are intrinsic to family ideology and to the even flow of family life in the community.

In the Antiguan lower class, men and women are held to have distinctly different natures. Although West Indians highly value individual autonomy and economic independence for both men and women, I found that Antiguans repeatedly stressed the biological and social differences between men and women and used those differences to support the premise that there is a proper domain for each sex. Both men and women distinguish between the "inside" world of women and the "outside" world of men, and neither views those two domains as equal in any respect. The creed of gender hierarchy within the family contributes to the subordinate position of women in this society. Nevertheless, as we shall see, a highly developed sense of justice ensures there are limits beyond which a man may not assert the special privileges accorded to his sex.

Antiguan men and women love and need each other—children are one consequence of that fact—but because their natures are so different, men and women parent in different ways. Women nurture children, cook for them, wash them, teach them, and discipline them. Men provide some of this care, but their primary responsibility is to "feed a child," which means that the man maintains a particular kind of relationship with the child and the mother. An alliance exists in the first place because the man and the child share the same blood. Antiguan men are proud of their children and boast about their number. As another indication of their willingness to accept fatherhood, men rarely deny paternity at court, even if there are raging disagreements about how much they can afford in weekly payments.

A child generally uses his or her father's surname in the community and is entitled to that man's attention and "support." Support may take the form of cash, gifts, food, clothing, school supplies, or services provided by either the man or members of his family. For example, a woman generally does not take a man to court if his mother babysits or provides clothing for her grandchild. In contrast to the law, community norms are flexible with respect to the amount and type of support due to an illegitimate child. Support may vary in amount or kind from month to month, but it must be given somewhat regularly to maintain the alliance.

Finally, in addition to support, a man owes the mother of his child "respect." Like the notion of feeding a child, respect embodies a host of expectations. It means that even after their separation the man speaks politely about his child's mother and the people she is close to, that he acknowledges them publicly if the occasion arises, that he acts with discretion, and that he never flaunts a new relationship in her presence.

Breaking the norms which govern the alliances between men, women and children sometimes results in a man being hauled to court. One woman I interviewed, for example, took the father of her child to court only after he had insulted her publicly in the market. Often, however, a norm involving respect is broken in conjunction with another which speaks directly about principles of hierarchy within the lower class. Consider the men whom Cicely and Evelyn brought to court: the bartender, the policeman, and Tyronne, the electrician. These men share a social stature that distinguishes them from the other fathers of Cicely's and Evelyn's illegitimate children. Locally, they are called "big men." A "big man" in Antigua has a respectable job with a steady income. Beyond this, he has won admiration by virtue of his leadership qualities, command of language, intelligence, wit, education, and generosity. He can maintain multiple unions, even when married, keep his women "in order," and father and "feed" many children. Big men uphold certain standards in their family relationships. They provide gifts to their wives and "outside" women and support all of their children in a manner which accords with their standing in the community.

Violating this code of behavior makes a big man an Antiguan woman's choice for a trip to the magistrate's court for a ritual shaming. The courtroom becomes for these men what Garfinkel[2] . . . calls a "degradation ceremony." When a man's name is called in court, his position as a big man is challenged. The trial indicates that he is not generous, not responsible, not a suitable father, and incapable of controlling his women.

By all accounts and my own observations, the shaming of men at the magistrate's court undeniably achieves this aim. Often a woman need only file legal papers and the man changes his ways. Those who come to court are chastised and warned that they may face prison if they fail to pay for their children. Some men refuse to attend, but in that case the suit is heard in their absence and the effect upon their reputation in the community is the same. The shaming ceremony, then, renews and validates legally constituted kinship responsibilities while mitigating the prestige of a big man.

INVERSION OF GENDER RELATIONS

The court ritual that challenges a man's personal competence and his status among his peers also inverts the usual hierarchical status between men and women. When she brings a man to the magistrate's court, a woman forces a conjuncture of the domestic and the public spheres; the dirty laundry is made public. During the case, she uses law, courts, forensic processes, and legal personnel to manage male behavior and to lay claim to the rights due her and her children. If only for the duration of the ritual, she is a status equal and the public spokesman and representative for her children. Such behavior has its costs. A woman may be chided for going to court; she may be accused of spite. Nonetheless, the achievement of equality, the validation of individual rights, and the recognition of moral duty—central elements of Antiguan family ideology—are proclaimed during the trial. These constitute a vital part of the "justice" for which Antiguan women go to court.

Ironically, the expressed intent of the lawmakers—the regular provision of support for illegitimate children—is not nearly as effective as the threat or the actual performance of the shaming ceremony. Almost every woman I spoke with during my follow-up study complained about not receiving weekly payments. Their complaints were borne out by the collecting officer's records. Most women waited weeks between payments; some waited months. Women who take policemen to court face an added diffi-

---

[2] H. Garfinkel, "Conditions of Successful Degradation Ceremonies," *The American Journal of Sociology* 61 (1956):89.

culty because officers are reluctant to hand warrants for failure to pay child support to fellow officers.

One last issue with respect to kinship cases at the magistrate's courts needs to be raised. There is a point at which a big man is too big a man to impugn in court, which accounts for the infrequency of inter-class family disputes in the lower courts. For at least three reasons, upper-middle-class status shields a man against the justice that lower-class women seek from the courts. First, charges of corruption against public officials occur frequently enough that the lower class remains cynical about the justice that poor people can expect at court when their opponents are wealthy and powerful people. In their view, pragmatism teaches that there is not much use in suing a middle-class man whose fancy lawyer will break your case or who is himself a friend of a friend of the judge. Second, rich and powerful men are likely to be married to rich and powerful women, who are formidable adversaries in their own right because they wield considerable influence over employment and educational opportunities in the community. Finally, some lower-class women do not take the wealthy fathers of their illegitimate children to court because they cherish the hope that some day these men will "rediscover" their children, come to love them, and provide them with their rightful due. That hope is part of the ideology of Antiguan family life and is crucial to understanding why a woman has a child "for" a man.

Although a maintenance case may appear to be a request for cash, it is in fact a way to substantiate familial alliances and to shame men who purport to be "big men" but who break a "big man's" code of conduct. A woman brings a case to magistrate's court to claim normative rights which regulate family, gender, and hierarchy within the lower class. Women rely on and use a literal translation of Antiguan kinship law to manage male behavior, to voice objections to their own inequality, and to reaffirm the rights of their children. They "carry" their cases for "justice."

REVIEW QUESTIONS

1. How is the Antiguan legal system organized, and how did it come to be this way?
2. What is the nature of the Antiguan class system, and how is it related to the kinds of cases heard in different courts?
3. What are the substantive rules that lower-class women use to take the fathers of their children to court?
4. What are the real reasons why women take the fathers of their children to court?
5. Which men are most likely to be taken to court for failure to pay child support?

27

Navigating Nigerian Bureaucracies

Elizabeth A. Eames

Anthropologists regularly study different political institutions, from the informal systems of foragers to the more highly structured organization of chiefdomships, kingdoms, and democracies. One important topic of anthropological study is the growth and operation of bureaucracies in complex societies, the subject of this selection by Elizabeth Eames. During fieldwork in Africa, Eames discovered that Nigerian bureaucracies work differently from those found in the west. Whereas the American plan is organized on the principle of what Max Weber called legal domination, *one characterized by impersonality and ideally the application of the same rules for everyone, the Nigerian system revolves around* patrimonial domination, *where transactions depend on establishing and cultivating social relations.*

Americans have a saying: "It's not *what* you know, it's *who* you know." This aphorism captures the usually subtle use of old-boy networks for personal advancement in the United States. But what happens when this principle becomes the primary dynamic of an entire social

From Elizabeth A. Eames, "Navigating Nigerian Bureaucracies, or 'Why Can't You Beg?' She Demanded," in *Work in Modern Society: A Sociology Reader.* Edited by Lauri Perman (Dubuque, IA: Kendall/Hunt, 1986). Copyright © 1985 by Elizabeth A. Eames. Reprinted by permission of the author.

system? The period of three years I spent pursuing anthropological field research in a small Nigerian city was one of continual adjustment and re-ordering of expectations. This paper discusses a single case—how I discovered the importance personal ties have for Nigerian bureaucrats—but also illustrates the *general process* by which any open-minded visitor to a foreign land might decipher the rules of proper behavior. I was already familiar with Max Weber's work on bureaucracy and patrimony, yet its tremendous significance and explanatory power only became clear to me following the incidents discussed below. Accordingly, the paper concludes with a discussion of Weber's concept of *patrimonial authority*.

I heard the same comment from every expatriate I met in Nigeria—U.S. foreign service officers, U.N. "experts," and visiting business consultants alike: "If you survive a stint in Nigeria, you can survive *anywhere*." The negative implications of this statement stem from outsiders' futile attempts to apply, in a new social setting, homegrown notions of how bureaucratic organizations function. This is indeed a natural inclination and all the more tempting where organizational structure *appears* bureaucratic. Yet in Nigeria, the office-holders behaved according to different rules; their attitudes and sentiments reflected a different moral code. A bureaucratic organizational structure coexisted with an incompatible set of moral imperatives. The resulting unwieldy, inflexible structure may be singled out as one of the British Colonialism's most devastating legacies.[1]

Please bear in mind, the problem of understanding another culture works both ways. Any Nigerian student reading for the first time the following passage by a prominent American sociologist would probably howl with laughter:

> The chief merit of a bureaucracy is its technical efficiency, with a premium placed on precision, speed, expert control, continuity, discretion and optimal returns on input. The structure is one which approaches the complete elimination of personalized relationships and nonrational considerations (hostility, anxiety, affectual involvements, etc.)[2]

Even those well-educated administrative officers who had once been required to incorporate such notions into their papers and exams do not *live* by them.

To many foreigners who have spent time in Nigeria, "the system" remains a mystery. What motivating principles explain the behavior of Nigerian administrative officers? How do local people understand the behavior of their fellow workers? Why do some people successfully maneuver their way through the system while others founder?

---

[1] One common misunderstanding must be clarified: *bureaucratic organization is not a recent Western invention*. Even during the Han Dynasty (3rd century B.C.), China had developed an efficient bureaucracy based on a system of official examinations. This was the start of a "modern" type of civil service system based on merit. It was almost two thousand years before the West adopted such a system, partly inspired by the Chinese example.

[2] Robert K. Merton, *Social Theory and Social Structure* (New York: Free Press, 1969), 250.

Recently I attended a party. As often happens at a gathering of anthropologists, we started swapping fieldwork stories, and meandered onto a topic of our most unpleasant sensation or unsettling experience. That night, I heard tales of surviving strange diseases, eating repulsive foods, losing one's way in the rain forest, being caught between hostile rebel factions or kidnapped by guerrilla fighters. As for me? All that came to mind were exasperating encounters with intransigent clerks and secretaries. I began to ponder why these interactions had proved so unsettling.

My discipline—social anthropology—hinges on the practice of "participant observation." To a fledgling anthropologist, the "fieldwork" research experience takes on all the connotations of initiation into full membership. For some, a vision-quest; for others, perhaps, a trial-by-ordeal: the goal is to experience another way of life from the inside and to internalize, as does a growing child, the accumulating lessons of daily life. But the anthropologist is not a child; therefore, he or she experiences not conversion, but self-revelation.

I came to understand my American-ness during the period spent coming to terms with Nigerian-ness. I found that I believed in my right to fair treatment and justice simply because I was a human being. I believed in equal protection under the law. But my Nigerian friends did not. What I found was a social system where status, relationships, and rights were fundamentally negotiable, and justice was *never* impartial. In the United States, impersonalized bureaucracies are the norm: we do not question them; our behavior automatically adjusts to them. But just imagine spending a year working in a corporation where none of these rules applied.

You see, a Nigerian immigration officer will only sign your form *if* doing so will perpetuate some mutually beneficial relationship or *if* he wishes to initiate a relationship by putting you in his debt. For those unlucky enough to be without connections (this must necessarily include most foreigners), the only other option is bribery—where the supplicant initiates a personal relationship of sorts and the ensuing favor evens matters up.[3]

Hence, Nigeria becomes labeled "inefficient," "tribalistic," and "corrupt." And so it is.[4] Yet this system exists and persists for a profound reason: Whereas in Europe and Asia, power and authority always derived

---

[3] Bribery exists for several reasons: it initiates a personal relationship, unlike a tip, which terminates all intimacy; if not dedicated to "duty," a worker must be given added incentive to perform a service; the poor salary scale aggravated by the unpredictable nature of extended kin obligations means everyone is desperately in search of extra cash.

[4] Corruption is condemned only in the abstract, when far removed and on a grand scale. But anyone and everyone knows someone "well-placed," and that person is now powerful precisely because he or she has been generous. Moreover, one is more likely to be condemned for going by the book than for corruption. If, for instance, the brother of the man married to one of my cousins (my mother's father's sister's daughter's husband's brother) did not see to it that his colleague signed my tax form with the minimum of fuss, life could be made quite miserable for him indeed!

from ownership of landed property, in West Africa the key ingredient was a large number of loyal dependents. Because land was plentiful and agriculture of the extensive slash-and-burn variety,[5] discontented subordinates could simply move on. The trick was to maintain power over subordinates through ostentatious displays of generosity. This meant more than simply putting on a lavish feast—you must demonstrate a willingness to use your influence to support others in times of need. Even now, all Nigerians participate in such patron-client relationships. In fact, *all legitimate authority derives from being in a position to grant favors and not the other way around.*

Actually, only a minuscule portion of my time in the field was spent dealing with Nigeria's "formal sector." My research entailed living within an extended family household (approximately a dozen adults and two dozen children), chatting with friends, visiting women in their market stalls, even at times conducting formal or informal interviews. And during the years spent researching women's economic resources and domestic responsibilities, I came to understand—indeed to deeply *admire*—their sense of moral responsibility to a wide-ranging network of kin, colleagues, neighbors, friends, and acquaintances. Even now, I often take the time to recall someone's overwhelming hospitality, a friendly greeting, the sharing and eating together. Such warm interpersonal relations more than made up for the lack of amenities.

The longer I stayed, however, the clearer it became that what I loved most and what I found most distressing about life in Nigeria were two sides of the same coin, inextricably related.

The first few months in a new place can be instructive for those with an open mind:

LESSON ONE: THE STRENGTH OF WEAK TIES

My first exposure to Nigerian civil servants occurred when, after waiting several months, I realized my visa application was stalled somewhere in the New York consulate. Letter-writing and telephoning proved futile, and as my departure date approached, panic made me plan a personal visit.

The waiting room was populated with sullen, miserable people—a roomful of hostile eyes fixed on the uniformed man guarding the office door. They had been waiting for hours on end. Any passing official was simultaneously accosted by half a dozen supplicants—much as a political celebrity is accosted by the news media. Everyone's immediate goal was to enter through that door

---

[5] Also known as shifting cultivation or swidden agriculture: small pieces of land are cultivated for a few years, until the natural fertility of the soil diminishes. When crop yields decline, the field must be abandoned. This has obvious implications for the concepts of private property, ownership, and monopoly.

to the inner sanctum—so far, they had failed. But I was lucky—I had the name of an acquaintance's wife's schoolmate currently employed at the consulate. After some discussion, the guard allowed me to telephone her.

Mrs. Ojo greeted me cordially, then—quickly, quietly—she coaxed my application forms through the maze of cubicles. It was a miracle!

"What a wonderful woman," I thought to myself. "She understands." I thought she had taken pity on me and acted out of disgust for her colleagues' mishandling of my application. I now realize that by helping me, she was reinforcing a relationship with her schoolmate. Needless to say, my gratitude extended to her schoolmate's husband, my acquaintance. As I later came to understand it, this natural emotional reaction—gratitude for favors granted—is the currency fueling the system. Even we Americans have an appropriate saying: "What goes around comes around." But at this point, I had merely learned that, here as elsewhere, connections open doors.

LESSON TWO: NO IMPERSONAL TRANSACTIONS ALLOWED

Once on Nigerian soil I confronted the mayhem of Muritala Muhammad airport. Joining the crowd surrounding one officer's station, jostled slowly forward, I finally confronted her face-to-face. Apparently I was missing the requisite currency form. No, sorry, there were none available that day. "Stand back," she declared: "You can't pass here today." I waited squeamishly. If I could only catch her eye once more! But then what? After some time a fellow passenger asked me what was the problem. At this point, the officer, stealing a glance at me while processing someone else, inquired: "Why can't you beg?" The person being processed proclaimed: "She doesn't know how to beg![6] Please, O! Let her go." And I was waved on.

A young post office clerk soon reinforced my conclusion that being employed in a given capacity did not in and of itself mean one performed it. Additional incentive was required. Again, I was confronted with a mass of people crowded round a window. Everyone was trying to catch the clerk's attention, but the young man was adept at avoiding eye contact. Clients were calling him by name, invoking the name of mutual friends, and so on. After some time, he noticed me, and I grabbed the opportunity to ask for stamps. In a voice full of recrimination yet tinged with regret, he announced more to the crowd than to me: "Why can't you greet?" and proceeded to ignore me. This proved my tip-off to the elaborate and complex cultural code of greetings so central to Nigerian social life.[7] In other words, a personal relationship is like a "jump-start" for business transactions.

---

[6] It turns out that "begging" means throwing yourself on someone's mercy, rubbing one's hands together, eyes downcast, even kneeling or prostrating if necessary, and literally begging for a favor.

[7] Nigerians coming to the United States are always taken aback by our positively inhuman greeting behavior.

LESSON THREE: EVERY CASE IS UNIQUE

Mrs. Ojo had succeeded in obtaining for me a three-month visa, but I planned to stay for over two years. Prerequisite for a "regularized" visa was university affiliation. This sounded deceptively simple. The following two months spent registering as an "occasional postgraduate student" took a terrible toll on my nervous stomach.[8] The worst feeling was of an ever-receding target, an ever-thickening tangle of convoluted mazeways. No one could tell me what it took to register, for in fact, no one could possibly predict what I would confront farther down the road. Nothing was routinized, everything personalized, no two cases could possibly be alike.

LESSON FOUR: "DASH" OR "LONG-LEG" GETS RESULTS

This very unpredictability of the process forms a cybernetic system with the strength of personal ties, however initiated. *Dash* and *Long-Leg* are the locally recognized means for cutting through red tape or confronting noncooperative personnel. *Dash* is local parlance for gift or bribe. *Long-Leg* (sometimes called *L-L* or *L-squared*) refers to petitioning a powerful person to help hack your way through the tangled overgrowth. To me, it evokes the image of something swooping down from on high to stomp on the petty bureaucrat causing the problem.

LESSON FIVE: EXERCISE KEEPS TIES LIMBER

During my drawn-out tussle with the registrar's office, I recounted my problem to anyone who would listen. A friend's grown son, upon hearing of my difficulties, wrote a note on his business card to a Mr. Ade in the Exams Section. Amused by his attempt to act important, I thanked Ayo politely. When I next saw him at his mother's home, he took the offensive, and accused me of shunning him. It came out that I had not seen Mr. Ade. But, I protested, I did not know the man. Moreover, he worked in exams not the registry. That, I learned, was not the point. I was supposed to assume that Mr. Ade would have known someone at the registry. Not only had I denied Ayo the chance to further his link to Mr. Ade, but ignoring his help was tantamount to denying any connection to him or—more important for me—his mother.

This revelation was reinforced when I ran into a colleague. He accused me of not greeting him very well. I had greeted him adequately, but apologized nonetheless. As the conversation progressed, he told me that he had heard I had had "some difficulty." He lamented the fact that I had not called on him, since as Assistant Dean of Social Science he could have helped me. His feelings were truly hurt, provoking his accusation of a lackluster greeting. Indeed, things were never the same between us again, for I had betrayed—or denied—our relationship.

---

[8] A few years later, I timed my registration as a graduate student at Harvard. The result: three offices in twelve minutes! Even a foreign graduate student could probably register in less than a day.

LESSON SIX: YOUR FRIENDS HAVE ENEMIES

Well, I did eventually obtain a regularized visa, and it came through *Long-Leg*.[9] But the problems inherent in its use derive from the highly politicized and factionalized nature of Nigerian organizations, where personal loyalty is everything:

Early on, I became friendly with a certain sociologist and his family. Thereby, I had unwittingly become his ally in a long, drawn-out war between himself and his female colleagues. The disagreement had its origins ten years before in accusations of sex discrimination, but had long since spilled over into every aspect of departmental functioning. Even the office workers had chosen sides, and would perform only for members of the proper faction. More significant, though, was the fact that my friend's chief antagonist and I had similar theoretical interests. Though in retrospect I regret the missed opportunity, I realize that I was in the thick of things before I could have known what was happening. Given the original complaint, my sympathies should have been with the other camp. But ambiguous loyalty is equivalent to none.

Early in the century, Max Weber, the great pioneering sociologist, articulated the difference between systems of *legal* and *patrimonial domination*. Within systems of legal domination, organized bureaucratically, authority is the property of a given office or position (not an attribute of the person) and is validated by general rules applying to the whole structure of offices. Assignment to an office is based on merit: rights and duties are properties of the office not its incumbent. The system functions according to routine and is therefore predictable and efficient. Great stress is placed on making relationships impersonal.

In contrast, patrimonial authority (from the Latin term for personal estate) pertains to the form of government organized as a more or less direct extension of the noble household, where officials originate as household servants and remain personal dependents of the ruler. Note how the following passage summarizing Weber's characterization of patrimonial administration fits with my own observations of Nigerian life:

First, whether or not the patrimonial ruler and his officials conduct administrative business is usually a matter of discretion; normally they do so only when they are paid for their troubles. *Second,* a patrimonial ruler resists the delimitation of his authority by the stipulation of rules. He may observe traditional or customary limitations, but these are unwritten: indeed, tradition endorses the principled arbitrariness of the ruler. *Third,* this combination of tradition and arbitrariness is reflected in the delegation and supervision of authority. Within the limits of sacred tradition the ruler decides whether or not to delegate authority, and his entirely personal recruitment of "officials" makes the supervision of their work a matter of personal preference and loyalty. *Fourth* and *fifth,* all administrative "offices" under patrimonial rule are a part of the ruler's personal household and private property: his "officials" are

---

[9] I never paid *dash* in Nigeria.

servants, and the costs of administration are met out of his treasury. *Sixth,* official business is transacted in personal encounter and by oral communication, not on the basis of impersonal documents.[10]

Weber himself believed that bureaucracy would supplant patrimonial authority. He believed that the world was becoming progressively more rationalized and bureaucratized. But there are several different dimensions along which I dispute this contention:

> Bureaucracy has been invented, declined, and re-invented, several times over the millennia.
>
> We have seen how patrimonial ties persisted within a bureaucratic structure of offices in Nigeria. This is also true in America. Within certain organizational structures, personal loyalty remains important, favoritism prevails, connections count, and nepotism or corruption abounds. For instance, urban "political machines" function according to a patrimonial logic. Bureaucracy and patrimonialism may be opposite poles on a continuum (Weber called them "ideal types"), but they are *not* mutually exclusive. Most institutions combine both types of authority structures, with a greater emphasis on one or the other. Personal connections can help in either society, but in America, their use is widely perceived as *illegitimate.*
>
> The system I have outlined is not irrational by any means—but rational actions are based on a different set of assumptions.
>
> Ties of kinship and clientship have an ally in human nature.

By the latter, I mean Weber's ideal types cannot be mutually exclusive for emotional/cognitive reasons: an individual's cognitive understanding of hierarchy is necessarily patterned on the relationship between infant and caretaker. Whatever the form of the earliest pattern (and child-rearing practices vary tremendously between and within cultures), it leaves a residual tendency for personal attachment to develop between authority figures and dependents. Clients in the Unemployment Office naturally wish to be considered individuals and resent cold, impersonal treatment. Each bureaucrat wages his or her own private struggle with the temptation to treat each case on its merits.

This is why most Nigerians' finely honed interpersonal skills stand them in good stead when they arrive in the United States. They easily make friends with whomever they run across, and naturally friends will grant you the benefit of the doubt *if* there is room to maneuver. The psychological need remains, even in our seemingly formalized, structured world, for a friendly, personable encounter. On the other hand, anyone adept at working this way suffers tremendous pain and anxiety from the impersonal enforcement of seemingly arbitrary rules. For instance, a Nigerian friend took it as a personal affront when his insurance agent re-

---

[10] Max Weber quoted from Reinhard Bendix, *Max Weber: An Intellectual Portrait* (Berkeley: University of California Press, 1960), 245; emphasis added.

fused to pay a claim because a renewal was past due.

Once I learned my lessons well, life became much more pleasant. True, every case was unique and personal relationships were everything. But as my friends and allies multiplied, I could more easily make "the system" work for me. As a result of my Nigerian experience, I am very sensitive to inflexible and impersonal treatment, the flip-side of efficiency.

Leaving Nigeria to return to Boston after 2½ years, I stopped for a week in London. I arrived only to find that my old college friend, with whom I intended to stay, had recently moved. Playing detective, I tried neighbors, the superintendent, directory assistance. Tired and bedraggled, I thought of inquiring whether a forwarding address had been left with the post office. Acknowledging me from inside his cage, the small, graying man reached for his large, gray ledger, peered in, slapped it shut, and answered:
"Yes."
"But . . . what is it?" I asked, caught off guard.
He peered down at me and replied: "I cannot tell you. We are not allowed. We must protect him from creditors."
I was aghast. In no way did I resemble a creditor. Noticing my reaction, he conceded:
"But, if you send him a letter, I will forward it."
Bursting into tears of frustration, in my thickest American accent, displaying my luggage and my air ticket, I begged and cajoled him, to no avail. I spent my entire London week in a Bed 'n Breakfast, cursing petty bureaucrats as my bill piled up. "THAT," I thought, "COULD NEVER HAPPEN IN NIGERIA!"

REVIEW QUESTIONS

1. What is the difference between American and Nigerian bureaucracies? How does this difference relate to Weber's concepts of *legal* and *patrimonial domination?*
2. If Nigerians use personal relationships to navigate through bureaucracies, why do such practices as *dash* and *Long-Leg* exist.
3. What are the six features of patrimonial domination suggested by Weber? Do all six apply to the Nigerians?
4. What problems do bureaucracies like the ones found in Nigeria pose for members of the international business world?

28

Kinship and Power on Capitol Hill

Jack McIver Weatherford

*As Elizabeth Eames points out in the previous article, Western bu-
reaucracies are predicated on formal rules and assumed impersonality. Logically, other American political institutions, such as the U.S.
Senate and House of Representatives, should reflect these principles
as well. Members of Congress must win election through the support of thousands of strangers to whom they appeal with ideas about
public policy and information on past achievement. Ideally, the U.S.
election process is open to all. Yet, the process may not be as open
and impersonal as Americans would like to believe, as Jack Weatherford notes in this original selection. He argues that, just as it does in
tribal and peasant societies, kinship, marriage, and adoption (in the
form of staff relationships) play a central part in the road to election
and power for many members of Congress. Lawmakers with family
or staff connections learn politics early, move into political office
young, and connect with a network of ready-made allies. Although
such connections may seem unfair in an elective system, kinship
functions to increase stability and continuity in the U.S. Congress
just as it does in the politics of tribal and peasant communities
around the world.*

Long ago, anthropologists discovered the importance of kinship as an organizing feature of many of the world's societies. Based on descent and marriage, and often extended to people outside these biological ties, kinship could be used to create groups such as families, lineages, and clans. Marriage tied together the kinship units, making them into a community. Kinship and marriage often provided the structure, and sometimes the motivation, for economic production and sharing.

It came as no surprise, then, to discover that kinship also plays an important role in politics in communities around the world. Many of the world's tribal communities relied on kinship to organize the political structure. In such societies, to understand how public policy was formed and enforced required careful understanding of kinship structure and ties. Take the Bhil tribals of India described by David McCurdy, for example. In the early 1960s, the Bhil community of Ratakote had an informal political system lead by a headman and serviced by a council or *panchayat* of important men. The headman was not just any ambitious villager; he came from the community's founding patrilineage, the *kataras*. Succession was not limited to the oldest male lineal descendant of the group, as it might be in the British royal family. The most suitable candidate from the lineage achieved the position by political skill. But the maintenance of power often required family support and alliances with other important village lineages.

Elders also represented lineages in Ratakote, and no community decision could be made without their agreement. The political process always considered the interests of different kinship groups, and the political careers of important men required the support of family and collateral kin.

Anthropologists have discovered that societies in many parts of the world have used kinship to build chiefdoms and kingdoms. Polynesian chiefs, such as the Hawaiian rulers, inherited their authority to rule according to rigid rules of descent. Polynesian chiefs often achieved political solidarity by marrying wives from important clans, arranging such marriages for their children, and generally demanding loyalty on the basis of kinship ties.

The European system of royalty has operated much like the royal clans of Polynesia. At the start of World War II in Europe, most of the crowned heads, such as the king of England, the kaiser of Germany and the czar of Russia, were cousins, the grandchildren of Queen Victoria.

While the importance of kinship appears obvious in the political life of tribal people or for European aristocrats, it seems much less obvious in democratic systems such as the United States, where power derives from election by the people. Yet, kinship plays a larger political role in countries such as the United States than at first seems obvious. Family ties often mean early entrance into the political arena. Political success often stems from family name recognition. Sons and daughters in political families learn the political culture early. They enter politics with a head start and understand the importance of continuing kinship relations through marriage and alliance. Many of the most powerful political figures in the United States have achieved their prominence at least partially because of their kin.

CONGRESSIONAL CULTURE

I began my research on congressional culture in 1978 as a member of the staff of Senator John Glen of Ohio. The first surprise I encountered on starting work in the Senate was to discover what a small and intimate community Washington is. As I wandered through the underground maze of tunnels, cafeterias, barbershops, and small candy stores stuck in little corners of the Capitol building, I felt very much at home, as I had on the small back streets of the Bavarian village of Kahl, where I had done my doctoral research a few years earlier. Even when I sat upstairs in the formal meeting and dining rooms, I sensed the same kinds of political maneuvering I had seen in the *barazas* and religious court sessions in a Swahili community I had visited in Mombasa, Kenya.

What surprised me most was the realization that marriage and kinship operated on Capitol Hill as a major part of the political system, just as they did in many of the traditional societies studied by anthropologists. In many ways, Congress was like the small Bhil community of Ratakote.

The importance of kinship and marriage first caught my attention in the case of Senator Howard Baker of Tennessee, who held the position of Senate majority leader from 1980 through 1984 and then became chief of staff in the Reagan White House. Baker first arrived in the Senate as a political professional; he was not simply a neophyte who had worked his way up through the ranks of Tennessee politics. Instead, he had followed in the steps of his father and his stepmother, both of whom had served in Congress before him.

Nor was he without family support in the Senate. In his early years there, he served with his brother-in-law, Representative William Wampler of Virginia, and with his father-in-law, Senator Everett Dirksen of Illinois, who was then Senate Minority Leader. After his father-in-law's death, Baker eventually succeeded him as Republican leader, and in 1982, Baker's daughter, Cissy, won the Republican nomination for the House of Representatives but lost in the general election to the grandson of the man whom her grandfather had defeated two generations earlier.

In the struggle to replace Howard Baker as Republican leader in 1985, Senator Robert Dole of Kansas soundly defeated his opponents. It may have been mere coincidence, but at the time of his election, he was married to Secretary of Transportation Elizabeth Dole. None of his opponents had such kinship ties.

By comparison with older families, Dole's kinship connections seemed quite minor. A succession of politicians, all with the name Hamilton Fish, has represented New York's Hudson district since 1842. The list includes Secretary of State Hamilton Fish (1869–1877); another Hamilton Fish left Congress to serve as assistant U.S. treasurer from 1903 to 1908. The next-to-the-last Hamilton Fish served in Congress from 1919 to 1945, when he was defeated by Katherine St. George, a cousin of the Fish family's arch-enemy, Franklin Roosevelt. After that defeat, the family did not regain its seat until the present Hamilton Fish was elected in 1968.

Generational succession regularly characterizes congressional kinship networks. In 1986, a new generation of the Kennedy family came to office in Massachusetts when 24-year-old Joseph P. Kennedy II won election to the seat of retiring House Speaker Tip O'Neill, Jr. North Dakota's Senator Quentin Burdick was preceded in his office by his father, Senator Usher Burdick. When Quentin died in 1992, he was replaced by his widow, thus temporarily extending the hold that this family has had on the seat until the next election. Other congressional sons include Alan Simpson of Wyoming, son of former Senator Milward Simpson, and Representative Charles J. Luken, who was elected to the House in 1990 to take the seat of his retiring father, Representative Thomas A. Luken.

Kinship has played a part in the election of America's most powerful political leaders. In the 1992 campaign for president and vice president of the United States, for example, both George Herbert Walker Bush and Albert Gore came from old congressional families. Before becoming vice president and then president of the United States, George Bush served in the House representing Houston, Texas. His father had served in the Senate representing Connecticut years earlier.

Albert Gore, elected vice president in 1992, served in the Senate representing Tennessee, the same state that his father, Thomas Gore, had represented as senator. In addition, another relative, Thomas Pryor Gore, served as senator from Oklahoma from 1907 to 1921 and again from 1931 to 1937 before becoming President Franklin Roosevelt's director of air commerce. Senator Thomas Gore's grandson, the novelist and sometime actor Gore Vidal, ran unsuccessfully for the House of Representatives in New York in 1960 and for the Senate in California in 1982. Although not a real senator, he managed to play one in the 1992 film *Bob Roberts*.

THE WEB OF KINSHIP

One way in which kinship functions in the American political process is to foster solidarity and support, and to interconnect senators and other political figures. The cases of Howard Baker and Robert Dole, both Republicans, mentioned earlier illustrate the importance of intraparty kinship ties. So do the family connections maintained by many top-ranking Democrats. For example, Russell Long of Louisiana was one of the most important senators in his position as top Democrat on the Senate Finance Committee. He first came to the Senate fresh out of law school and took the seat made vacant by the assassination of his father, Huey Long. For a while his mother, Rose Long, had also held the same seat. Other cousins and uncles of his served in virtually every elected office in Louisiana and in the U.S. Congress, all as Democrats.

Kin networks may also cut directly across party lines, making key members of both parties not only a part of the same political culture but, in many cases, part of the same extended kinship network. Jay Rockefeller (also known as John D. Rockefeller IV) arrived in the Senate in 1985 to represent West Virginia as a Democrat, the same year that his father-in-law, Republican Senator Charles Percy of Illinois, gave up his seat. Jay's uncles, Winthrop Rockefeller (former governor of Arkansas) and Nelson Rockefeller (former governor of New York and former vice president of the United States under Gerald Ford), had also won office as Republicans.

Political family ties easily transcend state and regional boundaries, politically linking different parts of the United States. John and Edward Kennedy represented Massachusetts in the Senate, and their brother, Robert, represented New York. In the 1970s, Barry Goldwater, Jr., won election in a California district while his father served as senator from Arizona.

Traditionally, women have not served in elected office as often as men in the United States. Although their numbers have increased recently, they have usually benefited less from kinship ties. In recent years, women have emerged as more important parts of these political dynasties, but their positions are often more tenuous than those of the men. In 1986, Elizabeth J. Patterson, the daughter of the late Senator Olin D. Johnston, won election to the House of Representatives from South Carolina. After only three terms in the House, however, she was defeated in the 1992 election. In 1990, a daughter followed her father into office when 32-year-old Republican Susan Molinari ran for the seat of her father, Representative Guy V. Molinari, who left Congress to become borough president of Staten Island.

Even though women find it difficult to follow their fathers into office, they can often follow their deceased husbands onto the congressional "widow's bench." Sometimes the widows have held the seat only until the next election, when a man took the job, but in other cases, the widows have gone on to have longer and more distinguished careers than their husbands. The classic case was that of Republican Senator Margaret Chase Smith of Maine, who replaced her deceased husband Clyde Smith in the House of Representatives in 1940. Later she won election to the Senate, and on June 1, 1950, she became the first senator brave enough to denounce anti-Communist crusader Senator Joseph McCarthy, and in doing so, she helped the United States to emerge from a long nightmare. After the career of Senator Margaret Chase Smith, the "widow's bench" took on a new meaning of power within Congress and has included Representative Lindy Boggs of Louisiana, Senator Muriel Humphrey of Minnesota, Representative Beverly Byron of Maryland, and Representative Cardiss Collins of Illinois.

Ideology, party affiliation, and geography all become a matter of simple manipulation for the individual with the right kinship and marriage connections. I soon found, however, that just as in New Guinea or Amazonia, these alliances are only as durable as the marriages that bind them. Divorce in twentieth-century American politics looms as threateningly as it did in the court of Henry VIII of England or as it does for the alliances of a 'big man' in Melanesia today.

When Kentucky congressman John Langley was sentenced to prison for trafficking in moonshine in 1924, his office was taken by his wife, Katherine Gudger Langley, the daughter of Congressman James Madison Gudger, Jr., of North Carolina. She served until her husband was released from prison in 1930, but she did not want to give up her seat. The two of them fought a deadly primary election, in which the disgusted voters turned both of them out of office.

An old example for the 1930s seems quaint by today's standards; yet, we see similar difficulties in the tragic career of presidential hopeful Gary Hart of Colorado. After he and his sister-in-law, Martha Keys, worked together on the George McGovern presidential campaign of 1972, Gary Hart and Martha Keys won election to Congress from Colorado and Kansas, respectively. Once in Congress, Martha Keys fell in love with Andrew Jacobs, Jr., a congressman from Indiana and son of former Indiana congressman Andrew Jacobs, Sr. Martha Keys divorced her political scientist husband in Kansas to marry Congressman Jacobs. This marriage started a great political clan stretching across the American heartland of Kansas, Colorado, and Indiana, a good all-American base for a presidential candidate. Representative Keys, however, failed to win reelection, and soon afterward she and second husband Jacobs divorced. The collapse of this congressional clan because of marital problems presaged the collapse of Gary Hart's presidential campaign in 1988 because of a disagreeable mixture of national and sexual politics.

FICTIVE KIN

Throughout the world, tribal people have ways of augmenting their kinship structures through adoption. Among the pastoral Nuer of the Sudan, families often adopted Dinka tribesmen into their lineage as needed. Among the ancient Iroquois of North America, the senior women could select any war captive for adoption to replace a lost member of her own family. These adopted relatives became full members of their new tribes and clans in every social and cultural sense.

Congress has instituted an adoptionlike process as well. It provides itself with supernumerary aides, or "staffers," who can inherit a position when one of the bosses dies or moves on to a higher office and does not have the right relative to take over the job. Senator Jesse Helms of North Carolina became such a successful congressional guerrilla after learning the inside workings of the system while serving on the staffs of two former senators.

In congressional politics, working on a staff functions as something like a fictive kinship or an adoption into the kin network. President Lyndon Johnson came into politics by first working as a congressional aide and learning the intimate details of congressional politics. Later, Walter Mondale began his political career working for Hubert Humphrey; in parallel careers, both of them went on to serve in the Senate, to become vice presidents of the United States, and to run unsuccessfully as Democratic candidates for the presidency. President Bill Clinton got his start in Washington politics working on the staff of Senator William Fulbright of Arkansas.

Increasingly, a bright, energetic young person who wants to enter national politics can do so more easily from a congressional staff position in Washington than by working up through the local ladder of school board, city council, and state legislature. Washington lobbyists offer more money for financing a campaign than local contacts back in the home district. With the demise of strong political machines at the local level, Washington has become increasingly more powerful in supplying young candidates with the needed resources for election.

Of course, the best route into office is to be related to other politicians and to be a congressional aide simultaneously. Senator Nancy Kassebaum is the daughter of the 1936 Republican presidential candidate Alf Landon, and she also worked in the Senate for several years before herself being elected in 1980. Similarly, Senator Sam Nunn, a major force as chairman of the Senate Armed Services Committee, worked for his great-uncle Carl Vinson, who chaired the House Armed Services Committee for many years. Then Nunn was elected to the Senate and immediately built himself a power base on the Senate Armed Services Committee. After serving 10 years as administrative assistant to Senator Nunn, Ray B. Richard won election to Congress in 1982, whereupon he immediately got a seat on the House Armed Services Committee.

Members of the congressional kinship networks have not only had the advantage of voter recognition at the polls but have a great advantage within the Congress itself. The congressional kin tend (1) to arrive in office at an earlier age, (2) to stay in office longer, (3) and to begin serving already knowing how the game is played and having the right contacts for advancement. They become committee chairs at an age when other politicians are just gaining their first seats in Congress.

The relatives and former aides of congressional members together control approximately 20 percent of the seats in the House of Representatives and the Senate. The 1992 election brought 17 more Congressional staffers to office as newly elected members. They arrived with great advantages, similar to those of other congressional kin. As newly elected representative John Mica said in an interview with *Roll Call* (November 9,

1992), being a former staffer "is an incredibly distinct advantage. You can already know you have to call one department to get a new light bulb and another to have it installed."

Even some of the people who seem most outside the congressional system already have deep ties within it. The 1992 election brought Barbara Boxer of California into the Senate after she had served five terms in the House. She got her start in congressional politics as an aide to former representative John Burton of Marin County, California, who was elected with the class of Watergate Babies of 1974 and who served in the House with his brother Phillip Burton of neighboring San Francisco.

CONCLUSIONS

Congressional kinship networks extend beyond the confines of Capitol Hill. They often include dozens of relatives who may be outside Congress but who are still important to the political process. These may include lobbyists, important business leaders, and even members of the press, as the case of Cokie Roberts illustrates. In 1990, when the editors of *Spy* magazine decided to make a diagram of the American political universe, they did not place the president of the United States at the center, nor the leaders of Congress, nor the richest person in the country, nor the strongest lobbyists. They selected radio and television reporter Cokie Roberts, who serves as a political reporter for ABC News after reporting for several years on National Public Radio. As a reporter, Cokie Roberts certainly is not the best known personality in the country, but her selection by *Spy* reveals an inside look at how Washington works, and at how broad the web of kinship really is. Let us look more closely at her genealogy.

Cokie Roberts is the daughter of Congresswoman Lindy Boggs who represented Louisiana's second district from 1972 until 1990. Cokie Roberts's father, Hale Boggs, represented the same New Orleans district until his death in an Alaska plane crash in 1972; he had served as the House majority leader. Cokie Roberts's brother is Tom Boggs, a major Washington lobbyist who once ran but lost an election for representative from Maryland. Cokie Roberts's sister is Barbara Boggs Sigmund, who ran for the Senate from New Jersey and later became mayor of Princeton, New Jersey.

On her mother's side, Cokie Roberts is related to Rhode Island's Senator Claiborne Pell; Cokie's full name is Mary Martha Corinne Morrison Claiborne Boggs Roberts. Senator Pell is the ranking Democrat on the Foreign Affairs Committee and the senator for whom student Pell Grants are named. His father, Representative Herbert Pell, served in the House, representing New York. Other political members of Cokie Roberts's family through the Claiborne and Pell connections include former senators William Claiborne and George Dallas. The ties stretch back to well before the founding of the country to John Pell, who served as a minister in the British court of Oliver Cromwell in the seventeenth century and whom history credits with introducing the mathematical notation for the division sign to the English-speaking world.

Growing up as a member of the congressional kids' club on Capitol Hill, Cokie Roberts knew the other kids in the club, such as young Al Gore, Jr., the son of Senator Al Gore, Sr., of Tennessee, and young Chris Dodd, Jr., son of Senator Christopher Dodd, Sr., of Connecticut. While Cokie Roberts pursued a career in broadcasting, these other children grew up to follow their fathers into political careers.

Cokie Roberts is married to Steven V. Roberts, senior editor of *U.S. News & World Report*. While Cokie Roberts serves as a commentator on ABC's "This Week with David Brinkley," her husband appears on PBS's "Washington Week in Review." In her capacity as a reporter for public television, Cokie Roberts worked under Sharon Percy Rockefeller, who chaired the Corporation for Public Broadcasting. Sharon Rockefeller, the daughter of former Senator Charles Percy of Illinois, was married to Senator and former West Virginia governor Jay Rockefeller. Although larger than most, Cokie Roberts's kinship network clearly illustrates the breadth of congressional family ties.

The press heralds the arrival of virtually every new congressional class as the sign of a major change in traditional politics; yet principles of kinship have endured and seem even more important in congressional politics in the 1990s than in the 1890s. The 110 new members who took their seats in 1993 represented one of the largest groups of new members since World War II. But the new Congress looks a lot like the old one, and some of the new members have very familiar names. Representative John Mica, a Republican of Florida, is the brother of former Representative Dan Mica, a Democrat from Florida. In the Senate, newly elected Bob Bennett, a Republican of Utah, is the son of former Senator Wallace Bennett of the same state and party.

The members of Congress and the Washington establishment share a common political culture, and as in many face-to-face communities around the world, kinship and marriage form an underlying framework for the social system. As the power of political parties has decreased in the twentieth century, much of that power has been taken over by small but tightly connected networks of individuals related by blood, marriage, and past employment. These ties give the structure stability over time, make them work more efficiently for the people in them, and constitute the informal structure underlying all the offices, committees, and caucuses.

The kinship networks of Washington also help to keep outsiders from penetrating very far into the system. Even when the outsiders have been duly elected by the citizens back home, they find their acceptance by these established networks to be slow and difficult. These older systems often make it impossible for newcomers to become effective and eventually force many of them out of the system. As in communities around the world, the kinship systems of Washington promote internal cohesion within the group, but they limit influence from outside the group.

In most tribes, kinship is only one resource used by rising leaders, but in Washington, kinship and marriage are fast becoming defining principles that determine who gets and holds power. Once families and their networks become as established and enduring as they now seem to be in American politics, they deviate from tribal politics and take a step toward the familial politics of reigning aristocracies and royal dynasties.

REVIEW QUESTIONS

1. What are the characteristics of local-level political systems such as that of the Bhils, according to Weatherford?
2. What groups and constituencies does kinship tie together in the American political system?
3. How do kinship relations give some members of Congress an advantage in the U.S. political system?
4. What positive functions does the existence of congressional kinship networks serve in the American political system?
5. Why do you think the U.S. Congress looks and often works as does a local-level system, such as the one that characterizes the Bhils?

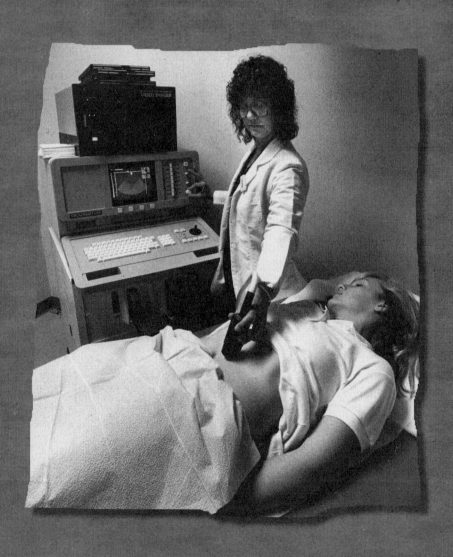

IX

RELIGION, MAGIC, AND WORLDVIEW

People seem most content when they are confident about themselves and the order of things around them. Uncertainty breeds debilitating anxiety; insecurity saps people's sense of purpose and their willingness to participate in social activity. Most of the time cultural institutions serve as a lens through which to view and interpret the world and respond realistically to its demands. But from time to time the unexpected or contradictory intervenes to shake people's assurance. A farmer may wonder about his skill when a properly planted and tended crop fails to grow. A wife may feel bewildered when the man she has treated with tenderness and justice for many years runs off with another woman. Death, natural disaster, and countless other forms of adversity strike without warning, eating away at the foundations of confidence. At these crucial points in life, many people use religion to help account for the vagaries of their experience.

Religion is the cultural knowledge of the supernatural that people use to cope with the ultimate problems of human existence.[1] In this definition, the term *supernatural* refers to a realm beyond normal experience. Belief in gods, spirits, ghosts, and magical power often defines the supernatural, but the matter is complicated by cultural variation and the lack of a clear distinction in many societies between the natural and the supernatural world. *Ultimate problems,* on the other hand, emerge from universal features of human life and include life's meaning, death, evil, and transcendent values. People everywhere wonder why they are alive, why they must die, and why evil strikes some individuals and not others. In every society, people's personal desires and goals may conflict with the values of the larger group. Religion often provides a set of *transcendent values* that override differences and unify the group.

---

[1] This definition draws on the work of Milton Yinger, *Religion, Society, and the Individual: An Introduction to the Sociology of Religion* (New York: Macmillan, 1957).

An aspect of religion that is more difficult to comprehend is its link to emotion. Ultimate problems "are more appropriately seen as deep-seated emotional needs," not as conscious, rational constructs, according to sociologist Milton Yinger.[2] Anthropologists may describe and analyze religious ritual and belief but find it harder to get at religion's deeper meanings and personal feelings.

Anthropologists have identified two kinds of supernatural power, personified and impersonal. *Personified supernatural force* resides in supernatural beings, in the deities, ghosts, ancestors, and other beings found in the divine world. For the Bhils of India, a *bhut*, or ghost, has the power to cause skin lesions and wasting diseases. *Bhagwan*, the equivalent of the Christian deity, controls the universe. Both possess and use personified supernatural force.

Impersonal supernatural force is a more difficult concept to grasp. Often called *mana*, the term used in Polynesian and Melanesian belief, it represents a kind of free-floating force lodged in many things and places. The concept is akin to the Western term *luck* and works like an electrical charge that can be introduced into things or discharged from them. Melanesians, for example, might attribute the spectacular growth of yams to some rocks lying in the fields. The rocks possess mana, which is increasing fertility. If yams fail to grow in subsequent years, they may feel that the stones have lost their power.

Supernatural force, both personified and impersonal, may be used by people in many societies. *Magic* refers to the strategies people use to control supernatural power. Magicians have clear ends in mind when they perform magic, and use a set of well-defined procedures to control and manipulate supernatural forces. For example, a Trobriand Island religious specialist will ensure a sunny day for a political event by repeating powerful sayings thought to affect the weather.

Sorcery uses magic to cause harm. For example, some Bhil *bhopas*, who regularly use magic for positive purposes, may also be hired to work revenge. They will recite powerful *mantras* (ritual sayings) over effigies to cause harm to their victims.

Witchcraft is closely related to sorcery because both use supernatural force to cause evil. But many anthropologists use the term to designate envious individuals who are born with or acquire evil power and who knowingly or unknowingly project it to hurt others. The Azande of Africa believe that most unfortunate events are due to witchcraft, and most Azande witches claim they were unaware of their power and apologize for its use.

Most religions possess ways to influence supernatural power or, if spirits are nearby, to communicate with it directly. For example, people may say *prayers* to petition supernatural beings. They may also give gifts

---

[2] Yinger, 9

in the form of *sacrifices* and offerings. Direct communication takes different forms. *Spirit possession* occurs when a supernatural being enters and controls the behavior of a human being. With the spirit in possession, others may talk directly with someone from the divine world. *Divination* is a second way to communicate with the supernatural. It usually requires material objects or animals to provide answers to human-directed questions. The Bhils of India, for example, predict the abundance of summer rainfall by watching where a small bird specially caught for the purpose lands when it is released. If it settles on something green, rainfall will be plentiful; if it rests on something brown, the year will be dry.

Almost all religions involve people with special knowledge who either control supernatural power outright or facilitate others in their attempt to influence it. *Shamans* are religious specialists who directly control supernatural power. They may have personal relationships with spiritual beings or know powerful secret medicines and sayings. They are usually associated with curing. *Priests* are religious specialists who mediate between people and supernatural beings. They don't control divine power; instead, they lead congregations in ceremonies and help others to petition the gods.

Worldview refers to a system of concepts and often unstated assumptions about life. It usually contains a *cosmology* about the way things are and a *mythology* about how things have come to be. World view presents answers to the ultimate questions: life, death, evil, and conflicting values.

The first article, by Robbie Davis-Floyd, deals with a central topic in the study of religion; the structure and impact of ritual. She identifies birthing in America as a rite of passage and analyzes the process using several important characteristics of all rituals. The second article, by Philip Newman, is a classic discussion of the functions of magic among a highland New Guinea society. He argues that not only is magic used to deal with anxiety-causing situation such as illness, but increasingly more powerful rituals are used when tensions rise because of previous failures. George Gmelch shows that Americans, who generally believe that magic is the province of primitive peoples, can also practice rituals of supernatural control. He looks in detail at the magical rituals practiced by American baseball players. Finally, a classic article by Peter Worsley describes how religion can be used to create new systems of meaning as cultures struggle with disruptions of acculturation and colonial rule. He specifically deals with the revitalization movements, called *cargo cults*, that once sprang up over and over again in Melanesia.

KEY TERMS

religion   prayer
supernatural   sacrifice
ultimate problems   spirit possession

transcendent values   divination
personified supernatural force   shaman
mana   priest
magic   worldview
sorcery   cosmology
witchcraft   mythology

READINGS IN THIS SECTION

29

The Ritual of Hospital Birth in America

Robbie E. Davis-Floyd

*Members of every society include ritual as part of their daily lives.
Although often associated with religion, ritual may also occur in
other settings, as Robbie Davis-Floyd shows in this selection. Using
several important elements of ritual, she shows how hospital birth in
America is structured as a transformative ritual designed to teach
and perpetuate the technocratic core values of American society.*

Why is childbirth, which should be such a unique and individual experience for the woman, treated in such a highly standardized way in the United States? No matter how long or short, how easy or hard their labors, the vast majority of American women are hooked up to an electronic fetal monitor and an IV (intravenously administered fluids and/or medication), are encouraged to use pain-relieving drugs, receive an episiotomy (a surgical incision in the vagina to widen the birth outlet in order to prevent tearing) at the moment of birth, and are separated from their babies shortly after birth. Most of them also receive doses of the synthetic hormone Pitocin to speed their labor, and give birth flat on their backs. Nearly one-quarter of them are delivered by cesarean section.

This article was written especially for this book. Copyright © 1994 by Robbie E. Davis-Floyd.

Many Americans, including most of the doctors and nurses who attend birth, view these procedures as medical necessities. Yet anthropologists regularly describe other, less technological ways to give birth. For example, the Mayan Indians of Highland Chiapas hold onto a rope while squatting for birth, a position that is far more physiologically efficacious than the flat-on-your-back-with-your-feet-in-stirrups (lithotomy) position. Mothers in many low-technology cultures give birth sitting, squatting, semireclining in their hammocks, or on their hands and knees, and are nurtured through the pain of labor by experienced midwives and supportive female relatives. What then might explain the standardization and technical elaboration of the American birthing process?

One answer emerges from the field of symbolic anthropology. Early in this century, Arnold van Gennep noticed that in many societies around the world, major life transitions are ritualized. These cultural *rites of passage* make it appear that society itself effects the transformation of the individual. Could this explain the standardization of American birth? I believe the answer is yes.

I came to this conclusion as a result of a study I conducted of American birth between 1983 and 1991. I interviewed over 100 mothers, as well as many of the obstetricians, nurses, childbirth educators, and midwives who attended them.[1] While poring over my interviews, I began to understand that the forces shaping American hospital birth are invisible to us because they stem from the conceptual foundations of our society. I realized that American society's deepest beliefs center around science, technology, patriarchy, and the institutions that control and disseminate them, and that there could be no better transmitter of these core values and beliefs than the hospital procedures so salient in American birth.

RITES OF PASSAGE

A *ritual* is a patterned, repetitive, and symbolic enactment of a cultural belief or value; its primary purpose is alignment of the belief system of the individual with that of society. A *rite of passage* is a series of rituals that moves individuals from one social state or status to another as, for example, from girlhood to womanhood, boyhood to manhood, or from the womb to the world of culture. Rites of passage transform both society's perception of individuals and individuals's perceptions of themselves.

Rites of passage generally consist of three stages, originally outlined by van Gennep: (1) *separation* of the individuals from their preceding social state; (2) a period of *transition,* in which they are neither one thing nor the other; and (3) an *integration* phase, in which, through various rites of

---

[1] The full results of this study appear in Robbie Davis-Floyd, *Birth as an American Rite of Passage* (University of California Press, 1992).

incorporation, they are absorbed into their new social state. In the year-long pregnancy-childbirth rite of passage in American society, the separation phase begins with the woman's first awareness of pregnancy; the transition stage lasts until several days after the birth; and the integration phase ends gradually in the newborn's first few months of life, when the new mother begins to feel that, as one woman put it, she is "mainstreaming it again."

Victor Turner, an anthropologist famous for his writings on ritual, pointed out that the most important feature of all rites of passage is that they place their participants in a transitional realm that has few of the attributes of either the past or the coming state. Existing in such a nonordinary realm, he argues, facilitates the gradual psychological opening of the initiates to profound interior change. In many initiation rites involving major transitions into new social roles (such as military basic training), ritualized physical and mental hardships serve to break down initiates' belief systems, leaving them open to new learning and the construction of new cognitive categories.

Birth is an ideal candidate for ritualization of this sort, and is, in fact, used in many societies as a model for structuring other rites of passage. By making the naturally transformative process of birth into a cultural rite of passage, a society can ensure that its basic values will be transmitted to the three new members born out of the birth process: the new baby, the woman reborn into the new social role of mother, and the man reborn as father. The new mother especially must be very clear about these values, as she is generally the one primarily responsible for teaching them to her children, who will be society's new members and the guarantors of its future.

THE CHARACTERISTICS OF RITUAL

Some primary characteristics of ritual are particularly relevant to understanding how the initiatory process of cognitive restructuring is accomplished in hospital birth. We will examine each of these characteristics in order to understand (1) how ritual works; and (2) how the natural process of childbirth is transformed in the United States into a cultural rite of passage.

Symbolism

Above all else, ritual is symbolic. Ritual works by sending messages in the form of symbols to those who perform and those who observe it. A *symbol* is an object, idea, or action that is loaded with cultural meaning. The left hemisphere of the human brain decodes and analyzes straightforward verbal messages, enabling the recipient to either accept or reject their content. Complex ritual symbols, on the other hand, are received by the right hemisphere of the brain, where they are interpreted holistically. Instead of being analyzed intellectually, a symbol's message will be *felt* through the body and the emotions. Thus, even though recipients may be unaware of incorporating the symbol's message, its ultimate effect may be extremely powerful.

Routine obstetric procedures are highly symbolic. For example, to be seated in a wheelchair upon entering the hospital, as many laboring women are, is to receive through their bodies the symbolic message that they are disabled; to then be put to bed is to receive the symbolic message that they are sick. Although no one pronounces, "You are disabled; you are sick," such graphic demonstrations of disability and illness can be far more powerful than words. One woman told me:

> I can remember just almost being in tears by the way they would wheel you in. I would come into the hospital, on top of this, breathing, you know, all in control. And they slap you in a wheelchair! It made me suddenly feel like maybe I wasn't in control anymore.

The intravenous (IV) drips commonly attached to the hands or arms of birthing women make a powerful symbolic statement: They are umbilical cords to the hospital. The cord connecting her body to the fluid-filled bottle places the woman in the same relation to the hospital as the baby in her womb is to her. By making her dependent on the institution for her life, the IV conveys to her one of the most profound messages of her initiation experience: in American society, we are all dependent on institutions for our lives. The message is even more compelling in her case, for *she* is the real giver of life. Society and its institutions cannot exist unless women give birth, yet the birthing woman in the hospital is shown, not that *she* gives life, but rather than the *institution* does.

A Cognitive Matrix

A *matrix* (from the Latin *mater*, mother), like a womb, is something from within which something else comes. Rituals are not arbitrary; they come from within the belief system of a group. Their primary purpose is to enact, and thereby, to transmit that belief system into the emotions, minds, and bodies of their participants. Thus, analysis of a culture's rituals can lead to a profound understanding of its belief system.

An analysis of the rituals of hospital birth reveals their cognitive matrix to be the *technocratic model* of reality which forms the philosophical basis of both Western biomedicine and American society. All cultures develop technologies. But most do not supervalue their technologies in the particular way that we do. This point is argued clearly by Peter C. Reynolds in his book *Stealing Fire: The Mythology of the Technocracy* (a tech-

nocracy is a hierarchical, bureaucratic society driven by an ideology of technological progress). There he discusses how we "improve upon" nature by controlling it through culture.

The technocratic model is the paradigm that charters such behavior. Its early forms were originally developed in the 1600s by René Descartes, Francis Bacon, and Thomas Hobbes, among others. This model assumes that the universe is mechanistic, following predictable laws that the enlightened can discover through science and manipulate through technology, in order to decrease their dependence on nature. In this model, the human body is viewed as a machine that can be taken apart and put back together to ensure proper functioning. In the seventeenth century, the practical utility of this body-as-machine metaphor lay in its separation of body, mind, and soul. The soul could be left to religion, the mind to the philosophers, and the body could be opened up to scientific investigation.

The dominant religious belief systems of western Europe at that time held that women were inferior to men—closer to nature and feebler both in body and in intellect. Consequently, the men who developed the idea of the body-as-machine also firmly established the male body as the prototype of this machine. Insofar as it deviated from the male standard, the female body was regarded as abnormal, inherently defective, and dangerously under the influence of nature.

The metaphor of the body-as-machine and the related image of the female body as a defective machine eventually formed the philosophical foundations of modern obstetrics. Wide cultural acceptance of these metaphors accompanied the demise of the midwife and the rise of the male-attended, mechanically manipulated birth. Obstetrics was thus enjoined by its own conceptual origins to develop tools and technologies for the manipulation and improvement of the inherently defective, and therefore anomalous and dangerous, process of birth.

The rising science of obstetrics ultimately accomplished this goal by adopting the model of the assembly-line production of goods as its template for hospital birth. Accordingly, a woman's reproductive tract came to be treated like a birthing machine by skilled technicians working under semiflexible timetables to meet production and quality control demands. As one fourth-year resident observed:

> We shave 'em, we prep 'em, we hook 'em up to the IV and administer sedation. We deliver the baby, it goes to the nursery, and the mother goes to her room. There's no room for niceties around here. We just move 'em right on through. It's hard not to see it as an assembly line.

The hospital itself is a highly sophisticated technocratic factory; the more technology the hospital has to offer, the better it is considered to be. Because it is an institution, the hospital constitutes a more significant social unit than an individual or a family. Therefore it can require that the birth process conform more to institutional than personal needs. As one resident explained,

> There is a set, established routine for doing things, usually for the convenience of the doctors and the nurses, and the laboring woman is someone you work around, rather than with.

The most desirable end-product of the birth process is the new social member, the baby; the new mother is a secondary by-product. One obstetrician commented, "It was what we were all trained to always go after—the perfect baby. That's what we were trained to produce. The quality of the mother's experience—we rarely thought about that."

Repetition and Redundancy

Ritual is marked by repetition and redundancy. For maximum effectiveness, a ritual concentrates on sending one basic set of messages, repeating it over and over again in different forms. Hospital birth takes places in a series of ritual procedures, many of which convey the same message in different forms. The open and exposing hospital gown, the ID bracelet, the intravenous fluid, the bed in which she is placed—all these convey to the laboring woman that she is dependent on the institution.

She is also reminded in myriad ways of the potential defectiveness of her birthing machine. These include periodic and sometimes continuous electronic monitoring of that machine, frequent manual examinations of her cervix to make sure that it is dilating on schedule, and, if it isn't, administration of the synthetic hormone Pitocin to speed up labor so that birth can take place within the required 26 hours.[2] All three of these procedures convey the same messages over and over: *Time is important, you must produce on time, and you cannot do that without technological assistance because your machine is defective.* In the technocracy, we supervalue time. It is only fitting that messages about time's importance should be repeatedly conveyed during the births of new social members.

Cognitive Reduction

In any culture, the intellectual abilities of ritual participants are likely to differ, often markedly. It is not practical for society to design different rituals for persons of different levels of intellectual ability. So ritual utilizes specific techniques, such as rhythmic repetition, to reduce all participants

---

[2] In Holland, by way of contrast, most births are attended by midwives who recognize that individual labors have individual rhythms. They can stop and start, can take a few hours or several days. If labor slows, the midwives encourage the woman to eat to keep up her strength, and then to sleep until contractions pick up again.

to the same narrower level of cognitive functioning. This low level involves thinking in either or patterns that do not allow for a consideration of options or alternative views.

Four techniques are often employed by ritual to accomplish this end. One is the *repetition* already discussed above. A second is *hazing,* which is familiar to undergraduates who undergo fraternity initiation rites but is also part of rites of passage all over the world. A third is *strange making*— making the commonplace appear strange by juxtaposing it to the unfamiliar. Fourth is *symbolic inversion*—metaphorically turning things upside-down and inside-out to generate, in a phrase coined by Roger Abrahams, "the power attendant upon confusion."

For example, in the rite of passage of military basic training, the initiate's normal patterns of action and thought are turned topsy-turvy. He is made strange to himself: his head is shaved, so that he does not even recognize himself in the mirror. He must give up his clothes, those expressions of his past individual identity and personality, and put on a uniform identical to that of the other initiates. Constant and apparently meaningless hazing, such as orders to dig six ditches and then fill them in, further breaks down his cognitive structure. Then through repetitive and highly symbolic rituals, such as sleeping with his rifle, the basic values, beliefs, and practices of the Marines are incorporated into his body and his mind.

In medical school and again in residency, the same ritual techniques that transform a youth into a Marine are employed to transform college students into physicians. Reduced from the high status of graduate to the lowly status of first-year medical student, initiates are subjected to hazing techniques of rote memorization of endless facts and formulas, absurdly long hours of work, and intellectual and sensory overload. As one physician explained:

> You go through, in a six-week course, a thousand-page book. You have pop quizzes in two or three courses every day the first year. We'd get up around 6, attend classes till 5, go home and eat, then head back to school and be in anatomy lab working with a cadaver, or something, until 1 or 2 in the morning, and then go home and get a couple of hours sleep and then go out again.

Subjected to such a process, medical students often gradually lose any broadminded goals of "helping humanity" they had upon entering medical school. A successful rite of passage produces new professional values structured in accordance with the technocratic and scientific values of the dominant medical system. The emotional impact of this cognitive narrowing is aptly summarized by a former resident:

> Most of us went into medical school with pretty humanitarian ideals. I know I did. But the whole process of medical education makes you inhuman . . . you forget about the rest of life. By the time you get to residency, you end up

not caring about anything beyond the latest techniques and most sophisticated tests.

Likewise, the birthing woman is socialized by ritual techniques of cognitive reduction. She is made strange to herself by being dressed in a hospital gown, tagged with an identification bracelet, and by the shaving or
clipping of her pubic hair, which symbolically de-sexualizes the lower
portion of her body, returning it to a conceptual state of childishness. (In
many cultures, sexuality and hair are symbolically linked.) Labor itself is
painful, and is often rendered more so by the hazing technique of frequent
and very painful insertion of someone's fingers into her vagina to see how
far her cervix has dilated. This technique also functions as a strange-mak-
ing device. Since almost any nurse or resident in need of practice may
check her cervix, the birthing women's most private parts are symbolically
inverted into institutional property. One respondent's obstetrician observed, "It's a wonder you didn't get an infection, with so many people
sticking their hands inside of you."

Cognitive Stabilization

When humans are subjected to extremes of stress and pain, they may become unreasonable and out of touch with reality. Ritual assuages this condition by giving people a conceptual handle-hold to keep them from
"falling apart" or "losing it." When the airplane starts to falter, even passengers who don't go to church are likely to pray! Ritual mediates between
cognition and chaos by making reality appear to conform to accepted cognitive categories. In other words, to perform a ritual in the face of chaos is
to restore order to the world.

Labor subjects most women to extremes of pain, which are often intensified by the alien and often unsupportive hospital environment. They
look to hospital rituals to relieve the distress resulting from their pain and
fear. They utilize breathing rituals taught in hospital-sponsored childbirth
education classes for cognitive stabilization. They turn to drugs for pain
relief, and to the reassuring presence of medical technology for relief from
fear. One woman expressed it this way:

> I was terrified when my daughter was born. I just knew I was going to split
> open and bleed to death right there on the table, but she was coming so fast,
> they didn't have any time to do anything to me . . . I like cesarean sections, be-
> cause you don't have to be afraid.

When you come from within a belief system, its rituals will comfort and
calm you. Accordingly, those women in my study who were in basic
agreement with the technocratic model of birth before going into the hospital (70 percent) expressed general satisfaction with their hospital births.

Order, Formality, and a Sense of Inevitability

Its exaggerated and precise order and formality set ritual apart from other modes of social interaction, enabling it to establish an atmosphere that feels both inevitable and inviolate. To perform a series of rituals is to feel oneself locking onto a set of "cosmic gears" that will safely crank the individual through danger to safety. For example, Trobriand sea fishermen described by anthropologist Bronislaw Malinowski regularly performed an elaborate series of rituals on the beach before embarking. The fishermen believed that these rituals, when carried out with precision, would obligate the gods of the sea to do their part to bring the fishermen safely home. Likewise, obstetricians, and many birthing women, feel that correct performance of standardized procedures ought to result in a healthy baby. Such rituals generate in humans a sense of confidence that makes it easier to face the challenge and caprice of nature.

When women who have placed their faith in the technocratic model are denied its rituals, they often react with fear and a feeling of being neglected:

> My husband and I got to the hospital, and we thought they would take care of everything. I kept sending my husband out to ask them to give me something for the pain, to check me, but they were short-staffed and they just ignored me until the shift changed in the morning.

Hospital rituals such as electronic monitoring work to give the laboring woman a sense that society is using the best it has to offer—the full force of its technology—to inevitably ensure that she will have a safe birth.

However, once those "cosmic gears" have been set into motion, there is often no stopping them. The very inevitability of hospital procedures makes them almost antithetical to the possibility of normal, natural birth. A "cascade of intervention" occurs when one obstetric procedure alters the natural birthing process, causing complications, and so inexorably "necessitates" the next procedure, and the next. Many of the women in my study experienced such a "cascade" when they received some form of pain relief, such as an epidural, which slowed their labor. Then Pitocin was administered through the IV to speed up the labor, but Pitocin very suddenly induced longer and stronger contractions. Unprepared for the additional pain, the woman asked for more pain relief, which ultimately necessitated more Pitocin. Pitocin-induced contractions, together with the fact that the mother must lie flat on her back because of the electronic monitor belts strapped around her stomach, can cause the supply of blood and oxygen to the fetus to drop, affecting the fetal heart rate. In response to the "distress" registered on the fetal monitor, an emergency cesarean is performed.

Acting, Stylization, and Staging

Ritual's set-apartness is enhanced by the fact that it is usually highly styl-
ized and self-consciously acted, like a part in a play. Most of us can easily
accept this view of the careful performances of TV evangelists, but it may
come as a surprise that those who perform the rituals of hospital birth are
often aware of their dramatic elements. The physician becomes the pro-
tagonist. The woman's body is the stage upon which he performs, often for
an appreciative audience of medical students, residents, and nurses. Here
is how one obstetrician played to a student audience observing the delivery he was performing:

> "In honest-to-God natural conditions babies were *sometimes* born without
> tearing the perineum and without an episiotomy, but without artificial things
> like anesthesia and episiotomy, the muscle is torn apart and if it is not cut, it
> is usually not repaired. Even today, if there is no episiotomy and repair, those
> women quite often develop a rectocoele and a relaxed vaginal floor. This is
> what I call the saggy, baggy bottom." Laughter by the students. A student
> nurse asks if exercise doesn't help strengthen the perineum. . . . "No, exercises
> may be for the birds, but they're not for bottoms. . . . When the woman is bear-
> ing down, the levator muscles of the perineum contract too. This means the
> baby is caught between the diaphragm and the perineum. Consequently,
> anesthesia and episiotomy will reduce the pressure on the head, and hope-
> fully, produce more Republicans." More laughter from the students.[3]

Cognitive Transformation

The goal of most initiatory rites of passage is cognitive transformation. It
occurs when the symbolic messages of ritual fuse with individual emotion
and belief, and the individual's entire cognitive structure reorganizes
around the newly internalized symbolic complex. The following quote
from a practicing obstetrician presents the outcome for him of such transformative learning:

> I think my training was valuable. The philosophy was one of teaching one
> way to do it, and that was the right way. . . . I like the set hard way. I like the
> riverbanks that confine you in a direction. . . . You learn one thing real well,
> and that's *the* way.

For both nascent physicians and nascent mothers, cognitive transformation of the initiate occurs when reality as presented by the technocratic
model and reality as the initiate perceives it become one and the same.
This process is gradual. Routine obstetrical procedures cumulatively map

---

[3] Nancy Stoller Shaw, *Forced Labor: Maternity Care in the United States* (New York: Perga-
mon Press, 1974), 90.

the technocratic model of birth onto the birthing woman's perceptions of her labor experience. They align her belief system with that of society.

Take the way many mothers come to think about the electronic fetal monitor, for example. The monitor is a machine that uses ultrasound to measure the rate of the baby's heartbeat through electrodes belted onto the mother's abdomen. This machine has become the symbol of high-technology hospital birth. Observers and participants alike report that the monitor, once attached, becomes the focal point of the labor. Nurses, physicians, husbands, and even the mother herself become visually and conceptually glued to the machine, which then shapes their perceptions and interpretations of the birth process. One woman described her experience this way:

> As soon as I got hooked up to the monitor, all everyone did was stare at it. The nurses didn't even look at me anymore when they came into the room—they went straight to the monitor. I got the weirdest feeling that *it* was having the baby, not me.

This statement illustrates the successful conceptual fusion between the woman's perceptions of her birth experience and the technocratic model. So thoroughly was this model mapped on to her psyche that she began to *feel* that the machine was having the baby, that she was a mere onlooker. Soon after the monitor was in place, she requested a cesarean section, declaring that there was "no more point in trying."

Consider the visual and kinesthetic images that the laboring woman experiences—herself in bed, in a hospital gown, staring up at an IV pole, bag, and cord, and down at a steel bed and a huge belt encircling her waist. Her entire sensory field conveys one overwhelming message about our culture's deepest values and beliefs: Technology is supreme, and the individual is utterly dependent upon it.

Internalizing the technocratic model, women come to accept the notion that the female body is inherently defective. This notion then shapes their perceptions of the labor experience, as exemplified by one woman's story:

> It seemed as though my uterus had suddenly tired! When the nurses in attendance noted a contraction building on the recorder, they instructed me to begin pushing, not waiting for the *urge* to push, so that by the time the urge pervaded, I invariably had no strength remaining but was left gasping and dizzy. . . . I felt suddenly depressed by the fact that labor, which had progressed so uneventfully up to this point, had now become unproductive.

Note that she did not say "The nurses had me pushing too soon," but "My uterus had tired," and her labor had "become unproductive." These responses reflect her internalization of the technocratic tenet that when something goes wrong, it is her body's fault.

Affectivity and Intensification

Rituals tend to intensify toward a climax. Behavioral psychologists have long understood that people are far more likely to remember, and to absorb lessons from, those events that carry an emotional charge. The order and stylization of ritual, combined with its rhythmic repetitiveness and the intensification of its messages, methodically create just the sort of highly charged emotional atmosphere that works to ensure long-term learning.

As the moment of birth approaches, the number of ritual procedures performed upon the woman will intensify toward the climax of birth, whether or not her condition warrants such intervention. For example, once the woman's cervix reaches full dilation (10 cm), the nursing staff immediately begins to exhort the woman to push with each contraction, whether or not she actually feels the urge to push. When delivery is imminent, the woman must be transported, often with a great deal of drama and haste, down the hall to the delivery room. Lest the baby be born *en route*, the laboring woman is then exhorted, with equal vigor, *not* to push. Such commands constitute a complete denial of the natural rhythms of the woman's body. They signal that her labor is a mechanical event and that she is subordinate to the institution's expectations and schedule. Similar high drama will pervade the rest of her birthing experience.

Preservation of the Status Quo

A major function of ritual is cultural preservation. Through explicit enactment of a culture's belief system, ritual works both to preserve and to transmit the culture. Preserving the culture includes perpetuating its power structure, so it is usually the case that those in positions of power will have unique control over ritual performance. They will utilize the effectiveness of ritual to reinforce both their own importance and the importance of the belief and value system that legitimizes their positions.

In spite of tremendous advances in equality for women, the United States is still a patriarchy. It is no cultural accident that 99 percent of American women give birth in hospitals, where only physicians, most of whom are male, have final authority over the performance of birth rituals—an authority that reinforces the cultural supervaluation of patriarchy for both mothers and their medical attendants.

Nowhere is this reality more visible than in the lithotomy position. Despite years of effort on the part of childbirth activists, including many obstetricians, the majority of American women still give birth lying flat on their backs. This position is physiologically dysfunctional. It compresses major blood vessels, lowering the mother's circulation and thus the baby's oxygen supply. It increases the need for forceps because it both narrows the pelvic outlet and ensures that the baby, who must follow the curve of the birth canal, quite literally will be born heading upward, against gravity.

This lithotomy position completes the process of symbolic inversion that has been in motion ever since the woman was put into that "upside-down" hospital gown. Her normal bodily patterns are turned, quite literally, upside-down—her legs are in the air, her vagina totally exposed. As the ultimate symbolic inversion, it is ritually appropriate that this position be reserved for the peak transformational moments of the initiation experience—the birth itself. The doctor—society's official representative—stands in control not at the mother's head nor at her side, but at her bottom, where the baby's head is beginning to emerge.

Structurally speaking, this puts the woman's vagina where her head should be. Such total inversion is perfectly appropriate from a social perspective, as the technocratic model promises us that eventually we will be able to grow babies in machines—that is, have them with our cultural heads instead of our natural bottoms. In our culture, "up" is good and "down" is bad, so the babes born of science and technology must be delivered "up" toward the positively valued cultural world, instead of down toward the negatively valued natural world. Interactionally, the obstetrician is "up" and the birthing woman is "down," an inversion that speaks eloquently to her of her powerlessness and of the power of society at the supreme moment of her own individual transformation.

The episiotomy performed by the obstetrician just before birth also powerfully enacts the status quo in American society. This procedure, performed on over 90 percent of first-time mothers as they give birth, expresses the value and importance of one of our technocratic society's most fundamental markers—the straight line. Through episiotomies, physicians can deconstruct the vagina (stretchy, flexible, part circular and part formless, feminine, creative, sexual, nonlinear), then reconstruct it in accordance with our cultural belief and value system. Doctors are taught (incorrectly) that straight cuts heal faster than the small jagged tears that sometimes occur during birth. They learn that straight cuts will prevent such tears, but in fact, episiotomies often cause severe tearing that would not otherwise occur. These teachings dramatize our Western belief in the superiority of culture over nature. Because it virtually does not exist in nature, the line is most useful in aiding us in our constant conceptual efforts to separate ourselves from nature.

Moreover, since surgery constitutes the ultimate form of manipulation of the human body-machine, it is the most highly valued form of medicine. Routinizing the episiotomy, and increasingly, the cesarean section, has served both to legitimize and to raise the status of obstetrics as a profession, by ensuring that childbirth will be not a natural but a surgical procedure.

Effecting Social Change

Paradoxically, ritual, with all of its insistence on continuity and order, can be an important factor not only in individual transformation but also in social change. New belief and value systems are most effectively spread through new rituals designed to enact and transmit them; entrenched belief and value systems are most effectively altered through alterations in the rituals that enact them.

Nine percent of my interviewees entered the hospital determined to avoid technocratic rituals in order to have "completely natural childbirth," yet ended up with highly technocratic births. These nine women experienced extreme cognitive dissonance between their previously held self-images and those internalized in the hospital. Most of them suffered severe emotional wounding and short-term postpartum depression as a result. But 15 percent did achieve their goal of natural childbirth, thereby avoiding conceptual fusion with the technocratic model. These women were personally empowered by their birth experiences. They tended to view technology as a resource that they could choose to utilize or ignore, and often consciously subverted their socialization process by replacing technocratic symbols with self-empowering alternatives. For example, they wore their own clothes and ate their own food, rejecting the hospital gown and the IV. They walked the halls instead of going to bed. They chose perineal massage instead of episiotomy, and gave birth like "primitives," sitting up, squatting, or on their hands and knees. One woman, confronted with the wheelchair, said "I don't need this," and used it for a luggage cart. This rejection of customary ritual elements is an exceptionally powerful way to induce change, as it takes advantage of an already charged and dramatic situation.

During the 1970s and early 1980s, the conceptual hegemony of the technocratic model in the hospital was severely challenged by the natural childbirth movement which these 24 women represent. Birth activists succeeded in getting hospitals to allow fathers into labor and delivery rooms, mothers to birth consciously (without being put to sleep), and mothers and babies to room together after birth. They fought for women to have the right to birth without drugs or interventions, to walk around or even be in water during labor (in some hospitals, Jacuzzis were installed). Prospects for change away from the technocratic model of birth by the 1990s seemed bright.

Changing a society's belief and value system by changing the rituals that enact it is possible, but not easy. To counter attempts at change, members of a society may intensify the rituals that support the status quo. Thus a response to the threat posed by the natural childbirth movement was to intensify the use of high technology in hospital birth. During the 1980s, periodic electronic monitoring of nearly all women became standard procedure, the epidural rate shot up to 80 percent, and the cesarean rate rose to nearly 25 percent. Part of the impetus for this technocratic intensification was the increase in malpractice suits against physicians. The threat of lawsuit forces doctors to practice conservatively—that is, in strict accordance with technocratic standards. As one of them explained:

> Certainly I've changed the way I practice since malpractice became an issue. I do more C-sections . . . And more and more tests to cover myself. More expensive stuff. We don't do risky things that women ask for—we're very conservative in our approach to everything. . . . In 1970 before all this came up, my C-section rate was around 4 percent. It has gradually climbed every year since then. In 1985 it was 16 percent, then in 1986 it was 23 percent.

The money goes where the values lie. From this macrocultural perspective, the increase in malpractice suits emerges as society's effort to make sure that its representatives, the obstetricians, perpetuate our technocratic core value system by continuing through birth rituals to transmit that system. Its perpetuation seems imperative, for in our technology we see the promise of our eventual transcendence of bodily and earthly limitations—already we replace body parts with computerized devices, grow babies in test tubes, build space stations, and continue to pollute the environment in the expectation that someone will develop the technologies to clean it up!

We are all complicitors in our technocratic system, as we have so very much invested in it. Just as that system has given us increasing control over the natural environment, so it has also given not only doctors but also women increasing control over biology and birth. Contemporary middle-class women *do* have much greater say over what will be done to them during birth than their mothers, most of whom gave birth during the 1950s and 1960s under general anesthesia. When what they demand is in accord with technocratic values, they have a much greater chance of getting it than their sisters have of achieving natural childbirth. Even as hospital birth still perpetuates patriarchy by treating women's bodies as defective machines, it now also reflects women's greater autonomy by allowing them conceptual separation from those defective machines.

Epidural anesthesia is administered in about 80 percent of American hospital births. So common is its use that many childbirth educators are calling the 1990s the age of the "epidural epidemic." As the epidural numbs the birthing woman, eliminating the pain of childbirth, it also graphically demonstrates to her through lived experience the truth of the Cartesian maxim that mind and body are separate, that the biological realm can be completely cut off from the realm of the intellect and the emotions. The epidural is thus the perfect technocratic tool, serving the interests of the technocratic model by transmitting it, and of women choosing to give birth under that model, by enabling them to use it to divorce themselves from their biology:

> Ultimately the decision to have the epidural and the Caesarean while I was in labor was mine. I told my doctor I'd had enough of this labor business and I'd like to . . . get it over with. So he whisked me off to the delivery room and we did it.

For many women, the epidural anesthesia provides a means by which they can actively witness birth while avoiding "dropping into biology." Explained Joanne, "I'm not real fond of things that remind me I'm a biological creature—I prefer to think and be an intellectual emotional person." Such women tended to define their bodies as tools, vehicles for their minds. They did not enjoy "giving in to biology" to be pregnant, and were happy to be liberated from biology during birth. And they welcomed advances in birth technologies as extensions of their own ability to control nature.

In dramatic contrast, six of my interviewees (6 percent), insisting that "I am my body," rejected the technocratic model altogether. They chose to give birth at home under an alternative paradigm, the *holistic model.* This model stresses the organicity and trustworthiness of the female body, the natural rhythmicity of labor, the integrity of the family, and self-responsibility. These homebirthers see the safety of the baby and the emotional needs of the mother as one. The safest birth for the baby will be the one that provides the most nurturing environment for the mother.[4] Said Ryla,

> I got criticized for choosing a home birth, for not considering the safety of the baby. But that's exactly what I was considering! How could it possibly serve my baby for me to give birth in a place that causes my whole body to tense up in anxiety as soon as I walk in the door?

Although homebirthers constitute only about 1 percent of the American birthing population, their conceptual importance is tremendous, as through the alternative rituals of giving birth at home, they enact—and thus guarantee the existence of—a paradigm of pregnancy and birth based on the value of connection, just as the technocratic model is based on the principle of separation.

The technocratic and holistic models represent opposite ends of a spectrum of beliefs about birth and about cultural life. Their differences are mirrored on a wider scale by the ideological conflicts between biomedicine and holistic healing, and between industrialists and ecological

---

[4] For summaries of studies that demonstrate the safety of planned, midwife-attended home birth relative to hospital birth, see *Birth as an American Rite of Passage,* Chapter 4.

activists. These groups are engaged in a core value struggle over the future—a struggle clearly visible in the profound differences in the rituals they daily enact.

CONCLUSION

Every society in the world has felt the need to socialize its citizens thoroughly into conformity with its norms, and citizens derive many benefits from such socialization. If a culture had to rely on police officers to make sure that everyone would obey its laws, it would disintegrate into chaos, as there would not be enough police officers to go around. It is much more practical for cultures to find ways to socialize their members from the *inside*, by making them *want* to conform to society's norms. Ritual is one major way through which such socialization can be achieved.

American obstetrical procedures can be understood as rituals that facilitate the internalization of cultural values. These procedures are patterned, repetitive, and profoundly symbolic, communicating messages concerning our culture's deepest beliefs about the necessity for cultural control of natural processes. They provide an ordered structure to the chaotic flow of the natural birth process. In so doing, they both enhance the natural affectivity of that process and create a sense of inevitability about their performance. Obstetrical interventions are also transformative in intent. They attempt to contain and control the process of birth, and to transform the birthing woman into an American mother who has internalized the core values of this society. Such a mother believes in science, relies on technology, and recognizes her inferiority (either consciously or unconsciously) and so at some level accepts the principles of patriarchy. She will tend to conform to society's dictates and meet the demands of its institutions, and will teach her children to do the same.

Yet it is important to note that human beings are not automatons. Human behavior varies widely even within the restraints imposed by particular cultures, including their rituals. As one woman sums it up:

> It's almost like programming you. You get to the hospital. They put you in this wheelchair. They whisk you off from your husband, and I mean just start in on you. Then they put you in another wheelchair, and send you home. And then they say, well, we need to give you something for the depression. [*Laughs*] Get away from me! That will help my depression!

Through hospital ritual procedures, obstetrics deconstructs birth, then inverts and reconstructs it as a technocratic process. But unlike most transformations effected by ritual, birth does *not* depend upon the performance of ritual to make it happen. The physiological process of labor itself transports the birthing woman into a naturally transitional situation that carries its own affectivity. Hospital procedures take advantage of that affectivity to transmit the core values of American society to birthing women. From society's perspective, the birth process will not be successful unless the woman and child are properly socialized during the experience, transformed as much by the rituals as by the physiology of birth.

REVIEW QUESTIONS

1. How does Davis-Floyd define the terms *ritual* and *rite of passage?*
2. What are the main elements of ritual discussed by Davis-Floyd?
3. What does Davis-Floyd mean by the *technocratic cognitive matrix?*
4. What evidences supports Davis-Floyd's assertion that hospital birth in America is part of a rite of passage?
5. How does ritual manage to transform individuals so that they come to internalize their society's values?

30

When Technology Fails:
Magic and Religion in New Guinea

Philip L. Newman

*All people experience anxiety when confronted with situations they
cannot control, and in many societies natural methods of influencing and predicting events work only part of the time. In such instances, supernatural forces may be invoked to account for such
events and our relation to them. In this article, Philip Newman describes the use of magic and witchcraft by a highland New Guinea
people and shows that they use such practices throughout their lives
whenever faced with uncertainty. He suggests that magical procedures can be ranked according to their ability to release tension, and
that the choice of particular magical practices correlates with the degree of anxiety to be reduced.*

Humans have created many forms in their quest for means of dealing with the world around them. Whether these forms be material
tools, social groups, or intangible ideas, they are all, in a sense, "instruments": each is a means to some end; each has a purpose that it fulfills.

Originally published as "Sorcery, Religion, and the Man." With permission from *Natural History*, February 1962. Copyright © the American Museum of Natural History, 1962.

When we think of such things as magical rites, a belief in ghosts, or accusations of sorcery, however, the matter of purpose becomes less obvious. In the descriptions and in the case history that follow, we will try both to show something of the magical and religious beliefs of a New Guinea people and to demonstrate the purposes that these beliefs have for the men who hold them.

In the mountainous interior of Australian New Guinea, the Asaro River has its headwaters some thirty miles to the north of Goroka, a European settlement that serves as the administrative center for the Central Highlands District. Near Goroka, the Asaro flows through a wide valley where the ground cover is mostly grasses and reeds. In its upper reaches, this valley narrows into a gorge where steep, heavily forested ridges reach out toward the river from mountain masses on either side. Some twelve thousand people live on this part of the river, occupying an area of approximately two hundred square miles. While these people are culturally and linguistically similar, they do not form a single political unit. Indeed, before contact with Europeans, the area was characterized by incessant intertribal warfare. Even now, when active warfare is no longer part of their lives, the pattern of alliances and animosities among the tribes is a factor in social intercourse.

Except for the cessation of warfare, life in the valley today is little changed from what it was before the Australian government began active pacification of the area after the end of World War II. Almost daily, the people climb up from the valley floor to enter the dense forest on the mountain slopes. It is here that building wood is gathered; birds and small marsupials are shot for meat, plumage, or fur; plants that provide for many needs are collected.

Below an altitude of some seven thousand feet, the forest has been cut back to make room for gardens that cling to the sides of steep ridges and crowd together in the narrow valley floors. These gardens provide the people's staple foods—sweet potatoes, yams, sugar cane, and a variety of green vegetables. A woman spends most of her time at garden work, preparing new planting areas, weeding the crop, and harvesting the mature plants. In fallow areas nearby she can turn loose the pigs her husband has entrusted to her care. If they wander too far afield by evening, her call will bring them back on the run. They know that a meal awaits them, as well as a snooze by the fire in their "mother's" house.

While each family may have one or more houses near the forest or in their garden, the center of social life is the village. The villages are located on the tops of ridges in spots usually selected with an eye to their defensibility against enemies. The fifteen to twenty houses that compose each village usually march in single file along the narrow ridge. But, if space permits, they are formed into a square. All the houses are much alike—round, about fifteen feet in diameter, made of double rows of five-foot stakes. The space between the stakes is filled with grass and the outside covered with strips of bark. The roof is thatched and topped with a long, tasseled pole.

Two or three houses always stand out. They are larger, they are not in line with the rest, and they may have as many as eight poles protruding through their roofs. These are the men's houses. As a rule, men and women do not live together, for the men fear that too much contact with women is weakening. For this reason, a man builds a house for his wife— or each of them, if he has more than one—and then helps in the construction of the larger house where he and the other men of the village will sleep apart. Ideally, all the men who live together in a single house can trace their descent back to a known, common ancestor. They thus constitute a lineage. Such a lineage is connected to the other village men's houses by descent links, but in many cases the links are so amorphous that no one can actually tell what they are. Similarly, several villages will be linked together into a clan, but genealogical ties may be more imputed than real.

Just as the forest and the garden represent the physical framework within which each individual lives, so too these various orders of grouping—the lineage, the village, the clan, and the tribe—represent the social framework of existence. The members of these groups are the people with whom each individual is in daily contact. They nurture him, teach him, and assist him in times of crisis. It is from these groups that he derives such things as his name, his rights to the land for gardening and hunting, and the financial help that he needs when it is time to purchase a wife. They hail his birth and mourn his death.

In turn, each individual has obligations to the other members of these groups. He acts as a representative of his group when dealing with outsiders. In this way, he enters into a whole series of relationships with individuals and groups outside his own immediate circle. He may visit a neighboring clan to help one of his own clansmen win the admiration of a prospective bride by sitting up all night near the hot fire singing love songs to her. Or a trip may take him to a nearby tribe, where he dances mightily with other men to show that his group is appreciative of the gift of food and valuables they are about to receive. He may walk several days over difficult ground to reach a completely alien group, where he can barter for shells, plumes, or foodstuffs not available in his own group. As in all societies, the groups comprising the society provide for the individual, while the individual, in turn, contributes some of his efforts to the life of the group.

Humans not only have their tools and their society to help cope with the world: they also have their ideas. There are some problems presented by the environment for which the people of the upper Asaro have not yet devised a mechanical or technical solution. There are other problems for which a technical solution seems not enough. Finally, there are problems for which an idea seems to be an inherently better solution than a physical or social tool. It is here that we enter the realm of magic and religion.

A great many of the activities among the upper Asaro people have a magical or religious component. When a child is born, it is cleaned, fed, and covered with grease to help protect it from the cool mountain air. It is also protected, nonphysically, by burying its umbilical cord in some secluded spot—so that sorcerers cannot later use this piece of the newformed being to cause illness or death by magical means. During the first few days of life, the infant is also made to accept, via magic, his first social responsibility—not to cry at night and disturb its mother. A small bundle of sweet-smelling grass is placed on the mother's head and her desire for uninterrupted slumber is blown into the grass by an attendant. The grass is then crushed over the head of the child and its pungent odor released so that the infant will breathe in the command along with the scent of the plant.

Throughout an individual's life there will be magical rites to protect him from various dangers, to overcome difficulties, and to assist his growth. When a young boy kills his first animal, his hand will be magically "locked" in the position that first sent an arrow on a true course. When he reaches puberty and moves out of his mother's house to begin his life in the men's house, he will be ritually cleansed of the contamination he has been subjected to during his years of association with women. If he were not so cleansed, he would never become strong enough to engage in men's activities. During the years when a young man is trying to win the favor of a girl, he not only relies on his prowess in singing love songs and his decorations, but on his knowledge of love magic as well. If all the usual spells and potions fail, he may utilize one especially powerful form that is thought to make him appear to his beloved with an entirely new face—the face of someone he knows she likes.

In his mature years, when a man's attention turns to the growth of pigs and gardens, he will have magical as well as technical skills to help him. Gardens are not difficult to grow in this fertile land, but it is still wise to put a certain series of leaves across one's fences, so that any thief will find his arms and legs paralyzed should he decide to raid the garden. It also behooves one whose gardens are near the main trails and settlements to give them magical assistance, for a slow-growing garden in such a conspicuous place could be an embarrassment.

The raising of pigs is a more difficult matter, and it is here that magical and religious rites become greatly elaborated. Some of these rites are performed by an individual for his own pigs. It may be a simple performance, as when smoke is blown into the ear of a wild pig to tame it. The theory is that the smoke cools and dries the pig's "hot" disposition. On the other hand, these individual rites may attain considerable complexity, as in the propitiation of forest spirits called *nokondisi*. These spirits are capricious in nature—sometimes playing malicious tricks on men and sometimes performing acts of kindness. Each man, therefore, maintains a small, fenced enclosure in which he builds a miniature earth oven and a tiny house. By placing food in the earth oven he may be able to entice a *nokon-disi* to come live near his pigs and watch after them. In return for the food, the spirit will help bring in lost pigs, protect the herd from thieves, and carry the animals safely across flooded streams during the rainy season.

In addition to the magic performed by an individual on behalf of his own pigs, some rather elaborate rites are performed by the lineage and clan for all the pigs belonging to these groups. The largest of these is the *gerua* ceremony, performed at intervals of from five to seven years. In this ritual, hundreds of pigs are killed and used to pay off various kinds of economic obligations to other clans. It is a time for feasting and dancing, for courting and reunion. It is also a time for propitiating the ghosts of the dead in the hope that they will help the living grow their pigs. All the pigs are killed in the name of particular ghosts. The songs are pleas for ghostly assistance. The wooden *gerua* boards, with their colorful geometric designs, are visible symbols to the ghosts that they have not been forgotten. It is not tender sentiment that motivates this display, however. Rather, it is the fear that failure to do so will engender the wrath of the ever-watchful dead.

The magical and religious beliefs that we have so far examined are all used in conjunction with other practices of a nonmagical nature. There are some areas, however, where no purely technical solutions are available, and where magic and religion are the only "tools" available. One such area is sickness. The people of the upper Asaro are not generally aware of modern medical practices, although efforts are being made in that direction. The nonmagical techniques available to them, such as inhaling the steam from fragrant plants to relieve a stopped-up nose, are few. These remedies do not extend to more serious maladies. When serious illness strikes, the only recourse is to magic.

The magical solutions available are many and varied. There are herbs with magical properties that are administered in much the same way as are medicines in our own society. I made a cursory check, however, which seems to show that few of the plants possess any curative value.

Ghosts and forest spirits are frequently thought to be the causes of illness, for they are deemed capable of entering the body and devouring a person's inner organs. Cures for such illnesses usually involve propitiation of the offending supernatural.

Witches and sorcerers are believed to be another major cause of illness, for they are supposedly capable of injecting foreign bodies into a victim, or performing black magic on objects that have been in association with the victim. To cure illness caused in this way involves calling in a magical specialist who can either extract the foreign bodies or retrieve the objects being operated upon.

While the ideas and rites listed here do not exhaust the entire inventory available to the group under discussion, they give some sense of the variety that exists. The notions are interesting in themselves, but the question of how an individual makes use of these notions is even more fascinating. Let us look at a crisis in the life of one of these people, and see how he picks and chooses among the various "tools" at his disposal.

Ombo was a young man in his early thirties. He had been married for about five years, but was childless. Early one April, it was announced in the traditional style that his wife, Magara, was with child. On such an occasion, a food distribution is held in the village and the announcement, along with gifts of food, is sent out to related villages. Ombo was instructed in the food taboos he would have to undergo during the period of his wife's pregnancy to protect himself from her increased contamination.

All went well for the first few weeks, and then Magara became ill. It is doubtful that her illness was associated with her pregnancy, for her symptoms were the classic signs of malaria—a rather rare disease in this part of the highlands. The first attempts to cure her involved a variety of highly regarded pseudomedications.

A potion of sweet-smelling leaves was administered. A command to the effect that the illness should depart was blown into the leaves, and the leaves were eaten. It was thought that the command, thus internalized, would drive out the illness.

At various other times, attempts were made to relieve her headaches and body pains by rubbing the afflicted areas with stinging nettles. It was held that when the welts and the pain caused by the nettles subsided, the pains in her body would also leave. On one occasion her husband blew smoke over her during a period of fever because, as we have seen, smoke is held to have a cooling and drying effect. He also painted various parts of her body with mud in an effort to cause the pain to dry up at the same time the mud dried.

This kind of treatment continued until early May without any noticeable improvement in Magara's condition. After almost a month had passed and it became apparent that the illness was not going away, Ombo began to speculate on a possible cause. During the next few weeks he came up with several solutions. While he had been away from the village, working for Europeans in Goroka, he had acquired some charms to help him win at a card game popular among the sophisticated younger men.

One of these charms was fairly new, and he was worried that he might not have gained sufficient control over it. Since he kept it hidden in his wife's house, his conclusion was that the charm was exerting its influence on her and causing the illness. He therefore removed it from her house and sent it away to a friend in another tribe. There was no improvement in his wife's condition.

Ombo's next action was to destroy his spirit house. He had not kept it in good repair and had not been diligent in feeding the *nokondisi* that lived there. His father suggested that the angered spirit was taking revenge on Magara. By destroying the house of the spirit, Ombo caused it to retreat to the forest, where it could do no harm. Finally, he burned the costly paraphernalia of a potent sorcery technique he had purchased some years before, fearing it affected his wife.

By now it was late in May. Magara had become so ill that she stopped all but the most minimal work in her garden. Concern about her illness began to increase, and people outside the immediate family began to speculate about its cause. Ombo's older brother mentioned one day that a malevolent ghost might be behind it. It was not long after this that a meeting was held in the men's house and Fumai, a member of the lineage, recounted a dream he had had the night before. In it, he had seen the ghost of Ombo's great-grandmother sitting in the forest near the spot where *gerua* boards are displayed for the ancestors. She had covered herself with ashes and, in a fit of self-pity, was wailing loudly because no one had made a *gerua* board in her honor at the last *gerua* ceremony, and no one had killed a pig in her name. Since ashes are put on at the death of a near relative as a sign of mourning, while clay is put on if the deceased is more distantly related, and since ghosts are thought to be capable of causing death, it was concluded that the dream was prophetic. It implied the imminent death of Magara at the great-grandmother's hands unless something were done.

The next day, Ombo and his wife, along with his parents and siblings, set out for the spot where the ghost had been "seen." A pig was killed there in honor of the ghost. It was cooked in an earth oven filled with valued food items—the largest sweet potatoes, the most succulent yams, and the most highly prized varieties of taro. While water was being poured into the oven, a speech was addressed to the ghost. It was pointed out that the food had been prepared and donated in her honor at considerable trouble to those present. The feeling was expressed that she should be satisfied with the amount and the quality of the offering. She was then told to refrain from causing trouble in the future. As the food steamed in the oven, a *gerua* board was made in the ghost's honor and placed among others in a nearby tree. Some of the food was eaten and the rest was later distributed among members of the lineage.

Things seemed to go well for the next few weeks. Magara improved and was able to return to her work in the garden. Discussion of the topic was dropped. Then, late in June, she suddenly became ill again. Ombo was greatly upset. I suggested to him that she might have malaria and should be taken to the medical aid post. But Ombo did not want to do this, for by now he was convinced that his wife was being attacked by a sorcerer. To deal with this threat, a magical specialist had to be called in. It was several days before he arrived, for he lived some distance away in another tribe. As with any good "doctor," his first acts were aimed at relieving his patient's pain and fever. With much physical strain, he literally pulled the pain from her body and cast it into the ground, where it could do no further harm. His next task was to find out what was causing her illness. For over two hours he sat chatting with Ombo and Magara, discussing the history of the illness, the treatments that had been used, and their own life histories. All the while, he puffed on a tobacco pipe made of a bamboo tube. The degree of irritation caused by the smoke in his throat signalized the appearance in the conversation of significant diagnostic events. Finally, he announced his conclusion—illness by black magic.

To eliminate the effects of the imputed black magic, the object being manipulated by the sorcerer had to be recovered. To do this, the magical specialist first had a bundle of long, thin leaves prepared. Into the bundle were put cooked pork and a variety of plants with magical properties. The specialist never directly touched the bundle himself, but directed Ombo in its preparation. When the bundle was completed, it and a specially prepared bamboo tube were both carried into Magara's house. She was given the tube to hold and the bundle was hung in the rafters near the center pole. After a rite to protect her from further sorcery, Ombo and Magara were locked together in the house.

The specialist remained outside. He walked round and round the house, reciting spells and whirling a special plant around his head. He was pulling the unknown object away from the sorcerer and bringing it back home. The ceremony became a real struggle: the object would come tantalizingly close, only to slip away. Then the specialist announced that the object had arrived. Magara was instructed to open the bundle in the rafters. Inside, among the bits of meat, were a small spider and a piece of string of the type used to hang ornaments around the neck.

The spider, Magara and Ombo were told, was an assistant to the specialist. It had taken the string out of the sorcerer's house and into the open where the specialist could reach it with his powers. The sorcerer was thought to be a young man who had once wanted to marry Magara. The existence of a disappointed suitor was one fact that had come out during the specialist's long interview. When Magara had married Ombo, the suitor had become angry and cut a bit of her necklace string to use for sorcery. The specialist placed the recovered string in the bamboo tube that Magara had been holding, and the tube was then hidden away among the thatch.

From that time until late September, when I left the area, Magara did not experience any further attacks of illness, although she was not in the best of health. The community considered her cured. Significantly, her child was born prematurely in September and died two days later, but no one saw any connection between this death and her illness.

What, then, can we say about the purpose of such ideas and behavior patterns? A situation such as Magara's creates a great deal of tension in an individual who experiences it. If magic does nothing more, it allows the bearer of this tension to act. Both the patient and those concerned feel that something is being done. The pioneer anthropologist Bronislaw Malinowski long ago made the point: "Magic expresses the greater value for man of confidence over doubt, of steadfastness over vacillation, of optimism over pessimism."

It is a rare man indeed, however, who can maintain his confidence and optimism in the face of repeated failure. The question then arises, Why is it that magic is not more readily given up? Three answers have traditionally been given to this question, all of them valid. In the first place, for people such as these, there is no alternative. Secondly, for the believer in the efficacy of magic, the occasional chance successes are more significant than repeated failure. Finally, explanations for failures are always at hand. Inadvertent errors in spells or formulas that must be performed precisely, or imagined countermagic, are ready explanations that are necessarily built into the very nature of magic.

The case history we have seen suggests still a fourth answer. This answer becomes apparent, however, only if we examine the way in which an individual makes use of the magical notions available to him. In the progression of the various magical techniques and explanations employed by Ombo, we can see that they call for behavior patterns allowing for increasingly aggressive release of the tension built up in him by the failure of previously selected techniques.

The simple pseudomedicinal rites, such as rubbing with nettles and painting with mud, were enough to reduce the tension of the initial crisis. The treatment was symptomatic and there was no attempt to identify the cause of the illness. When it became apparent that these techniques had failed, we find Ombo resorting to the more drastic measure of destroying valuable property. The frustration was not yet great enough to cause him to seek outlets in other people: that which he destroyed and removed from his use belonged only to him. In the next phase, we find that a ghost is predicated as the causative agent. One need not be nice to ghosts. They, like the living, are thought to be a mercenary lot who do not much care what is said about them as long as they get their just due. The speech made to the great-grandmother was studded with commands and expressions of anger at the trouble the ghost had caused. This was an excellent mechanism for the release of tension, just as was the physical act of killing the pig.

Finally, we see the most aggressive act of all—accusing a specific individual of sorcery. The accused individual was a member of an enemy tribe and lived some distance away. It was, therefore, unlikely that accuser and accused would often meet. But if the two had come together, a fight would have been inevitable. In former times, this could have led to open warfare. Thus, Ombo not only used magic as a tool against disease, but also selected the magical tools in such an order that his own increasing anxiety was relieved by increasingly aggressive actions. It is thus not only the forms created by humans that enable them to cope with the world they meet, but the very way in which they manipulate those forms that are available to them.

REVIEW QUESTIONS

1. According to Newman, what is the function of magic?
2. Why do the Asaro use magic? What kinds of things do they use it on?
3. Why did the husband depicted in this article use stronger and stronger magic to cure his wife as time went by?
4. How does Newman explain the fact that people continue to use magic even when it fails?

31

Ritual and Magic in American Baseball

George Gmelch

Americans pride themselves on their "scientific" approach to life and problem solving. But as George Gmelch demonstrates in this article, American baseball players, much like the New Guinea highlanders described in the previous article, by Philip Newman, also depend to a great extend on supernatural forces to ensure success in their athletic endeavors. Gmelch demonstrates that the findings of anthropologists in distant cultures shed light on our own cultural practices.

On each pitching day for the first three months of a winning season, Dennis Grossini, a pitcher on a Detroit Tiger farm team, arose from bed at exactly 10:00 A.M. At 1:00 P.M. he went to the nearest restaurant for two glasses of iced tea and a tuna fish sandwich. Although the afternoon was free he changed into the sweatshirt and supporter he wore during his last winning game, and one hour before the game he chewed a wad of Beech-Nut chewing tobacco. During the game he touched his letters (the

Adapted from "Baseball Magic," *Human Nature*, 1(8): 1978. Copyright © 1993 by George Gmelch. Reprinted by permission of the author.

team name on his uniform) after each pitch and straightened his cap after each ball. Before the start of each inning he replaced the pitcher's rosin bag next to the spot where it was the inning before. And after every inning in which he gave up a run, he would wash his hands.

I asked him which part of the ritual was most important. He responded, "You can't really tell what's most important so it all becomes important. I'd be afraid to change anything. As long as I'm winning, I do everything the same. Even when I can't wash my hands (this would occur when he had to bat), it scares me going back to the mound. . . . I don't feel quite right."

Trobriand Islanders, according to anthropologist Bronislaw Malinowski, felt the same way about their fishing magic. Among the Trobrianders, fishing took two forms. In the inner lagoon fish were plentiful and there was little danger; on the open sea fishing was dangerous and yields varied widely. Malinowski found that magic was not used in lagoon fishing, where men could rely solely on their knowledge and skill. But when fishing on the open sea, Trobrianders used a great deal of magical ritual to ensure safety and increase their catch.

Baseball, the American national sport, is an arena in which the players behave remarkably like Malinowski's Trobriand fishermen. To professional baseball players, baseball is more than a game. It is an occupation. Since their livelihood depends on how well they perform, they use magic to try to control or eliminate the chance and uncertainty built into baseball.

To control uncertainty Chicago White Sox shortstop Ozzie Guillen doesn't wash his underclothes after a good game. The Boston Red Sox's Wade Boggs eats chicken before every game (that's 162 meals of chicken per year). Ex-San Francisco Giant pitcher Ron Bryant added a new stick of bubble gum to the collection in his bulging back pocket after each game he won. Jim Ohms, my teammate on the Daytona Beach Islanders in 1966, used to put another penny in the pouch of his supporter after each win. Clanging against the hard plastic genital cup, the pennies made an audible sound as the pitcher ran the bases toward the end of a winning season.

Whether they are professional baseball players, Trobriand fishermen, soldiers, or farmers, people resort to magic in situations of chance, when they believe they have limited control over the success of their activities. In technologically advanced societies that pride themselves on a scientific approach to problem solving, as well as in simple societies, rituals of magic are common. Magic is a human attempt to impose order and certainty on a chaotic, uncertain situation. This attempt is irrational in that there is no causal connection between the instruments of magic and the desired consequences of the magical practice. But it is rational in that it creates in the practitioner a sense of confidence, competence, and control, which in turn is important to successfully executing a specific activity and achieving a desired result.

I have long had a close relationship with baseball, first as a participant and then as an observer. I devoted much of my youth to the game and played professionally as first baseman for five teams in the Detroit Tiger organization over three years. I also spent two years in the Quebec Provincial League. For additional information about baseball magic I interviewed twenty-eight professional ballplayers and sportswriters.

There are three essential activities in baseball—pitching, hitting, and fielding. The first two, pitching and hitting, involve a great deal of chance and are comparable to the Trobriand fishermen's open sea; in them, players use magic and ritual to increase their chances for success. The third activity, fielding, involves little uncertainty and is similar to the Trobriander inner lagoon; fielders find it unnecessary to resort to magic.

The pitcher is the player least able to control the outcome of his own efforts. His best pitch may be hit for a home run, and his worst pitch may be hit directly into the hands of a fielder for an out or be swung at and missed for a third strike. He may limit the opposing team to a few hits yet lose the game, or he may give up a dozen hits and win. Frequently pitchers perform well and lose, and perform poorly and win. One has only to look at the frequency with which pitchers end a season with poor won-lost records but good earned run averages, or vice versa. For example, in 1990 Dwight Gooden gave up more runs per game than his teammate Sid Fernandez but had a won-lost record nearly twice as good. Gooden won nineteen games and lost only seven, one of the best records in the National League, while Sid Fernandez won only nine games while losing fourteen. They pitched for the same team—the New York Mets—and therefore had the same fielders behind them. Regardless of how well he performs, on every outing the pitcher depends upon the proficiency of his teammates, the inefficiency of the opposition, and caprice.

An incredible example of bad luck in pitching occurred some years ago involving former Giant outfielder Willie Mays. Mays intentionally "dove for the dirt" to avoid being hit in the head by a fastball. While he was falling the ball hit his bat and went shooting down the left field line. Mays jumped up and ran, turning the play into a double. Players shook their heads in amazement—most players can't hit when they try to, but Mays couldn't avoid hitting even when he tried not to. The pitcher looked on in disgust.

Hitting is also full of risk and uncertainty—Red Sox outfielder and Hall of Famer Ted Williams called it the most difficult single task in the world of sports. Consider the forces and time constraints operating against the batter. A fastball travels from the pitcher's mound to the batter's box, just sixty and one-half feet, in three to four tenths of a second. For only three feet of the journey, an absurdly short two-hundredths of a second, the ball is in a position where it can be hit. And to be hit well the ball must be neither too close to the batter's body nor too far from the "meat" of his bat. Any distraction, any slip of a muscle or change in stance, can throw a swing off. Once the ball is hit chance plays a large role in determining where it will go—into a waiting glove, whistling past a fielder's diving stab, or into the wide open spaces. While the pitcher who threw the fastball to Mays was suffering, Mays was collecting the benefits of luck.

Batters also suffer from the fear of being hit by a pitch—specifically, by a fastball that often travels at speeds exceeding ninety miles per hour. Throughout baseball history the great fastball pitchers like Sandy Koufax, Bob Gibson, Nolan Ryan, and Roger Clemens have thrived on this fear and on the level of distraction it causes hitters. The well-armed pitcher inevitably captures the advantage in the psychological war of nerves that characterizes the ongoing tension between pitcher and hitter, and that determines who wins and loses the game. If a hitter is crowding the plate in order to reach balls on the outside corner, or if the batter has been hitting unusually well, pitchers try to regain control of their territory. Indeed, many pitchers intentionally throw at or "dust" a batter in order to instill this sense of fear (what hitters euphemistically call "respect") in him. On one occasion Dock Ellis of the Pittsburgh Pirates, having become convinced that the Cincinnati Reds were dominating his team, intentionally hit the first three Reds batters he faced before his manager removed him from the game.

In fielding, on the other hand, the player has almost complete control over the outcome. Once a ball has been hit in his direction, no one can intervene and ruin his chances of catching it for an out. Infielders have approximately three seconds in which to judge the flight of the ball, field it cleanly, and throw it to first base. Outfielders have almost double that amount of time to track down a fly ball. The average fielding percentage (or success rate) of .975, compared with a .250 success rate for hitters (the average batting percentage), reflects the degree of certainty in fielding. Compared with the pitcher or the hitter, the fielder has little to worry about. He knows that in better than 9.7 times out of 10, he will execute his task flawlessly.

In keeping with Malinowski's hypothesis about the relationship between magic and uncertainty, my research shows that baseball players associate magic with hitting and pitching, but not with fielding. Despite the wide assortment of magic—which includes rituals, taboos, and fetishes—associated with both hitting and pitching, I have never observed any directly connected to fielding. In my experience I have known only one player, a shortstop with fielding problems, who reported any ritual even remotely connected with fielding.

The most common form of magic in professional baseball is personal ritual—a prescribed form of behavior that players scrupulously observe in an effort to ensure that things go their way. These rituals, like those of Malinowski's Trobriand fishermen, are performed in a routine, unemotional manner, much as players do nonmagical things to improve their play: rubbing pine tar on the hands to improve a grip on the bat, or rubbing a new ball to make it more comfortable and responsive to the pitcher's grip. Rituals are infinitely varied since ballplayers may formalize any activity that they consider important to performing well.

Rituals usually grow out of exceptionally good performances. When a player does well he seldom attributes his success to skill alone. Although his skill remains constant, he may go hitless in one game and in the next get three or four hits. Many players attribute the inconsistencies in their performances to an object, item of food, or form of behavior outside their play. Through ritual, players seek to gain control over their performance. In the 1920s and 1930s sportswriters reported that a player who tripped en route to the field would often retrace his steps and carefully walk over the stumbling block for "insurance."

The word taboo comes from a Polynesian term meaning prohibition. Failure to observe a taboo or prohibition leads to undesirable consequences or bad luck. Most players observe a number of taboos. Taboos usually grow out of exceptionally poor performances, which players often attribute to a particular behavior or food. Certain uniform numbers may become taboo. If a player has a poor spring training season or an unsuccessful year, he may refuse to wear the same number again. During my first season of professional baseball I ate pancakes before a game in which I struck out four times. Several weeks later I had a repeat performance, again after eating pancakes. The result was a pancake taboo—I never ate pancakes during the season from that day on. Another personal taboo, against holding a baseball during the national anthem (the usual practice for first basemen, who must warm up the other infielders), had a similar origin.

In earlier decades some baseball players believed that it was bad luck to go back and fasten a missed buttonhole after dressing for a game. They simply left missed buttons on shirts or pants undone. This taboo is not practiced by modern ballplayers.

Fetishes or charms are material objects believed to embody supernatural powers that aid or protect the owner. Good luck fetishes are standard equipment for many ballplayers. They include a wide assortment of objects: horsehide covers from old baseballs, coins, crucifixes, and old bats. Ordinary objects acquire power by being connected to exceptionally hot batting or pitching streaks, especially ones in which players get all the breaks. The object is often a new possession or something a player finds and holds responsible for his new good fortune. A player who is in a slump might find a coin or an odd stone just before he begins a hitting streak, attribute an improvement in his performance to the influence of the new object, and regard it as a fetish.

While playing for Spokane, a Dodger farm team, Alan Foster forgot his baseball shoes on a road trip and borrowed a pair from a teammate.

That night he pitched a no-hitter, which he attributed to the borrowed shoes. After he bought them from his teammate, they became a prized possession.

During World War II American soldiers used fetishes in much the same way. Social psychologist Samuel Stouffer and his colleagues found that in the face of great danger and uncertainty, soldiers developed magical practices, particularly the use of protective amulets and good-luck charms (crosses, Bibles, rabbits' feet, medals), and jealously guarded articles of clothing they associated with past experiences of escape from danger. Stouffer also found that prebattle preparations were carried out in a fixed "ritual" order, much as ballplayers prepare for a game.

Because most pitchers play only once every four days, they perform rituals less frequently than hitters. The rituals they do perform, however, are just as important. A pitcher cannot make up for a poor performance the next day, and having to wait three days to redeem oneself can be miserable. Moreover, the team's win or loss depends more on the performance of the pitcher than on any other single player. Considering the pressures to do well, it is not surprising that pitchers' rituals are often more complex than those of hitters.

A seventeen-game winner in the Texas Rangers organization, Mike Griffin begins his ritual preparation a full day before he pitches, by washing his hair. The next day, although he does not consider himself superstitious, he eats bacon for lunch. When Griffin dresses for the game he puts on his clothes in the same order, making certain he puts the slightly longer of his two outer, or "stirrup," socks on his right leg. "I just wouldn't feel right mentally if I did it the other way around," he explains. He always wears the same shirt under his uniform on the day he pitches. During the game he takes off his cap after each pitch, and between innings he sits in the same place on the dugout bench.

Tug McGraw, formerly a relief pitcher for the Phillies, slapped his thigh with his glove with each step he took leaving the mound at the end of an inning. This began as a means of saying hello to his wife in the stands, but it then became ritual as McGraw slapped his thigh whether his wife was there or not.

Many of the rituals pitchers engage in—tugging their caps between pitches, touching the rosin bag after each bad pitch, smoothing the dirt on the mound before each new batter or inning—take place on the field. Most baseball fans observe this behavior regularly, never realizing that it may be as important to the pitcher as actually throwing the ball.

Uniform numbers have special significance for some pitchers. Many have a lucky number which they request. Since the choice is usually limited, pitchers may try to get a number that at least contains their lucky number, such as fourteen, four, thirty-four, or forty-four for the pitcher whose lucky number is four. Oddly enough, there is no consensus about the effect of wearing number thirteen. Some pitchers will not wear it; others such as the Mets' David Cone and Oakland's John "Blue Moon" Odom prefer it. (During a pitching slump, however, Odom asked for a new number. Later he switched back to thirteen.)

The way in which number preferences emerge varies. Occasionally a pitcher requests the number of a former professional star, hoping that—in a form of imitative magic—it will bring him the same measure of success. Or he may request a favorite number that he has always associated with good luck. Vida Blue, former Athletic and Giant, changed his uniform number from thirty-five to fourteen, the number he wore as a high-school quarterback. When the new number did not produce the better pitching performance he was looking for, he switched back to his old number.

One of the sources of his good fortune, Blue believed, was the baseball hat he had worn—since 1974. Several American League umpires refused to let him wear the faded and soiled cap. When Blue persisted he was threatened with a fine and suspension from a game. Finally he conceded, but not before he ceremoniously burned the hat on the field before a game. On the days they are scheduled to appear, many pitchers avoid activities that they believe sap their strength and therefore detract from their effectiveness, or that they otherwise generally link with poor performance. (Many pitchers avoid eating certain foods on their pitching days; actually, some food taboos make good physiological sense.) Some pitchers do not shave on the day of a game. In fact, Oakland's Dave Stewart and St. Louis's Todd Worrell don't shave as long as they are winning. Early in the 1989 season Stewart had six consecutive victories and a beard before he finally lost. Ex-St. Louis Cardinal Al Hrabosky took this taboo to extreme lengths; Samsonlike, he refused to cut his hair or beard during the entire season—hence part of the reason for his nickname, the "Mad Hungarian." Many hitters go through a series of preparatory rituals before stepping into the batter's box. These include tugging on their caps, touching their uniform letters or medallions, crossing themselves, tapping or bouncing the bat on the plate, swinging the weighted warm-up bat a prescribed number of times, and smoothing the dirt in the box.

There were more than a dozen individual elements in the batting ritual of Mike Hargrove, former Cleveland Indian first baseman. And after each pitch he would step out of the batter's box and repeat the entire sequence. His rituals were so time consuming that he was called "the human rain delay."

Clothing, both the choice of clothes and the order in which they are put on, is often ritualized. During a batting streak many players wear the same clothes and uniforms for each game and put them on in exactly the same order. Once I changed sweatshirts midway through the game for seven consecutive games to keep a hitting streak going. During a sixteen-game winning streak in 1954, the New York Giants wore the same clothes in each game and refused to let them be cleaned for fear that their good fortune might be washed away with the dirt. Taking this ritual to the extreme, Leo Durocher, managing the Brooklyn Dodgers to a pennant in 1941, spent three and a half weeks in the same black shoes, gray slacks, blue coat, and knitted blue tie.

The opposite may also occur. Several of the Oakland A's players bought new street clothing in an attempt to break a fourteen-game losing streak. Most players, however, single out one or two lucky articles or quirks of dress rather than ritualizing all items of clothing. After hitting two home runs in a game, infielder Jim Davenport of the San Francisco Giants discovered that he had missed a buttonhole while dressing for the game. For the remainder of his career he left the same button undone.

A popular ritual associated with hitting is tagging a base when leaving and returning to the dugout during each inning. Mickey Mantle was in the habit of tagging second base on the way to or from the outfield. During a successful month of the season, one player stepped on third base on his way to the dugout after the third, sixth, and ninth innings of each game. Asked if he ever purposely failed to step on the bag, he replied, "Never! I wouldn't dare. It would destroy my confidence to hit." A hitter who is playing poorly may try different combinations of tagging and not tagging particular bases in an attempt to find a successful combination.

When their players are not hitting some managers will rattle the bat bin, the large wooden box containing the team's bats, as if the bats were in a stupor and could be aroused by a good shaking. Similarly, some hitters rub their hands along the handles of the bats protruding from the bin, presumably in hopes of picking up some power or luck from bats that are getting hits for their owners.

There is a taboo against crossing bats, against permitting one bat to rest on top of another. Although this superstition appears to be dying out among ballplayers today, it was religiously observed by some of my teammates. And in some cases it was elaborated even further. One former Detroit minor leaguer became quite annoyed when a teammate tossed a bat from the batting cage and it landed on top of his bat. Later he explained that the top bat might steal hits from the lower one. In his view, bats contained a finite number of hits, a sort of baseball "image of limited good." For Pirate shortstop Honus Wagner, a charter member of baseball's Hall of Fame, each bat contained only a certain number of hits, and never more than 100. Regardless of the quality of the bat, he would discard it after its 100th hit.

Hall of Famer Johnny Evers, of the Cub double-play trio Tinker to Evers to Chance, believed in saving his luck. If he was hitting well in practice, he would suddenly stop and retire to the bench to "save" his batting for the game. One player told me that many of his teammates on the Asheville Tourists in the Class A Western Carolinas League would not let pitchers touch or swing their bats, not even to loosen up. The traditionally poor-hitting pitchers were believed to pollute or weaken the bats.

Food often forms part of a hitter's ritual repertoire. Eating certain foods before a game is supposed to give the ball "eyes," that is, the ability to seek the gaps between fielders after being hit. In hopes of maintaining a batting streak I once ate chicken every day at 4:00 P.M. until the streak ended. Yankee catcher Jim Leyritz eats turkey before every game. Hitters, like pitchers, also avoid certain foods that are believed to sap their strength during the game.

There are other examples of hitters' ritualized behavior. I once kept my eyes closed during the national anthem in an effort to prolong a batting streak. A friend of mine refused to read anything on the day of a game because he believed that reading weakened his eyesight when batting.

These are personal taboos. There are some taboos, however, that all players hold and that do not develop out of individual experiences or misfortunes. These taboos are learned, some as early as Little League. Mentioning a no-hitter while one is in progress is a widely known example. It is believed that if a pitcher hears the words "no-hitter," the spell will be broken and the no-hitter lost. This taboo is still observed by many sports broadcasters, who use various linguistic subterfuges to inform their listeners that the pitcher had not given up a hit, never mentioning "no-hitter."

But superstitions, like most everything else, change over time. Many of the rituals and beliefs of early baseball are no longer remembered. A century ago players spent time off the field and on looking for items that would bring them luck. For example, to find a hairpin on the street assured a batter of hitting safely in that day's game (today women don't wear hairpins—a good reason why the belief has died out). To catch sight of a white horse or a wagonload of barrels was also good omens. In 1904 the manager of the New York Giants, John McGraw, hired a driver and a team of white horses to drive past the Polo Grounds around the time his players were arriving at the ballpark. He knew that if his players saw white horses they'd have more confidence and that could only help them play better. Belief in the power of white horses survived in a few backwaters until the 1960s. A gray haired manager of a team I played for in Quebec would drive around the countryside before important games and during the playoffs looking for a white horse. When he was successful, he'd announce it to everyone in the clubhouse before the game.

Today most professional baseball coaches or managers will not step on the chalk foul lines when going onto the field to talk to their pitcher. Detroit's manager Sparky Anderson jumps over the line. Others follow a different ritual. They intentionally step on the lines when they are going to take a pitcher out of a game.

How do these rituals and taboos get established in the first place? B. F. Skinner's early research with pigeons provides a clue. Like human beings, pigeons quickly learn to associate their behavior with rewards or punishment. By rewarding the birds at the appropriate time, Skinner taught them such elaborate games as table tennis, miniature bowling, or to play simple tunes on a toy piano.

On one occasion he decided to see what would happen if pigeons were rewarded with food pellets every fifteen seconds, regardless of what they did. He found the the birds tended to associate the arrival of the food with a particular action—tucking the head under a wing, hopping from side to side, or turning in a clockwise direction. About ten seconds after the arrival of the last pellet, a bird would begin doing whatever it had associated with getting the food and keep it up until the next pellet arrived.

In the same way, baseball players tend to believe there is a causal connection between two events that are linked only temporally. If a superstitious player touches his crucifix and then gets a hit, he may decide the gesture was responsible for his good fortune and follow the same ritual the next time he comes to the plate. If he should get another hit, the chances are good that he will begin touching the crucifix each time he bats and that he will do so whether or not he hits safely each time.

The average batter hits safely approximately one quarter of the time. And if the behavior of Skinner's pigeons—or of gamblers at a Las Vegas slot machine—is any guide, that is more often than necessary to keep him believing in a ritual. Skinner found that once a pigeon associated one of its actions with the arrival of food or water, sporadic rewards would keep the connection going. One pigeon, apparently believing that hopping from side to side brought pellets into its feeding cup, hopped ten thousand times without a pellet before it gave up.

Since the batter associates his hits at least in some degree with his ritual touching of a crucifix, each hit he gets reinforces the strength of the ritual. Even if he falls into a batting slump and the hits temporarily stop, he will persist in touching the crucifix in the hope that this will change his luck.

Skinner's and Malinowski's explanations are not contradictory. Skinner focuses on how the individual comes to develop and maintain a particular ritual, taboo, or fetish. Malinowski focuses on why human beings turn to magic in precarious or uncertain situations. In their attempts to gain greater control over their performance, baseball players respond to chance and uncertainty in the same way as do people in simple societies. It is wrong to assume that magical practices are a waste of time for either group. The magic in baseball obviously does not make a pitch travel faster or more accurately, or a batted ball seek the gaps between fielders. Nor does the Trobriand brand of magic make the surrounding seas calmer and more abundant with fish. But both kinds of magic give their practitioners a sense of control—and an important element in any endeavor is confidence.

REVIEW QUESTIONS

1. What is magic and why do people practice it, according to Gmelch?
2. In what ways does the magic used by baseball players illustrate the 12 characteristics of ritual describe by Davis-Floyd in Selection 29?
3. What parts of baseball are most likely to lead to magical practice? Why?
4. How are Malinowski's and Skinner's theories of magic alike and different? What is each designed to explain?
5. Can you think of other areas of American life where magic is practiced? Does the same theory used in this article account for these examples, too?

32

Cargo Cults

Peter M. Worsley

When one cultural group becomes dominated by another, its original meaning system may seem thin, ineffective, and contradictory. The resulting state of deprivation often causes members to rebuild their culture along more satisfying lines. In this article, Peter Worsley describes a religious movement among the peoples of New Guinea and adjacent islands, an area where Western influence has caused cultural disorientation and where cargo cults have provided the basis for reorganization.

Patrols of the Australian government venturing into the "uncontrolled" central highlands of New Guinea in 1946 found the primitive people there swept up in a wave of religious excitement. Prophecy was being fulfilled: The arrival of the whites was the sign that the end of the world was at hand. The natives proceeded to butcher all of their pigs—animals that were not only a principal source of subsistence but also symbols of social status and ritual preeminence in their culture. They killed

From "Cargo Cults," by Peter M. Worsley, *Scientific American* 200 (May 1959): 117–128.
Reprinted with permission. Copyright © 1959 by Scientific American, Inc. All rights reserved.
Illustrations are omitted.

these valued animals in expression of the belief that after three days of darkness "Great Pigs" would appear from the sky. Food, firewood, and other necessities had to be stockpiled to see the people through to the arrival of the Great Pigs. Mock wireless antennae of bamboo and rope had been erected to receive in advance the news of the millennium. Many believed that with the great event they would exchange their black skins for white ones.

This bizarre episode is by no means the single event of its kind in the murky history of the collision of European civilization with the indigenous cultures of the southwest Pacific. For more than one hundred years traders and missionaries have been reporting similar disturbances among the people of Melanesia, the group of Negro-inhabited islands (including New Guinea, Fiji, the Solomons, and the New Hebrides) lying between Australia and the open Pacific Ocean. Though their technologies were based largely upon stone and wood, these peoples had highly developed cultures, as measured by the standards of maritime and agricultural ingenuity, the complexity of their varied social organizations, and the elaboration of religious belief and ritual. They were nonetheless ill prepared for the shock of the encounter with the whites, a people so radically different from themselves and so infinitely more powerful. The sudden transition from the society of the ceremonial stone axe to the society of sailing ships and now of airplanes has not been easy to make.

After four centuries of Western expansion, the densely populated central highlands of New Guinea remain one of the few regions where the people still carry on their primitive existence in complete independence of the world outside. Yet as the agents of the Australian government penetrate into ever more remote mountain valleys, they find these backwaters of antiquity already deeply disturbed by contact with the ideas and artifacts of European civilization. For "cargo"—Pidgin English for trade goods—has long flowed along the indigenous channels of communication from the seacoast into the wilderness. With it has traveled the frightening knowledge of the white man's magical power. No small element in the white man's magic is the hopeful message sent abroad by his missionaries: the news that a Messiah will come and that the present order of Creation will end.

The people of the central highlands of New Guinea are only the latest to be gripped in the recurrent religious frenzy of the "cargo cults." However variously embellished with details from native myth and Christian belief, these cults all advance the same central theme: the world is about to end in a terrible cataclysm. Thereafter God, the ancestors, or some local culture hero will appear and inaugurate a blissful paradise on earth. Death, old age, illness, and evil will be unknown. The riches of the white man will accrue to the Melanesians.

Although the news of such a movement in one area has doubtless often inspired similar movements in other areas, the evidence indicates that these cults have arisen independently in many places as parallel responses to the same enormous social stress and strain. Among the movements best known to students of Melanesia are the "Taro Cult" of New Guinea, the "Vailala Madness" of Papua, the "Naked Cult" of Espiritu Santo, the "John Frum Movement" of the New Hebrides, and the "Tuka Cult" of the Fiji Islands.

At times the cults have been so well organized and fanatically persistent that they have brought the work of government to a standstill. The outbreaks have often taken the authorities completely by surprise and have confronted them with mass opposition of an alarming kind. In the 1930s, for example, villagers in the vicinity of Wewak, New Guinea, were stirred by a succession of "Black King" movements. The prophets announced that the Europeans would soon leave the island, abandoning their property to the natives, and urged their followers to cease paying taxes, since the government station was about to disappear into the sea in a great earthquake. To the tiny community of whites in charge of the region, such talk was dangerous. The authorities jailed four of the prophets and exiled three others. In yet another movement, which sprang up in declared opposition to the local Christian mission, the cult leader took Satan as his god.

Troops on both sides in World War II found their arrival in Melanesia heralded as a sign of the Apocalypse. The G.I.'s who landed in the New Hebrides, moving up for the bloody fighting on Guadalcanal, found the natives furiously at work preparing airfields, roads, and docks for the magic ships and planes that they believed were coming from "Rusefel" (Roosevelt), the friendly king of America.

The Japanese also encountered millenarian visionaries during their southward march to Guadalcanal. Indeed, one of the strangest minor military actions of World War II occurred in Dutch New Guinea, when Japanese forces had to be turned against the local Papuan inhabitants of the Geelvink Bay region. The Japanese had at first been received with great joy, not because their "Greater East Asia Co-Prosperity Sphere" propaganda had made any great impact upon the Papuans, but because the natives regarded them as harbingers of the new world that was dawning, the flight of the Dutch having already given the first sign. Mansren, creator of the islands and their peoples, would now return, bringing with him the ancestral dead. All this had been known, the cult leaders declared, to the crafty Dutch, who had torn out the first page of the Bible where these truths were inscribed. When Mansren returned, the existing world order would be entirely overturned. White men would turn black like Papuans, Papuans would become whites; root crops would grow in trees, and coconuts and fruits would grow like tubers. Some of the islanders now began to draw together into large "towns"; others took biblical names such as "Jericho" and "Galilee" for their villages. Soon they adopted military uniforms and began drilling. The Japanese, by now highly unpopular, tried to disarm and disperse the Papuans; resistance inevitably developed. The climax of this tragedy came when several canoe-loads of fanatics sailed out to attack Japanese warships, believing themselves to be invulnerable by virtue of the holy water with which they had sprinkled themselves. But the bullets of the Japanese did not turn to water, and the attackers were mowed down by machine-gun fire.

Behind this incident lay a long history. As long ago as 1857 missionaries in the Geelvink Bay region had made note of the story of Mansren. It is typical of many Melanesian myths that became confounded with Christian doctrine to form the ideological basis of the movements. The legend tells how long ago there lived an old man named Manamakeri ("he who itches"), whose body was covered with sores. Manamakeri was extremely fond of palm wine, and used to climb a huge tree every day to tap the liquid from the flowers. He soon found that someone was getting there before him and removing the liquid. Eventually he trapped the thief, who turned out to be none other than the Morning Star. In return for his freedom, the Star gave the old man a wand that would produce as much fish as he liked, a magic tree, and a magic staff. If he drew in the sand and stamped his foot, the drawing would become real. Manamakeri, aged as he was, now magically impregnated a young maiden; the child of this union was a miracle-child who spoke as soon as he was born. But the maiden's parents were horrified, and banished her, the child, and the old man. The trio sailed off in a canoe created by Mansren ("The Lord"), as the old man now became known. On this journey Mansren rejuvenated himself by stepping into a fire and flaking off his scaly skin, which changed into valuables. He then sailed around Geelvink Bay, creating islands where he stopped, and peopling them with the ancestors of the present-day Papuans.

The Mansren myth is plainly a creation myth full of symbolic ideas relating to fertility and rebirth. Comparative evidence—especially the shedding of his scaly skin—confirms the suspicion that the old man is, in fact, the Snake in another guise. Psychoanalytic writers argue that the snake occupies such a prominent part in mythology the world over because it stands for the penis, another fertility symbol. This may be so, but its symbolic significance is surely more complex than this. It is the "rebirth" of the hero, whether Mansren or the Snake, that exercises such universal fascination over men's minds.

The nineteenth-century missionaries thought that the Mansren story would make the introduction of Christianity easier, since the concept of "resurrection," not to mention that of the "virgin birth" and the "second coming," was already there. By 1867, however, the first cult organized around the Mansren legend was reported.

Though such myths were widespread in Melanesia, and may have sparked occasional movements even in the pre-white era, they took on a new significance in the late nineteenth century, once the European powers had finished parceling out the Melanesian region among themselves. In many coastal areas the long history of "blackbirding"—the seizure of islanders for work on the plantations of Australia and Fiji—had built up a reservoir of hostility to Europeans. In other areas, however, the arrival of the whites was accepted, even welcomed, for it meant access to bully beef and cigarettes, shirts and paraffin lamps, whisky and bicycles. It also meant access to the knowledge behind these material goods, for the Europeans brought missions and schools as well as cargo.

Practically the only teaching the natives received about European life came from the missions, which emphasized the central significance of religion in European society. The Melanesians already believed that human activities—whether gardening, sailing canoes, or bearing children—needed magical assistance. Ritual without human effort was not enough. But neither was human effort on its own. This outlook was reinforced by mission teaching.

The initial enthusiasm for European rule, however, was speedily dispelled. The rapid growth of the plantation economy removed the bulk of the able-bodied men from the villages, leaving women, children, and old men to carry on as best they could. The splendid vision of the equality of all Christians began to seem a pious deception in face of the realities of the color bar, the multiplicity of rival Christian missions, and the open irreligion of many whites.

For a long time the natives accepted the European mission as the means by which the "cargo" would eventually be made available to them. But they found that acceptance of Christianity did not bring the cargo any nearer. They grew disillusioned. The story now began to be put about that it was not the whites who made the cargo, but the dead ancestors. To people completely ignorant of factory production, this made good sense. White men did not work; they merely wrote secret signs on scraps of paper, for which they were given shiploads of goods. On the other hand, the Melanesians labored week after week for pitiful wages. Plainly the goods must be made for Melanesians somewhere, perhaps in the Land of the Dead. The whites, who possessed the secret of the cargo, were intercepting it and keeping it from the hands of the islanders, to whom it was really consigned. In the Madang district of New Guinea, after some forty years' experience of the missions, the natives went in a body one day with a petition demanding that the cargo secret should now be revealed to them, for they had been very patient.

So strong is this belief in the existence of a "secret" that the cargo cults generally contain some ritual in imitation of the mysterious European customs which are held to be the clue to the white man's extraordinary power over goods and men. The believers sit around tables with bottles of flowers in front of them, dressed in European clothes, waiting for the cargo ship or airplane to materialize; other cultists feature magic pieces of paper and cabalistic writing. Many of them deliberately turn their backs on the past by destroying secret ritual objects, or exposing them to the gaze of uninitiated youths and women, for whom formerly even a glimpse of the sacred objects would have meant the severest penalties, even death. The belief that they were the chosen people is further reinforced by their reading of the Bible, for the lives and customs of the people in the Old Testament resemble their own lives rather than those of the Europeans. In the New Testament they find the Apocalypse, with its prophecies of destruction and resurrection, particularly attractive.

Missions that stress the imminence of the Second Coming, like those of the Seventh Day Adventists, are often accused of stimulating millenarian cults among the islanders. In reality, however, the Melanesians themselves rework the doctrines the missionaries teach them, selecting from the Bible what they themselves find particularly congenial in it. Such movements have occurred in areas where missions of quite different types have been dominant, from Roman Catholic to Seventh Day Adventists. The reasons for the emergence of these cults, of course, lie far deeper in the life experience of the people.

The economy of most of the islands is very backward. Native agriculture produces little for the world market, and even the European plantations and mines export only a few primary products and raw materials: copra, rubber, gold. Melanesians are quite unable to understand why copra, for example, fetches thirty pounds sterling per ton one month and but five pounds a few months later. With no notion of the workings of world-commodity markets, the natives see only the sudden closing of plantations, reduced wages, and unemployment, and are inclined to attribute their insecurity to the whim or evil in the nature of individual planters.

Such shocks have not been confined to the economic order. Governments, too, have come and gone, especially during the two world wars: German, Dutch, British, and French administrations melted overnight. Then came the Japanese, only to be ousted in turn largely by the previously unknown Americans. And among these Americans the Melanesians saw Negroes like themselves, living lives of luxury on equal terms with white G.I.'s. The sight of these Negroes seemed like a fulfillment of the old prophecies to many cargo cult leaders. Nor must we forget the sheer scale of this invasion. Around a million U.S. troops passed through the Admiralty Islands, completely swamping the inhabitants. It was a world of meaningless and chaotic changes, in which anything was possible. New ideas were imported and given local twists. Thus in the Loyalty Islands people expected the French Communist Party to bring the millennium. There is no real evidence, however, of any Communist influence in these movements, despite the rather hysterical belief among Solomon Island planters that the name of the local "Masinga Rule" movement was derived from the word "Marxian"! In reality the name comes from a Solomon Island tongue, and means "brotherhood."

Europeans who have witnessed outbreaks inspired by the cargo cults are usually at a loss to understand what they behold. The islanders throw away their money, break their most sacred taboos, abandon their gardens, and destroy their precious livestock; they indulge in sexual license or, alternatively, rigidly separate men from women in huge communal establishments. Sometimes they spend days sitting gazing at the horizon for a glimpse of the long-awaited ship or airplane; sometimes they dance, pray, and sing in mass congregations, becoming possessed and "speaking with tongues."

Observers have not hesitated to use such words as "madness," "mania," and "irrationality" to characterize the cults. But the cults reflect quite logical and rational attempts to make sense out of a social order that appears senseless and chaotic. Given the ignorance of the Melanesians about the wider European society, its economic organization and its highly developed technology, their reactions form a consistent and understandable pattern. They wrap up all their yearning and hope in an amalgam that combines the best counsel they can find in Christianity and their native belief. If the world is soon to end, gardening or fishing is unnecessary; everything will be provided. If the Melanesians are to be part of a much wider order, the taboos that prescribe their social conduct must now be lifted or broken in a newly prescribed way.

Of course the cargo never comes. The cults nonetheless live on. If the millennium does not arrive on schedule, then perhaps there is some failure in the magic, some error in the ritual. New breakaway groups organize around "purer" faith and ritual. The cult rarely disappears, so long as the social situation which brings it into being persists.

At this point it should be observed that cults of this general kind are not peculiar to Melanesia. People who feel themselves oppressed and deceived have always been ready to pour their hopes and fears, their aspirations and frustrations, into dreams of a millennium to come or of a golden age to return. All parts of the world have had their counterparts of the cargo cults, from the American Indian ghost dance to the Communist-millenarist "reign of the saints" in Münster during the Reformation, from medieval European apocalyptic cults to African "witch-finding" movements and Chinese Buddhist heresies. In some situations men have been content to wait and pray; in others they have sought to hasten the day by using their strong right arms to do the Lord's work. And always the cults serve to bring together scattered groups, notably the peasants and urban plebians of agrarian societies and peoples of "stateless" societies where the cult unites separate (and often hostile) villages, clans, and tribes into a wider religio-political unity.

Once the people begin to develop secular political organizations, however, the sects tend to lose their importance as vehicles of protest. They begin to relegate the Second Coming to the distant future or to the next world. In Melanesia ordinary political bodies, trade unions, and native councils are becoming the normal media through which the islanders express their aspirations. In recent years continued economic prosperity and political stability have taken some of the edge off their despair. It now seems unlikely that any major movement along cargo-cult lines will recur in areas where the transition to secular politics has been made, even if the insecurity of prewar times returned. I would predict that the embryonic nationalism represented by cargo cults is likely in future to take forms familiar in the history of other countries that have moved from subsistence agriculture to participation in the world economy.

REVIEW QUESTIONS

1. What did the Melanesians mean by cargo, and why was it so important to them?
2. What were the main features of cargo cults? What was their purpose?
3. Why did so many cargo cults, each remarkably similar to the others, appear in so many different places in Melanesia?
4. How did cargo cults contribute to cultural change in Melanesia?

CULTURE CHANGE AND APPLIED ANTHROPOLOGY

Nowhere in the world do human affairs remain precisely constant from year to year. New ways of doing things mark the history of even the most stable groups. Change occurs when an Australian aboriginal dreams about a new myth and teaches it to the members of his band; when a loader in a restaurant kitchen invents a way to stack plates more quickly in the dishwasher; or when a New Guinea Big Man cites the traditional beliefs about ghosts to justify the existence of a new political office devised by a colonial government. Wherever people interpret their natural and social worlds in a new way, cultural change has occurred. Broad or narrow, leisurely or rapid, such change is part of life in every society.

Culture change can originate from two sources: innovation and borrowing. *Innovation* is the invention of qualitatively new forms. It involves the recombination of what people already know into something different. For example, Canadian Joseph-Armand Bombardier became an innovator when he mated tracks, designed to propel earth-moving equipment, to a small bus that originally ran on tires, producing the first snowmobile in the 1950s. Later, the Skolt Lapps of Finland joined him as innovators when they adapted his now smaller, more refined snowmobile for herding reindeer in 1961. The Lapp innovation was not the vehicle itself. That was borrowed. What was new was the use of the vehicle in herding, something usually done by men on skis.

Innovations are more likely to occur and to be adopted during stressful times when traditional culture no longer works well. Bombardier, for example, began work on his snowmobile after he was unable to reach medical help in time to save the life of his critically ill son during a Canadian winter storm. Frustrated by the slowness of his horse and sleigh, he set out to create a faster vehicle.

The other basis of culture change is *borrowing*. Borrowing—or *diffusion,* as it is sometimes called—refers to the adoption of something new from another group. Tobacco, for example, was first domesticated and grown in the New World but quickly diffused to Europe and Asia after 1492. Such items as the umbrella, pajamas, Arabic numerals, and perhaps even the technology to make steel came to Europe from India. Ideologies and religions may diffuse from one society to another.

An extreme diffusionist view has been used to explain most human achievements. For example, author Erik Von Däniken argues that features of ancient New World civilizations were brought by space invaders. Englishman G. Elliot Smith claimed that Mayan and Aztec culture diffused from Egypt. Thor Heyerdahl sailed a reed boat, the *Ra II*, from Africa to South America to prove that an Egyptian cultural origin was possible for New World civilization.

Whether something is an innovation or borrowed, it must pass through a process of *social acceptance* before it can become part of a culture. Indeed many, if not most, novel ideas and things remain unattractive and relegated to obscurity. To achieve social acceptance, an innovation must become known to the members of a society, must be accepted as valid, and must fit into a system of cultural knowledge revised to accept it.

Several principles facilitate social acceptance. If a change wins the support of a person in authority, it may gain the approval of others. Timing is also important. It would have made little sense for a Lapp to attempt the introduction of snowmobiles when there was no snow or when the men who do the reindeer herding were scattered over their vast grazing territory. Other factors also affect social acceptance. Changes have a greater chance of acceptance if they meet a felt need, if they appeal to people's prestige (in societies where prestige is important), and if they provide some continuity with traditional customs.

Change may take place under a variety of conditions, from the apparently dull day-to-day routine of a stable society to the frantic climate of a revolution. One situation that has occupied many anthropologists interested in change is *cultural contact*, particularly situations of contact where one society politically dominates another. World history is replete with examples of such domination, which vary in outcome from annihilation, in the case of the Tasmanians and hundreds of tribes in North and South America, Africa, Asia, and even ancient Europe, to the political rule that indentured countless millions of people to colonial powers.

The study of change caused by these conditions is called *acculturation*. Acculturation is the process of change that results from cultural contact. Acculturative change may affect dominant societies as well as subordinate ones. After their ascendance in India, for example, the British came to wear *khaki* clothes, live in *bungalows*, and trek through *jungles*—all Indian concepts.

But those who are subordinated experience the most far-reaching changes in their way of life. From politically independent, self-sufficient people, they usually become subordinate and dependent. Sweeping changes in social structure and values may occur, along with a resulting social disorganization.

Although the age of colonial empires is largely over, the destruction of tribal culture continues at a rapid pace today. As we saw in Reed's article in Part IV of this book, hundreds of thousands of Amazonian Indians have already perished in the last few years because of intrusive frontier and development programs. Following almost exactly the pattern of past colonial exploitation, modern governments bent on "progress" displace and often kill off indigenous tribal populations. The frequent failure of development, coupled with its damaging impact on native peoples, has caused many anthropologists to reassess their role. As a result, more and more anthropologists have become part of native resistance to outside intrusion.

A less dramatic, but in many ways no less important, agent of change is the world economy. No longer can most people live in self-sufficient isolation. Their future is inevitably tied in with an overall system of market exchange. Take the Marshall Islanders described by anthropologist Michael Rynkiewich, for example. Although they cultivate to meet their own subsistence needs, they also raise coconuts for sale on the world market. Receipts from the coconut crop go to pay for outboard motors and gasoline, cooking utensils, and a variety of other goods they don't manufacture themselves but have come to depend on. Recently several major American food companies have eliminated coconut oil from their products because of its high level of saturated fat. This loss has created lower demand for copra (dried coconut meat), from which the oil is pressed. Reduced demand, in turn, may cause substantial losses to the Marshall Islanders. A people who once could subsist independently have now become prisoners of the world economic system.

Anthropologists may themselves become agents of change, applying their work to practical problems. Applied anthropology, as opposed to academic anthropology, includes any use of anthropological knowledge to influence social interaction, to maintain or change social institutions, or to direct the course of cultural change. There are four basic uses of anthropology contained within the applied field: adjustment anthropology, administrative anthropology, action anthropology, and advocate anthropology.

Adjustment anthropology uses anthropological knowledge to make social interaction more predictable among people who operate with different cultural codes. For example, take the anthropologists who consult with companies and government agencies about intercultural communication. It is often their job to train Americans to interpret the cultural rules that govern interaction in another society. For a business person who will work in Latin America, the anthropologist may point out the appropriate culturally defined speaking distances, ways to sit, definitions of time, topics of conversation, times for business talk, and so on. All of these activities would be classified as adjustment anthropology.

Administrative anthropology uses anthropological knowledge for planned change by those who are external to the local cultural group. It is the use of anthropological knowledge by a person with the power to make decisions. If an anthropologist provides to a mayor knowledge about the culture of constituents, he or she is engaged in administrative anthropology. So would advisers to chief administrators of U.S. trust territories such as once existed in places like the Marshall Islands.

Action anthropology uses anthropological knowledge for planned change by the local cultural group. The anthropologist acts as a catalyst, providing information but avoiding decision making, which remains in the hands of the people affected by the decisions.

Advocate anthropology uses anthropological knowledge by the anthropologist to increase the power of self-determination of a particular cultural group. Instead of focusing on the process of innovation, the anthropologist centers attention on discovering the sources of power and how a group can gain access to them. James Spradley took such action when he studied tramps in 1968. He discovered that police and courts systematically deprived tramps of their power to control their lives and of the rights accorded normal citizens. By releasing his findings to the Seattle newspapers, he helped tramps gain additional power and weakened the control of Seattle authorities.

Whether they are doing administrative, advocate, adjustment, or action anthropology, anthropologists take, at least in part, a qualitative approach. They do ethnography, discover the cultural knowledge of their informants, and apply this information in the ways discussed previously. In contrast to the quantitative data so often prized by other social scientists, they use the insider's viewpoint to discover problems, to advise, and to generate policy.

The articles in this section illustrate several aspects of cultural change and applied anthropology. The first, by Lauriston Sharp, reveals how the introduction of a tool as simple as a hatchet-sized steel axe can destroy a functionally integrated society. John Bodley's piece describes the process of tribal destruction as it has happened over and over again at the hands of more powerful governments. Bodley, a pioneer spokesperson for tribal rights, argues that progress means the destruction of indigenous culture and society. The selection by Anne Sutherland serves as an example of applied anthropology. Written for doctors, it advises physicians about the aspects of American Gypsy culture they need to know to treat these mobile people. Finally, David McCurdy discusses the modern uses of anthropology. From studies of General Motors workers, to program assessment for people with AIDS, to participation in government health projects, to international counseling, professional anthropologists put their discipline to work. In this article, McCurdy looks at one way in which the ethnographic perspective can be put to work in a business setting.

KEY TERMS

innovation
borrowing
diffusion
social acceptance
cultural contact
acculturation

applied anthropology
adjustment anthropology
administrative anthropology
action anthropology
advocate anthropology

READINGS IN THIS SECTION

33

Steel Axes
for Stone-Age Australians

Lauriston Sharp

*Anthropologists regularly look at how societies are functionally
integrated.* Functional integration *refers to how the various
aspects of a society, such as its culturally defined behaviors, beliefs,
and artifacts, affect and support each other to create an organized
system. This approach is useful in the understanding and prediction
of the effects of change, for a particular alteration often changes the
relationships inside a system. This is the topic of Lauriston Sharp's
classic article about the impact of hatchet-sized steel axes on the
traditional functional integration of an Australian aboriginal society in the 1930s. Introduced by missionaries without reference
to traditional Yir Yoront social organization, the axe replaced its
stone counterpart, with dramatic results.*

Reproduced by permission of the Society for Applied Anthropology from *Human Organization* 11 (2): 17–22, 1952.

I.

L ike other Australian aboriginals, the Yir Yoront group which lives at the mouth of the Coleman River on the west coast of Cape York Peninsula originally had no knowledge of metals. Technologically their culture was of the old Stone Age or paleolithic type. They supported themselves by hunting and fishing, and obtained vegetables and other materials from the bush by simple gathering techniques. Their only domesticated animal was the dog; they had no cultivated plants of any kind. Unlike some other aboriginal groups, however, the Yir Yoront did have polished stone axes hafted in short handles which were most important in their economy.

Toward the end of the nineteenth century metal tools and other European artifacts began to filter into the Yir Yoront territory. The flow increased with the gradual expansion of the white frontier outward from southern and eastern Queensland. Of all the items of Western technology thus made available, the hatchet, or short-handled steel axe, was the most acceptable to and the most highly valued by all aboriginals.

In the mid-1930s an American anthropologist lived alone in the bush among the Yir Yoront for thirteen months without seeing another white man. The Yir Yoront were thus still relatively isolated and continued to live an essentially independent economic existence, supporting themselves entirely by means of their old Stone Age techniques. Yet their polished stone axes were disappearing fast and being replaced by steel axes which came to them in considerable numbers, directly or indirectly, from various European sources to the south.

What changes in the life of the Yir Yoront still living under aboriginal conditions in the Australian bush could be expected as a result of their increasing possession and use of the steel axe?

II. THE COURSE OF EVENTS

Events leading up to the introduction of the steel axe among the Yir Yoront begin with the advent of the second known group of Europeans to reach the shores of the Australian continent. In 1623 a Dutch expedition landed on the coast where the Yir Yoront now live.[1] In 1935 the Yir Yoront were still using the few cultural items recorded in the Dutch log for the aboriginals they encountered. To this cultural inventory the Dutch added beads and pieces of iron which they offered in an effort to attract the frightened "Indians." Among these natives metal and beads have disappeared, together with any memory of this first encounter with whites.

---

[1] An account of this expedition from Amboina is given in R. Logan Jack, *Northmost Australia*, 2 vols. (London, 1921), vol. 1, 18–57.

The next recorded contact in this area was in 1864. Here there is more positive assurance that the natives concerned were the immediate ancestors of the Yir Yoront community. These aboriginals had the temerity to attack a party of cattlemen who were driving a small herd from southern Queensland through the length of the then unknown Cape York Peninsula to a newly established government station at the northern tip.[2] Known as the "Battle of the Mitchell River," this was one of the rare instances in which Australian aboriginals stood up to European gunfire for any length of time. A diary kept by the cattlemen records that:

> 10 carbines poured volley after volley into them from all directions, killing and wounding with every shot with very little return, nearly all their spears having already been expended. . . . about 30 being killed, the leader thought it prudent to hold his hand, and let the rest escape. Many more must have been wounded and probably drowned, for 59 rounds were counted as discharged.

The European party was in the Yir Yoront area for three days; they then disappeared over the horizon to the north and never returned. In the almost three-year-long anthropological investigation conducted some seventy years later—in all the material of hundreds of free association interviews, in texts of hundreds of dreams and myths, in genealogies, and eventually in hundreds of answers to direct and indirect questioning on just this particular matter—there was nothing that could be interpreted as a reference to this shocking contact with Europeans.

The aboriginal accounts of their first remembered contact with whites begin in about 1900 with references to persons known to have had sporadic but lethal encounters with them. From that time on whites continued to remain on the southern periphery of Yir Yoront territory. With the establishment of cattle stations (ranches) to the south, cattlemen made occasional excursions among the "wild black-fellows" in order to inspect the country and abduct natives to be trained as cattle boys and "house girls." At least one such expedition reached the Coleman River, where a number of Yir Yoront men and women were shot for no apparent reason.

About this time the government was persuaded to sponsor the establishment of three mission stations along the seven-hundred-mile western coast of the Peninsula in an attempt to help regulate the treatment of natives. To further this purpose a strip of coastal territory was set aside as an aboriginal reserve and closed to further white settlement.

In 1915, an Anglican missions station was established near the mouth of the Mitchell River, about a three-day march from the heart of the Yir Yoront country. Some Yir Yoront refused to have anything to do with the mission, others visited it occasionally while only a few eventually settled more or less permanently in one of the three "villages" established at the mission.

---

[2] Logan Jack, 298–335.

Thus the majority of the Yir Yoront continued to live their old self-supporting life in the bush, protected until 1942 by the government reserve and the intervening mission from the cruder realities of the encroaching new order from the south. To the east was poor, uninhabited country. To the north were other bush tribes extending on along the coast to the distant Archer River Presbyterian mission with which the Yir Yoront had no contact. Westward was the shallow Gulf of Carpentaria, on which the natives saw only a mission lugger making its infrequent dry season trips to the Mitchell River. In this protected environment for over a generation the Yir Yoront were able to recuperate from shocks received at the hands of civilized society. During the 1930s their raiding and fighting, their trading and stealing of women, their evisceration and two- or three-year care of their dead, and their totemic ceremonies continued, apparently uninhibited by Western influence. In 1931 they killed a European who wandered into their territory from the east, but the investigating police never approached the group whose members were responsible for the act.

As a direct result of the work of the Mitchell River mission, all Yir Yoront received a great many more Western artifacts of all kinds than ever before. As part of their plan for raising native living standards, the missionaries made it possible for aboriginals living at the mission to earn some Western goods, many of which were then given or traded to natives still living under bush conditions; they also handed out certain useful articles gratis to both mission and bush aboriginals. They prevented guns, liquor, and damaging narcotics, as well as decimating diseases, from reaching the tribes of this area, while encouraging the introduction of goods they considered "improving." As has been noted, no item of Western technology available, with the possible exception of trade tobacco, was in greater demand among all groups of aboriginals than the short-handled steel axe. The mission always kept a good supply of these axes in stock; at Christmas parties or other mission festivals they were given away to mission or visiting aboriginals indiscriminately and in considerable numbers. In addition, some steel axes as well as other European goods were still traded in to the Yir Yoront by natives in contact with cattle stations in the south. Indeed, steel axes had probably come to the Yir Yoront through established lines of aboriginal trade long before any regular contact with whites had occurred.

III. RELEVANT FACTORS

If we concentrate our attention on Yir Yoront behavior centering about the original stone axe (rather than on the axe—the object—itself) as a cultural trait or item of cultural equipment, we should get some conception of the role this implement played in aboriginal culture. This, in turn, should enable us to foresee with considerable accuracy some of the results stemming from the displacement of the Stone Age by the steel axe.

The production of a stone axe required a number of simple technological skills. With the various details of the axe well in mind, adult men
could set about producing it (a task not considered appropriate for women
or children). First of all, a man had to know the location and properties of
several natural resources found in his immediate environment: pliable
wood for a handle, which could be doubled or bent over the axe head and
bound tightly; bark, which could be rolled into cord for the binding; and
gum, to fix the stone head in the haft. These materials had to be correctly
gathered, stored, prepared, cut to size, and applied or manipulated. They
were in plentiful supply, and could be taken from anyone's property without special permission. Postponing consideration of the stone head, the
axe could be made by any normal man who had a simple knowledge of nature and of the technological skills involved, together with fire (for heating the gum), and a few simple cutting tools—perhaps the sharp shells of
plentiful bivalves.

The use of the stone axe as a piece of capital equipment used in producing other goods indicates its very great importance to the subsistence
economy of the aboriginal. Anyone—man, woman, or child—could use
the axe; indeed, it was used primarily by women, for theirs was the task of
obtaining sufficient wood to keep the family campfire burning all day, for
cooking, or other purposes, and all night against mosquitoes and cold (for
in July, winter temperature might drop below 40 degrees). In a normal lifetime a woman would use the axe to cut or knock down literally tons of firewood. The axe was also used to make other tools or weapons, and a variety of material equipment required by the aboriginal in his daily life. The
stone axe was essential in the construction of the wet season domed huts
which keep out some rain and some insects; of platforms which provide
dry storage; or shelters which give shade in the dry summer when days
are bright and hot. In hunting and fishing and in gathering vegetable or
animal food the axe was also a necessary tool, and in this tropical culture,
where preservatives or other means of storage are lacking, the natives
spend more time obtaining food than in any other occupation—except
sleeping. In only two instances was the use of the stone axe strictly limited
to adult men: for gathering wild honey, the most prized food known to the
Yir Yoront; and for making the secret paraphernalia for ceremonies. From
this brief listing of some of the activities involving the use of the axe, it is
easy to understand why there was at least one stone axe in every camp, in
every hunting or fighting party, and in every group out on a "walkabout"
in the bush.

The stone axe was also prominent in interpersonal relations. Yir
Yoront men were dependent upon interpersonal relations for their stone
axe heads, since the flat, geologically recent alluvial country over which
they range provides no suitable stone for this purpose. The stone they
used came from quarries four hundred miles to the south, reaching the Yir
Yoront through long lines of male trading partners. Some of these chains

terminated with the Yir Yoront men, others extended on farther north to other groups, using Yir Yoront men as links. Almost every older adult man had one or more regular trading partners, some to the north and some to the south. He provided his partner or partners in the south with surplus spears, particularly fighting spears tipped with the barbed spines of stingray which snap into vicious fragments when they penetrate human flesh. For a dozen such spears, some of which he may have obtained from a partner to the north, he would receive one stone axe head. Studies have shown that the stingray barb spears increased in value as they moved south and farther from the sea. One hundred and fifty miles south of the Yir Yoront one such spear may be exchanged for one stone axe head. Although actual investigations could not be made, it was presumed that farther south, nearer the quarries, one stingray barb spear would bring several stone axe heads. Apparently people who acted as links in the middle of the chain and who made neither spears nor axe heads would receive a certain number of each as a middleman's profit.

Thus trading relations, which may extend the individual's personal relationships beyond that of his own group, were associated with spears and axes, two of the most important items in a man's equipment. Finally, most of the exchanges took place during the dry season, at the time of the great aboriginal celebrations centering about initiation rites or other totemic ceremonials which attracted hundreds and were the occasion for much exciting activity in addition to trading.

Returning to the Yir Yoront, we find that adult men kept their axes in camp with their other equipment, or carried them when traveling. Thus a woman or child who wanted to use an axe—as might frequently happen during the day—had to get one from a man, use it promptly, and return it in good condition. While a man might speak of "my axe," a woman or child could not.

This necessary and constant borrowing of axes from older men by women and children was in accordance with regular patterns of kinship behavior. A woman would expect to use her husband's axe unless he himself was using it; if unmarried, or if her husband was absent, a woman would go first to her older brother or to her father. Only in extraordinary circumstances would she seek a stone axe from other male kin. A girl, a boy, or a young man would look to a father or an older brother to provide an axe for their use. Older men, too, would follow similar rules if they had to borrow an axe.

It will be noted that all these social relationships in which the stone axe had a place are pair relationships and that the use of the axe helped to define and maintain their character and the roles of the two individual participants. Every active relationship among the Yir Yoront involved a definite and accepted status of superordination or subordination. A person could have no dealings with another on exactly equal terms. The nearest approach to equality was between brothers, although the older was always superordinate to the younger. Since the exchange of goods in a trading relationship involved a mutual reciprocity, trading partners usually stood in a brotherly type of relationship, although one was always classified as older than the other and would have some advantage in case of dispute. It can be seen that repeated and widespread conduct centering around the use of the axe helped to generalize and standardize these sex, age, and kinship roles both in their normal benevolent and exceptional malevolent aspects.

The status of any individual Yir Yoront was determined not only by sex, age, and extended kin relationships, but also by membership in one of two dozen patrilineal totemic clans into which the entire community was divided.[3] Each clan had literally hundreds of totems, from one or two of which the clan derived its name, and the clan members their personal names. These totems included natural species or phenomena such as the sun, stars, and daybreak, as well as cultural "species": imagined ghosts, rainbow serpents, heroic ancestors; such eternal cultural verities as fires, spears, huts; and such human activities, conditions, or attributes as eating, vomiting, swimming, fighting, babies and corpses, milk and blood, lips and loins. While individual members of such totemic classes or species might disappear or be destroyed, the class itself was obviously ever-present and indestructible. The totems, therefore, lent permanence and stability to the clans, to the groupings of human individuals who generation after generation were each associated with a set of totems which distinguished one clan from another.

The stone axe was one of the most important of the many totems of the Sunlit Cloud Iguana clan. The names of many members of this clan referred to the axe itself, to activities in which the axe played a vital part, or to the clan's mythical ancestors, with whom the axe was prominently associated. When it was necessary to represent the stone axe in totemic ceremonies, only men of this clan exhibited it or pantomimed its use. In secular life, the axe could be made by any man and used by all; but in the sacred realm of the totems it belonged exclusively to the Sunlit Cloud Iguana people.

Supporting those aspects of cultural behavior which we have called technology and conduct is a third area of culture, which includes ideas, sentiments, and values. These are most difficult to deal with, for they are latent and covert, and even unconscious, and must be deduced from overt actions and language or other communicating behavior. In this aspect of

---

[3] The best, although highly concentrated, summaries of totemism among the Yir Yoront and the other tribes of north Queensland will be found in R. Lauriston Sharp, "Tribes and Totemism in Northeast Australia," *Oceania* 8 (1939):254–275 and 439–461 (especially pp. 268–275); also "Notes on Northeast Australian Totemism," in *Papers of the Peabody Museum of American Archaeology and Ethnology*, Vol. 20, *Studies in the Anthropology of Oceania and Asia* (Cambridge, 1943), 66–71.

the culture lies the significance of the stone axe to the Yir Yoront and to their cultural way of life.

The stone axe was an important symbol of masculinity among the Yir Yoront (just as pants or pipes are to us). By a complicated set of ideas the axe was defined as "belonging" to males, and everyone in the society (except untrained infants) accepted these ideas. Similarly spears, spear throwers, and fire-making sticks were owned only by men and were also symbols of masculinity. But the masculine values represented by the stone axe were constantly being impressed on all members of society by the fact that females borrowed axes but not other masculine artifacts. Thus the axe stood for an important theme of Yir Yoront culture: the superiority and rightful dominance of the male, and the greater value of his concerns and of all things associated with him. As the axe also had to be borrowed by the younger people it represented the prestige of age, another important theme running through Yir Yoront behavior.

To understand the Yir Yoront culture it is necessary to be aware of a system of ideas which may be called their totemic ideology. A fundamental belief of the aboriginal divided time into two great epochs: (1) a distant and sacred period at the beginning of the world when the earth was peopled by mildly marvelous ancestral beings or culture heroes who are in a special sense the forebears of the clans; and (2) a period when the old was succeeded by a new order, which includes the present. Originally there was no anticipation of another era supplanting the present. The future would simply be an eternal continuation and reproduction of the present, which itself had remained unchanged since the epochal revolution of ancestral times.

The important thing to note is that the aboriginal believed that the present world, as a natural and cultural environment, was and should be simply a detailed reproduction of the world of the ancestors. He believed that the entire universe "is now as it was in the beginning," when it was established and left by the ancestors. The ordinary cultural life of the ancestors became the daily life of the Yir Yoront camps, and the extraordinary life of the ancestors remained extant in the recurring symbolic pantomimes and paraphernalia found only in the most sacred atmosphere of the totemic rites.

Such beliefs, accordingly, opened the way for ideas of what *should be* (because it supposedly *was*) to influence or help determine what actually *is*. A man called Dog-chases-iguana-up-a-tree-and-barks-at-him-all-night had that and other names because he believed his ancestral alter ego had also had them; he was a member of the Sunlit Cloud Iguana clan because his ancestor was; he was associated with particular countries and totems of this same ancestor; during an initiation he played the role of a dog and symbolically attacked and killed certain members of other clans because his ancestor (conveniently either anthropomorphic or kynomorphic) really did the same to the ancestral alter egos of these men; and he would avoid his mother-in-law, joke with a mother's distant brother, and make spears in a certain way because his and other people's ancestors did these things. His behavior in these specific ways was outlined, and to that extent determined for him, by a set of ideas concerning the past and the relation of the present to the past.

But when we are informed that Dog-chases-etc. had two wives from the Spear Black Duck clan and one from the Native Companion clan, one of them being blind, that he had four children with such and such names, that he had a broken wrist and was left-handed, all because his ancestor had exactly these same attributes, then we know (though he apparently didn't) that the present has influenced the past, that the mythical world has been somewhat adjusted to meet the exigencies and accidents of the inescapably real present.

There was thus in Yir Yoront ideology a nice balance in which the mythical was adjusted in part to the real world, the real world in part to the ideal preexisting mythical world, the adjustments occurring to maintain a fundamental tenet of native faith that the present must be a mirror of the past. Thus the stone axe, in all its aspects, uses, and associations, was integrated into the context of Yir Yoront technology and conduct because a myth, a set of ideas, had put it there.

IV. THE OUTCOME

The introduction of the steel axe indiscriminately and in large numbers into the Yir Yoront technology occurred simultaneously with many other changes. It is therefore impossible to separate all the results of this single innovation. Nevertheless, a number of specific effects of the change from stone to steel axes may be noted, and the steel axe may be used as an epitome of the increasing quantity of European goods and implements received by the aboriginals and of their general influence on the native culture. The use of the steel axe to illustrate such influences would seem to be justified. It was one of the first European artifacts to be adopted for regular use by the Yir Yoront, and whether made of stone or steel, the axe was clearly one of the most important items of cultural equipment they possessed.

The shift from stone to steel axes provided no major technological difficulties. While the aboriginals themselves could not manufacture steel axe heads, a steady supply from outside continued; broken wooden handles could easily be replaced from bush timbers with aboriginal tools. Among the Yir Yoront the new axe was never used to the extent it was on mission or cattle stations (for carpentry work, pounding tent pegs, as a hammer, and so on); indeed, it had so few more uses than the stone axe that its practical effect on the native standard of living was negligible. It did some jobs better, and could be used longer without breakage. These factors were sufficient to make it of value to the native. The white man believed that a shift from steel to stone axe on his part would be a definite regression. He was convinced that his axe was much more efficient, that its use would save time, and that it therefore represented technical "progress" toward goals which he had set up for the native. But this assumption was hardly borne out in aboriginal practice. Any leisure time the Yir Yoront might gain by using steel axes or other Western tools was not invested in "improving the conditions of life," nor, certainly, in developing aesthetic activities, but in sleep—an art they had mastered thoroughly.

Previously, a man in need of an axe would acquire a stone axe head through regular trading partners from whom he knew what to expect, and was then dependent solely upon a known and adequate natural environment, and his own skills or easily acquired techniques. A man wanting a steel axe, however, was in no such self-reliant position. If he attended a mission festival when steel axes were handed out as gifts, he might receive one either by chance or by happening to impress upon the mission staff that he was one of the "better" bush aboriginals (the missionaries' definition of "better" being quite different from that of his bush fellows). Or, again, almost by pure chance, he might get some brief job in connection with the mission which would enable him to earn a steel axe. In either case, for older men a preference for the steel axe helped change the situation from one of self-reliance to one of dependence, and a shift in behavior from well-structured or defined situations in technology or conduct to ill-defined situations in conduct alone. Among the men, the older ones whose earlier experience or knowledge of the white man's harshness made them suspicious were particularly careful to avoid having relations with the mission, and thus excluded themselves from acquiring steel axes from that source.

In other aspects of conduct or social relations, the steel axe was even more significantly at the root of psychological stress among the Yir Yoront. This was the result of new factors which the missionary considered beneficial: the simple numerical increase in axes per capita as a result of mission distribution, and distribution directly to younger men, women, and even children. By winning the favor of the mission staff, a woman might be given a steel axe which was clearly intended to be hers, thus creating a situation quite different from the previous custom which necessitated her borrowing an axe from a male relative. As a result a woman would refer to the axe as "mine," a possessive form she was never able to use of the stone axe. In the same fashion, young men or even boys also obtained steel axes directly from the mission, with the result that older men no longer had a complete monopoly of all the axes in the bush community. All this led to a revolutionary confusion of sex, age, and kinship roles, with a major gain in independence and loss of subordination on the part of those who now owned steel axes when they had previously been unable to possess stone axes.

The trading partner relationship was also affected by the new situation. A Yir Yoront might have a trading partner in a tribe to the south whom he defined as a younger brother and over whom he would therefore have some authority. But if the partner were in contact with the mission or had other access to steel axes, his subordination obviously decreased. Among other things, this took some of the excitement away from the dry season fiesta-like tribal gatherings centering around initiations. These had traditionally been the climactic annual occasions for exchanges between trading partners, when a man might seek to acquire a whole year's supply of stone axe heads. Now he might find himself prostituting his wife to almost total strangers in return for steel axes or other white man's goods. With trading partnerships weakened, there was less reason to attend the ceremonies, and less fun for those who did.

Not only did an increase in steel axes and their distribution to women change the character of the relations between individuals (the paired relationships that have been noted), but a previously rare type of relationship was created in the Yir Yoront's conduct toward whites. In the aboriginal society there were few occasions outside of the immediate family when an individual would initiate action to several other people at once. In any average group, in accordance with the kinship system, while a person might be superordinate to several people to whom he could suggest or command action, he was also subordinate to several others with whom such behavior would be taboo. There was thus no overall chieftainship or authoritarian leadership of any kind. Such complicated operations as grass-burning animal drives or totemic ceremonies could be carried out smoothly because each person was aware of his role.

On both mission and cattle stations, however, the whites imposed their conception of leadership roles upon the aboriginals, consisting of one person in a controlling relationship with a subordinate group. Aboriginals called together to receive gifts, including axes, at a mission Christmas party found themselves facing one or two whites who sought to control their behavior for the occasion, who disregarded the age, sex, and kinship variables of which the aboriginals were so conscious, and who considered them all at one subordinate level. The white also sought to impose similar patterns on work parties. (However, if he placed an aboriginal in charge of a mixed group of post-hole diggers, for example, half of the group, those subordinate to the "boss," would work while the other half, who were superordinate to him, would sleep.) For the aboriginal, the steel axe and other European goods came to symbolize this new and uncomfortable form of social organization, the leader-group relationship.

The most disturbing effects of the steel axe, operating in conjunction with other elements also being introduced from the white man's several subcultures, developed in the realm of traditional ideas, sentiments, and values. These were undermined at a rapidly mounting rate, with no new conceptions being defined to replace them. The result was the erection of a mental and moral void which foreshadowed the collapse and destruction of all Yir Yoront culture, if not, indeed, the extinction of the biological group itself.

From what has been said it should be clear how changes in overt behavior, in technology and conduct, weakened the values inherent in a reliance on nature, in the prestige of masculinity and of age, and in the various kinship relations. A scene was set in which a wife, or a young son whose initiation may not yet have been completed, need no longer defer to the husband or father who, in turn, became confused and insecure as he was forced to borrow a steel axe from them. For the woman and boy the steel axe helped establish a new degree of freedom which they accepted readily as an escape from the unconscious stress of the old patterns—but they, too, were left confused and insecure. Ownership became less well defined with the result that stealing and trespassing were introduced into technology and conduct. Some of the excitement surrounding the great ceremonies evaporated and they lost their previous gaiety and interest. Indeed, life itself became less interesting, although this did not lead the Yir Yoront to discover suicide, a concept foreign to them.

The whole process may be most specifically illustrated in terms of totemic system, which also illustrates the significant role played by a system of ideas, in this case a totemic ideology, in the breakdown of a culture.

In the first place, under pre-European aboriginal conditions where the native culture has become adjusted to a relatively stable environment, few, if any, unheard of or catastrophic crises can occur. It is clear, therefore, that the totemic system serves very effectively in inhibiting radical cultural changes. The closed system of totemic ideas, explaining and categorizing a well-known universe as it was fixed at the beginning of time, presents a considerable obstacle to the adoption of new or the dropping of old culture traits. The obstacle is not insurmountable and the system allows for the minor variations which occur in the norms of daily life. But the inception of major changes cannot easily take place.

Among the bush Yir Yoront, the only means of water transport is a light wood log to which they cling in their constant swimming of rivers, salt creeks, and tidal inlets. These natives know that tribes forty-five miles further north have a bark canoe. They know these northern tribes can thus fish from midstream or out at sea, instead of clinging to the river banks and beaches, that they can cross coastal waters infested with crocodiles, sharks, stingrays, and Portuguese men-of-war without danger. They know the materials of which the canoe is made exist in their own environment. But they also know, as they say, that they do not have canoes because their own mythical ancestors did not have them. They assume that the canoe was part of the ancestral universe of the northern tribes. For them, then, the adoption of the canoe would not be simply a matter of learning a number of new behavioral skills for its manufacture and use. The adoption would require a much more difficult procedure; the acceptance by the entire society of a myth, either locally developed or borrowed, to explain the presence of the canoe, to associate it with some one or more of the several hundred mythical ancestors (and how decide which?), and thus establish it as an accepted totem of one of the clans ready to be used by the whole community. The Yir Yoront have not made this adjustment, and in this case we can only say that for the time being at least, ideas have won out over very real pressures for technological change. In the elaborateness and explicitness of the totemic ideologies we seem to have one explanation for the notorious stability of Australian cultures under aboriginal conditions, an explanation which gives due weight to the importance of ideas in determining human behavior.

At a later stage of the contact situation, as has been indicated, phenomena unaccounted for by the totemic ideological system begin to appear with regularity and frequency and remain within the range of native experience. Accordingly, they cannot be ignored (as the "Battle of the Mitchell" was apparently ignored), and there is an attempt to assimilate them and account for them along the lines of principles inherent in the ideology. The bush Yir Yoront of the mid-thirties represent this stage of the acculturation process. Still trying to maintain their aboriginal definition of the situation, they accept European artifacts and behavior patterns, but fit them into their totemic system, assigning them to various clans on a par with original totems. There is an attempt to have the myth-making process keep up with these cultural changes so that the idea system can continue to support the rest of the culture. But analysis of overt behavior, of dreams, and of some of the new myths indicates that this arrangement is not entirely satisfactory, that the native clings to his totemic system with intellectual loyalty (lacking any substitute ideology), but that associated sentiments and values are weakened. His attitude toward his own and toward European culture is found to be highly ambivalent.

All ghosts are totems of the Head-to-the-East Corpse clan, are thought of as white, and are of course closely associated with death. The white man, too, is closely associated with death, and he and all things pertaining to him are naturally assigned to the Corpse clan as totems. The steel axe, as a totem, was thus associated with the Corpse clan. But as an "axe," clearly linked with the stone axe, it is a totem of the Sunlit Cloud Iguana clan. Moreover, the steel axe, like most European goods, has no distinctive origin myth, nor are mythical ancestors associated with it. Can anyone, sitting in the shade of a *ti* tree one afternoon, create a myth to resolve this confusion? No one has, and the horrid suspicion arises as to the authenticity of the origin myths, which failed to take into account this vast new universe of the white man. The steel axe, shifting hopelessly between one clan and the other, is not only replacing the stone axe physically, but is hacking at the supports of the entire cultural system.

The aboriginals to the south of the Yir Yoront have clearly passed beyond this stage. They are engulfed by European culture, either by the mission or cattle station subcultures or, for some natives, by a baffling, paradoxical combination of both incongruent varieties. The totemic ideology can no longer support the inrushing mass of foreign culture traits, and the myth-making process in its native form breaks down completely. Both intellectually and emotionally a saturation point is reached so that the myriad new traits which can neither be ignored nor any longer assimilated simply force the aboriginal to abandon his totemic system. With the collapse of this system of ideas, which is so closely related to so many other aspects of the native culture, there follows an appallingly sudden and complete cultural disintegration, and a demoralization of the individual such as has seldom been recorded elsewhere. Without the support of a system of ideas well devised to provide cultural stability in a stable environment, but admittedly too rigid for the new realities pressing in from outside, native behavior and native sentiments and values are simply dead. Apathy reigns. The aboriginal has passed beyond the realm of any outsider who might wish to do him well or ill.

Returning from the broken natives huddled on cattle stations or on the fringes of frontier towns to the ambivalent but still lively aboriginals settled on the Mitchell River mission, we note one further devious result of the introduction of European artifacts. During a wet season stay at the mission, the anthropologist discovered that his supply of toothpaste was being depleted at an alarming rate. Investigation showed that it was being taken by old men for use in a new toothpaste cult. Old materials of magic having failed, new materials were being tried out in a malevolent magic directed toward the mission staff and some of the younger aboriginal men. Old males, largely ignored by the missionaries, were seeking to regain some of their lost power and prestige. This mild aggression proved hardly effective, but perhaps only because confidence in any kind of magic on the mission was by this time at a low ebb.

For the Yir Yoront still in the bush, a time could be predicted when personal deprivation and frustration in a confused culture would produce an overload of anxiety. The mythical past of the totemic ancestors would disappear as a guarantee of a present of which the future was supposed to be a stable continuation. Without the past, the present could be meaningless and the future unstructured and uncertain. Insecurities would be inevitable. Reaction to this stress might be some form of symbolic aggression, or withdrawal and apathy, or some more realistic approach. In such a situation the missionary with understanding of the processes going on about him would find his opportunity to introduce his forms of religion and to help create a new cultural universe.

REVIEW QUESTIONS

1. What part did traditional stone axes play in the social integration of Yir Yoront society?
2. How could a simple tool such as a small steel axe disrupt Yir Yoront social organization?
3. How did the way the missionaries gave out steel axes contribute to Yir Yoront social disorganization?
4. Can the model of change be applied to other cases? What are some examples?

34

Progress and Tribal Peoples

John H. Bodley

As John Bodley points out in this selection, tribal peoples have been virtually wiped out in the last two hundred years. Until that time, several million tribals, usually hunter-gatherers and horticulturalists, inhabited a large area of the world. But the onset of industrialization meant a run on local resources for many nations and the need to exploit untapped territory. Tribals paid the price. Bodley discusses the process of world detribalization, looking at everything from the ethnocentrism of nation-states to the question of tribal self-determination.

Tribal peoples are being drastically affected by civilization, and their cultural patterns and, in many cases, the peoples themselves are disappearing as civilization advances. For many years anthropologists have made this topic a special field of study, but many seem to have missed its larger significance by failing to stress that the ecological irresponsibility of modern industrial nations and the reckless pursuit of progress are the basic causes of the continuing destruction of tribal peoples. . . .

At the outset the problem must be viewed in long-term perspective as a struggle between two incompatible cultural systems—tribes and states. For the purpose of understanding the interaction between these two systems, the most critical features of tribal groups are their political independence, reliance on local natural resources, and relative internal social equality. Tribes are small-scale sovereign nations that tend to manage local ecosystems for long-term sustained use. In comparison with states, and especially industrial states, tribal systems tend to expand more slowly and have been environmentally less destructive. Maintaining a greater internal social equality translates into less incentive for tribes to elevate economic production and consumption beyond local subsistence demands and more uniformly satisfies basic human needs. These differences explain why territories still controlled by tribal groups are so attractive to "developing nations"—because tribal territories contain "underutilized" resources.

The struggle between tribes and states has been over conflicting systems of resource management and internal social organization. Tribes represent small-scale, classless societies, with decentralized, communal, long-term resource management strategies, whereas states are class-based societies, with centralized management systems that extract resources for the short-term profit of special interest groups. Understandably, then, the political conquest of tribal areas often brings rapid environmental deterioration and may impoverish tribal peoples.

I am speaking here in global terms about a generalized tribal system for the purpose of understanding the causes and consequences of the incorporation and conquest of tribes by states. There are many exceptions to this ideal tribal model, and any specific culture exists at some point along a continuum between tribal and state organization. I am not assuming that tribes were ever isolated or completely self-sufficient, or existed in perfect equality, harmony, and absolute "balance" with nature. Nor would I argue that tribes are inherently good and states inherently evil. Both systems have advantages and disadvantages. However, given this disclaimer, significant qualitative differences between tribes and states remain, and these differences illuminate the recent fate of tribals along the frontiers of national expansion. The most advantageous unique qualities of tribal systems will need to be acknowledged and safeguarded by national governments if the future of indigenous peoples is to be secured.

People have led a tribal existence for at least the past half million years, and only for the past ten thousand years or so have any people lived in cities or states. Since the first appearance of urban life and state organization, the earlier tribal cultures were gradually displaced from the world's most productive agricultural lands and were relegated to marginal areas. Tribal peoples persisted for thousands of years in a dynamic equilibrium or symbiotic relationship with civilizations that had reached and remained within their ecological boundaries. But this situation shifted abruptly a mere five hundred years ago as Europeans began to expand beyond the long-established frontiers separating tribal peoples from states. However, by 1750, after two hundred and fifty years of preindustrial European expansion, tribal peoples still seemed secure and successfully adapted to their economically "marginal" refuges—but industrialization suddenly reduced the possibilities for the continued existence of politically independent tribal groups.

PROGRESS: THE INDUSTRIAL EXPLOSION

In the mid-eighteenth century the industrial revolution launched the developing Western nations on an explosive growth in population and consumption called "progress," which led to an unprecedented assault on the world's tribal peoples and their resources. Within the two hundred and fifty years since then the world has been totally transformed, many self-sufficient tribal cultures have disappeared, and dramatic resource shortages and environmental disasters have materialized. Now that many researchers are struggling to explain why industrial civilization seems to be floundering in its own success, anthropologists are beginning to realize that the first and most ominous victims of industrial progress were the several million tribal people who still controlled over half the globe in 1820 and who shared a relatively stable, satisfying, and proven cultural adaptation. It is highly significant and somewhat unsettling to realize that the cultural systems of these first victims of progress present a striking contrast to the characteristics of industrial civilization.

The industrial revolution is nothing less than an *explosion* because of the unparalleled scope and the catastrophic nature of the transformations that it has initiated. Phenomenal increases in both population and per-capita consumption rates were the two most critical correlates of industrialization because they quickly led to overwhelming pressure on natural resources.

The acceleration in world population growth rates and their relationship to industrial progress have been well documented. Immediately prior to the industrial revolution, for example, the doubling time of the world's population was approximately two hundred and fifty years. However, after industrialization was under way, the European population of 1850 doubled in just over eighty years, and the European populations of the United States, Canada, Australia, and Argentina tripled between 1851 and 1900. The doubling time of the world's population reached its lowest point of about thirty-three years (an annual growth rate of over 2 percent) during the period 1965–1973. By 1986 the global rate of population growth had declined only slightly to 1.8 percent a year. In contrast, clear anthropological evidence shows that tribal populations grow slowly and use their natural resources conservatively. The relative stability of tribal populations is due only partly to higher mortality rates; it is also attributed to social, economic, and religious controls on fertility, the significance of which is still not fully understood. Although tribal populations have the capacity for growth, and may expand rapidly into empty lands, they are politically and economically designed to operate most effectively at low densities and low absolute size.

THE CULTURE OF CONSUMPTION

The increased rates of resource consumption accompanying industrialization have been even more critical than mere population increase. Above all else, industrial civilization is a culture of *consumption,* and in this respect it differs most strikingly from tribal cultures. Industrial economies are founded on the principle that consumption must be ever expanded, and complex systems of mass marketing and advertising have been developed for that specific purpose. Social stratification in industrial societies is based primarily on inequalities in material wealth and is both supported and reflected by differential access to resources. Industrial ideological systems stress belief in continual economic growth and progress and characteristically measure "standard of living" in terms of levels of material consumption.

Tribal cultures contrast strikingly in all of these aspects. Their economies are geared to the satisfaction of basic subsistence needs, which are assumed to be fixed, while a variety of cultural mechanisms serve to limit material acquisitiveness and to redistribute wealth. Wealth itself is rarely the basis of social stratification, and there is generally free access to natural resources for all. These contrasts are the basis for the incompatibility between tribal and industrial cultures, and are the traits that are the sources of particular problems during the modernization process.

The most obvious consequences of tribal consumption patterns are that these cultures tend to be highly stable, make light demands on their environments, and can easily support themselves within their own boundaries. The opposite situation prevails for the culture of consumption. Almost overnight the industrialized nations quite literally ate up their own local resources and outgrew their boundaries. This was dramatically apparent in England, where local resources comfortably supported tribal cultures for thousands of years, but after a hundred years of industrial progress the area was unable to meet its basic needs for grain, wood, fibers, and hides. Between 1851 and 1900 Europe was forced to export 35 million people because it could no longer support them. In the United States, where industrial progress has gone the furthest, since 1970 Americans have been consuming per capita some fifteen times more energy than neolithic agriculturalists and seven times the world average in nonrenewable resources. They were also importing vast tonnages of food, fuels, and other resources to support themselves.

Indeed few, if any, industrial nations can now supply from within their own boundaries the resources needed to support further growth or even to maintain current consumption levels. It should not be surprising, then, that the "underdeveloped" resources controlled by the world's self-sufficient tribal peoples were quickly appropriated by outsiders to support their own industrial progress.

RESOURCE APPROPRIATION AND ACCULTURATION

In case after case, government programs for the progress of tribal peoples directly or indirectly force culture change, and these programs in turn are linked invariably to the extraction of tribal resources to benefit the national economy. From the strength of this relationship between tribal "progress" and the exploitation of tribal resources, we might even infer that tribal peoples would not be asked to surrender their resources and independence if industrial societies learned to control their own culture of consumption. This point must be made explicit, because considerable confusion exists in the enormous culture change literature regarding the basic question of why tribal cultures seem inevitably to be acculturated or modernized by industrial civilization. The consensus, at least among economic development writers (and the view often expressed in introductory textbooks), is the ethnocentric view that contact with superior industrial culture causes tribal peoples to voluntarily reject their own cultures in order to obtain a better life. Other writers, however, have seemed curiously mystified by the entire process. An example of this latter position can be seen in Julian Steward's summary of a monumental study of change in traditional cultures in eleven countries. Steward concluded that while many startling parallels could be identified, the causal factors involved in the modernization process were still "not well conceptualized."

This inability to conceptualize the causes of the transformation process in simple, nonethnocentric terms—or indeed the inability to conceptualize the causes at all—may be due to the fact that the analysts are members of the culture of consumption that today is the dominant world culture type. The most powerful cultures have always assumed a natural right to exploit the world's resources wherever they find them, regardless of the prior claims of indigenous populations. Arguing for efficiency and survival of the fittest, early colonialists elevated this "right" to the level of an ethical and legal principle that could be invoked to justify the elimination of any cultures that were not making "effective" use of their resources. . . .

Apart from the obvious ethical implications involved here, upon close inspection . . . theories expounding the greater adaptability, efficiency, and survival value of the dominant industrial culture prove to be misleading. Of course, as a culture of consumption, industrial civilization is uniquely capable of consuming resources at tremendous rates, but this does not make it a more *effective* culture than low-energy tribal cultures, if stability or long-run ecological success is taken as the criterion for "effectiveness."

Likewise, the assumption that a given environment is not being exploited effectively by a traditional culture may merely reflect the unwillingness of national political authorities to allow local tribal groups to manage their own resources for their own interests. We should expect, then, that members of the culture of consumption would probably consider another culture's resources to be underexploited and to use this as a justification for appropriating them. . . .

THE ROLE OF ETHNOCENTRISM

Although resource exploitation is clearly the basic cause of the destruction of tribal peoples and cultures, it is important to identify the underlying ethnocentric attitudes that are often used to justify what are actually exploitative policies. *Ethnocentrism,* the belief in the superiority of one's own culture, is vital to the integrity of any culture, but it can be a threat to the well-being of other peoples when it becomes the basis for forcing irrelevant standards upon tribal cultures. Anthropologists may justifiably take credit for exposing the ethnocentrism of nineteenth-century writers who described tribal peoples as badly in need of improvement, but they often overlook the ethnocentrism that occurs in the modern professional literature on economic development. This is ironic because ethnocentrism threatens tribal peoples even today by its support of culturally insensitive government policies.

Ethnocentrism and Ethnocide

Anthropologists have been quick to stress the presumed deficiencies of tribal cultures as a justification for externally imposed change or a rejection of proposals that tribals be granted political autonomy. For example, in 1940 British anthropologist Lord Fitzroy Raglan, who later became president of the Royal Anthropological Institute, declared that tribal beliefs in magic were a chief cause of "folly and unhappiness" and the "worst evils of the day." He argued that, as long as tribals persist in such beliefs, the rest of the world cannot be considered civilized. In his view, existing tribes constituted "plague spots" that threatened to reinfect civilized areas, and the rapid imposition of civilization was the only solution. He declared:

> We should bring to them our justice, our education, and our science. Few will deny that these are better than anything which savages have got.[1]

More recently, American anthropologist Arthur Hippler echoed Raglan's remarks. In a debate with Gerald Weiss over the merits of tribal

---

[1] Lord Fitzroy R. S. Raglan, "The Future of the Savage Races," *Man* 40 (1940):62.

autonomy, Hippler argued that national religions are superior to the "terrors of shamanism." He found "our own culture" more exciting, interesting, and varied, and better at promoting human potential than are "backward" tribal cultures, and he assumed that all tribals would inevitably be drawn to it. Hippler suggested that only internal oppression from tribal elders prevents tribals from improving their culture. Not surprisingly, Hippler specifically opposed autonomy proposals for the defense of tribal groups because autonomy would keep people "backward" against their will. Furthermore, he argued that "culture" is an abstraction, not something that can be defended or "saved" from extinction. Thus, ethnocide, the destruction of a cultural or an ethnic group, could not occur. In his response, Weiss exposed the ethnocentrism of Hippler's position point by point. . . .

Technological Ethnocentrism

Development writers with tractors and chemicals to sell have expressed more ethnocentrism in their treatment of traditional economic systems than for any other aspect of tribal culture. These writers automatically assume that tribal economies must be unproductive and technologically inadequate and therefore consistently disregard the abundant evidence to the contrary. It has long been fashionable to attack the supposed inefficiency of shifting cultivation and pastoral nomadism and the precariousness of subsistence economies in general. But it could be argued that it is industrial subsistence techniques that are inefficient and precarious. Mono-crop agriculture, with its hybrid gains and dependence on chemical fertilizers, pesticides, and costly machinery, is extremely expensive in terms of energy demands and is highly unstable because of its susceptibility to disease, insects, and the depletion of critical minerals and fuels. The complexity of the food distribution system in industrial society also makes it highly vulnerable to collapse because of the breakdowns in the long chain from producer to consumer. In contrast, tribal systems are highly productive in terms of energy flow and are ecologically much stabler, while they enjoy efficient and reliable distribution systems.

Cultural reformers almost unanimously agree that all people share our desire for what we define as material wealth, prosperity, and progress and that others have different cultures only because they have not yet been exposed to the superior technological alternatives offered by industrial civilization. Supporters of this view seem to minimize the difficulties of creating new wants in a culture and at the same time make the following highly questionable and clearly ethnocentric assumptions:

1. The materialistic values of industrial civilization are cultural universals.
2. Tribal cultures are unable to satisfy the material needs of their peoples.
3. Industrial goods are, in fact, always superior to their handcrafted counterparts.

Unquestionably, tribal cultures represent a clear rejection of the materialistic values of industrial civilization, yet tribal individuals can be made to reject their traditional values if outside interests create the necessary conditions for this rejection. Far more is involved here than a mere demonstration of the superiority of industrial civilization.

The ethnocentrism of the second assumption is obvious. Clearly, tribal cultures could not have survived for half a million years if they did not do a reasonable job of satisfying basic human needs.

The third assumption—the superiority of industrial goods and techniques—deserves special comment because abundant evidence indicates that many of the material accouterments of industrial civilization may not be worth their real costs regardless of how appealing they may seem initially. To cite a specific example, it could be argued that the bow is superior to a gun in certain cultural and environmental contexts, because it is far more versatile and more efficient to manufacture and maintain. A single bow can be used for both fishing and hunting a variety of animals. Furthermore, bow users are not dependent on an unpredictable external economy, because bows can be constructed of local materials and do not require expensive ammunition. At the same time, use of the bow places some limits on game harvesting and demands a closer relationship between man and animal, which may have great adaptive significance. Hames has shown that Amazon Indians who have adopted shotguns have dramatically increased their hunting yields, but these gains do not entirely offset the extra labor that must go into raising the money to support the new technology. Furthermore, the increased hunting efficiency also means that certain vulnerable species are more likely to be depleted.

Many of the ethnocentric interpretations of tribal cultures are understandable when we realize that development writers often mistakenly attribute to them the conditions of starvation, ill health, and poverty, which are actually related to civilization and industrialization. Self-sufficient tribal peoples do not belong in the underdeveloped category. "Poverty" is an irrelevant concept in tribal societies, and poverty conditions do not result from subsistence economies per se.

Tribal Wards of the State

Writers on international law and colonial experts often called on the *wardship principle* in an effort to justify harsh government programs of culture change directed against tribal peoples. This so-called legal principle reflects the grossest ethnocentrism in that it considers tribal peoples to be incompetent or even retarded children. It defines the relationship between tribal peoples and the state as that of a benevolent parent-guardian and a ward who must be protected from his or her own degrading culture and gradually reformed or corrected. According to the wardship principle, the state is under a moral obligation to make all tribal peoples share in the benefits of civilization—that is, in health, happiness, and prosperity as defined primarily in terms of consumption.

This legal inferiority of tribal peoples has contributed significantly to the speed with which their acculturation or "reform" can occur and has worked marvelously to satisfy both the conscience and the economic needs of modern states.

Placing tribal peoples in the legal category of incompetent children reflects a tendency to view tribal culture as abnormal, sick, and mentally retarded. This obviously ethnocentric theme runs throughout the colonial literature, in which the civilization process is often described as *mental* correction, but this same theme has continued to appear in the modern literature. Some recent economic development writers have lumped tribal peoples indiscriminately with underdeveloped peoples, referred explicitly to economic underdevelopment as a "sickness," spoken of the "medicine of social change," and compared change agents to brain surgeons. It appears that the basic attitudes of some modern cultural reformers were unaffected by the discovery of ethnocentrism.

A Sacred Trust of Civilization

As we have seen, the modern civilizing mission undertaken by governments against tribal peoples was supported by a variety of ethnocentric assumptions, some of which were recognized as principles of international law. Not surprisingly, therefore, prestigious international organizations such as the United Nations also threw their support behind official attempts to bring civilization to all peoples—whether or not they desired it.

During the second half of the nineteenth century the colonizing industrial nations began to justify their scramble for foreign territories as a fulfillment of a sacred duty to spread their form of civilization to the world. When the major imperialist powers met in 1884–1885 at Berlin to set guidelines for the partitioning of Africa, they pledged support for the civilizing crusade and promised to assist missionaries and all institutions "calculated to educate the natives and to teach them to understand and appreciate the benefits of civilization." This position was reiterated and took on a more militant tone in Article Two of the Brussels Act of 1892, which called on the colonial powers to raise African tribal peoples to civilization and to "bring about the extinction of barbarous customs." This constituted an internationally approved mandate for ethnocide in the interests of progress.

Whereas such attitudes are perhaps to be expected from colonial nations at the height of their power, they seem inappropriate when expressed by world organizations dedicated to peace and self-determination of peoples. Nevertheless, the 1919 League of Nations Covenant in Article 22 gave "advanced nations" responsibility for "peoples not yet able to stand by themselves under the strenuous conditions of the modern world," thereby placing many tribal peoples officially under tutelage as "a sacred trust of civilization." In fact, this sacred trust proved to be a profitable colonial booty for the trust powers because it gave them the internationally recognized right to exploit the resources of thousands of square kilometers of formerly nonstate territory while making only token allowance for the wishes of the native peoples involved. Under the 1945 United Nations Charter, many of these same tribal peoples were identified as "peoples who have not yet attained a full measure of self-government," and their continued advancement was to be promoted by their guardians "by constructive measures of development" (Articles 73 and 76, UN Charter). Here again, responsibility for deciding what constitutes a tribal people's welfare is effectively taken from them and is legally placed in the hands of outside interests. The carefully worded and seemingly nonderogatory phrases "peoples not yet able to stand by themselves" and "nonself-governing" are glaringly ethnocentric and derogatory because these peoples have governed themselves for thousands of years without the support of civilization. Of course, they were unable to defend themselves against the incursions of militant, resource-hungry states. But many modern nations exist only at the discretion of more powerful nations, and the UN Charter would not advocate making all militarily weak nations surrender their political autonomy to their stronger neighbors.

CIVILIZATION'S UNWILLING CONSCRIPTS

It now seems appropriate to ask the obvious question: How do autonomous tribal peoples themselves feel about becoming participants in the progress of industrial civilization? Because of the power at their disposal, industrial peoples have become so aggressively ethnocentric that they have difficulty even imagining that another life-style—particularly one based on fundamentally different premises—could possibly have value and personal satisfaction for the peoples following it. Happily arrogant in their own supposed cultural superiority, industrial peoples assume that those in other cultures perhaps realize their obsolescence and inferiority and eagerly desire progress toward the better life. This belief persists in the face of abundant evidence that independent tribal peoples are not anxious to scrap their cultures and would rather pursue their own form of the good life undisturbed. Peoples who have already chosen their major cultural patterns and who have spent generations tailoring them to local conditions are probably not even concerned that another culture might be superior to theirs. Indeed, it can perhaps be assumed that people in any autonomous, self-reliant culture would prefer to be left alone. Left to their own devices, tribal peoples are unlikely to volunteer for civilization or acculturation. Instead:

Acculturation has always been a matter of conquest . . . refugees from the foundering groups may adopt the standards of the more potent society in order to survive as individuals. But these are conscripts of civilization, not volunteers.[2]

Free and Informed Choice

The question of choice is a critical point because many development authorities have stressed that tribal peoples should be allowed to choose progress. This view was obvious at a 1936 conference of administrators, educators, and social scientists concerning education in Pacific colonial dependencies, where it was stated that choices regarding cultural directions "must lie with the indigenous peoples themselves." Anthropologists at a more recent international conference in Tokyo took the same position when they called for "just and scientifically enlightened programs of acculturation which allow the peoples concerned a free and informed basis for choice." Apparently no one noticed the obvious contradiction between a scientific culture change program and free choice, or even the possible conflict between free and informed. The official position of the Australian government on free choice for the aborigine in 1970 indicates the absurdities to which such thinking can lead:

> The Commonwealth and State governments have adopted a common policy of assimilation which seeks that all persons of Aboriginal descent will choose to attain a similar manner and standard of living to that of other Australians and live as members of a single Austalian community.[3]

Those who so glibly demand choice for tribal peoples do not seem to realize the problems of directly instituting such a choice, and at the same time they refuse to acknowledge the numerous indicators that tribal peoples have already chosen their own cultures instead of the progress of civilization. In fact, the question of choice itself is probably ethnocentric and irrelevant to the peoples concerned. Do we choose civilization? is not a question that tribal peoples would ask, because they in effect have already answered it. They might consider the concept of choosing a way of life to be as irrelevant in their own cultural context as asking a person if he or she would choose to be a tree.

It is also difficult to ask whether tribal peoples desire civilization or economic development because affirmative responses will undoubtedly be from individuals already alienated from their own cultures by culture modification programs, and their views may not be representative of their still autonomous tribal kin.

---

[2] Stanley Diamond, "Introduction: The Uses of the Primitive" in *Primitive Views of the World*, edited by Stanley Diamond (New York: Columbia University Press, 1960), vi.

[3] Australia. Commonwealth Bureau of Census and Statistics, 1970, 976.

Other problems are inherent in the concept of free and informed choice. Even when free to choose, tribal peoples would not generally be in a position to know what they were choosing and would certainly not be given a clear picture of the possible outcomes of their choice, because the present members of industrial cultures do not know what their own futures will be. Even if tribal peoples could be given a full and unbiased picture of what they were choosing, obtaining that information could destroy their freedom to choose, because participation in such an "educational" program might destroy their self-reliance and effectively deny them their right to choose their own tribal culture. An obvious contradiction exists in calling for culture change in order to allow people to choose or not to choose culture change. The authorities at the 1936 conference referred to earlier were caught in just such Alice-in-Wonderland doubletalk when they recommended the promotion of formal education programs (which would disrupt native culture) so that the people could freely decide whether they wanted their cultures disrupted:

> It is the responsibility of the governing people, through schools and other means, to make available to the native an adequate understanding of non-native systems of life so that these can be ranged alongside his own in order that his choices may be made.[4]

Such a program of education might sound like a sort of "cultural smorgasbord," but in fact there is really only one correct choice allowed—tribal peoples must choose progress.

One further problem overlooked in the "free choice" approach is that of the appropriateness of industrial progress or of any foreign cultural system in a given cultural and environmental context—even if freely chosen. Should Eskimos be encouraged to become nomadic camel herders or to develop a taste for bananas? Does the American "car complex" belong on a Micronesian coral atoll of four square kilometers? What will be the long-term effects of a shift from a self-reliant subsistence economy to a cash economy based on the sale of a single product on the uncertain world market? There are inescapable limits to what can constitute a successful human adaptation in a given cultural and environmental setting.

We Ask To Be Left Alone

At this point we will again ask the question posed earlier regarding whether tribal peoples freely choose progress. This question has actually been answered many times by independent tribal peoples who, in confrontations with industrial civilization, have (1) ignored it, (2) avoided it, or (3) responded with defiant arrogance. Any one of these responses could be interpreted as a rejection of further involvement with progress.

---

[4] Cited in Felix M. Keesing, *The South Seas in the Modern World* (Institute of Pacific Relations International Research Series. New York: John Day, 1941), 84.

Many of the Australian aborigines reportedly chose the first response in their early contacts with members of Western civilization. According to Captain Cook's account of his first landing on the Australian mainland, aborigines on the beach ignored both his ship and his men until they became obnoxious. Elkin confirms that this complete lack of interest in white people's habits, material possessions, and beliefs was characteristic of aborigines in a variety of contact settings. In many cases, tribal peoples have shown little interest in initial contacts with civilized visitors because they simply assumed that the visitors would soon leave and they would again be free to pursue their own way of life undisturbed.

Among contemporary tribal peoples who still retain their cultural autonomy, rejection of outside interference is a general phenomenon that cannot be ignored. The Pygmies of the Congo represent a classic case of determined resistance to the incursions of civilization. Turnbull, who studied the Pygmies intensively in their forest environment, was impressed with the fact that in spite of long contact with outsiders they had successfully rejected foreign cultural domination for hundreds of years. Attempts of Belgian colonial authorities to settle them on plantations ended in complete failure, basically because the Pygmies were unwilling to sacrifice their way of life for one patterned for them by outsiders whose values were irrelevant to their environment and culture. According to Turnbull, the Pygmies deliberated over the changes proposed by the government and opted to remain within their traditional territory and pursue their own way of life. Their decision was clear:

> So for the Pygmies, in a sense, there is no problem. They have seen enough of the outside world to feel able to make their choice, and their choice is to preserve the sanctity of their own world up to the very end. Being what they are, they will doubtless play a masterful game of hide-and-seek, but they will not easily sacrifice their integrity.[5]

Anthropologist Cavalli-Sforza, who coordinated a long-term series of multidisciplinary field studies of Pygmies throughout Africa beginning in 1966, confirmed Turnbull's basic conclusion about the Pygmy rejection of directed change. He attributes the remarkable two-thousand-year persistence of Pygmies as a distinct people to the attractiveness of their way of life and the effectiveness of their enculturation practices. But like Turnbull, he also cites the importance of the forest itself and the Pygmies' successful symbiosis with their village-farmer neighbors. The most critical threat to Pygmies is now deforestation and disruption of their exchange relationships caused by the invasion of new colonists and the development of large-scale coffee plantations. As the forest shrinks, there simply will be no place for Pygmies as forest peoples. Bailey warns, "Unless sufficient areas

---

[5] Colin M. Turnbull, "The Lessons of the Pygmies," *Scientific American*, 1963, 208.

of forest are set aside, a unique subsistence culture based on hunting and gathering forest resources will be lost in the Ituri [rain forest] and throughout central Africa forever."[6]

Avoiding Progress: Those Who Run Away

Direct avoidance of progress represents what is a widespread, long-established pattern of cultural survival whose implications should not be ignored by those who promote culture change.

Throughout South America and many other parts of the world, many nonhostile tribal peoples have made their attitudes toward progress clear by choosing to follow the Pygmies' game of hide-and-seek and actively avoiding all contact with outsiders. In the Philippines, a special term meaning "those who run away" has been applied to tribal peoples who have chosen to flee in order to preserve their cultures from government influence.

Many little-known tribal peoples scattered in isolated areas around the world have, in fact, managed to retain their cultural integrity and autonomy until recently by quietly retreating farther and farther into more isolated refuge areas. As the exploitative frontier has gradually engulfed these stubborn tribes, the outside world periodically has been surprised by the discovery of small pockets of unknown "Stone-Age" peoples who have clung tenaciously to their cultures up to the last possible moment. . . .

Some observers argue that these cases do not represent real rejections of civilization and progress, because these people were given no choice by their hostile neighbors, who refused to share the benefits of civilization and so they were forced to pretend that they didn't desire these benefits. Critics point out that such people often eagerly steal or trade for steel tools. This argument misses the real point and represents a misunderstanding of the nature of culture change. Stability and ethnocentrism are fundamental characteristics of all cultures that have established a satisfactory relationship with their environment. Some degree of change, such as adopting steel tools, may well occur to enhance an ongoing adaptation and to prevent greater change from occurring.

CULTURAL PRIDE VERSUS PROGRESS

The pride and defiance of numerous tribal peoples in the face of forced culture change are unmistakable and have often been commented upon by outsiders. The ability of these cultures to withstand external intrusion is related to their degree of ethnocentrism or to the extent to which tribal in-

---

[6] Robert Bailey, "Development in the Ituri Forest of Zaire," *Cultural Survival Quarterly*, 6(2) (1982): 23–25.

dividuals feel self-reliant and confident that their own culture is best for them. The hallmark of such ethnocentrism is the stubborn unwillingness to feel inferior even in the presence of overwhelming enemy force.

A case of calm but defiant self-assurance of this sort is offered by a warrior-chief of the undefeated Xavante (Shavante) of central Brazil, who had personally participated in the 1941 slaying of seven men of a "pacification" mission sent by the Brazilian government to end the Xavante's bitter fifty-year resistance to civilization. As further evidence of their disdain for intruders, the Xavante shot arrows into an air force plane and burned the gifts it dropped. After one Xavante community finally accepted the government's peace offers in 1953, the air force flew the chief to Rio de Janeiro in order to impress him with the superiority of the Brazilian state and the futility of further resistance. To everyone's amazement, he observed Rio, even from the air, with absolute calm. He was then led into the center of a soccer field to be surrounded by thousands of applauding fans, and it was pointed out to him how powerful the Brazilian state was and how unwise it was for the Xavante to be at war with it. The chief remained unmoved and responded simply: "This is the white man's land, mine is Xavante land." The Xavante have been militant in defense of their lands since "pacification" and have forcibly expelled settlers and occupied government offices to force the authorities to fulfill their promise of legal protections. A Xavante leader, Mario Juruna, carried the struggle further into the political arena by winning election to Brazil's House of Representatives in 1982. Juruna has campaigned effectively for the land rights of Brazilian Indians at both the national and international level.

THE PRINCIPLE OF STABILIZATION

According to theories of cultural evolution, adaptation, and integration, resistance to change is understandable as a natural cultural process. If the technological, social, and ideological systems of a culture gradually specialize to fit the requirements of successful adaptation to a specific environment, other cultural arrangements become increasingly difficult, if not impossible, to accommodate without setting in motion major disruptive changes that have unforeseen consequences. Resistance to change— whether it be direct avoidance of new cultural patterns, overt ethnocentrism, or open hostility to foreigners—may thus be seen to be a significant means of adaptation because it operates as a "cultural isolating mechanism" to protect successfully established cultures from the disruptive effects of foreign cultural elements. The resulting "stability" refers to a relative lack of change in the major cultural patterns and does not imply complete changelessness in all the nuances of culture, because minor changes probably occur constantly in all cultures. Stability is such a fundamental characteristic of cultures that it has been formulated as a general principle: "A culture at rest tends to remain at rest."[7] A corollary of this so-called principle of stabilization states:

> When acted upon by external forces a culture will, if necessary, undergo specific changes only to the extent of and with the effect of *preserving* unchanged its fundamental structure and character.[8]

As change agents are well aware, resistance to change is based not only on the natural resistance or inertia of already established cultural patterns, but also on the realization by the people concerned of the risks of experimenting with unproven cultural patterns. Either the rewards of adopting new ways must appear to be worth the risks, or some form of coercion must be applied. However, change agents who are convinced of their own cultural superiority tend to overlook the fact that native fears about the dangers of untested innovations may be justified. Peoples that reject such unproven cultural complexes as miracle grains, pesticides, and chemical fertilizers may prove in the long run to be wiser and better adapted to their natural environments.

For peoples in relatively stable, self-reliant cultures, resistance to change is a positive value. It is only in industrial cultures that such emphasis is placed on change for its own sake, and among those who make a profession of promoting change, that cultural stability is given a negative connotation and is identified as backwardness and stagnation.

REVIEW QUESTIONS

1. What has been the effect of industrialization on the tribal peoples of the world?
2. What is meant by the term *acculturation?* What has acculturation meant for most tribal peoples?
3. What part has ethnocentrism played in the formulation and implementation of development programs? How is ethnocentrism expressed?
4. What should the policy of nation-states be toward tribals, according to Bodley? Do you think there is a realistic answer to the problems of tribes?
5. What should anthropologists do about the plight of tribals? Can they continue ethnographic research among tribals under present circumstances?

---

[7] Thomas G. Harding, "Adaptation and Stability," in *Evolution and Culture*, edited by Marshall Sahlins and Elman R. Service (Ann Arbor: University of Michigan Press, 1960), 54.

[8] Harding, 54.

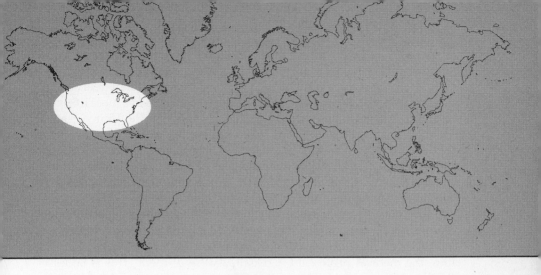

35

Gypsies and Health Care

Anne Sutherland

Applied anthropologists work in a variety of settings, from interna-
tional consulting to corporate ethnography. One especially impor-
tant area is medicine. For years, anthropologists have researched dis-
ease in cross-cultural settings, have studied cultural definitions of
disease, and have examined indigenous remedies and curing prac-
tices. They have also increasingly used their training to advise med-
ical professionals about patients from different cultural back-
grounds. This article, by Anne Sutherland, fits the last model nicely.
Published in a medical journal, it advises doctors about how to relate
to American Gypsies. Sutherland notes that Gypsies can seem to be
difficult patients to those ignorant of Gypsy culture. She suggests
that doctors pay attention to Gypsy notions of disease, pollution, so-
cial support, lifestyle, and traditional treatments if they are to treat
these patients successfully.

G ypsies are a largely unknown ethnic population in the United
States. Lacking census data, most estimates suggest there are between 200,000 and 500,000 members of various Gypsy groups living in all
regions of the United States. Not all Gypsies belong to the same group or

From *The Western Journal of Medicine*, September 1992. Copyright © by Anne Sutherland,
1992. Reprinted by permission of the author.

speak the same dialect or language. The data presented here refer to the largest group, the Rom, which is the group physicians are most likely to see and to recognize as Gypsy.[1] The Rom live all over the United States. The specific group this article is based on live in the San Francisco Bay Area of California. The Rom are originally from India, migrated through the Middle East and Europe over the past 800 years, and arrived in the United States primarily at the end of the 19th century. The Rom speak Romany as a first language and English as a second language. Older Rom are generally not literate, but younger members of the family usually have some schooling and can read important documents to older members.

Although most Americans hardly know that Gypsies live in their cities, the medical profession is usually aware of them. This is because Gypsies are generally not healthy and because they are assertive in seeking medical care. Gypsies have an unusual ability to maneuver within a complex medical system and to get attention from medical personnel. The Gypsy "style" of seeking help is often frustrating and confusing to health care professionals. Gypsies often request specific "famous name" physicians and demand specific treatment they have heard of even when the treatment or specific physician is inappropriate. Gypsies frequently request specific colored pills that they share with their relatives. They prefer older, "big" (well-known) physicians over younger ones. They often do not comply with preventive and long-term treatment. When a relative is sick, they come to the hospital in alarmingly large numbers, sometimes camp on hospital grounds, disregard visiting rules, and generally create chaos in the corridors of the hospital. Hospital personnel are often at a loss in knowing how to deal with Gypsies.

Gypsies can be cooperative, interesting patients, however. They respect authority in their own families, they are eager to learn about the best treatment for themselves and their relatives, and they have a large support network of relatives. All of these factors can be called on by medical professionals to assist them in providing treatment to Gypsies while reducing the disruption that results from a sick Gypsy's desire to have relatives nearby.

In this article I provide information about Gypsy culture that will be useful for understanding how to interact with them in medical situations. This article contains guidelines, but not every Gypsy follows every single custom or rule. Families and individual members have varied practices. Some Gypsies are more old-fashioned than others; some are more fastidious; some, generally older ones, are more informed; and some are sicker and have more experience with physicians. Nonetheless, these general guidelines should ease some of the frustration between Gypsy patients and health professionals.

---

[1] A. Sutherland, *Gypsies, the Hidden Americans* (Chicago: Waveland Press, 1986).

GYPSY CULTURE

Gypsies live in urban areas, usually on main streets, in the poorer parts of towns. They are not always recognizable as such, especially the men who wear American clothes; however, women, in particular older women, often wear long colorful skirts and low-cut sleeveless blouses. Gypsies often prefer to pass as another ethnic group and may claim to be American Indian, Mexican, or Romanian. They are accustomed to discrimination and stereotyping by those who often see them either romantically as free spirits or as contemptible thieves. Neither stereotype is accurate. If a medical professional indicates that it would help to know if a patient is Gypsy, the family may freely admit to it.

Gypsies live in households with somewhat fluid membership because they generally belong to large extended families. Dating back to the days when they all shared one camp, members of extended families will eat and sleep at each other's homes as if they were their own. The men work in groups of relatives and friends. Their usual work involves soliciting body and fender repair jobs, buying and selling cars, or helping women with their fortune-telling businesses. The women (mothers, daughters, and daughters-in-law) often share a storefront office or room at the front of a house, where they tell fortunes. Gypsies prefer to keep to themselves and to avoid contact with non-Gypsies. As a cultural group, they have survived hundreds of years living by their wits.

ILLNESS IS SOCIAL

For Gypsies, illness is not just the concern of the individual, it is a problem of broader social importance. A serious illness always elicits deep concern from a wide circle of relatives willing to drop everything and rush to the bedside of the stricken. The gathering of Gypsies in the vicinity of a seriously ill person is partly socially mandated by custom but also is a genuine expression of concern for both the afflicted and his or her immediate relatives. Families coming together when someone is ill is one of the strongest values in Gypsy culture.

A knowledge of certain basic beliefs and behaviors of Gypsies in relation to sickness and health and the sociocultural context of health care is essential to effectively interact with Gypsies. The social context of Gypsy medical and religious knowledge begins with Gypsy attitudes in general toward health and illness, auspiciousness and inauspiciousness, and cleanliness and uncleanliness.[2] These attitudes are reflected in certain key concepts, presented in complementary opposition in Table I.

---

[2] A. Sutherland, "Health and Illness Among the Rom of California," *Journal of Gypsy Lore*, Series 5, *Vol. II, No. 1* (1992):19–59.

Table I Key Concepts in Gypsy Thought

Positive Concepts	Negative Concepts
Romania (social order)	
Rom (Gypsy)	Gaje (non-Gypsy)
Traveling	Sedentary
Sastimos (good health)	Naswalemos (illness)
BaXt (good fortune)	Prikaza (bad luck)
Wuzho (purity)	Marime (impurity; exclusion)

FORTUNE AND HEALTH

Good fortune and good health are closely associated for Gypsies, as expressed in their most common blessing, "May God give you luck and health." Those who enjoy good health also have been blessed with good fortune; those who are ill have lost their good luck. To some extent everyone can influence their own fortunes. By their actions they either promote their own health or cause their own illness. Illness can be caused by actions that are considered contaminating or polluting. Returning to a state of purity and conforming to correct social behavior are necessary to cure these conditions. For example, a young person who exhibits rebellious behavior and may be in danger of pollution through illicit sexual relations can be "cured" by marriage.

Perhaps the most frustrating belief physicians encounter is that the larger a person is, the luckier, healthier, and happier that person will be. A fat person is perceived as healthy and fortunate, and a thin person is pitied as either ill or too poor to eat, both of which indicate a lack of good luck. Wealth is also partly attributed to luck because although each family develops similar economic skills, some are more fortunate than others. Some families enjoy good health, grow to a large size, and prosper, whereas others are plagued with illness, family troubles, and economic failure. In such a situation persons must take action to change their fate. Personal cleanliness, proper social attitudes, and behavior—generosity and virtue—should bring good luck. In a more general sense, traveling as opposed to living in one place is considered auspicious.

Marime, meaning polluted, defiled, or unclean, is used to indicate uncleanliness or impurity of a physical as well as a ritual or moral nature. To be "clean," the top half of the body from the waist up ideally must be kept separate from the bottom half of the body, which is considered polluted and is an area associated with feelings of shame.[3] The source of pollution of the lower body is the genitoanal area and its emissions and secretions.

---

[3] A. Sutherland, "The Body as a Social Symbol Among the Rom," in *The Anthropology of the Body*, edited by J. Blacking (New York: Academic Press, 1977), 375–390.

Secretions from the upper half of the body are not polluting or shameful. For example, spittle is viewed as a clean and curative substance that may be used to clean cuts or scratches. This viewpoint conflicts with medical practice, which sees spittle as a possible source of contagion. Separate soap and towels are allocated for use on either the upper or the lower part of the body, and they must not be allowed to mix. Bathing in a hospital can be easily accommodated to Gypsy beliefs by providing them with separate soaps and towels for the upper and lower parts of the body.

A failure to keep the two sections of the body separate in everyday living can result in serious illness. A large number of practical guidelines are necessary to keep the upper half of the body separate and pure. At the least, it is important to wash the hands after touching the lower body and before touching the upper body. Body separation is a general cultural ideal that comes into play more in public situations than in private ones, and it has implications for a physician wishing to examine the lower body. Most Gypsy women will not agree to a gynecologic examination or a Papanicolaou smear unless the necessity of the procedure is clearly explained as essential to a woman's well-being.

Marime can also mean rejection because to become physically or morally impure could mean being rejected by the entire group. Rejection is a serious punishment for a Gypsy because it means social isolation.

MARIME AND NON-GYPSIES

The use of *marime* as a defining term for a whole series of social boundaries gives it much importance for the Rom. The most important boundary is that between Gypsy and non-Gypsy. Because they do not observe body separation, non-Gypsies are a source of impurity and disease. Public places where non-Gypsies predominate such as public toilets, hospitals, buses, schools, offices, jails, and non-Gypsy homes are also potential sources of disease. All these places are less "clean" than the home of a Gypsy or open outdoor spaces such as parks and woods. When they must be in non-Gypsy places, Gypsies generally avoid touching as many impure surfaces as possible, but, of course, prolonged occupation of a non-Gypsy place such as a hospital means certain impurity. In this case the person tries to lessen the pollution risk by using disposable paper cups, plates, and towels—that is, things not used by non-Gypsies.

AGE-RELATED CLEANLINESS

Concern for a person's health begins at birth and is most active during the days or weeks of confinement (from 9 days to 6 weeks) of the mother. In the past, infant mortality for Gypsies has been high. This may be somewhat improved nowadays because more women give birth in hospitals;

however, the crucial period of prenatal care is still entirely neglected because few women will accept a vaginal examination. One of the reasons Gypsies have turned to hospital birth is the advantage to them of avoiding the impure birth substances.

Gypsies recognize that a baby is vulnerable in the first weeks of life and take precautions to protect the child. A new baby is immediately swaddled tightly and handled only by his or her mother. The woman avoids certain foods, such as green vegetables and tomatoes, so that the nursing baby will not get colic. The child's navel is carefully cleaned and protected with ashes, and amulets are sewn into the baby's clothing for protection. In the first weeks at night, no member of the family is allowed to go in and out, and all windows and doors are kept shut lest a spirit of death, called "the night," enters to harm the baby. Crying and fear are prevented in a child by placing a small piece of *johai* ("ghost vomit," a curative substance) on their tongue. Visitors are carefully watched lest they give the baby the evil eye. If the baby fusses or becomes ill, the giver of the evil eye must make a cross with spittle on the forehead of the baby.

If despite these precautions a baby dies, this is bad luck for the parents. They must avoid the baby's body, which is buried in a secret place by the grandparents. Another way to avoid the bad luck of death of a baby is to leave the funeral and burial to the hospital authorities.

After the period of pollution of birth has passed (more or less 6 weeks), children are considered basically pure in body and action. They can enjoy freedom from most social restraints and are not expected to understand or demonstrate "shame" in their actions. Physical contacts defiling to adults are not necessarily defiling to children, who need not take many of the precautions that adults do to ensure cleanliness in their daily lives. Children, for example, may eat food handled and prepared by non-Gypsies that postpuberty juveniles would reject.

At puberty, boys and girls are introduced to the idea of personal shame. Now both their bodies and their actions will be judged in terms of control of their own polluting secretions (menstrual blood, semen) and of "shameful" and polluting actions (sexual contact). The control of sexual relations and body cleanliness is modified by marriage and childbirth, but basically such controls last throughout married life until old age.

Women have a particular need to keep clean. Menstruation, for example, is surrounded by a number of rules to control the ill effects of this potentially polluting bodily function. When a girl first menstruates she is introduced to shame and must observe the washing, dressing, cooking, eating, and behavioral rules of adult women, partly for her own protection and partly for the protection of men. Her clothes must be washed separately from those of men and children, and she cannot cook food for others during menstruation. She must show respect to men by not passing in front of them, stepping over their clothes, or allowing her skirts to touch them.

At old age, after menopause and when sexual relations are assumed to have ceased, many of these regulations are relaxed. The aged are venerated and respected persons, both because they are politically powerful (political authority is vested in the aged) and because they now enjoy a "clean" status. When in contact with a group of Gypsies, it is always wise to seek out older authority figures and to communicate problems in their presence because they have authority and exert influence over younger Gypsies. Also, without the approval of older relatives, many young Gypsies will not agree to medical procedures considered risky.

FOOD AND HEALTH

Gypsies try to eat only food that is known to be pure and clean. Consequently, there are many regulations regarding the preparation and handling of food. There are no foods that are always prohibited, although some adult Gypsies fast on Fridays. Some foods—pepper, salt, vinegar, garlic, and onions—are considered lucky. To eat them encourages good health.

Eating together is imbued with great social significance. To share food with someone demonstrates respect, friendship, and acknowledgement of their cleanliness. Refusing to share food is a serious affront, implying a person is not pure and clean. The most serious punishment Gypsies as a group can impose on anyone is to refuse to eat with the person. To be prohibited commensality is social death. All rituals at which the Gypsies express important unifying social values involve the sharing of food at a feast.

All food must be carefully prepared to avoid any *marime* contacts. Cooking and eating utensils are always washed in a special separate basin reserved only for that purpose. In many households, a separate soap is reserved for food-related items, and even the hands are washed only with that soap before handling food. Women in birth confinement and menstruating women do not handle food. Food prepared by non-Gypsies is *marime* and is avoided. This avoidance is not always possible, such as when in a hospital, but it can be aided by eating wrapped take-away foods, drinking from cartons or bottles, and using disposable eating implements. Gypsies may simply eat with their hands rather than use utensils that may not have been properly washed.

CAUSES OF ILLNESS

Gypsies make a distinction between illnesses that originate from the non-Gypsies (*gaje*) and illnesses that are exclusively part of their own world. The former can be cured by non-Gypsy doctors, but the latter can only be tackled by the *drabarni*, their own medical practitioners. A knowledge of

Gypsy medicine is the prerogative almost exclusively of the oldest women. They are both respected and feared because of this knowledge.

Gypsies do not have a scientific understanding of how the body functions. To them American physicians simply have a special knowledge of (*gaje*) illnesses and cures, a store of lore on medicines, and diagnostic and curing techniques. Not all physicians have the same knowledge or ability. To a Gypsy, a "big" doctor is one who cures, and a bad doctor is one whose medicine does not work.

Hospitals are feared and avoided whenever possible. Most Gypsies will go to a hospital only if they are in serious danger of dying or if they view the situation as a crisis. Furthermore, a hospital is a hostile place for the Gypsies, full of non-Gypsies, unclean, and completely removed from Gypsy society. Too few visitors are allowed, so for the Gypsies, who want to be with their kin when ill, a hospital is close to a state of exile from their own society. For these reasons, many Gypsies suffer great pain rather than go to a hospital. If they have to be admitted, the one thing they know for certain is that they do not want to be alone, to be without their relatives.

Gypsy and non-Gypsy diseases overlap, but their causes are different (Table II). Most Gypsies prefer to try several different cures for any single illness to combat the different causes. A person who has convulsions, for example, may be rushed to a hospital where a physician can attend but will also be given asafetida by relatives. Physicians, therefore, are not in competition with Gypsy *drabarni*.

Table II Disease Causation and Treatment

Disease	Cause	Cure
***Gaje* (non-Gypsy) diseases**		
Flu, "fevers," gonorrhea, syphilis, hernias, hemorrhoids	*Marime* from contact with *gaje;* germs	Avoid *gaje; gaje* physicians
Gypsy diseases		
Mental illness; mental retardation	Denial of cultural rules	Observe cultural rules, such as marriage
Grave illness, such as polio, serious influenza, pneumonia, and hemorrhages	*Mamioro,* a spirit who visits places that are unclean and brings illness	*Johai* ("ghost vomit"), *Fuligo septica,* a slime mold, is curative
Tosca (nerves); convulsions	*O Beng,* the Devil, the source of evil	*Khantino drab* ("Devil's dung") or asafetida
General illness and bad luck (*prikaza*)	*Mule,* spirits or ghosts; not necessarily harmful, but Gypsies are afraid of them	Prevented by showing respect to the dead; observing *pomana* (death ritual); avoiding places *mule* may visit; traveling

HEALTH STATUS OF GYPSIES

Many Gypsies claim that they are sicker now than they used to be. They believe it is because they travel less and live in houses instead of separate from non-Gypsies in camps. They think that the closer contact with non-Gypsies is having a deleterious effect on their health. Recent work on the medical condition of Gypsies would indicate that their medical problems are in fact serious.[4] In a study of 58 Gypsies in the Boston area, Thomas found that 41 of 56 (73%) had hypertension, 24 of 52 (46%) diabetes mellitus, 32 of 40 (80%) hypertriglyceridemia, 26 of 39 (67%) hypercholesterolemia, 20 of 51 (39%) occlusive vascular disease, and 8 of 40 (20%) chronic renal insufficiency. A combination of diet, which is extremely high in fat, and genetics could be leading to the high cholesterol levels and hypertension. In this group, 50 (86%) smoked cigarettes and 49 (84%) were obese. The life expectancy of a Gypsy in the United States is between 48 and 55 years.[5]

To combat non-Gypsy diseases, the Gypsies logically turn to non-Gypsy physicians and hospitals. Although they are eager to try any cure that they think might work, they are suspicious of physicians and tend to "shop around." A physician who acquires the reputation of being effective will find Gypsy patients flocking to the office. Physicians whose Gypsy patients die under their care will probably never see another in their practice.

Surgery is feared, especially when general anesthesia is required, as Gypsies believe a person under anesthesia undergoes a "little death." Thus, Gypsies will gather around the bedside to muster support and help the patient come out of the anesthesia.

Despite their fear of hospitals, Gypsies are in general extremely knowledgeable of hospital procedure. They know what services are available and who are the best physicians for specific problems. They learn of famous clinics and learn the complicated hospital regulations, how to get around them, and how to get what they want. One study concluded that Gypsies receive better medical care than other urban minorities because they have figured out effective ways to use medical services.[6] In the same way that they are willing to try physicians and hospitals to cure them, they will also try cures and medicines advertised by Mexican *curanderos*, faith healers, and patented miracle cures. These are all *gaje* remedies. Nothing that might work is to be scorned.

Gypsy diseases have no connection with non-Gypsies or with germs and therefore cannot be cured by non-Gypsy physicians. For these dis-

---

[4] J. Thomas, "Gypsies and American Medical Care," *Annals of Internal Medicine* 102 (1985): 842–845.

[5] J. Thomas, "Disease, Lifestyle and Consanguinity in 58 American Gypsies," *Lancet* 2 (1987): 377–379.

[6] J. Salloway, "Medical Care Utilization Among Urban Gypsies," *Urban Anthropology* 2(1) (1973): 113–126.

eases the Gypsies must turn to their own knowledge and their own medical practitioners, the *drabarni* (literally, "women who have knowledge of medicines"). The knowledge of spirits and medicines that old women have is a great source of power for them.

Serious Gypsy diseases are caused either by a spirit called *Mamioro* or the Devil. *Mamioro*, a specific spirit who has become a disease carrier, causes illness simply by visiting the homes of Gypsies. Fortunately, she only visits dirty houses, so by keeping a clean house, the Gypsy can keep her away. *Johai*, her vomit, is found most frequently in garbage dumps, and it is the most powerful and valuable cure the Gypsies have.*

Several important diseases are caused by the Devil. *Tosca* is a disease that the Gypsies translate as "nerves." People who are nervous, fidgety, and worry excessively have *tosca*. A lot of Gypsies get *tosca*, especially the less aggressive and more sensitive ones who find it hard to keep up with the demanding, noisy, fast pace of Gypsy social life. *Khantino drab* will cure *tosca*. *Khantino drab* is also said to be found near the place where a person has been seized with a convulsion or epileptic seizure. It is believed that convulsions occur when a person is possessed by the Devil and that usually the Devil defecates during the convulsion. Locating the *Khantino drab* and giving it to the convulsed person will make the Devil *marime* and drive him away.

DEATH

Gypsies can never be sure that they have done everything possible to keep pure, to promote auspiciousness, and in general to live up to the ideals of correct behavior; therefore, it is not surprising when someone becomes ill or suffers misfortune. For the Gypsies, illness and death are not only a personal crisis, they introduce a social crisis as well. Reporters, physicians, hospital staff, social workers, and police are all aware of a great happening when a Gypsy becomes seriously ill and dies. When they ask what is going on, they may be told, "a Gypsy king (queen, prince) has died." This reply is a way of satisfying reporters and providing a reasonable explanation to hospital staff and police of why the Gypsies are flocking into town in large numbers, camping on hospital grounds, and in general breaking rules and creating havoc. Although there are no kings and queens, only leaders of the large Gypsy extended family, death is a major crisis in a Gypsy family that must be dealt with in ritual.

When a young person dies unexpectedly, the relatives are so griefstricken that their behavior can become extremely wild. In one case, after

---

*Rena Gropper, PhD, Professor of Anthropology at Hunter College and a gypsiologist, discovered "ghost vomit" on some wood chips in her garden in new York City. Thomas H. Delendick, PhD, associate taxonomist at the Brooklyn Botanic Garden, identified it as a slime mold, *Fuligo septica*. A literature search showed that heretofore there had been no known economic or folklore uses of this slime mold (written communication, July 1983).

the accidental death of a young man, the relatives were so distraught that they threatened physicians for "letting him die." The relatives scratched their faces, drawing blood, beat themselves on the chest and head, wailed, and screamed. This behavior was an expression of extreme grief. Even in the case of a death that has been anticipated, however, it is culturally acceptable for relatives to moan and shout out to the deceased, scratch their faces, or pull out their own hair.

Death at an old age is generally perceived as part of the natural and acceptable course of events, and the attitudes and feelings toward the death of an old person are very different from those toward early death. The main preoccupation of the relatives of an old person, as well as the dying person, is to see that all preparations for the person's eventual demise have been arranged. For the Lowara Gypsies, Yoors said, "the Gypsies yearned for what they called 'a great death' for which they could prepare and which they could share with their households, relatives and friends. They feared most that kind of death which came when one was unprepared."[7]

John Davis, also known as Rattlesnake Pete, had a "great" death. His funeral was the greatest spectacle since Big George Adams hired an entire movie studio to provide props for his funeral in Los Angeles. John Davis had a brass band playing Dixieland in the funeral cortege, a horse-drawn hearse complete with black enameled scrollwork and silver lanterns and drawn by two gray Appaloosas. His grave was a red-carpeted crypt with a chandelier inside in a grave site surrounded by full-sized statues of the Apostles. In front of the casket was a flower arbor with the words "Welcome to Heaven, John Davis," in gold letters. He also had flowers in the shape of his favorite fishing chair with a pole and line dangling into a flower-edged pool, the American flag, a clock with the time of his death, a car, an airplane, and a ship (because he liked to travel), a barrel of beer and beer mugs (he liked a drink), and a little white house (he was a property owner). The newspaper the next day ran a picture of the funeral cortege with the caption, "Death of a Gypsy King" (Janet Tompkins, Contra Costa County Social Service, written communication, July 1976).

CONCLUSIONS

To help physicians and hospital personnel interact effectively with Gypsies, I have some specific suggestions.

- Older relatives have an important role in the decision-making process of a patient. Try to include them and treat them with the respect they are due as elders in the community. Older relatives can be of great help in ensuring the cooperation of younger ones.

---

[7] J. Yoors, *The Gypsies* (London: Allen & Unwin, 1967).

- Gypsies can alternate rapidly between moods or styles of interpersonal interaction from extreme assertion to plaintive begging. Medical personnel should appeal to the strong desire of Gypsies to obtain the best medical treatment and assure them that cooperation will work best for them.
- English is a second language. Explain clearly without resorting to too many technical terms the procedures the patient will undergo. Then ask if there is anything that is against the patient's religion. If there is something they do not want done, explain why it is necessary for their health or allow them to forgo it.
- Many Gypsies cannot read, but it would be a mistake to assume that they are therefore less intelligent. Read important instructions (particularly at intake) to a patient or ask a translator to read out loud to the patient. They are accustomed to dealing with complex bureaucracies and policies.
- Gypsies accept emergency measures more readily than they accept proscriptions to undertake changes in diet or lifestyle; however, instruction in long-term health goals is crucial. They need education on the connection between diets high in animal fats, heavy smoking, drinking, and no exercise and the health problems they cause.
- A Gypsy patient does not want to be alone and will be fearful and agitated if forced to be without family. Allowing some relatives in the room with the patient on a rotation basis will keep the chaos to a minimum. Allow someone to stay overnight with the patient. If the patient is dying, it is essential that relatives be allowed to be present at the moment of death.

REVIEW QUESTIONS

1. How do Gypsies live and work in the United States, according to Sutherland?
2. What is the Gypsy concept of *marime,* and how does it relate to Gypsy views of disease causation, treatment, and hospitals?
3. How are Gypsy views of good health and good fortune related to their health?
4. What main pieces of advice does Sutherland have for doctors about treating Gypsies?

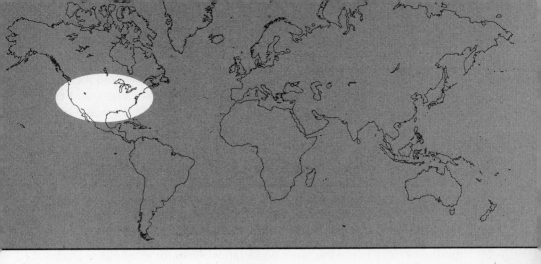

36

Using Anthropology

David W. McCurdy

*Some disciplines, such as economics, have an obvious relationship to
the nonacademic world. Economic theory, although generated as
part of basic research, may often prove useful for understanding the
"real" economy. Anthropology, on the other hand, does not seem so
applicable. In this article, David McCurdy discusses some of the
professional applications of anthropology and argues that there is a
basic anthropological perspective that can help anyone cope with the
everyday world. He uses the case of a company manager to illustrate
this point, asserting that ethnographic "qualitative" research is an
important tool for use in the nonacademic world.*

Recently, a student, whom I had not seen for fifteen years, stopped
by my office. He had returned for his college reunion and thought
it would be interesting to catch up on news about his (and my) major department, anthropology. The conversation, however, soon shifted from
college events to his own life. Following graduation and a stint in the
Peace Corps, he noted, he had begun to study for his license as a ship's

This article was adapted from "The Shrink-Wrap Solution: Anthropology and Business," by David W. McCurdy and Donna F. Carlson in *Conformity and Conflict: Readings in
Cultural Anthropology*, 5th ed. (Boston: Little, Brown and Company, 1983). It was written especially for this volume. Copyright © 1990 by David W. McCurdy.

engineer. He had attended the Maritime Academy, and worked for years on freighters. He was finally granted his license, he continued, and currently held the engineer's position on a container ship that made regular trips between Seattle and Alaska. He soon would be promoted to chief engineer and be at the top of his profession.

As he talked, he made an observation about anthropology that may seem surprising. His background in the discipline, he said, had helped him significantly in his work. He found it useful as he went about his daily tasks, maintaining his ship's complex engines and machinery, his relationships with the crew, and his contacts with land-based management.

And his is not an unusual case. Over the years, several anthropology graduates have made the same observation. One, for example, is a community organizer who feels that the cross-cultural perspective he learned in anthropology helps him mediate disputes and facilitate decision making in a multiethnic neighborhood. Another, who works as an advertising account executive, claims that anthropology helps her discover what products mean to customers. This, in turn, permits her to design more effective ad campaigns. A third says she finds anthropology an invaluable tool as she arranges interviews and writes copy. She is a producer for a metropolitan television news program. I have heard the same opinion expressed by many others, including the executive editor of a magazine for home weavers, the founder of a fencing school, a housewife, a physician, several lawyers, the kitchen manager for a catering firm, and a high school teacher.

The idea that anthropology can be useful is also supported by the experience of many new Ph.D.'s. A recent survey has shown, for the first time, that more new doctorates in anthropology find employment in professional settings than in college teaching or scholarly research, and the list of nonacademic work settings revealed by the survey is remarkably broad. There is a biological anthropologist, for example, who conducts research on nutrition for a company that manufactures infant formula. A cultural anthropologist works for a major car manufacturer, researching such questions as how employees adapt to working overseas, and how they relate to conditions on domestic production lines. Others formulate government policy, plan patient care in hospitals, design overseas development projects, run famine relief programs, consult on tropical forest management, and advise on product development, advertising campaigns, and marketing strategy for corporations.

This new-found application of cultural anthropology comes as a surprise to many Americans. Unlike political science, for example, which has a name that logically connects it with practical political and legal professions, there is nothing in the term *anthropology* that tells most Americans how it might be useful.

The research subject of anthropology also makes it more difficult to comprehend. Political scientists investigate political processes, structures, and motivations. Economists look at the production and exchange of goods and services. Psychologists study differences and similarities among individuals. The research of cultural anthropologists, on the other hand, is more difficult to characterize. Instead of a focus on particular human institutions, such as politics, law, and economics, anthropologists are interested in cross-cultural differences and similarities among the world's many groups.

This interest produces a broad view of human behavior that gives anthropology its special cross-cultural flavor. It also produces a unique research strategy, called *ethnography*, that tends to be qualitative rather than quantitative. Whereas other social sciences moved toward *quantitative methods* of research designed to test theory by using survey questionnaires and structured, repetitive observations, most anthropologists conduct *qualitative research* designed to elicit the cultural knowledge of the people they seek to understand. To do this, anthropologists often live and work with their subjects, called *informants* within the discipline. The result is a highly detailed ethnographic description of the categories and rules people consult when they behave, and the meanings that things and actions have for them.

It is this ethnographic approach, or cultural perspective, that I think makes anthropology useful in such a broad range of everyday settings. I particularly find important the special anthropological understanding of the culture concept, ethnographic field methods, and social analysis. To illustrate these assertions, let us take a single case in detail, that of a manager working for a large corporation who consciously used the ethnographic approach to solve a persistent company problem.

THE PROBLEM

The manager, whom we will name Susan Stanton, works for a large multinational corporation called UTC (not the company's real name). UTC is divided into a number of parts, including divisions, subdivisions, departments, and other units designed to facilitate its highly varied business enterprises. The company is well diversified, engaging in research, manufacturing, and customer services. In addition to serving a wide cross-section of public and private customers, it also works on a variety of government contracts for both military and nonmilitary agencies.

One of its divisions is educational. UTC has established a large number of customer outlets in cities throughout the United States, forming what it calls its "customer outlet network." They are staffed by educational personnel who are trained to offer a variety of special courses and enrichment programs. These courses and programs are marketed mainly to other businesses or to individuals who desire special training or practical information. For example, a small company might have UTC provide its employees with computer training, including instruction on hardware, programming, computer languages, and computer program applications. Another company might ask for instruction on effective management or accounting procedures. The outlets' courses for individuals include such topics as how to get a job, writing a resume, or enlarging your own business.

To organize and manage its customer outlet network, UTC has created a special division. The division office is located at the corporate headquarters and is responsible for developing new courses, improving old ones, training customer outlet personnel, and marketing customer outlet courses, or "products" as they are called inside the company. The division also has departments that develop, produce, and distribute the special learning materials used in customer outlet courses. These include books, pamphlets, video and audio tapes and cassettes, slides, overlays, and films. These materials are stored in a warehouse and are shipped, as they are ordered, to customer outlets around the country.

It is with this division that Susan Stanton first worked as a manager. She had started her career with the company in a small section of the division that designed various program materials. She had worked her way into management, holding a series of increasingly important positions. She was then asked to take over the management of a part of the division that had the manufacture, storage, and shipment of learning materials as one of its responsibilities.

But there was a catch. She was given this new management position with instructions to solve a persistent, although vaguely defined, problem. "Improve the service," they had told her, and "get control of the warehouse inventory." In this case, "service" meant the process of filling orders sent in by customer outlets for various materials stored in the warehouse. The admonition to improve the service seemed to indicate that service was poor, but all she was told about the situation was that customer outlet personnel complained about the service; she did not know exactly why or what "poor" meant.

In addition, inventory was "out of control." Later she was to discover the extent of the difficulty.

> We had a problem with inventory. The computer would say we had two hundred of some kind of book in stock, yet it was back ordered because there was nothing on the shelf. We were supposed to have the book but physically there was nothing there. I'm going, "Uh, we have a small problem. The computer never lies, like your bank statement, so why don't we have the books?"

If inventory was difficult to manage, so were the warehouse employees. They were described by another manager as "a bunch of knuckle draggers. All they care about is getting their money. They are lazy and don't last long at the job." Strangely, the company did not view the actions of the warehouse workers as a major problem. Only later did Susan Stanton tie in poor morale in the warehouse with the other problems she had been given to solve.

MANAGEMENT BY DEFENSE

Although Stanton would take the ethnographic approach to management problems, that was not what many other managers did. They took a defensive stance, a position opposite to the discovery procedures of ethnography. Their major concern—like that of many people in positions of leadership and responsibility—was to protect their authority and their ability to manage and to get things done. Indeed, Stanton also shared this need. But their solution to maintaining their position was different from hers. For them, claiming ignorance and asking questions—the hallmark of the ethnographic approach—is a sign of weakness. Instead of discovering what is going on when they take on a new management assignment, they often impose new work rules and procedures. Employees learn to fear the arrival of new managers because their appearance usually means a host of new, unrealistic demands. They respond by hiding what they actually do, withholding information that would be useful to the manager. Usually, everyone's performance suffers.

Poor performance leads to elaborate excuses as managers attempt to blame the troubles on others. Stanton described this tendency.

> When I came into the new job, this other manager said, "Guess what? You have got a warehouse. You are now the proud owner of a forklift and a bunch of knuckle draggers." And I thought, management's perception of those people is very low. They are treating them as dispensable, that you can't do anything with them. They say the workers don't have any career motives. They don't care if they do a good job. You have to force them to do anything. You can't motivate them. It's only a warehouse, other managers were saying. You can't really do that much about the problems there so why don't you just sort of try to keep it under control.

Other managers diminished the importance of the problem itself. It was not "poor service" that was the trouble. The warehouse was doing the best it could with what it had. It was just that the customers—the staff at the customer outlets—were complainers. As Susan Stanton noted:

> The people providing the service thought that outlet staff were complainers. They said, "Staff complain about everything. But it can't be that way. We have checked it all out and it isn't that bad."

Making excuses and blaming others lead to low morale and a depressed self-image. Problems essentially are pushed aside in favor of a "let's just get by" philosophy.

ETHNOGRAPHIC MANAGEMENT

By contrast, managers take the offensive when they use ethnographic techniques. That is what Stanton did when she assumed her new managerial assignment over the learning materials manufacturing and distribution system. To understand what the ethnographic approach means, however, we must first look briefly at what anthropologists do when they conduct ethnographic field research. Our discussion necessarily involves a look at the concepts of culture and microculture as well as ethnography. For as we will shortly point out, companies have cultures of their own, a point that has recently received national attention; but more important for the problem we are describing here, companies are normally divided into sub-groups, each with its own microculture. It is these cultures and microcultures that anthropologically trained managers can study ethnographically, just as fieldworkers might investigate the culture of a !Kung band living in the Kalahari Desert of West Africa or the Gypsies living in San Francisco.

Ethnography refers to the process of discovering and describing culture, so it is important to discuss this general and often elusive concept. There are numerous definitions of culture, each stressing particular sets of attributes. The definition we employ here is especially appropriate for ethnographic fieldwork. We may define culture as the acquired knowledge that people use to generate behavior and interpret experience. In growing up, one learns a system of cultural knowledge appropriate to the group. For example, an American child learns to chew with a closed mouth because that is the cultural rule. The child's parents interpret open-mouthed chewing as an infraction and tell the child to chew "properly." A person uses such cultural knowledge throughout life to guide actions and to give meaning to surroundings.

Because culture is learned, and because people can easily generate new cultural knowledge as they adapt to other people and things, human behavior and perceptions can vary dramatically from one group to another. In India, for example, children learn to chew "properly" with their mouths open. Their cultural worlds are quite different from the ones found in the United States.

Cultures are associated with groups of people. Traditionally, anthropologists associated culture with relatively distinctive ethnic groups. Culture referred to the whole life-way of a society and particular cultures could be named. Anthropologists talked of German culture, Ibo culture, and Bhil culture. Culture was everything that was distinctive about the group.

Culture is still applied in this manner today, but with the advent of complex societies and a growing interest among anthropologists in understanding them, the culture concept has also been used in a more limited way. Complex societies such as our own are composed of thousands of groups. Members of these groups usually share the national culture, including a language and a huge inventory of knowledge for doing things, but the groups themselves have specific cultures of their own. For example, if you were to walk into the regional office of a stock brokerage firm, you would hear the people there talking an apparently foreign language.

You might stand in the "bull pen," listen to brokers make "cold calls," "sell short," "negotiate a waffle," or get ready to go to a "dog and pony show." The fact that events such as this feel strange when you first encounter them is strong evidence to support the notion that you don't yet know the culture that organizes them. We call such specialized groups *microcultures*.

We are surrounded by microcultures, participating in a few, encountering many others. Our family has a microculture. So may our neighborhood, our college, and even our dormitory floor. The waitress who serves us lunch at the corner restaurant shares a culture with her coworkers. So do bank tellers at our local savings and loan. Kin, occupational groups, and recreational associations each tend to display special microcultures. Such cultures can be, and now often are, studied by anthropologists interested in understanding life in complex American society.

The concept of microculture is essential to Susan Stanton as she begins to attack management problems at UTC because she assumes that conflict between different microcultural groups is most likely at the bottom of the difficulty. One microculture she could focus on is UTC company culture. She knows, for example, that there are a variety of rules and expectations—written and unwritten—for how things should be done at the company. She must dress in her "corporates," for example, consisting of a neutral-colored suit, bow tie, stockings, and conservative shoes. UTC also espouses values about the way employees should be treated, how people are supposed to feel about company products, and a variety of other things that set that particular organization apart from other businesses.

But the specific problems that afflicted the departments under Stanton's jurisdiction had little to do with UTC's corporate culture. They seemed rather to be the result of misunderstanding and misconnection between two units, the warehouse and the customer outlets. Each had its own microculture. Each could be investigated to discover any information that might lead to a solution of the problems she had been given.

Such investigation would depend on the extent of Stanton's ethnographic training. As an undergraduate in college, she had learned how to conduct ethnographic interviews, observe behavior, and analyze and interpret data. She was not a professional anthropologist, but she felt she was a good enough ethnographer to discover some relevant aspects of microcultures at UTC.

Ethnography is the process of discovering and describing a culture. For example, an anthropologist who travels to India to conduct a study of village culture will use ethnographic techniques. The anthropologist will move into a community, occupy a house, watch people's daily routines, attend rituals, and spend hours interviewing informants. The goal is to discover a detailed picture of what is going on by seeing village culture through the eyes of informants. The anthropologist wants the insider's perspective. Villagers become teachers, patiently explaining different aspects of their culture, praising the anthropologist for acting correctly and appearing to understand, laughing when the anthropologist makes mistakes or seems confused. When the anthropologist knows what to do and can explain in local terms what is going on or what is likely to happen, real progress has been made. The clearest evidence of such progress is when informants say, "You are almost human now," or "You are beginning to talk just like us."

The greatest enemy of good ethnography is the preconceived notion. Anthropologists do not conduct ethnographic research by telling informants what they are like based on earlier views of them. They teach the anthropologist how to see their world: the anthropologist does not tell them what their world should really be like. All too often in business, a new manager will take over a department and begin to impose changes on its personnel to fit a preconceived perception of them. The fact that the manager's efforts are likely to fail makes sense in light of this ignorance. The manager doesn't know the microculture. Nor have they been asked about it.

But can a corporate manager really do ethnography? After all, managers have positions of authority to maintain, as we noted earlier. It is all right for professional anthropologists to enter the field and act ignorant; they don't have a position to maintain and they don't have to continue to live with their informants. The key to the problem appears to be the "grace period." Most managers are given one by their employees when they are new on the job. A new manager cannot be expected to know everything. It is permissible to ask basic questions. The grace period may last only a month or two, but it is usually long enough to find out valuable information.

This is the opportunity that Susan Stanton saw as she assumed direction of the warehouse distribution system. As she described it:

> I could use the first month, actually the first six weeks, to find out what was going on, to act dumb and find out what people actually did and why. I talked to end customers. I talked to salespeople, people who were trying to sell things to help customer outlets with their needs. I talked to coordinators at headquarters staff who were trying to help all these customer outlets do their jobs and listened to what kinds of complaints they had heard. I talked to the customer outlet people and the guys in the warehouse. I had this six-week grace period where I could go in and say, "I don't know anything about this. If you were in my position, what would you do, or what would make the biggest difference, and why would it make a difference?" You want to find out what the world they are operating in is like. What do they value. And people were excited because I was asking and listening and, by God, intending to do something about it instead of just disappearing again.

As we shall see shortly, Stanton's approach to the problem worked. But it also resulted in an unexpected bonus. Her ethnographic approach symbolized unexpected interest and concern to her employees. That, combined with realistic management, gave her a position of respect and authority. Their feelings for her were expressed by one warehouse worker when he said:

> When she [Susan] was going to be transferred to another job, we gave her a party. We took her to this country-and-western place and we all got to dance with the boss. We told her that she was the first manager who ever tried to understand what it was like to work in the warehouse. We thought she would come in like the other managers and make a lot of changes that didn't make sense. But she didn't. She made it work better for us.

PROBLEMS AND CAUSES

An immediate benefit of her ethnographic inquiry was a much clearer view of what poor service meant to customer outlet personnel. Stanton discovered that learning materials, such as books and cassettes, took too long to arrive after they were ordered. Worse, material did not arrive in the correct quantities. Sometimes there would be too many items, but more often there were too few, a particularly galling discrepancy since customer outlets were charged for what they ordered, not what they received. Books also arrived in poor condition, their covers ripped or scratched, edges frayed, and ends gouged and dented. This, too, bothered customer outlet staff because they were often visited by potential customers who were not impressed by the poor condition of their supplies. Shortages and scruffy books did nothing to retain regular customers either.

The causes of these problems and the difficulties with warehouse inventory also emerged from ethnographic inquiry. Stanton discovered, for example, that most customer outlets operated in large cities, where often they were housed in tall buildings. Materials shipped to their office address often ended up sitting in ground-level lobbies, because few of the buildings had receiving docks or facilities. Books and other items also arrived in large boxes, weighing up to a hundred pounds. Outlet staff, most of whom were women, had to go down to the lobby, open those boxes that were too heavy for them to carry, and haul armloads of supplies up the elevator to the office. Not only was this time-consuming, but customer outlet staff felt it was beneath their dignity to do such work. They were educated specialists, after all.

The poor condition of the books was also readily explained. By packing items loosely in such large boxes, warehouse workers ensured trouble in transit. Books rattled around with ease, smashing into each other and the side of the box. The result was torn covers and frayed edges. Clearly no one had designed the packing and shipping process with customer outlet staff in mind.

The process, of course, originated in the central warehouse, and here as well, ethnographic data yielded interesting information about the causes of the problem. Stanton learned, for example, how materials were stored in loose stacks on the warehouse shelves. When orders arrived at the warehouse, usually through the mail, they were placed in a pile and filled in turn (although there were times when special preference was given to some customer outlets). A warehouse employee filled an order by first checking it against the stock recorded by the computer, then going to the appropriate shelves and picking the items by hand. Items were packed in the large boxes and addressed to customer outlets. With the order complete, the employee was supposed to enter the number of items picked and shipped in the computer so that inventory would be up to date.

But, Stanton discovered, workers in the warehouse were under pressure to work quickly. They often fell behind because materials the computer said were in stock were not there, and because picking by hand took so long. Their solution to the problem of speed resulted in a procedure that even further confused company records.

> Most of the people in the warehouse didn't try to count well. People were looking at the books on the shelves and were going, "Eh, that looks like the right number. You want ten? Gee, that looks like about ten." Most of the time the numbers they shipped were wrong.

The causes of inaccurate amounts in shipping were thus revealed. Later, Stanton discovered that books also disappeared in customer outlet building lobbies. While staff members carried some of the materials upstairs, people passing by the open boxes helped themselves.

Other problems with inventory also became clear. UTC employees, who sometimes walked through the warehouse, would often pick up interesting materials from the loosely stacked shelves. More important, rushed workers often neglected to update records in the computer.

THE SHRINK-WRAP SOLUTION

The detailed discovery of the nature and causes of service and inventory problems suggested a relatively painless solution to Stanton. If she had taken a defensive management position and failed to learn the insider's point of view, she might have resorted to more usual remedies that were impractical and unworkable. Worker retraining is a common answer to corporate difficulties, but it is difficult to accomplish and often fails. Pay incentives, punishments, and motivation enhancements such as prizes and quotas are also frequently tried. But they tend not to work because they don't address fundamental causes.

Shrink-wrapping books and other materials did. Shrink-wrapping is a packaging device that emerged a few years ago. Clear plastic sheeting is placed around items to be packaged, then through a rapid heating and cooling process, shrunk into a tight covering. The plastic molds itself like a tight skin around the things it contains, preventing any internal movement or external contamination. Stanton described her decision.

I decided to have the books shrink-wrapped. For a few cents more, before the books ever arrived in the warehouse, I had them shrink-wrapped in quantities of five and ten. I made it part of the contract with the people who produced the books for us.

On the first day that shrink-wrapped books arrived at the warehouse, Stanton discovered that they were immediately unwrapped by workers who thought a new impediment had been placed in their way. But the positive effect of shrink-wrapping soon became apparent. For example, most customer outlets ordered books in units of fives and tens. Warehouse personnel could now easily count out orders in fives and tens, instead of having to count each book or estimate numbers in piles. Suddenly, orders filled at the warehouse contained the correct number of items.

Employees were also able to work more quickly, since they no longer had to count each book. Orders were filled faster, the customer outlet staff was pleased, and warehouse employees no longer felt the pressure of time so intensely. Shrink-wrapped materials also traveled more securely. Books, protected by their plastic covering, arrived in good condition, again delighting the personnel at customer outlets.

Stanton also changed the way materials were shipped, based on what she had learned from talking to employees. She limited the maximum size of shipments to twenty-five pounds by using smaller boxes. She also had packages marked "inside delivery" so that deliverymen would carry the materials directly to the customer outlet offices. If they failed to do so, boxes were light enough to carry upstairs. No longer would items be lost in skyscraper lobbies.

Inventory control became more effective. Because they could package and ship materials more quickly, the workers in the warehouse had enough time to enter the size and nature of shipments in the computer. Other UTC employees no longer walked off with books from the warehouse, because the shrink-wrapped bundles were larger and more conspicuous, and because taking five or ten books is more like stealing than "borrowing" one.

Finally, the improved service dramatically changed morale in the division. Customer outlet staff members, with their new and improved service, felt that finally someone had cared about them. They were more positive and they let people at corporate headquarters know about their feelings. "What's happening down there?" they asked. "The guys in the warehouse must be taking vitamins."

Morale soared in the warehouse. For the first time, other people liked the service workers there provided. Turnover decreased as pride in their work rose. They began to care more about the job, working faster with greater care. Managers who had previously given up on the "knuckle draggers" now asked openly about what had got into them.

Stanton believes the ethnographic approach is the key. She has managers who work for her read anthropology, especially books on ethnography, and she insists that they "find out what is going on."

CONCLUSION

Anthropology is, before all, an academic discipline with a strong emphasis on scholarship and basic research. But, as we have also seen, anthropology is a discipline that contains several intellectual tools—the concept of culture, the ethnographic approach to fieldwork, a cross-cultural perspective, a holistic view of human behavior—that make it useful in a broad range of nonacademic settings. In particular, it is the ability to do qualitative research that makes anthropologists successful in the professional world.

A few years ago an anthropologist consultant was asked by a utility company to answer a puzzling question: Why were its suburban customers, whose questionnaire responses indicated an attempt at conservation, failing to reduce their consumption of natural gas? To answer the question, the anthropologist conducted ethnographic interviews with members of several families, listening as they told him about how warm they liked their houses and how they set the heat throughout the day. He also received permission to install several video cameras aimed at thermostats in private houses. When the results were in, the answer to the question was deceptively simple: Fathers fill out questionnaires and turn down thermostats; wives, children, and cleaning workers, all of whom, in this case, spent time in the houses when fathers were absent, turn them up. Conservation, the anthropologist concluded, would have to involve family decisions, not just admonitions to save gas. The key to this anthropologist's success, and indeed to the application of cultural anthropology by those acquainted with it, is the ethnographic approach. For it is people with experience in the discipline who have the special background needed to, in the words of Susan Stanton, "find out what is going on."

REVIEW QUESTIONS

1. What kinds of jobs do professional anthropologists do?
2. What is special about anthropology that makes it suitable for some jobs?
3. What is meant by *qualitative research?* Why is such research valuable to business and government?
4. What difficulties did the company manager described in this article face? What solutions did she invent to deal with them? How did her knowledge of anthropology help her with this problem?
5. Why is ethnography useful in everyday life? Can you think of situations in which you could use ethnographic research?

GLOSSARY

Acculturation. The process that takes place when groups of individuals having different cultures come into first-hand contact, which results in change to the cultural patterns of both groups.

Action Anthropology. Any use of anthropological knowledge for planned change by the members of a local cultural group.

Adjustment Anthropology. Any use of anthropological knowledge that makes social interaction between persons who operate with different cultural codes more predictable.

Administrative Anthropology. The use of anthropological knowledge for planned change by those who are external to a local cultural group.

Advocate Anthropology. Any use of anthropological knowledge by the anthropologist to increase the power of self-determination for a particular cultural group.

Affinity. A fundamental principle of relationship linking kin through marriage.

Agriculture. A subsistence strategy involving intensive farming of permanent fields through the use of such means as the plow, irrigation, and fertilizer.

Allocation of Resources. The knowledge people use to assign rights to the ownership and use of resources.

Applied Anthropology. Any use of anthropological knowledge to influence social interaction, to maintain or change social institutions, or to direct the course of cultural change.

Bilateral (Cognatic) Descent. A rule of descent relating someone to a group of consanguine kin through both males and females.

Caste. A form of stratification defined by unequal access to economic resources and prestige, which is acquired at birth and does not permit individuals to alter their rank.

Clan. A kinship group normally comprising several lineages; its members are related by a unilineal descent rule, but it is too large to enable members to trace actual biological links to all other members.

Class.   A system of stratification defined by unequal access to economic resources and prestige, but permitting individuals to alter their rank.

Consanguinity.   The principle of relationship linking individuals by shared ancestry (blood).

Contest.   A method of settling disputes requiring disputants to engage in some kind of mutual challenge such as singing (as among the Inuit).

Cosmology.   A set of beliefs that defines the nature of the universe or cosmos.

Court.   A formal legal institution in which at least one individual has authority to judge and is backed up by a coercive system to enforce decisions.

Cultural Contact.   The situation that occurs when two societies with different cultures somehow come in contact with each other.

Cultural Ecology.   The study of the way people use their culture to adapt to particular environments, the effects they have on their natural surrounding, and the impact of the environment on the shape of culture, including its long-term evolution.

Cultural Environment.   The categories and rules people use to classify and explain their physical environment.

Culture.   The knowledge that is learned, shared, and used by people to interpret experience and generate behavior.

Culture Shock.   A form of anxiety that results from an inability to predict the behavior of others or act appropriately in cross-cultural situations.

Descent.   A rule of relationship that ties people together on the basis of reputed common ancestry.

Descent Groups.   Groups based on a rule of descent.

Detached Observation.   An approach to scientific inquiry stressing emotional detachment and the construction of categories by the observer in order to classify what is observed.

Diffusion.   The passage of a cultural category, culturally defined behavior, or culturally produced artifact from one society to another through borrowing.

Distribution.   The strategies for apportioning goods and services among the members of a group.

Divination.   The use of supernatural force to provide answers to questions.

Division of Labor.   The rules that govern the assignment of jobs to people.

Ecology.   The study of the way organisms interact with each other within an environment.

Economic System.   The provision of goods and services to meet biological and social wants.

Egalitarian Societies.   Societies that, with the exception of ranked differences between men and women and adults and children, provide all people an equal chance at economic resources and prestige. Most hunter-gatherer societies are egalitarian by this definition.

Endogamy.   Marriage within a designated social unit.

Ethnocentrism.   A mixture of belief and feeling that one's own way of life is desirable and actually superior to others'.

Ethnography.   The task of discovering and describing a particular culture.

Exogamy.   Marriage outside any designated group.

Explicit Culture.   The culture that people can talk about and of which they are aware. Opposite of tacit culture.

Extended Family.   A family that includes two or more married couples.

Extralegal Dispute.   A dispute that remains outside the process of law and develops into repeated acts of violence between groups, such as feuds and wars.

Family.   A residential group composed of at least one married couple and their children.

Functional Integration.   The various aspects of a society, such as its culturally defined behaviors, beliefs, and artifacts, that affect and support each other to create an organized system.

Go-Between.   An individual who arranges agreements and mediates disputes.

Grammar.   The categories and rules for combining vocal symbols.

Horticulture.   A kind of subsistence strategy involving semi-intensive, usually shifting, agricultural practices. Slash-and-burn farming is a common example of horticulture.

Hunting and Gathering.   A subsistence strategy involving the foraging of wild, naturally occurring foods.

Incest Taboo.   The cultural rule that prohibits sexual intercourse and marriage between specified classes of relatives.

Industrialism.   A subsistence strategy marked by intensive, mechanized food production and elaborate distribution networks.

Inequality.   A human relationship marked by differences in power, authority, prestige, and access to valued goods and services, and by the payment of deference.

Informant.   A person who teaches his or her culture to an anthropologist.

Infralegal Dispute.   A dispute that occurs below or outside the legal process without involving regular violence.

Innovation.   A recombination of concepts from two or more mental configurations into a new pattern that is qualitatively different from existing forms.

Kinship.   The complex system of social relationships based on marriage (affinity) and birth (consanguinity).

Language.   The system of cultural knowledge used to generate and interpret speech.

Law.   The cultural knowledge that people use to settle disputes by means of agents who have recognized authority.

Lineage.   A kinship group based on a unilineal descent rule that is localized, has some corporate powers, and whose members can trace their actual relationships to each other.

Magic.   Strategies people use to control supernatural power to achieve particular results.

Mana.   An impersonal supernatural force inherent in nature and in people. Mana is somewhat like the concept of "luck" in American culture.

Market Economies.   Economies in which production and exchange are motivated by market factors: price, supply, and demand. Market economies are associated with large societies where impersonal exchange is common.

Market Exchange.   The transfer of goods and services based on price, supply, and demand.

Marriage.   The socially recognized union between a man and a woman that accords legitimate birth status rights to their children.

Matrilineal Descent.   A rule of descent relating a person to a group of consanguine kin on the basis of descent through females only.

Microculture.   The system of knowledge shared by members of a group that is part of a larger national society or ethnic group.

Monogamy.   A marriage form in which a person is allowed only one spouse at a time.

Moot.   A community meeting held for the informal hearing of a dispute.

Morpheme.   The smallest meaningful category in any language.

Mythology.   Stories that reveal the religious knowledge of how things have come into being.

Naive Realism.   The notion that reality is much the same for all people everywhere.

Nonlinguistic Symbols.   Any symbols that exist outside the system of language and speech; for example, visual symbols.

Nuclear Family.   A family composed of a married couple and their children.

Ordeal.   A supernaturally controlled, painful, or physically dangerous test, the outcome of which determines a person's guilt or innocence.

Pastoralism.   A subsistence strategy based on the maintenance and use of large herds of animals.

Patrilineal Descent.   A rule of descent relating consanguine kin on the basis of descent through males only.

Personified Supernatural Force.   Supernatural force inherent in Supernatural beings such as goddesses, gods, spirits, and ghosts.

Phoneme.   The minimal category of speech sounds that signals a difference in meaning.

Phonology.   The categories and rules for forming vocal symbols.

Phratry.   A group composed of two or more clans. Members acknowledge unilineal descent from a common ancestor but recognize that their relationship is distant.

Physical Environment.   The world as people experience it with their senses.

Policy.   Any guideline that can lead directly to action.

Political System.   The organization and process of making and carrying out public policy according to cultural categories and rules.

Polyandry.   A form of polygamy in which a woman has two or more husbands at one time.

Polygamy.   A marriage form in which a person has two or more spouses at one time. Polygyny and polyandry are both forms of polygamy.

Polygyny.   A form of polygamy in which a man is married to two or more wives at one time.

Prayer.   A petition directed at a supernatural being or power.

Priest.   A full-time religious specialist who intervenes between people and the supernatural, and who often leads a congregation at regular cyclical rites.

Production.   The process of making something.

Public.   The group of people a policy will affect.

Racial Inequality.   Inequality based on reputed biological characteristics of the members of different groups.

Ramage.   A cognatic (bilateral) descent group that is localized and holds corporate responsibility.

Rank Societies.   Societies stratified on the basis of prestige only.

Reciprocal Exchange.   The transfer of goods and services between two people or groups based on their role obligations. A form of nonmarket exchange.

Redistribution.   The transfer of goods and services between a group of people and a central collecting service based on role obligation. The U.S. income tax is a good example.

Religion.   The cultural knowledge of the supernatural that people use to cope with the ultimate problems of human existence.

Respondent.   An individual who responds to questions included on questionnaires; the subject of survey research.

Rite of Passage.   A series of rituals that move individuals from one social state or status to another.

Role.   The culturally generated behavior associated with particular statuses.

Sacrifice.   The giving of something of value to supernatural beings or forces.

Self-redress.   The actions taken by an individual who has been wronged to settle a dispute.

Semantics.   The categories and rules for relating vocal symbols to their referents.

Sexual Inequality.   Inequality based on gender.

Shaman.   A part-time religious specialist who controls supernatural power, often to cure people or affect the course of life's events.

Slash-and-Burn Agriculture.   A form of horticulture in which wild land is cleared and burned over, farmed, then permitted to lie fallow and revert to its wild state.

Social Acceptance.   A process that involves learning about an innovation, accepting an innovation as valid, and revising one's cultural knowledge to include the innovation.

Social Situation.   The categories and rules for arranging and interpreting the settings in which social interaction occurs.

Social Stratification.   The ranking of people or groups based on their unequal access to valued economic resources and prestige.

Sociolinguistic Rules.   Rules specifying the nature of the speech community, the particular speech situations within a community, and the speech acts that members use to convey their messages.

Sorcery.   The malevolent practice of magic.

Speech.   The behavior that produces meaningful vocal sounds.

Spirit Possession.   The control of a person by a supernatural being in which the person becomes that being.

Status.   A culturally defined position associated with a particular social structure.

Stratified Societies.   Societies that are at least partly organized on the principle of social stratification. Contrast with egalitarian and rank societies.

Subject.   The person who is observed in a social or psychological experiment.

Subsistence Economies.   Economies that are local and that depend largely on the nonmarket mechanisms, reciprocity and redistribution, to motivate production and exchange.

Subsistence Strategies.   Strategies used by groups of people to exploit their environment for material necessities. Hunting and gathering, horticulture, pastoralism, agriculture, and industrialism are subsistence strategies.

Substantive Law.   The legal statutes that define right and wrong for members of a society.

Supernatural.   Things that are beyond the natural. Anthropologists usually recognize a belief in such things as goddesses, gods, spirits, ghosts, and *mana* to be signs of supernatural belief.

Support.   Anything that contributes to the adoption of public policy and its enforcement.

Symbol.   Anything that humans can sense that is given an arbitrary relationship to its referent.

Tacit Culture.   The shared knowledge of which people usually are unaware and do not communicate verbally.

Technology.   The part of a culture that involves the knowledge that people use to make and use tools and to extract and refine raw materials.

Transcendent Values.   Values that override differences in a society and unify the group.

Ultimate Problems.   Universal human problems, such as death, the explanation of evil and the meaning of life, and transcendent values that can be answered by religion.

Unit of Production.   The group of people responsible for producing something.

Witchcraft.   The reputed activity of people who inherit supernatural force and use if for evil purposes.

Worldview.   The way people characteristically look out on the universe.

INDEX